AMERICAN MiG PILOT

AMERICAN MiG PILOT

INSIDE THE TOP SECRET USAF "RED EAGLES" MiG SQUADRON

ROB "Z-MAN" ZETTEL

OSPREY PUBLISHING
Bloomsbury Publishing Plc
Kemp House, Chawley Park, Cumnor Hill, Oxford OX2 9PH, UK
Bloomsbury Publishing Ireland Limited
29 Earlsfort Terrace, Dublin 2, D02 AY28, Ireland

Bloomsbury Publishing Inc.,
1359 Broadway, 12th Floor, New York, NY 10018, USA
E-mail: info@ospreypublishing.com
www.ospreypublishing.com

OSPREY is a trademark of Osprey Publishing Ltd

First published in Great Britain in 2026

© Rob Zettel, 2026

Rob Zettel has asserted his right under the Copyright, Designs and Patents Act, 1988, to be identified as Author of this work.

For legal purposes the Acknowledgments on p. 7–11 constitute an extension of this copyright page.

All rights reserved. No part of this publication may be: i) reproduced or transmitted in any form, electronic or mechanical, including photocopying, recording or by means of any information storage or retrieval system without prior permission in writing from the publishers; or ii) used or reproduced in any way for the training, development or operation of artificial intelligence (AI) technologies, including generative AI technologies. The rights holders expressly reserve this publication from the text and data mining exception as per Article 4(3) of the Digital Single Market Directive (EU) 2019/790.

A catalog record for this book is available from the British Library

ISBN: HB 9781472808554; eBook 9781472808578; ePDF 9781472808561;
XML 9781472822031; Audio 9781472875105

26 27 28 29 30 10 9 8 7 6 5 4 3 2 1

Edited by Tony Holmes
Index by Fionbar Lyons

Typeset by Lumina Datamatics Ltd
Printed and bound in Great Britain by Clays Ltd, Elcograf S.p.A.

Osprey Publishing supports the Woodland Trust, the UK's leading woodland conservation charity.

To find out more about our authors and books visit www.ospreypublishing.com. Here you will find extracts, author interviews, details of forthcoming events and the option to sign up for our newsletter.

For product safety related questions contact productsafety@bloomsbury.com

Contents

Acknowledgments   7
Foreword   12
List of Illustrations   15
Prologue   21

1. Like Ice Skating — 26
2. A Distant Memory — 32
3. Improbable Odds — 41
4. Tweets and Talons — 54
5. F-4 Phantom II – The Beast — 63
6. A Vector — 71
7. The Fork in the Road — 82
8. Sharpening the Edge — 89
9. Inherent Risks and Cheating Death — 95
10. Right Place, Right Time — 106
11. "How'd You Get this Assignment?" — 113
12. Going Up North — 117
13. The Assets — 126
14. Light the Rocket — 137
15. "I'm Not Him" — 148
16. Behind the "Black Curtain" — 152
17. "Stink Bugs" — 162
18. The Aggressors — 170
19. The Crapper — 184
20. "You're Grounded!" — 190
21. TOPGUN — 203
22. Coincidence or a Prelude to History? — 212

23	MiG-21 vs F-15	219
24	"Sir, Can He Do That?"	228
25	"Flogger!"	237
26	"Knock It Off!"	252
27	"We Lost One"	263
28	Pushing the Envelope	272
29	The Final Push	287
30	Going Back	297

Epilogue	309
Appendices	325
Glossary	339
Abbreviations	353
Index	359

Acknowledgments

"When you support others, you become part of their success story."
UNKNOWN

When I began writing this section of the book, I quickly related to the struggle that has afflicted so many Academy Award winners over the years when they have to thank everyone who played a part in their success within the 45 seconds allotted to them. Simply stated, it is just impossible. So too, in my attempt to list all of those who contributed to this work, I will apologize at the outset as I will surely fail to acknowledge someone who, in whatever small way, helped shape this story.

Unlike many stories, this one did not initially grow out of a plan to write a book at all. However, it started as a simple interest in jotting down a few unique stories of my time as a "Red Eagle" with the 4477th Test and Evaluation Squadron (TES), which then germinated into something resembling "chapters," eventually growing into the work it became. All, I might add, at the insistence and encouragement of many squadron mates who were witnesses to many of the same experiences I have penned here.

Throughout the research and writing of this book, I had the good fortune to record more than 35 video and audio interviews with fellow "Red Eagles" pilots, maintenance squadron mates, fighter pilots from other squadrons, and friends and neighbors who, over the years, all had some impact on me along this journey of mine. Additionally, there were countless exchanges over the telephone and via e-mail and text that contributed immeasurably to the story you are about to read. In an effort to add authenticity to the book with respect to events, the dates on which they took place, and the aircraft flown at the time, I have relied extensively on both personal and USAF flight records to ensure accuracy.

For their efforts, I wish to thank the following for their contribution to this work *(Note – all listed ranks for officers/NCOs reflect their retirement rank, and individuals are listed alphabetically, rank notwithstanding)*:

Family and Friends – First and foremost, any measure of success I may have had I owe to the selfless example of love, honesty, hard work, and discipline embodied by my mother, Harriet. While she has passed, her legacy lives on in the people she touched through her countless acts of love and friendship. To my brothers, Chuck and Mark, for their support and help over the years, during which I looked up to them and the example they set, providing a path for me to follow. To Rich Hofman, the "big kid" next door, who, through his example and coaching on the ball diamond, taught me more than just the game of baseball. The core tenets of his life – hard work, discipline, honesty, and a "never give up" attitude – instilled in me from my earliest memories of playing ball, have helped me throughout my entire life. While Alex Rodriguez may be the most famous player he ever coached, I was one of his very first! Thanks, Rich.

4477th TES "Red Eagles" – Lt Col Bill "Billy" Bayer, Lt Col John "Bama" Bermingham, MSgt Jim "J. B." Bell, SMSgt Mike Beverlin, Col Tom "Boomer" Boma, Cdr Guy "Brudog" Brubaker, Gen Herbert "Hawk" Carlisle, VADM Marty "Streak" Chanik, Col Jim "Meat" Day, Lt Col Ted "Gabby" Drake, MSgt Jerry Fields, Maj Dan "Truck" Futryk, Col Frank "Paco" Geisler, Col George "G2" Gennin, SMSgt Bob Gibeault, CMSgt Buster Helms, Lt Col Dudley "Dud" Larsen, MSgt Don Lyon, Lt Col Jim "Smack" MacDonald, Col Marty "Fog" Macy, Col Jack "Mad Jack" Manclark, SMSgt Larry Mason, Lt Col Jim "Thug" Matheny, Brig Gen David "Marshall" McCloud, Capt (US Navy) Dan "Bad Bob" McCort, Capt Brian "Lazmo" McCoy, Lt Col Burt "Buffalo" Myers, ADM John "Black" Nathman, Maj John "Admiral" Nelson, Zara Newton-Pyatt, Col Gail "Evil" Peck, Col Denny "Hog" Phelan, Col Mike "Bat" Press, RADM Jim "Rookie" Robb, Lt Col Mike "Mach" Roy, Col John "Sax" Saxman, Col Mike "Scotty" Scott, Capt Bob "Catfish" Sheffield, Lt Col Larry "Shy" Shervanick, Capt (US Navy) Cary "Dollar" Silvers, Lt Col John "Skid" Skidmore, Lt Col Paul "Stook" Stucky, Lt Col Jon "Jaws" Waldrop, and Lt Col Bruce "B. W." Walls.

Three "Red Eagles" who warrant special mention are Ted "Gabby" Drake, Frank "Paco" Geisler, and Jim "Smack" MacDonald. Ted was the squadron expert on the MiG-23 and, without doubt, has probably forgotten more about that aircraft than I ever knew. I want to thank him for tolerating countless calls, texts, and e-mails from me while I was researching every facet of squadron life. Along the way, we shared a lot of laughs and stories too numerous to capture in the allotted space given. Thanks, Ted.

"Paco" Geisler is a breed all of his own, and besides being "a fighter pilot's fighter pilot," he's an even better friend. "Paco's" input on what was going on within the squadron behind the scenes was priceless, and often had us laughing during our countless telephone calls over the years of this project. Need I mention that he's one of the biggest practical jokers around? Thanks, "Paco," you rock, dude!

Jim MacDonald was invaluable in not only proofreading the seemingly endless drafts I sent his way, but also providing insight on the role that he and the rest of our Ground-Controlled Interception (GCI) controllers at Bandit Control played in making our mission a success. I believe I speak for all "Red Eagles" pilots in saluting their professionalism and importance. Without them, there is no story. Thanks, Jim.

How I was fortunate enough to be in the same squadron with these three is beyond comprehension and most certainly had to have been the result of divine intervention. This work owes much of its authenticity to their help and support.

USAF Aggressors – Lt Col Larry "Dirt" Austin, Lt Col John "Bomber" Bomberger, Maj Aric "Redeye" Johnson, Lt Col Matt "Skunk" Skundrick, all of whom added immeasurably to Chapter 18 on the Aggressors during a particularly turbulent period at Nellis AFB in 1983–84. I owe you all a huge "thank you" for being brutally honest in voicing your assessments of life in the 57th Fighter Weapons Wing (FWW) at that time.

Notables – To Steve Davies, author of *Red Eagles – America's Secret MiGs*, for his encouragement, support, and friendship over the years. Steve's book is the gold standard for the definitive history of the 4477th TES, and is therefore a must-read work. Along with Steve, my good friend and supporter Col Gail "Evil" Peck, author of *America's Secret MiG Squadron*, was among the very first to champion me writing this book. Not only was he the brainchild behind the concept of *Constant Peg*, he was also one I could always count on for words of encouragement when it came to pursuing the goal of finishing the manuscript.

Next, I would be remiss if I did not mention my good fortune in crossing paths with best-selling author Louella Bryant (*Sheltering Angel* and 11 other novels) at a local Starbucks in Annapolis, Maryland, who took it upon herself to offer advice and encouragement to this struggling writer, and in the process has become a good friend along the way. Thanks, Ellie. Your expertise is priceless.

I would also like to give a big shout out to all the baristas at that same Starbucks who served up hundreds of cups of coffee, along with encouragement and smiles, over the many months I camped out every morning at the same table in their cafe working on this book, and providing countless "pup cups" without fail to my Golden Retriever, "MiGs."

A special thanks to Chloe McCubbin for taking such good care of "MiGs." I don't think he's ever had so many belly rubs!

To my good friend and "Dutch Connection," Jan-Peter van Viegen, who, from across the Atlantic, never failed to patiently wade through the many chapters of this book, which were rarely in chronological order, yet somehow made sense of them all. Having relied heavily on his input to keep this project on course, we have become good friends along the way. Thanks, "J. P."!

Proofreaders and guinea pigs – Whenever I needed to test my writing skills (or lack thereof!), I had a team of friends who were all more than willing to wade through my drafts and, in turn, were not afraid to point out errors, suggest course corrections and highlight areas needing improvement and clarity – trust me, there were quite a few! Many thanks to Maj Gen David Eichhorn, Lt Col Keith Miller, Lt Col John Pasqual, and Lt Col Dennis Ward for filling in the blanks of the formative year spent together earning our wings at Vance AFB, Oklahoma, as members of Undergraduate Pilot Training (UPT) class 78–04.

Additionally, thank you to three of my closest friends and fellow 94th Tactical Fighter Squadron (TFS) F-15 Eagle squadron mates, Lt Col Jim "Boots" Bowman, Lt Col John "Gash" Caudill, and Lt Col Clarke "Frog" Peele, for never failing to give me feedback on my latest writing. Their continual support and encouragement for the book over the many years I subjected them to regular "progress reports" was nothing short of miraculous. It is only fitting that I single out "Frog" for being a mentor and best friend who helped shape me as a young Aggressor pilot, who, despite some talent, needed direction. Without his tutelage, it is doubtful I would have developed into the fighter pilot I became, much less a "Red Eagle."

Thanks also Lt Col Dick "Tooey" Hoey for his steadfast friendship over the many years since first being squadron mates in the 12th TFS at Kadena AB, Okinawa, and my first flight in the F-4D. Dick was one of the initial cadre of pilots in the F-117 stealth fighter program at Tonopah Test Range (TTR), Nevada, and helped immensely in walking me through the operations and internal growing pains of being a member of the 4450th Tactical Group (TG) during the infancy of that program.

Additionally, I'd like to add my special thanks to Lt Col Greg "Curly" Nicholl and his wife, Marcie, who were the best neighbors possible and dear friends on North Straight Street in Las Vegas, Nevada. Curly and Marcie's input on the events surrounding the loss of the first F-117 during the early morning hours of July 11, 1986 (Chapter 27) were invaluable in piecing together events as they happened that fateful day.

ACKNOWLEDGMENTS

I next need to mention and thank my very good friend, warrior, and MiG-killer, Capt Rhory "Hoser" Draeger. The catalyst for this book stemmed from my initial discussion with Rhory about his two MiG kills during Operation *Desert Storm* in January 1991. Over two days in the vault of the Portland Air National Guard (ANG) in the fall of 1994, with maps, line-up cards, and mission notes arrayed before him, "Hoser" walked me through each of his MiG-29 and MiG-23 kills. What turned out to be the Epilogue of this book is Rhory's account of that first encounter with the enemy over the skies of Iraq on that historic afternoon on January 17, 1991. Sadly, just months following my discussions with Rhory, he was tragically taken from us and would never see his story shared with the readers of this book. Draeger was, without a doubt, the single-best fighter pilot I ever flew with or against. I count myself blessed to have known him as both a good friend and squadron mate.

And finally, this whole project would not have been possible without the unwavering love, support, encouragement, and patience of my best friend in life, my wife, Ann Marie. Her tolerance of the many hours I spent working on this book, from the early hours of most mornings and often into the wee hours of the night, was simply astounding. Her love knows no limits, and to her, I will be forever indebted.

Rob Zettel
Annapolis, Maryland
August, 2025

Foreword

The concept of air power in warfare was born in World War I, with brave and intrepid aviators like Eddie Rickenbacker and Frank Luke. During the interwar period, air power advocates were often met with skepticism – even ridicule – but pioneers such as Billy Mitchell persevered. By the time World War II broke out, they were vindicated. Air power had come of age, proving itself a decisive element of joint warfighting and ultimately contributing to victory. This success gave rise to a separate Service – the United States Air Force (USAF) – along with robust aviation arms within the US Navy, US Army, and US Marine Corps.

Air power continued to evolve in the Korean War, where US aviators achieved an impressive air-to-air kill ratio and refined air-to-ground tactics. The Vietnam conflict, however, was a sobering setback. Overconfidence, insufficient innovation, and inadequate aircraft, weapons, and tactics denied that generation of aviators the means to dominate. In the aftermath, as defense budgets were slashed during the 1970s, the US military drifted into what became known as a "hollow force."

Fortunately, visionary leaders like Gen Bill Creech and Col Gail Peck recognized that a dominant air power capability was not only a warfighting necessity but also a powerful deterrent. They drove three critical initiatives that ensured US air power would again rise to unrivaled dominance – especially against the Soviet Union and the Warsaw Pact.

First, we needed a cadre of "PhD-level" tactical aviators who could lead and teach at squadron level. This led to the growth and evolution of the USAF Fighter Weapons Instructor Course (FWIC), the US Navy Fighter Weapons School TOPGUN course, and the US Marine Corps' Marine Aviation Weapons and Tactics Squadron One (MAWTS-1). These programs/units produced graduates who were the best of the best – tactical experts who would ultimately shape combat execution across their Services.

Second, lessons from the Vietnam War showed that most combat losses occurred during the first ten missions in-theater. The solution was a training environment that realistically replicated the stress and complexity of air combat, with adversary aircraft that mirrored real-world threats. Out of this need came the *Red Flag* exercises and the Aggressor squadrons – built to replicate adversary tactics. Both programs were established to prepare aircrews to fight and survive from their very first mission.

Finally, we needed to understand the true capabilities of adversary aircraft and teach our aviators how to defeat them. Realism was Gail Peck's vision, and it gave birth to the 4477th Test and Evaluation Squadron (TES), the legendary "Red Eagles." This secret flying squadron, comprising Air Force, Navy, and Marine pilots, brought together graduates of FWIC, TOPGUN, and MAWTS-1, as well as Aggressor pilots, supported by some of the best maintainers, intelligence specialists, and air controllers in the US military. Operating from a remote base near Tonopah, Nevada, the squadron flew actual Soviet and Communist Bloc MiG aircraft (without manuals, often improvising maintenance and operations), providing American aviators with priceless experience.

Life in the "Red Eagles" was unique. Imagine a group of young captains, a few majors and lieutenant commanders, and a couple of lieutenant colonels, living and working in secrecy, flying airplanes no one admitted we had. The stories practically write themselves. Rob "Z-Man" Zettel has done just that in this book. To be candid, I never expected "Z-Man" to emerge as such an accomplished author, but he has brilliantly captured the spirit, challenges, and camaraderie of life in our secret MiG squadron.

There were practical jokes, rowdy parties, and the occasional lapse in judgment, but above all, there was professionalism, teamwork, and an unbreakable bond. We invented things like the "SAD" (screaming ass dive) arrival, threw legendary (toga) parties, and kept each other sharp and safe. The camaraderie was extraordinary, and the friendships endure to this day.

The flying was equally unforgettable. You can't imagine the looks from F-15, F-16, or F/A-18 pilots when a MiG-21 or MiG-23 slid into formation alongside them. We ran side-by-side performance profiles, executed one-on-one dogfights, and flew two-versus-two engagements where "Blue Air" (the good guys) never knew what would appear at the merge. In *Red Flag* exercises, we brought the unknown into the fight, forcing American aviators to contend with the reality of facing foreign jets in combat.

Being part of the "Red Eagles" was an extraordinary experience – not just because of the airplanes, but because of the people. It was a tight-knit squadron, bound by secrecy and purpose, and those bonds remain strong to this day.

Most importantly, I believe history will show that the combination of FWIC, TOPGUN, MAWTS-1, *Red Flag*, and the "Red Eagles" laid the foundation for US air power's overwhelming success in Operation

Desert Storm, the air war over Serbia (Operation *Allied Force*), and later in Operations *Enduring Freedom*, *Iraqi Freedom*, and even *Midnight Hammer*. These programs built the combat credibility that ensured America fielded the world's greatest air power. And it is a legacy we must preserve.

General (Ret) Herbert "Hawk" Carlisle
Commander, Air Combat Command, 2014–17
"Bandit 54"
Alexandria, Virginia
September, 2025

List of Illustrations

1 The author is seen seated here in a Christmas 1958 photograph with his two older brothers, Mark (left) and Chuck (right), and our mother, Harriet. I was four years old at the time, and I had already seen my first aircraft, which had left a lasting impression on me. (*Rob Zettel collection*)
2 My mother does the honors of pinning on my second lieutenant bars following my USAF commissioning at the College of Saint Thomas, in Saint Paul, Minnesota, on May 22, 1976. (*Rob Zettel collection*)
3 On the flightline at Vance AFB, Oklahoma, next to a T-38 Talon "White Rocket." The first time I sat in the aircraft, I knew this was where I belonged. I would solo in the T-38 on November 18, 1977. (*Rob Zettel collection*)
4 My mother pins on my wings following graduation from USAF UPT at Vance AFB on March 17, 1978. (*Rob Zettel collection*)
5 With brothers Mark (left) and Chuck (right) at the UPT graduation banquet at the Vance AFB O'Club in Enid, Oklahoma. (*Rob Zettel collection*)
6 311th TFTS, Luke AFB, Arizona, January 1979. I'm seated atop the F-4C's left intake, fifth from the left. Our class comprised all pilots, no WSOs. Lt Larry "Murph" Murphy (top row, far left) and I were the only two assigned to PACAF and the 18th TFW at Kadena AB, Okinawa. (*Rob Zettel collection*)
7 Standing before a 12th TFS F-4D at Kadena AB in July 1979, I'm posing here with my WSO, Capt John Sheekly. We were about to take off for Clark AB, in the Philippines, for two weeks of TDY, participating in *Cope Thunder 79-8*. (*Rob Zettel collection*)
8 Seen standing atop my F-4E in the revetments at Osan AB, Republic of Korea, after joining the 36th TFS "Flying Fiends."

This photograph was taken in spring 1981. I had just made captain a couple of months earlier. (*Rob Zettel collection*)

9   After making my final flight in the F-4E with the 36th TFS on August 20, 1981, at Osan AB, I shared a traditional bottle of "bubbly" with my WSO, Lt Tom "Mayberry" Griffith. Ten years later, then Maj Griffith spent 42 days as a PoW following the downing of his F-15E on January 17, 1991, during Operation *Desert Storm*. Tom was among the best WSOs I ever flew with. (*Rob Zettel collection*)

10 When I posed in my aircraft, F-5E 75-0612, at Clark AB in November 1982, little did I know that just weeks later, while back at Nellis AFB on holiday leave, I would be asked to interview for a position as a member of the 4477th TES. (*Rob Zettel collection*)

11 F-5E 75-0612 was photographed on short final approach at Kadena AB, Japan, in its distinctive "Lizard" camouflage. I was at the controls when this shot was taken. (*Rob Zettel collection*)

12 Capt Clarke "Frog" Peele, next to his Aggressor F-5E at Kadena AB in June 1983. The "Frog" was both a best friend and mentor. I owe much of my skills as a fighter pilot to his patience in molding me to his high standards. He was, without a doubt, one of the very best fighter pilots I ever flew with. (*Rob Zettel collection*)

13 Unbeknownst to me at the time, this USAF photograph was part of a package forwarded by the commanding officer of the 3rd TFW to his equivalent at the 57th FWW, recommending this young Aggressor to be part of the 4477th TES. (*Rob Zettel collection*)

14 This was the letter handed to me when I was called to report to Col Chuck "Brows" Holden, the Deputy Commander of Operations for the 3rd TFW. Thinking I was about to be called on the carpet for some flying infraction, I was instead told I'd been selected to be a "Red Eagle." (*Rob Zettel collection*)

15 4477th TES "Red Eagles" in June 1984, in a photograph featured in a slideshow for the farewell party of squadron commander, Lt Col George Gennin. These pilots are, from left to right, Capt Gary "Goldie" Craig, Maj John "Skid" Skidmore, Capt Jim "Wiley" Green, Capt Steve "Brownie" Brown, Lt Cdr Orville

LIST OF ILLUSTRATIONS

"Orv" Prins, Capt Rob "Z-Man" Zettel, Lt Cdr Jim "Rookie" Robb, Capt Paul "Stook" Stucky, Maj Dave "Blazo" Bland, Maj Larry "Shy" Shervanick, Maj Ted "Gabby" Drake, and Maj Frank "Paco" Geisler. (*Rob Zettel collection*)

16 The cockpit of the MiG-21F-13 was a less than stellar example of human engineering. Being used to Western-designed fighters, new "Red Eagles" found it a shock. Except for a different altimeter, airspeed indicator, transponder, G-suit fitting, and radio, the aircraft was vintage Soviet. (*USAF*)

17 The MiG-21F-13 was simply a pleasure to fly, excelling in the vertical. The large rudder allowed for superb high AOA control. Oddly enough, handling the aircraft on the ground was just the opposite, for its pneumatic brakes proved quite a challenge for new "Red Eagles" to become accustomed to. (*USAF*)

18 4477th TES commander Lt Col George Gennin leads a tour of the "Red Eagles'" VIP hangar for US Secretary of Defense Caspar Weinberger (right), with Assistant Secretary of Defense Frank Carlucci (far left) and TAC vice commander Lt Gen Bob Russ looking on. (*Photo courtesy of Laureen Gennin*)

19 Maj "Paco" Geisler, Lt Cdr "Orv" Prins, and Capt Billy Bayer of the "Red Eagles" are seen here with Laureen Gennin, wife of 4477th TES commander Lt Col George Gennin, at one of many parties hosted by the couple. (*Photo courtesy of Laureen Gennin*)

20 A 4477th TES MiG-21F-13 on a low-altitude run over the Nellis AFB ranges. (*USAF*)

21 Chinese-built F-7B Bort number "96" on the flightline at TTR. The 4477th TES would end up operating eight F-7Bs as part of *Constant Peg*, all of them brand new. I once opened the logbook for one I'd never seen before, and it revealed a total flight time of only 3.5 hours. (*USAF*)

22 Lt Cdr Guy "Brudog" Brubaker flies an immaculate T-38 over Cactus Peak, returning to TTR from one of many cross-country flights he and I made – I was flying the lead jet here. Note the absence of any identifying tail letters or fin flash. (*Rob Zettel collection*)

23 This US Navy Fighter Weapons School A-4E "Mongoose," complete with the famous TOPGUN insignia on its fin, is

an example of the aircraft Lt Cdr Greg "Hollywood" Dishart was flying when he and I knocked heads (I was flying a MiG-21F-13 at the time) over Range 76 in the Nellis AFB Range Complex in the fall of 1985. (*US Navy*)

24 A rare photograph of a "Red Eagles" pilot and a squadron MiG-23, in this case a "Flogger-E." It was taken one spring day in 1986 while I was checking out as an FCF in the MiG-23MS. (*Rob Zettel collection*)

25 Maj Ted "Gabby" Drake, "Bandit 42," was instrumental in turning the MiG-23 program into the success it was, and many "Flogger" pilots who flew the aircraft with the "Red Eagles" owe him a debt of gratitude for making it safer by doing so. (*Ted Drake collection*)

26 Learning and mastering this complicated cockpit presented another challenge for those who flew the MiG-23. It was but one week from my last flight in the MiG-21 until the first in the "Flogger," and the transition was made without the benefit of a simulator or two-seat trainer. (*National Museum of the Air Force*)

27 The only thing that made the transition from the MiG-21 to the MiG-23 a bit easier was the general placement of the engine and flight instruments. The visibility hadn't improved, and there were a few new items, namely radar, wing-sweep controls/indicator, stick grip, INS, and a throttle that slid along a rail. (*National Museum of the Air Force*)

28 The AOA gauge in the MiG-23 was indispensable in helping the pilot get maximum performance out of his airplane. Starting at 18 units of AOA, the "knuckle-rapper" on the control stick would begin rhythmic tapping on your knuckles, tactily making the pilot aware he was entering the high AOA region. (*Rob Zettel collection*)

29 MiG-23 flap and wing-sweep controls. The three-position flap control buttons (left to right, down–half–up) are just outboard of the wing-sweep control handle. Wing-sweep was manual, with detents at the 72°, 45°, and 16° settings. The standard wing-sweep rate was 3.1° per second. The actual wing-sweep position was verified by an indicator low and to the right of the gunsight. (*Rob Zettel collection*)

LIST OF ILLUSTRATIONS

30   MiG-23MS "Flogger-E" Bort number "39" on final approach to land. It was one of several MiG-23s I flew while a member of the 4477th TES. Here, you can see the ventral fin retracted for landing. It retracted whenever the landing gear handle was placed in the down position. (*USAF*)

31   Best party ever! I am seen here (center) in the O'Club at NAS Miramar at the Second Annual Toga Party, held on August 9, 1986. I'm flanked by "Red Eagles" Lt Cdr Marty "Streak" Chanik (second from left) and Capt "Hawk" Carlisle (second from right). Entertainment was provided by Otis Day and the Knights from the 1978 movie *National Lampoon's Animal House*. (*Rob Zettel collection*)

32   Just weeks following my last sortie in the MiG-23, I am seen here in the cockpit of an F-15 during transition training at Luke AFB, Arizona, as a member of the 426th TFTS in January 1987. (*Rob Zettel collection*)

33   The author in the 94th TFS's flagship F-15C over Jordan during Exercise *Coronet Archer* in July 1988. This was just months after the 94th had participated in one of the last *Constant Peg* deployments by any squadron before the 4477th flew its final official MiG sorties on March 4, 1988. (*Rob Zettel collection*)

34   The author poses with the commander of Air Combat Command, Gen "Hawk" Carlisle, while attending the October 2016 "Red Eagles" reunion at the National Museum of the USAF in Dayton. (*Rob Zettel collection*)

35   Rich Hofman, neighbor, coach, friend. He didn't know it at the time, but as the "big kid" next door, when Rich taught me how to play baseball, he instilled in me much more than how to just throw a ball and swing a bat. Discipline, hard work, and teamwork were values he imparted that helped shape me throughout my entire life. (*Rob Zettel collection*)

36   The author stands next to a MiG-23MS in the National Museum of the USAF in Dayton. This was one of many "Fishbeds" and "Floggers" the author flew during Project *Constant Peg* while a pilot with the 4477th TES. Lt Col Zettel would finish his assignment with the unit having completed a combined total of 476 sorties in both MiG aircraft. (*Rob Zettel collection*)

Prologue

"No Shots Taken"

"Ability is nothing without opportunity."

NAPOLEON BONAPARTE

October 7, 1983
20,000ft AGL (above ground level) over the South China Sea
45 miles west of Clark Air Base (AB), Republic of the Philippines

The high-G turn into the sleek fighter at my immediate "nine o'clock" for 500ft pushed my torso back into the ejection seat even farther. Sweat from beneath my helmet ran down my face, impeded only by my oxygen mask. The sounds of my hurried breathing and guttural straining against the G-force muffled out any sound of my fighter's engines at full afterburner. The throttles were "parked" at the forward stop of the throttle quadrant as I asked for every ounce of power they could muster. My opponent had mirrored my initial move, our two fighters closing the distance between us in seconds. Each pilot sought an advantage to press home his attack and defeat the other. Now on a collision course, neither one giving any quarter.

As our agile fighters drew nearer, my feet and hands acted instinctively. Gently moving the control stick slightly to the right, I placed the lift vector of my hard-turning jet imperceptibly above the missile rail on the tip of my opponent's left wing. My mind mentally crunched the closure rate of our two aircraft and prepared to reverse the hard turn, this time blending in smooth top rudder and full aft right stick. It was something you felt, almost sensed, rather than mechanically applied. We were both committed to an engagement; neither could afford to leave without the risk of being shot. Drawing nearer, I could discern his masked face, his helmet visor in the raised position, eyeing me precisely as I was him. Each of us was looking for that elusive "eye of the needle" advantage.

While still 100ft from his fighter, I began my lead-turn of him, not wanting to give away any undue advantage in turning room. Quickly reversing direction, I swung my head to the right just as his shiny silver fighter appeared below my canopy rail, a mere 200ft away. Having anticipated my move, he'd already begun his pull-up to his left to counter me. Within seconds, we'd each bled off 150KIAS (knots indicated airspeed) of energy, and the airspeed indicator quickly decreased through 250KIAS.

Once more, our aircraft crossed paths painfully close, with me maintaining a slightly higher position, both aircraft slowing still further. My body, attuned to the sensation of diminished G authority in the control stick, could tell we were nearing 150KIAS, and about to slow even further. There is no escape from such an engagement, only victory or defeat at the receiving end of the ravaging impact of 20mm cannon rounds ripping into your aircraft.

Not about to settle for being "tree'd" above his fighter, I abruptly applied full left rudder and full left and aft stick to roll off inverted and duck under him, quickly changing the dynamic of the fight. If this was where we were to lock horns, I was intent on driving the fight.

My adversary, nestled in the other cockpit, had immediately rolled off, countering my aggressive move. This guy was better than good. He was superb, handling his fighter at these high angles of attack (AOA) and now only at 120KIAS. I was now locked in a "rolling scissors" with my opponent. This was a corkscrew sort of maneuver where altitude and airspeed were traded for an opening to press home a gun attack on your opponent. Our proximity to each other was just too close to employ our heat-seeking missiles.

In short order, we were well into a left descending pirouette, each trying desperately to flush the other out front to bring our guns to bear. The maneuver had us canopy to canopy, eyeing each other from a distance of just a few hundred feet, each looking for his opponent to make a fatal mistake.

A glance at the rapidly retreating altimeter dials told me we were now descending through 15,000ft AGL, our attitude inconsequential as we continued our spiral down towards the calm surface of the flat Pacific Ocean that was looming beneath us. Such was the three-dimensional joust of air combat, our aircraft, our trusty steeds. Any delay of aircraft control inputs or miscalculation of your opponent meant inevitable defeat. There was no escape, except for hoping the other guy made the first mistake, allowing you to slide aft of his wing line and saddle up to employ your cannons at a range too close to miss. This engagement was what I'd trained for. This was what I was – a fighter pilot intent on winning.

The pitched fight continued its descent, the altimeter fast approaching 10,000ft. Still, there was no advantage; no shots were available to tip the battle in either direction, and fuel and altitude were running out. Nearing 10,000ft, I had enough altitude for one more roll before I'd be forced to transition back to a "flat scissors" above the "hard deck." I leveled out with

PROLOGUE

mere feet to spare before the no-nonsense limit of 10,000ft. Like me, my adversary had done the same, wallowing just above the altitude limit at 110KIAS off my right wing and desperately trying to gain energy. We were at a stalemate. No shots had been taken.

"Knock it off [KIO], knock it off. 'Baron Two-One,' knock it off," I radioed my opponent.

"Roger, 'Baron Two-Two' copies, knock it off," came his reply.

Within seconds of the call to stop the fight, I rocked the wings of my snake-camouflaged Northrop F-5E fighter, the signal for my "opponent," Capt Clarke "Frog" Peele, in his nearly identical F-5E, to join up on my right wing. Moments later, with him tucked in alongside me in close formation, I gave him an approving "thumbs up" as I turned our formation east and began our return for a landing at Clark AB, in the Republic of the Philippines.

This had been my last flight before heading back stateside following my nearly two-year assignment as a member of the USAF's 26th Aggressor Squadron (AS) at Clark AB. And for this flight, where it was customary to fly a scenario of your choice, I'd asked the squadron commander for only two things: two jets and the opportunity to fight "Frog" one last time.

A seasoned aviator with more than 2,000 hours as an Aggressor pilot in the F-5E, Peele had taken me under his wing 18 months earlier and mentored me to be the best fighter pilot I could be in that period. Along the way, he had kicked my ass on any number of occasions during our innumerable one-versus-one (1-v-1) engagements. During that time, I had made great strides and had, of late, been nearly his equal. Notice I said "nearly." Today, my final flight in the squadron was my last chance to test myself against arguably one of the best in the USAF. And I had more than held my own, having pushed Peele to the limit during our exhausting airborne duel. We were homeward bound on my final flight as an Aggressor pilot at Clark AB. It would be the last time that I ever flew with "Frog."

Once on the ground and back in the squadron building, a thorough debrief of the mission ensued. As the flight lead, I went through the sortie point by point, from engine start to shut down, focusing mostly on the engagement itself. Who did what, opportunities missed, lessons learned to take with us in subsequent engagements, and for me, to my next assignment.

I was about to head back to Nellis Air Force Base (AFB), Nevada, which was known as the "Home of the Fighter Pilot" in USAF parlance. To every USAF fighter pilot for decades, "Nellis" was simply Mecca, where it all happened. The base was home to the prestigious USAF Fighter Weapons School (FWS), two Aggressor squadrons similar to the one I was about to leave, the *Red Flag* combat training group, the USAF's Air Demonstration

Squadron, better known as the Thunderbirds, and an entire wing of operational F-16s. To say the place was a beehive of activity would be a gross understatement, and fighter pilots throughout the USAF would measure their careers by whether they had been a part of this place. High testosterone levels and equally inflated egos abounded.

I was about to embark on the next leg of my career as a fighter pilot. But it wasn't to any of the previously mentioned units I would be assigned. I had orders for a squadron that was even more unusual. Several weeks before my last flight with "Frog," I was told to report to the 4477th TES, a unit whose mission was shrouded in secrecy and which operated aircraft that no one could discuss freely. This was the USAF's top secret MiG squadron, and the aviators who flew the jets were all selected from the best fighter pilots the USAF, US Navy and US Marine Corps had to offer. I was to be one of them, a "Red Eagle."

So it was in this light that my debrief with Peele continued. With my "turn at the chalkboard" complete and celebratory cold beers already in hand, I deferred the remainder of the debrief to my mentor. A downhome native son of Richmond, Virginia, and proud graduate of the Virginia Military Institute, "Frog," known for his "Southern Talk," was brief.

"'Z-Man', I don't have much to say. You covered all the points. I flew the best airplane I could today, and I never had the slightest chance of a shot," Peele drawled. "Eighteen months ago, you came in here as a new 'puppy' Aggressor, and I spanked you in the same setup." He paused to laugh while he recounted our first 1-v-1 engagement and a couple of the bone-headed moves I'd made. All in vain, he was quick to add with a throaty laugh. Peele continued, "I had to work my ass off today to stay with you. No shots taken, 'Z-Man.' It doesn't get any better than that." With that, he reached forward to clink beer bottles with me and, as a toast, offered the following.

"You're ready, 'Z-Man.' You go back to Nellis and show them how it's done. The guys there are damn good, but they've got nothing on you. You can go there with your head high, knowing you belong there. And don't take any shit from anyone there; you can hang with the best. However, remember that you can still improve. There's still more to learn. I'm proud of you, boy. Good on ya!" And with that, it was over. I would soon return to Nellis AFB to join a new squadron and face new challenges.

This is my story of what it was like to be on the "inside" of a squadron whose collection of Russian-built MiGs was for years officially denied. Stories and myths abounded about who we were, what we did, and what we flew. During the heart of the Reagan years, the program, known simply as *Constant Peg* within the Department of Defense (DoD), flourished and grew from a handful of pilots and aircraft into a complete squadron (the 4477th TES), eventually totaling 30 pilots and 27 aircraft.

Among those of my former squadron mates, I'm sure my recollections are not unique, just different from the standard tales you might expect to hear when talking with fighter pilots of other squadrons, discussing their aircraft, and what they did with them. Our stories were inherently different due to the nature of our mission. What we had in common with our brethren in other US fighter squadrons was a shared passion for living on the edge, being incredibly competitive, and striving to be the best we could be at what we did.

After all, we're Americans! Cut from the same cloth as earlier generations of US fighter pilots who flew SPADs and Nieuports, Mustangs and Hellcats, and Sabres and Panthers into harm's way and back. Those who went before us were the stuff of legend, and we intended to carry on that proud tradition in our machines. You could say it was in our blood.

In most cases, we were the typical all-American boys who "grew up next door," went to academies, colleges, and universities, received our commissions as new second lieutenants and ensigns, went on to pilot training and, a year later, found ourselves pinning on our wings at the top of our respective classes and then on our way to an assignment flying our Phantom IIs, Tomcats or Eagles in our first operational fighter squadrons. From there, we never looked back; we only moved forward, higher and faster, tackling the challenges and taking the opportunities that came our way.

I realize that some or all of this may sound cocky and arrogant. Were we good? You bet we were. Just ask us! Tragically, along the way, we lost some squadron mates who were equally talented, deserving, and as dedicated to our cause and country as the rest. To them, I dedicate this book. So, kick back with a "cold one" and immerse yourself in a story of fast-living and hard-flying American fighter jocks and our secret MiG fighters – the likes of which our country will never see again.

Rob Zettel
Lieutenant Colonel, USAF (Ret)

1

Like Ice Skating

"Most healthy young men or women from 16 to 40 years of age can be taught to fly an ordinary airplane. A great majority of these may become very good pilots for transport- or passenger-carrying machines in times of peace, but the requirements for a military aviator call for more concentrated physical and mental ability in the individual than has ever been necessary in any calling heretofore."

BRIG GEN WILLIAM "BILLY" MITCHELL, SKYWAYS, 1930

Ever watch, seriously watch, any professional hockey player play the game and bring the puck up-ice? If you have, you'll notice a couple of things. Firstly, the guy has to skate incredibly well to make things happen. While he's skating, of course, he's doing all sorts of other stuff, like handling the puck, and sighting the defenders in his path to the goal, the position of his teammates and, finally, the goalie. Not only the position of the goalie in front of the net, but also mentally calculating the exact position around the goalie that he's planning to shoot the puck at, giving him the highest probability of scoring. Okay, now let's go back to the first thing I mentioned. He's doing all this while he's got a pair of blades strapped to his feet, and it happens in seconds in a very dynamic and energy-charged environment.

In describing flying a fighter aircraft to someone who's never been in one, much less in aerial combat, whether actual or simulated, I like to use the following analogy – *physically flying the airplane to a fighter pilot is what skating is to the hockey player.*

The mere act of actually flying in itself isn't that hard. Once you get the aircraft off the ground and up to altitude, I'm sure you could keep it reasonably straight and level. With some practice obtained from something as simple as the various flight simulator games on your home computer, you could probably do some basic maneuvers without losing control. Similarly, once you get a Formula 1 race car onto the track, I'm sure most could make it around without hitting any barriers. But that's all you'll do. Now, let's take

LIKE ICE SKATING

this analogy back to the role of the fighter pilot about to go head-to-head with an equally matched opponent.

Employing a high-performance fighter as a weapon system requires a unique skill set. Remember the hockey player blazing up the ice with the puck on his stick? Do you think he's wondering about what his feet are doing? No way!

Well, imagine yourself in the cockpit of a high-performance fighter in the middle of a gut-wrenching dogfight with another reasonably skilled opponent. First off, you don't have time to think about physically flying the airplane. Either it happens, or you'll quickly find yourself losing out to your opponent. Press on in such a fight when you're losing precious airspeed, altitude, and turning room, or all three, to your adversary, and you'll soon find yourself fighting for your very life in a contest where only the victor comes home.

From the time you "eyeball" your opponent from whatever distance, you're increasingly in a mode of trying to position yourself, and by extension your aircraft, in a place where you can employ any of the weapons you're carrying to shoot him down in the least amount of time. Allow your opponent to do it first, and you'll quickly be on the receiving end of the devastating effectiveness of a high-explosive missile as it slices through your aircraft, or the withering fire from his high-velocity cannon impacting your aircraft and tearing both it and your body to pieces.

Let's take this scenario a bit further and use it as a precursor. Let's make it easier for you and say it's only you and your opponent in the skies today. Lucky you. You don't have to worry about his wingman trying to shoot you down, or your wingman accidentally doing the same to you or having a mid-air collision with you as you both vie for position to kill your opponent. So, it's just the two of you. And to make it even easier, we won't even consider the complexity that goes into the same equation if you throw in radar-guided and/or heat-seeking missiles to employ or defend against. In today's scenario, you and your adversary are armed with just your cannons. So, it's "guns versus guns" in our aerial dogfight scenario. It's just like back in the days of von Richthofen and Rickenbacker. Well, sort of.

Back then, they flew at airspeeds generally less than 120KIAS in aircraft that could barely sustain a couple of Gs, and rarely engaged one another at higher than 5,000ft AGL. In today's air-to-air battles, you're often supersonic, your aircraft and powerful engines can develop and sustain more Gs than your body can withstand, and you will engage your opponent at altitudes anywhere from mere feet above the ground up to 50,000ft AGL.

Once you've visually acquired your enemy, the work begins in earnest. In an instant, you're assessing his and your energy states. By that, I mean how much potential energy you each have at this very instant, and how that will factor into everything you do from here on out. Your machine subtly whispers to you, the feel of the control stick in your right hand relaying the aerodynamic forces on your flight controls. Eyes sweep the Heads-Up Display (HUD) and instruments, confirming what your hands are sensing. You're verifying your airspeed, altitude, attitude, heading, fuel, and weapons, while keeping an eye on your opponent and continuing to determine his intentions as you close the miles between you. All of this the mind absorbs in an instant.

To the uninitiated, speed is the first thing that is entirely mind-boggling. In aviation, it's measured in knots of indicated airspeed (KIAS) or simply "knots," not miles per hour (mph). Most people's day-to-day lives aren't filled with making split-second decisions that their survival depends on. In this environment, it's a constant. For example, if you're both doing 500KIAS, you're closing on each other at 1,000KIAS, "eating up" a nautical mile between you every 3.6 seconds.

How about a figure you can relate to? At 500KIAS, you're doing the equivalent of 575mph. The 16-mile separation you had between you and your adversary a minute ago has just evaporated in the time it takes most people to stir the cream and sugar into their morning tea or coffee. There's not much time to get your act together and figure out if you're either going to "bug-out" (leave the fight and separate) and live to fight another day, or stay and fight until someone gets shot down or one or both of you run out of fuel. There are few options, and, as you can see, everything happens quickly. This is no place for the faint of heart or, in fighter pilot terminology, a "weak dick" (aka, a "Whiskey Delta").

The pilot in the other cockpit is doing precisely the same kind of assessment as he closes on you. You are assessing and reassessing, and so is he. It's the ultimate chess game, played in three dimensions and often at supersonic speeds. You're both quickly adjusting any or all of the above variables to find that one combination that will allow you a single ounce of advantage. Once you get it, you press it home and make the other guy pay. A single mistake in the air will cost you your life in combat.

Add to this mix the factors of weather, sun position, camouflage of each fighter, and aircraft size, and the problem suddenly becomes incredibly complex. And this is all happening in the first 60 seconds of your fight, and you haven't even merged with your adversary yet.

An additional variable of this aerial chess game that the average reader doesn't often consider is the altitude at which we will engage. In combat, anything is fair; there are no rules, just results. Anywhere between the Earth's surface and 50,000ft AGL is pretty realistic. If you are screaming along at just a few hundred feet, the surrounding landscape is nothing but a blur. At higher altitudes, the mosaic below is not unlike the one you see out of your typical airline window. Of course, like everything in life, there are trade-offs for choosing one or the other. Pick the wrong one and you might give undue advantage to your opponent, again possibly costing you your life.

At lower altitudes, you'll be able to get the maximum performance from your airplane due to the increased air density, enabling your wings and engines to deliver more performance than the human body can withstand in terms of the gravitational forces (Gs) you're likely to pull in a hard turning fight. All this is at the cost of higher fuel consumption, shorter weapons employment ranges, and the ever-present danger of hitting terra firma.

Conversely, in the rarefied air at 40,000ft AGL, your aircraft cannot develop or sustain the optimal performance you previously enjoyed at the lower altitudes, and a turning engagement with another fighter of similar design will quickly be going "downhill" to maintain the aforementioned critical energy state. Once again, lose out here to your opponent and you'll pay with your life.

See a common thread here? Holding an advantage over your opponent means survival, or at least the likelihood of it. And this isn't to say that seemingly small or large advantages can't quickly be lost to a costly error in judgment or something as fundamental as losing sight of your enemy. As you close with your opponent, you're not thinking about the good ole USA, mom, or apple pie. Survival means killing the other guy as quickly as possible because it must be assumed that he's trying to do the same thing to you.

In your mind, you have to respect every enemy opponent, and his fighter, that you're about to meet. No assumptions, no quarter given. Doing anything less may unknowingly give away some subtle advantage that could cost you your life. Right now, it means getting him sufficiently in your sights to enable you to employ your 20mm cannon, remembering full well that if he's flying anything other than a US-made fighter, he's probably carrying even larger armament: 23mm, 30mm, perhaps even a 37mm cannon. There's no room for error. Any hits that find their mark at this speed will mean almost certain loss of either fighter. A single hit to the cockpit will be fatal.

As you get closer, you must determine if you can see him sufficiently well enough to allow you to employ your cannon as you meet. Closing this fast, you'll have to open fire while still two miles apart and try to concentrate your fire into a very narrow window if you have any hope of hitting him. And remember, if he's worth a damn, he'll probably be trying to do the same to you. So not only must you think offensively, but you'll also have to be prepared to evade if you see his "nose on fire" before you open up with your guns as well.

You'll merge with him from two miles out in less than eight seconds. Each precious second, you analyze every conceivable variable of this equation to find the answer. And then, in a flash, he's past you. Today, off your left side, passing so close you couldn't fit another fighter in between you. Giving him any available room to turn is criminal, and you try to steal all the space you can from him at the pass, hopefully getting precious degrees of turn, sometimes measured in single digits, in your favor as you pass. If you've waited until now to start your max-G turn to pursue him, allow me to let you in on something – you're already behind the fight, and if not corrected soon, it will soon mark your end.

The following 10–15 seconds are crucial to winning and your survival. As he blazes past you, those foreign to this environment would find something else missing. Sound! There are no roaring jet engines that would deafen you like at an airshow. There is no sensation of rushing air as you likewise flash past him. The only sounds registering are those of your own making. The sounds of grunting and heavy breathing that fill your ears are you. You're working against the 7–9G turn to keep the blood in your head from draining to your lower extremities. Failing to do this will rob you of your eyesight ("gray-out") and, eventually, actual consciousness ("black-out") – this last phenomenon is commonly known in the fighter world as G-induced loss of consciousness.

This you do instinctively, your abdominal muscles having tightened like you're ready to absorb a stomach punch from Muhammad Ali, forcefully exerting pressure in your diaphragm while keeping your throat closed, stealing gasps of precious oxygen every couple of seconds to stay conscious. Your neck is twisted like it's never been twisted before, all to keep sight of your enemy. Your head is back against the ejection seat, and you're fighting to keep it from dropping into your chest. At this moment, the 8G load of your hard turn exerts eight times the force of gravity on your body, and your head is now the equivalent of an 80lb barbell! The sweat that's been building over the past several minutes beneath your helmet runs down your forehead, through your eyes, and down your face. You're soaked. While you're subconsciously aware of this, you're focused, not caring that you will lose three to five pounds in weight on this flight despite the frigid cold temperatures outside your cockpit. All the while, you're one with your machine, going where you command it. No thinking, just doing. You're Wayne Gretzky coming up-ice with the puck, times ten!

Your airplane is bleeding energy fast in the first few seconds of the turning engagement. At altitude, with 7–9Gs on the airframe and in full afterburner,

LIKE ICE SKATING

you're bleeding off anywhere from 30 to 50KIAS per second, depending on the wing-loading of your aircraft. Your airplane can withstand more than the human body at low altitudes, and you're not losing airspeed as fast.

As you keep your eyes on your opponent, you turn your fighter at a rate of 18–22 degrees per second. If your airplane can't sustain this at medium to high altitudes, you will soon be either out of airspeed to fight or descending like a rock, possibly both. But whatever happens to you is also happening to your opponent in the other cockpit. You must both manage a highly fluid, dynamic, and changing aerial duel. As the airspeed bleeds off, so do the G loads, for without the airspeed, your aircraft can't sustain the Gs and the turn rates generated at a fighter's optimal "corner velocity."

The pressure you exert on your body from your abdominal "crunches" eases as the Gs subside. You can manage to take mostly full, but hurried, breaths. If you've grayed out, your eyesight returns, and you can focus on your quarry again. Physically, it's as demanding a workout as you've ever had. And you've just started. This is part of what I did almost daily for more than three years as a pilot flying Soviet MiGs as a member of the 4477th TES.

This story is a window into that world, specifically mine. Becoming a fighter pilot, or more importantly, becoming arguably one of the best, isn't a destination as much as it is a journey that can't be mapped out in advance. It's full of triumphs, disappointments, twists and turns, detours, and obstacles. And if I'm being brutally honest, it isn't something obtained without ample measures of luck and good fortune. It is a matter of good fortune to sometimes be in the right place at the right time, and fortunate to have lived through countless close calls and emergencies while flying some of the world's highest-performance fighter aircraft.

To be sure, those of us who became fighter pilots had to have some talent – some would even call it natural talent. I've known aviators who were incredibly gifted when it came to aerial combat. The majority of us mere mortals had to work at it.

I mentioned it as a journey, perhaps one without a destination. In my experience, you never quite know when the journey is over. While that may be the case throughout a career, in this instance, I'll explain how I stepped foot in the squadron that once seemed so remote and out of reach that when I arrived, I still could hardly believe I was there.

2

A Distant Memory

"You cannot control everything that happens to you; you can only control the way you respond to what happens. In your response is your power."

ANONYMOUS

A person's first memories are difficult to define; much less certain is that they definitively have anything to do with shaping one's future. For most, searching the cobwebbed attic of our memory will likely turn up faint scenes, such as a parent's loving embrace, with siblings at a playground, or perhaps an emotional event that is etched forever in the cerebral cortex of our brain. However unlikely, it doesn't erase the fact that one, if not the earliest, memory I have is that of an airplane. Make that a row of airplanes. While this may sound fabricated and all too convenient, it is the simple truth. For me, whatever one chooses to call it, whether it be a prologue to a career in aviation or mere coincidence, it was part of what later unfolded and can't be dismissed entirely.

That memory is of me as a very small boy, perhaps no more than three years old, sitting in the back seat of our family's 1951 Mercury Coupé, looking ahead from where we had parked and seeing a row of shiny aircraft. I don't remember buildings or people; I just remember the airplanes. While the circumstances are a blur, the most significant and lasting image is of the bright orange tip-tanks attached to their wings. All I can remember is being in this car with my mom and two older brothers, standing on the back seat and looking out beyond the cyclone fence ahead to the flightline beyond, perhaps just 50 yards away. I don't recall the sound of jet engines or the smell of jet fuel – just the bright orange tip-tanks.

The year had to have been 1957, definitely no later than 1958. The location was Mitchell Field Airport in Milwaukee, Wisconsin. Where my mother, Harriet, had parked the car had to have been just outside the Wisconsin ANG's flightline. Why there? I have no idea. I just remember looking out with my two brothers and seeing those aircraft. I don't even remember us getting out of the car to stretch our legs, although I'm sure we had. I just don't remember. In retrospect, those aircraft were most likely F-89s of the 126th Fighter Interceptor Squadron (FIS) of the Wisconsin ANG. But that's largely irrelevant. All my tiny brain registered were the bright orange tip-tanks.

The reason why we were there is a longer story. The short answer is that my mother, being relatively new to driving, would take short trips to gain experience and, more likely, boost her confidence. This 30-mile drive was undoubtedly one of those, and it was also borne of necessity. You see, my father, Andrew, had tragically been killed in an industrial accident just weeks before my second birthday, leaving my mother a widow with three small boys, the oldest of whom had just turned five at the time. Some might say such events shape people. Or, perhaps, you allow them to shape you. Ironically, because I grew up not knowing what life was like with a father, you could say I was spared the emotional pain and trauma that would accompany the sudden loss of mine. For me, it was all I ever knew.

Most importantly, my mother didn't let that tragedy shape who she was or what her sons would become. I owe her considerable gratitude for being the rock and presence she was for me and my brothers throughout her life. However, before I delve into how I began this journey, which itself was improbable, it's essential to understand where I came from and the people and circumstances that helped shape the environment in which I was raised.

My mother and father had humble beginnings, growing up on small dairy farms in northeastern Wisconsin. Respectively, they were the children of Belgian and German emigrants, who, like thousands before them, had come to the USA in the early 1900s, dreaming of opportunities beyond reach in their native homelands. While these immigrants initially couldn't speak English, they made up for it with their work ethic and devotion to faith and family. Moreover, they were so proud of their newly adopted country and citizenship that many never taught their children their native language but instead insisted on the strict use of English in their homes.

Although most had limited education, they were skilled dairy farmers, and the land my grandparents settled in was similar to what they had left behind in Europe. Unknowingly, at the time, my parents had grown up less than 15 miles apart on separate farms surrounded by their Belgian and German enclaves. While their families might have come from different countries and backgrounds, they shared similar values: a strong faith in God centered on the Catholic Church, a reliance on hard work and discipline, and an absolute contempt for self-pity and complaining.

When the Great Depression hit in 1929, my parents were in their teens. The sudden economic hardships hit home hard, even on the farm. When President Franklin D. Roosevelt took office in 1933, unemployment in the US was nearing 25 percent. The grim reality was that, due to their family's financial hardships, neither of my parents could afford to be spared from the farm to attend high school. An eighth-grade education was the highest they were allowed to achieve, their presence being needed that much back home on the farms in order to make ends meet. Despite this, my mother continued to read and learn as much as possible, with the hope of returning to school one day. For her and so many others at the time, that opportunity never happened.

When the Japanese attacked Pearl Harbor on December 7, 1941, my parents had only just started dating, having met at a local dance hall mere weeks before. While my mother described it as a budding romance, it was put on hold when my father enlisted in the US Navy to serve his country, like millions of other young men across the country. He did this despite being eligible for a deferment as a farmer, which was deemed vital to the economy and the war effort.

Months later, following his induction into service and completion of training, my father received orders that he and his ship, the battle damage repair vessel USS *Phaon* (ARB-3), would depart for the South Pacific, where the war had, by that time, been raging for over a year. Ironically, being of German descent, my father was prohibited from serving in the European theater.

While they weren't married and unsure if he'd return, my father summoned his courage and asked my mom to wait for him. He also told her he'd understand if she didn't. My mom told me years later that she didn't hesitate in her answer, promised him she'd stay and wait, and prayed that he'd someday come home again. In early 1943, he left for the war, not knowing if he'd ever return. Over the next two-and-a-half years, half-a-world apart, they kept their romance going, held together by the occasional letter in the mail – two young hearts separated by war. Years later, following my mother's passing, my brothers and I discovered, neatly tucked away in a shoebox and hidden from us for more than 60 years, every letter she'd received from the young man who would someday be my father. They remain today my most treasured possession.

As fortune would have it, he returned from the war the first week in August 1945. Just four days before Victory over Japan Day, they were married, Andy, a decorated Chief Petty Officer, resplendent in his US

A DISTANT MEMORY

Navy uniform, and my mother, Harriet, a beautiful and smiling bride in an expensive dress my grandfather, Charles, deemed worth the hefty expense following years of war (their wedding photo still sits on a bookshelf in my office today).

With the war over, the new couple didn't return to the farms they had grown up on. Instead, like many GIs returning from the war with newfound skills and aspirations, made their way to the big cities and their factories that were fast becoming part of the postwar industrial boom in the US. Within months of his return, my father had found work in the small but growing town of Racine, Wisconsin, three hours south of where they'd grown up.

Situated between Chicago, Illinois, and Milwaukee, Wisconsin, Racine was part of the industrial belt that stretched along the southwestern corner of Lake Michigan. There, he went to work for Massey Ferguson, a huge tractor and farm machinery company that, having produced tanks for the US Army during the war, had retooled for peacetime production and needed skilled workers. Andy was exactly what they were looking for, having become a master welder repairing ships damaged in combat during the war.

Over the next several years, Andy and Harriet started a family, built a new and larger home in the country for their growing family of three boys, and provided space for my father to start and establish his own welding business. For Harriet, with everything going so well, the lean years during the Depression and those spent alone during the war seemed a distant and forgotten memory. And then, it all was shattered with a knock on the door one spring day, with police officers informing her that her husband, Andy, wouldn't be coming home.

Suddenly, the world, as she had known it, ceased to exist and became something unexpected, the unknown of what lay ahead of her undoubtedly daunting and frightening. Dreams and plans for a life as she once imagined were gone in an instant. The grim reality she faced was stark. She was now a single mother of three young boys, the oldest of whom had just turned five years old, the youngest not yet two years old, and still in diapers.

For the past 11 years, she'd been a housewife and a homemaker. She hadn't worked outside the home since the years during the war in the plywood factories in Algoma, Wisconsin, where women filled jobs previously held by men who were off to the war in uniform. As such, she had no marketable skills, even if she had been able to leave her young boys at home, which was impossible, given that she had no family or friends nearby to watch them. The year was 1956, and my mother didn't even know how to drive a car. The Mercury Coupé my father had bought new, right off the showroom floor, sat idle in the garage. Her ability to provide for her family had to have weighed heavily on her.

So, how did she cope and manage what, at the time, must have seemed like insurmountable odds? She fell back on what she had been raised on: her strong Catholic faith, hard work, discipline, and never giving in to self-pity or complaint.

Her faith provided the bedrock to press ahead during the darkest chapter in her life. Over the years, Saint Edward's Catholic Parish, its priests, and Dominican nuns became the support center that undoubtedly kept her going, while its grade school provided foundation and structure for me and my brothers. Although there was no way she could afford to send us to Saint Edward's private school, somehow, we were enrolled every year with apparently few questions asked. How she did it, I'll never know. But I received a first-class parochial education for which I'll forever be indebted to the parishioners of Saint Edwards.

Still, I remember countless nights passing her open bedroom door when I saw her silhouette kneeling by her bedside in the darkness, silently praying her rosary, undoubtedly asking for help and guidance to make it through yet another day. How many nights she wept silently, out of sight of her young boys, I'll never know. It's emotional for me today just thinking of it.

Hard work was something Harriet was accustomed to, growing up on my grandparents' farm, and it was not foreign to her. Up early to milk the cows before heading to work for an eight-hour shift at the plywood factory, and then milking them again when she returned was the routine she had grown accustomed to. All done without complaint. It was all she had known.

Now, unable to leave her boys to look for a job, she did what she knew; she took in people's laundry every week. Mind you, this was well before automatic washers and dryers were common household appliances. Some of my earliest memories were of her doing loads of laundry, carrying heavy baskets up from the basement to the clotheslines in our backyard, where she hung them to dry. And that was when the weather in Wisconsin allowed it. When it didn't, our basement was a maze of sheets, blankets, and personal laundry items hanging from a dozen clotheslines that stretched across its length. As a young toddler, I found this to be an endless source of fun as my brothers and I would run up and down the rows of drying clothes, hiding from each other.

From shortly after breakfast until late at night, my mom washed, ironed, and folded laundry. She did all this and everything else required to support her family. If there had been more than 24 hours each day, she would've found a way to fill them. Her selflessness knew no bounds.

Beyond her work ethic, her discipline in whatever she did helped shape me in the years ahead. Our household was not one where you were in bed past 6.30 am. I still remember hearing her alarm clock go off well before we awoke each morning, and her footsteps down the hall to the kitchen, where she would prepare breakfast for us or, more often than not, iron another basket of clothes for customers before my brothers and I got up.

There was no dilly-dallying when it was time for us to get up for school or daily mass. It was either you got up or you heard about it. To this day, I never lounge in bed when my alarm sounds. What's more, she purposely set the clocks in the house five minutes ahead of actual time to ensure we would never be late for anything. As the saying in the military goes, "If you're not five minutes early, you're late!" I'm not sure my mother hadn't coined that phrase much earlier.

Discipline went hand in hand with hard work and was one of her core beliefs, evident in her approach to everything in life. She left nothing to chance and followed a pattern she could count on to help her get through every day, week after week, month after month, year after year. This pattern enabled her to raise us as she did, with us following a fairly strict regimen. As you can imagine, a combination of three growing boys and no structural or behavioral discipline would have been a disaster waiting to happen. It never did.

While my mother was small in stature, soft-spoken, and had a caring nature, she wasn't lax in setting the rules and enforcing them. As a young boy, I recall spending many a time in a corner of the kitchen or hallway on my knees for 10–15 minutes for some infraction of the house rules or misbehavior. Oh, and there was to be no sitting back on your heels. Kneel straight up with your nose in the corner, and no talking. My brothers and I stayed in line pretty well. That discipline kept us out of trouble, and it served us well long after we left for college years later.

Her attention to detail, of necessity, was astounding when it came to anything related to finances. With minimal financial resources, she was a master at stretching a dollar, never wasting a penny, and knowing exactly where every dollar was going. While Harriet may only have attended school through the eighth grade, she could teach a master class on economics and the value of a dollar. Many evenings, I recall sitting at the kitchen table after dinner and watching her go through all the bills and deposits she had taken from doing clients' laundry, then balancing her checkbook to the penny. If it didn't balance, Mom worked at it until it did. She did all this relying solely on meticulously written notes. Do I need to mention that calculators did not yet exist? For her entire life, Harriet never had an unbalanced checkbook.

As you might imagine, having grown up as my parents did and what they had been through, there was never a thought about self-pity or complaining. When everyone around you is in the same boat as you, it's senseless to complain, as no one will be listening to you, much less giving you any sympathy. While you might think my mother would occasionally give in to self-pity or complaint, you'd be wrong. Furthermore, she didn't tolerate it from my brothers or me. That was a sign of weakness to her; it had no room in our family or house. If you wanted to complain, you'd better do it outside her presence.

With that as a foundation, what came next was the catalyst that helped my brothers and me develop the traits of discipline, hard work, and never giving in to whining or complaint, which our mother had instilled in us. What was needed, in those formative years of ours, was a person or program who could channel our energy into something productive, worthwhile, and lasting. Call it sheer luck or perhaps fate, the answer just happened to live right next door. For my brothers and me, we simply knew the big kid who lived next to us as "Rich." Little did any of us know at the time that in the decades ahead, thousands of ballplayers from Little League to Major League Baseball would respectfully call him by one name only – "Coach Hofman."

Summertime 1960
Backyard ball field
7009 Washington Ave
Racine, Wisconsin

With a distinct crack, the baseball rocketed off the barrel of the bat just swung by my oldest brother, Chuck, who lined a speeding ground ball my way at shortstop in the infield. As I positioned myself to field the ball, in a booming voice, Rich Hofman shouted from the pitcher's mound, "Robbie, get down in front of that ball – glove down, head up, eye on the ball. Don't let that ball get past you!"

From the pitcher's mound, Hofman was, as he always did, "coaching" me to make the play. Assuming I fielded the ball, I next had to throw it back to Rich to force my brother out, who, in the meantime, was speeding on his way to first base. This rule of "Pitcher's Hand" backyard baseball was one Rich had taught us. We didn't have enough neighborhood kids to dedicate a teammate to the pitcher's role, much less first base, so Rich himself filled that position. It was the singular role he would voluntarily fill for years to follow, teaching the "little kids" next door all about the game of baseball, which even then, as a 16-year-old, was his passion.

As the "designated pitcher," Rich was also the umpire, calling balls and strikes, ruling on foul balls, the scorekeeper, and tactician, offering his thoughts on what to hit, how to hit it, where to place it and, more importantly, the why behind all of the above! It was Rich who had laid out the ball diamond on a field where alfalfa had been mowed just a year earlier and paced off the distances between the bases. If it involved the game of baseball, he was all over it. In a nutshell, he was everything but the groundskeeper!

I positioned myself, ready to make the play, as the ball came at me skipping across the uneven "infield." I use that term loosely. Our ball field was the vacant half-acre former hayfield that my parents had bought adjacent to the property our home was on, which constituted the neighborhood's "all-sports" facility: baseball in the spring and summer, football in the fall, and occasionally, if the weather cooperated, a hockey rink in the winter. Oh, and there was the basketball "court" in the driveway where the backboard and basket hung on the garage wall when we were so inclined.

As the ball neared me and I prepared to scoop it up in my glove, it took one of those "hayfield hops," and instead of following a predictable path along the ground, it bounced and made a beeline straight to my lower lip. It hit me square, but I had stopped it, and with no time to waste, picked it up and threw, for me, a rocket to Rich on the mound, throwing my brother, Chuck, out before he reached first base. The ball had not gotten past me.

"Great job, Robbie. Way to stay with it." Rich offered it as a way of approval for handling a hot grounder.

"Hey, are you okay? Looks like that grounder caught you square on your lower lip," he added, approaching me to take a look.

I reached up with my throwing hand and wiped it across my mouth. Yes, there was a substantial amount of blood there. I ran my tongue over the source of the stinging pain and could both feel and taste it. After spitting out a mouthful of blood, followed by wiping my mouth on my shirt sleeve, I was ready to continue playing. No complaining, no whining allowed.

"Atta boy, Robbie. Way to be fearless out there. That's how it's done." With those words of encouragement and praise from Rich, which meant more to me than winning the game, it was next batter up. The game continued.

I'm sure that at the time, Rich had no idea of the impact he was having on the future of the three young boys living next door when he simply taught them how to hold a baseball bat, throw, catch, and field ground balls. Despite Rich being anywhere from seven to ten years older than my brothers and me, we were eager participants. What we lacked in size and skills was made up for with a zeal to play the game like him. Even though I was the youngest and could hardly hold the bat or the ball in my small hands when I first started playing sports at the age of five, I never gave up or complained. It was just another opportunity to try harder and listen to what Rich had to share with me.

To us, learning the game and how to play it, like Rich, was everything. At the time, Rich, a varsity baseball player at Washington Park High School in Racine, was unknowingly instilling in my brothers and me a love for sports, hard work, discipline, and a hearty competitive attitude, something that we would carry with us long after we moved on from sandlot ballgames and on to high school and eventually college.

Reflecting on it, those lessons aligned perfectly with how our mother was raising us. We then had an outlet in which to channel our seemingly boundless energy and focus those traits: team sports. In essence, it was a roadmap to success in life, literally being played out in the form of a game. It is a miracle that we were fortunate enough to have Rich Hofman as our neighbor at a time when we needed inspiration and guidance the most, without a father.

For Hofman, it was just the start of a lifelong love affair with the game itself, one that would eventually lead to him becoming the highest achieving high school baseball coach of all time in the state of Florida with 1,020 victories, 12 State Championships, four National Championships, and named high school "Coach of the Decade" for the 1990s by Baseball America – all records that would one day find him inducted into eight different Baseball Halls of Fame. I often remind "Coach Hofman" that while I may not have developed into a Major League Baseball star, like his former player Alex Rodriguez and others, I was one of his very first!

To be sure, my brothers and I would go on to play and participate in various sports, have other great coaches, and achieve success in all of them. But it was those formative years, spent on an old hayfield with Rich Hofman, that cemented in me traits that would stay with me and allow me to overcome hurdles for a lifetime.

So, you may be asking yourself, how does this all tie into the airplane I remembered seeing as a toddler? Subconsciously, growing up, I think my fascination with aircraft and flight, despite never having been around them, had always been with me as a kid. Perhaps, it had always been a dream, much like hitting a home run before one could even hold a bat properly. Whatever one chooses to call it, it was there in every airplane model I built, movies I watched about flying, like "Twelve O'clock High," or the simple sighting of one flying overhead on a warm summer's day while out playing baseball in a hayfield in Racine. Little did I know at the time that this fascination would someday become a dream fueled by passion. It would be years before all that became clear, but it was one borne on a solid foundation of hard work, discipline, and never giving in to self-pity or complaint. I had indeed been well coached.

3

Improbable Odds

"It's difficult to follow your dream. It's a tragedy not to."

RALPH MARSTON

May 13, 1971
J. I. Case High School
Racine, Wisconsin

I remember sitting patiently outside the Guidance Counselor's office, located amongst the administrative offices on the first floor at the east end of J. I. Case High School, awaiting Mr. David Liljegren to finish with the previous student's appointment before my turn came. Mr. Liljegren was one of a handful of school guidance counselors who, every year, in addition to his other job as a music teacher, sat down with students of the Junior Class for a 30-minute guidance session and asked them what they had in mind after receiving their diplomas the following year. J. I. Case High School, or more simply, Case, was one of three public high schools in Racine, each with an enrollment of roughly 2,000–2,200 students in grades 10–12.

With more than 700 students in my class, Mr. Liljegren and his fellow guidance counselors had been conducting these sessions for the other members of the Class of '72 for the past eight to ten weeks to ensure every pupil would cycle through before school let out for the summer, scheduled to occur just a few weeks from now. With a last name that starts with "Z" and accustomed to being at the end of almost every line since I could remember, I figured they must be about finished with their counseling sessions for the school year.

After being summoned in and offered a chair opposite his desk, Mr. Liljegren began with some small talk about the current track season, plans for the summer, and so on. After a couple of minutes, he cut to the chase.

"Okay, Rob, let's talk about your plans for what you'd like to do after graduation this time next year. It'll be here before you know it."

At the time, I was about three weeks shy of my 17th birthday, and any thoughts or plans beyond that and summer vacation were sketchy and vague at best.

"Well, I'm pretty sure I'd like to go to college," I replied – a good and reasonable answer, I thought. My oldest brother, Chuck, was about to finish his sophomore year at the University of Notre Dame, and my brother Mark had recently been accepted there and would be starting his first year in September. So, it only seemed reasonable, in my simplistic way of thinking, that I'd follow a similar route. After all, how hard could it be?

"That's great to hear. But I'm talking about beyond college, wherever that might be. What sort of career aspirations do you have? Is there anything of interest beyond just going to college?"

Whoa! What? Beyond college? That's at least five years away. I need to decide that now?

This was the first time anyone had ever asked me that. Until now, I'd just assumed that if I plodded along, the answers to these questions would somehow sort themselves out, and things would magically fall into place. Planning wasn't something I did beyond the next week or two, and typically centered on weekend work schedules and track practice. I sensed he sought a well-thought-out, reasoned answer, so, not having one, I hurriedly blurted out what subconsciously had been on my mind.

"Well, I think I'd like to be a pilot."

I must have looked surprised, possibly unsure of my answer, as Mr. Liljegren paused and sat up a bit straighter in his chair, seemingly taken aback by my response. I'm sure this was not a response he had often heard, if ever.

My answer to his question had to have come from somewhere unknown and much deeper inside me, as neither I nor anyone in my family had any knowledge or background in aviation, whether military or civilian. My exposure to anything dealing with flying was limited to what I'd read about or seen in the movies. At this point, I hadn't even been on an airplane, and the look on my face must've also been evident to Mr. Liljegren. Of course, my surprised look led to the next, more challenging question.

"Okay, Rob, that sounds exciting. What sort of pilot?"

Damn! I hadn't thought of that. How many different types of pilots are there?

At this point in my life, my only exposure to anything remotely associated with flying had been watching the airliners flying overhead of where we lived, just a few miles west of Racine, beneath the flight corridor between Chicago's O'Hare Field and Milwaukee's Mitchell Field. And except for a visit to an airport as a toddler, which I only vaguely remembered, I hadn't ever even been to an airport to watch airplanes take off and land.

However, while operating the big tractors for the neighboring dairy farmer I occasionally worked for, I often remember thinking that if driving those machines was incredible, how awesome it would be to pilot a sleek jet like those regularly flying overhead. But it was never anything more than a fantasy. Daydreaming, if you will, while working in the fields with little else on my mind. And now, here I am, telling the guidance counselor I want to be one without any clue how to get there.

"Ahh . . . I don't know. Air Force? Navy?" came my timid, almost sheepish response.

I subconsciously knew that people paid for flying lessons and became pilots that way. Still, I'd never seriously considered it, probably because I knew I didn't have the money I imagined would be required. However, by my reasoning, I was certain that the Air Force or Navy would teach me to fly, which might be the most accessible route to becoming a pilot. But I did not know how to get there from where I sat in Mr. Liljegren's office.

He drew in his breath, paused for a few seconds, and began.

"Well, Rob, to get there, you'll probably have to go to one of the service academies: Colorado Springs or Annapolis. Mind you, it's very competitive to get an appointment at one of those schools. And, assuming you did, the screening and attrition that comes with flight training at that level is intense. A lot of guys wash out going through the programs."

He went on for the next several minutes, detailing the process he knew that led to pilot training, much less making it through and earning one's wings. The more he talked, the more daunting it seemed to me. After a while, I wondered who he was trying to convince, me or himself. Then, he summed up all this discussion with a single searing sentence.

"Perhaps you might want to consider another career path, as this one looks like a tough journey."

What? Is that it? That's the only pathway to learning to fly and earning my wings?

I'm sure Mr. Liljegren had my best interests at heart. Sitting there as a naive high school student, I thought he was giving me sound advice, albeit disappointing. I'm sure before I walked into his office, he'd already taken a look at my grades over the past two years. While a solid student, he most assuredly knew I was not a viable candidate for either academy.

Also, and I'll never really know if this was a factor, but the US combat involvement in Vietnam had by then been going on for six years. Footage of ground combat, B-52 air strikes, and the rundown of daily American casualties was part of the nightly news. Back then, the familiar voice of Walter Cronkite on CBS was still one of the primary and trusted sources of information for millions of Americans. Perhaps this was a subtle way of dissuading me from pursuing such a career. Or, more likely, it was all just coincidental. I'll never know.

"Alright, I guess I'll give it some thought and see about something else."

With that, Mr. Liljegren stood and thanked me for coming in. I took that as my cue that our talk was over, politely thanked him for his advice, and exited his office into the now half-deserted main hallway, classes having been dismissed with the 2.30 pm bell I'd heard going off minutes earlier. Up and down the hallway, just a few students lingered at their lockers in small groups, the rest having made their way home or to other after-school events.

I went down the long hallway adjacent to the school's administrative offices and turned left at the end, out the exit leading to Oakes Road. Left on Oakes and then right on Washington Avenue for a quarter-mile before arriving home. It was my usual route back home – a mere half-mile. Over the past two years, I had taken this route several hundred times. I probably could have made it with my eyes closed. Today, I thought about what had occurred in Mr. Liljegren's office. If I wasn't going to be a pilot, then what?

Well, now what am I going to do? No hope of becoming an Air Force or Navy pilot? Oh well, I'm sure it'll all work out, and by this time next year, I'll have my answer. But it doesn't sound like it'll be in aviation.

August 7, 1971
Racine, Wisconsin

It was late afternoon on a warm, lazy summer's day in Racine. I remember being in the kitchen of our modest home when my brother Mark stepped in from outside, having just returned from retrieving the mail from our mailbox, located just down the driveway from our house. In his hand were several letter-sized envelopes, plus one sizable brown envelope. I wasn't paying close attention as I had just returned from a ten-mile workout in preparation for the upcoming high school cross-country season and was cooling down with several glasses of ice water when he walked in.

I noted that he casually sorted through the mail and hesitated briefly when he came to the single large envelope. He glanced at it briefly and then took it and a couple of others to the kitchen closet, tossed them into the large garbage bin, and returned to pull up a chair at the kitchen table.

"What was that you just threw out?" I asked inquisitively.

"I don't know. Some Air Force crap from some outfit at Notre Dame," came his quick response. Everything in his reply told me he couldn't care less.

Air Force crap? What would the Air Force be sending my brother Mark? And from Notre Dame?

While Mark had zero interest in anything related to the USAF, mentioning anything remotely associated with it got my attention as I still harbored a deep-seated interest in flying. At this point, I didn't know how or even where to start. I opened the closet, reached into the bin, pulled out the previously discarded envelope, and examined it.

There, in the upper left-hand corner of the envelope, was the return address of the sender:

AFROTC, Det 225
University of Notre Dame
South Bend, IN 46556

Mark was weeks away from starting his first year at the University of Notre Dame. As had been the case over the past several weeks, it was not uncommon for him to receive mail from various organizations located at or affiliated with the University, inviting him to join their group or club or offering items for sale. It was a steady stream of mostly junk mail. I sensed he was long over the barrage of solicitations he was receiving.

"Hey, do you mind if I open this?" I quickly asked Mark.

"Sure, go ahead. I don't think I'm interested in anything related to the Air Force."

Having his permission to open what had been addressed to him, it wasn't long before I slit open the envelope and emptied its contents onto the kitchen table. There, spread out before me, were several glossy color brochures and a letter addressed to my brother and signed by a lieutenant colonel, USAF, with the title of Professor of Aerospace Studies (PAS).

What is all this stuff, and what does it have to do with Notre Dame?

The enclosed letter described the Air Force Reserve Officer Training Corps (AFROTC) and its purpose in training and providing newly commissioned Reserve Officers to the USAF following graduation from a university. This commissioning program was separate and distinct from the US Air Force Academy, and it was offered at hundreds of public and private colleges and universities nationwide. Among the many career opportunities listed, the one that caught my attention was the reference to pilot training. The accompanying brochures sported an array of photos showing jet fighters, trainers, transports, and shiny silver wings being pinned on new pilots upon graduation. Assuming the officers met qualification standards, they would attend USAF Undergraduate Pilot Training (UPT) as new second lieutenants following their commission.

Pilot training? UPT? And I don't need to go to one of the academies? Could this possibly be true?

Astonished, I continued to read more about the program and what it took to apply. The accompanying pamphlets provided a detailed description of the program. Almost in disbelief, I turned to Mark,

"Hey, am I reading this correctly? If I qualify for the program and finish college in four years, the Air Force will train me to be a pilot." I said, waving the color brochure in my hand.

He looked up from what he was doing and asked what I was talking about. I showed him the brochures and program description. He looked over the info for a few minutes and replied, "Yeah. That's how I read it," he said. "But you've got to finish in four years, and there's a service commitment afterward. Six years. Is that something you're really interested in?" It then dawned on me that I'd never previously shared my interest in becoming a pilot with either of my brothers or even my mother, for that matter.

The even better news was that AFROTC offered a scholarship program whereby they would pay for all your tuition, books, and lab fees, plus a monthly stipend for the entire time you were in the program and remained qualified. The more I read, the better it sounded. This program seemed to fit the bill perfectly for a guy who had had no clue months earlier.

Inside one of the brochures was a tear-out postcard for applicants to request more information. It was simple enough to fill out and tell the USAF you were interested in the program, and then leave the rest to them and chance.

What could be easier? In less than ten minutes, I'd filled out the postcard indicating my interest in the Pilot Candidate Program and requesting that I be contacted with additional information regarding when I'd be graduating from high school and where I intended to attend college. It didn't even require a stamp! As soon as I'd finished filling it out, I walked out and placed it in the mailbox, fully expecting that someone, somewhere, would receive it and the rest would take care of itself. As they say, ignorance is bliss. Like most things I did back then, what was on my mind one day would simply be forgotten and replaced by something else the following week. This was no different.

Months passed, and between school studies, cross-country season, chasing girls, and my part-time job on weekends, I had forgotten about the small postcard I'd sent to the Air Force seemingly eons ago. Then, late one December day, I received a large envelope with the following return address:

Department of the Air Force
Air University
Headquarters, Air Force ROTC
Maxwell AFB, Alabama 36113

Its contents informed me of the process to be followed if I wanted to apply for the AFROTC scholarship.

Whoa. What? Oh, yeah, that program I sent away to ask for more information about. This is wild.

The instructions were pretty detailed and straightforward. If I was interested in applying for an AFROTC four-year college scholarship, I would need to report to K. I. Sawyer AFB, Michigan, at the appointed time and date listed, and be prepared to take the Air Force Officer Qualifying Test (AFOQT), as well as undergo a pilot flight physical. Based on my test score and assuming I met the physical standards, the Air Force would let me know if I qualified for the program and possibly earn a scholarship. The best part was that it was a pathway to becoming an Air Force pilot.

You've got to be kidding me. That's all I have to do? Wait a moment! Where is K. I. Sawyer AFB? Marquette, Michigan.

I had no idea where Marquette, Michigan, was, much less having ever been there or having even heard of the Air Force Base located 16 miles to its south. Moreover, for that matter, I'd never been to any military installation. In this regard, I was a true neophyte and pretty clueless about how the Air Force thing was about to unfold. This was decades before the internet came along, when one's answer to such simple questions wasn't just a few clicks away on Wikipedia and Google Maps. Consequently, it took some time on a road map of the upper Midwest to even find K. I. Sawyer AFB.

In answer to my first question, Marquette was located on the south shore of Lake Superior on Michigan's Upper Peninsula, roughly 320 miles north of our home in Racine. Not having a car of my own, and having just obtained my driver's license months before, my mother was not about to entrust me to make that drive myself in our family's only vehicle. Six weeks later, as I approached the appointed date to be at K. I. Sawyer AFB, I rode with my mother up to Green Bay, Wisconsin. There, I boarded a Greyhound bus for the scheduled five-hour trip to Marquette, while she stayed behind with relatives in the area. Getting to K. I. Sawyer AFB was quite an adventure for someone whose farthest trip away from home up to this point had been with his family to visit Notre Dame in South Bend, Indiana, a relatively short two-and-a-half-hour drive away.

The instructions included as part of the packet I'd received had some basic information on K. I. Sawyer AFB, a handful of numbers to call for transportation, billeting, etc., the location of the medical clinic and the time and room to be at for the flight physical scheduled for the morning on day one of the two-day AFROTC scholarship application process. Basically, if you wanted this to happen, you were on your own to find your way there, put yourself up, and then do well on the test and physical.

There were no guarantees. I had no idea if there were any preparatory study guides for what to expect on the AFOQT, so again I figured it would all take care of itself and made my way to Marquette.

Stepping off the bus, which had its stop at the Landmark Inn in downtown Marquette, I was welcomed by the reality of wintertime in late January on the Upper Peninsula – bitter cold and seemingly mountains of snow everywhere. I had no idea where or how to get to the Air Force base, but I did have a number for transportation. The concierge at the hotel offered to call the base on my behalf, and an hour later, a dark blue USAF 48-passenger school bus pulled up, with the driver asking if I was the one who called for a lift.

I looked at him, dumbfounded, expecting a sedan or something way smaller. Moreover, this bus was empty. I looked around, thinking there must be others either on board or to be picked up elsewhere. No, I was it, the driver told me, and shortly after I'd climbed aboard, we were off to the base, which, in those wintertime conditions, was about a 30-minute drive away. A short time later, we passed the entrance to K. I. Sawyer AFB and the prominent signs out front welcoming those entering the base to the 410th Bomb Wing, a proud member of the USAF's Strategic Air Command (SAC) and home to B-52 bombers and KC-135 tankers. I knew nothing at all about their mission, but the mere mention of B-52s was familiar from the seemingly endless reports on the evening news covering the air war in Vietnam.

The driver dropped me at the entrance to the Visiting Officers Quarters and wished me luck pursuing my dream. I thanked him for the lift, grabbed my small suitcase, and quickly went inside, glad to be out of the near-zero temperatures outside. Moments later, the Airman working the registration desk gave me a quizzical look when I told him I was there for the AFROTC application process, most likely trying hard to imagine this high school senior standing before him as an officer someday.

Luckily for me, he had been briefed to expect a group of us to be staying there for the next few days while we went through the testing and physical exams. Better yet, he handed me a schedule of events for the next two days and pickup times for the 10–12 of us they expected to be going through the same process. Indeed, later that afternoon, I met most of the others, who, like me, had traveled there from across Wisconsin and Michigan to begin the first step in pursuing our dreams of becoming Air Force pilots.

Over the next two days, in between testing and the required physical exam appointments, we got to know each other, traded stories of where we were from, where we planned to attend college, and, of course, what we'd like to fly when we eventually got our wings. Fearing ridicule, I didn't dare tell them I'd never been on an airplane, fully assuming I was the only one who had not.

Collectively, we were an incredibly presumptuous and naive bunch, full of dreams and innocent aspirations, without much concept of the hurdles and dangers ahead, which was probably a blessing. Many would have probably quit had anyone told us about the odds stacked against any of us earning our Air Force wings, much less flying a fighter. But optimism and hope spring eternal. I often wonder how many, if any, of the young men I met back then actually served in the USAF, let alone earned their wings. Chances are good that I was the only one.

Two days later, having finished up our initial screening for selection for an AFROTC scholarship, we all headed our separate ways. Having compared notes with my newfound friends the previous evening while grabbing dinner at the nearby Officers' Club (O'Club), I felt good about my first exposure to the Air Force and confident I'd compete well. I was even more excited about pursuing this endeavor when a couple of young F-106 pilots from the 87th FIS offered to give us a tour of their fighters at their nearby alert facility. I even had an opportunity to sit in the simulator. It was not only the first airplane I'd ever had a chance to look at up close and personal, but it was an imposing-looking machine to boot. This was the stuff that fueled dreams for a young kid from Racine who had never before been around an airplane, much less a Mach 2+ fighter.

The following morning, I boarded the familiar Greyhound bus back to Green Bay, where my mom awaited my arrival, followed by the three-hour drive back to our home in Racine. During the drive home, I distinctly remember sharing everything I'd experienced over the past few days with her. The people I'd met, the testing, the air base, and most importantly, to me, at least, the airplanes. True to her nature, my mother listened intently to my tales without much comment or question and no doubt noted my heightened excitement at this seemingly newfound fascination I was intent on pursuing. Perhaps she was just pleased I had finally found a career path to focus on, having never seriously shown interest in anything else until now. The hours and the miles went by, and I'm pretty sure I rarely paused with my speculation about what it would be like to fly and what such a career would entail. Despite my ramblings, my mother said very little.

Then, during a stretch of silence, my mom broke the calm and softly shared a secret she had harbored for a long time and something I'd never heard her utter in my 17 years: had she been a man during World War II, she would've joined the Army Air Corps and become a pilot! I was simply speechless. Little had I or my brothers known that our meek, gentle mother, deep down, had an unwavering fascination with flying. Only now, so many years later, did that explain some things and make others clear. The trips to the airport when she was first learning to drive, the aviation books, the aircraft models, the movies, etc., were all perhaps a subconscious way of satisfying her curiosity about flying. Make no mistake, never, in all that time, was there ever a hint or even subtle prod to pursue such a career path. Whatever happened occurred naturally. Or did it?

The final months of my senior year passed quickly, with graduation coinciding with my 18th birthday in early June 1972. Just weeks before, I had received the letter I'd anxiously awaited from the Air Force. In short, I hadn't been selected as a primary AFROTC Four-Year Scholarship recipient. Instead, I was designated an alternate selectee. I had no idea where that put me on any sort of national list, or the likelihood of being offered a scholarship at a later date, if ever. But at least I was in the hunt. I had scored well enough on the AFOQT and passed the physical exam to be a contender. Despite my non-selection, I was still fully committed and intent on joining the AFROTC when I entered college that fall.

In the meantime, I applied to and was accepted at The College of Saint Thomas in Saint Paul, Minnesota, and I had already enrolled for studies there starting at the beginning of September 1972. The dream hadn't disappeared and was still foremost in my mind.

On August 27th, I boarded a North Central Airlines DC-9 for the one-hour flight from Milwaukee's Mitchell Field to Minneapolis/Saint Paul International Airport to begin my freshman year at the College of Saint Thomas. Little did I know at the time that it would be the first step of a journey leading to an Air Force career. Ironically, this was the same airport where I had seen my first airplane so many years before, when I was no more than three years old. And now, it was where I'd experience my very first flight. Naturally, I didn't know what lay before me as I settled into my window seat on the starboard side of the airplane. What captivated me was the excitement and anticipation of my first flight on an aircraft. Everything surrounding the experience was new and exciting, from the airport ticket counter to the gate area to the uniformed crew members and the airplane itself.

Before long, we were airborne, and while I don't remember much about what was said by the crew, or the in-flight service, I distinctly recall spending almost the entirety of the flight with my nose pressed up against the cabin window. I was captivated by the sight of the countryside as it slipped beneath us, homes and cars becoming increasingly smaller as we gained altitude, yet still surprisingly distinct thousands of feet below on that clear Wisconsin afternoon. Figuratively speaking, it was the shortest flight of my life, as I was so enthralled with what I was experiencing that I didn't want it to end. But like all good things, it did, and with it, my arrival into the twin cities of Minneapolis–Saint Paul to begin my collegiate years and the next step in chasing my dream.

Just hours later, following a 20-minute cab ride from the airport, I arrived at Saint Thomas and entered Dowling Hall as a wide-eyed and long-haired 18-year-old eager to begin the orientation process for all incoming first-year students in the Class of '76. Between adjusting to life in a dormitory, a roommate, social mixers with the nearby women's college, and a schedule full of events, the first few days flew past. To my surprise, out of the dozens of friends I quickly made, I soon found that none of them expressed even the slightest interest in AFROTC or becoming a pilot, as I did. Regardless, that did not dissuade me from my objective, which I was already fixated on but seemed light years away. Nevertheless, just days later, with a renewed focus on the present, I set that plan in motion in a significant and irreversible way.

That Tuesday, looking more like a kid off the beaches of southern California than from the farmlands of southern Wisconsin, I walked into the campus barber shop in the basement of Murray Hall and told the barber to cut off my sun-bleached shoulder-length blond hair. He looked at me in disbelief and asked if he had heard me correctly. After all, this was the fall of 1972, at the height of the Vietnam anti-war movement on campuses all across America, and the sight of a young man such as me coming in and asking for a military-grade haircut was almost unheard of. It was such an unprecedented sight that the other barber stopped what he was doing to take in the event and left them shaking their heads in amazement.

Twenty minutes later, having left my golden locks on the barbershop floor, I walked out and went straight to the offices of AFROTC Detachment 410, where I introduced myself to the PAS, Lt Col Fromm, and enrolled. It was that simple, that quick. Later that day, I was fitted for and issued with a uniform. By the end of my second week on campus, I was fully immersed in the program, learning about the Air Force and its diverse missions, structure, and aircraft. Additionally, there was a healthy dose of marching drills in the nearby armory, the timing of which often required me to wear my uniform to my full complement of classes several times each week.

With students enrolled in AFROTC making up less than three percent of the student body at Saint Thomas, you couldn't help but stick out wherever you went, whether in or out of uniform. Regardless, I was never jeered at or harassed for my connection with the program. I attribute this to Saint Thomas's historically long affiliation with the USAF. It also meant that anti-war protests were minimal compared to those on many larger public campuses throughout the US.

Months later, as if I needed any additional incentive to continue with the program, I was offered an AFROTC scholarship as a pilot candidate for my final three-and-a-half years at Saint Thomas. Enough of the original primary recipients either had not accepted their scholarships or had opted out of the program, triggering my name as an alternate. Needless to say, I jumped at the offer and, within an hour, had signed the contract, which, in exchange for the Air Force paying for almost all of my remaining years of school, stipulated I would be joining the Undergraduate Pilot Training (UPT) course as a newly commissioned second lieutenant months after graduation. If I hadn't been all in before, contractually and emotionally I was now. The odds had broken in my favor yet again.

My following years in school were typical for any college-aged young man, both on and off campus: a full slate of academics, parties, ball games, shenanigans in the dorm, dating, and so on. In the big scheme of things, it was pretty unremarkable to be quite honest.

With the start of my final year, and commissioning less than a year away, things began to pick up in earnest in anticipation of me attending UPT following graduation. For starters, the Air Force required all cadets who were pilot candidates to complete the AFROTC Flight Instruction Program, which is essentially a screening program. Let's face it, before the USAF committed more than a million dollars to commence training you in supersonic jets, they needed to know that you had the aptitude to at least competently fly a light airplane. So, during the fall of 1975, I regularly made the 16-mile drive to the University of Minnesota's flight facilities at Anoka County Airport, where I first learned to fly in a Piper PA-28-140 Cherokee.

Despite having a full course load of regular college classes, I seemed to spend every other minute focused on some aspect of flying. Sixteen days after my first instructional flight, with 11 hours of flight time, I soloed when my instructor stepped out of the airplane at nearby Crystal Airport and told me to take it for three circuits around the pattern. In addition to being my newfound love, and yet another step closer to UPT, the Air Force paid for all 25 hours of private instruction, including certain "progress checks" to ensure the student was what it deemed "trainable."

By the end of October, having finished the course and logged 25 hours, I found it relatively easy to complete the additional 15 hours of instruction required by the Federal Aviation Administration (FAA) to obtain my Private Pilot's License (PPL). And just a few months later, with a whopping total of 44.7 hours, I passed the FAA practical test and walked away with my PPL.

At the time, I thought I was somebody. In retrospect, I was too green even to begin to know what I didn't know.

Graduation day, May 22, 1976, was a gorgeous spring Saturday in the Twin Cities, with the campus in full bloom and temperatures in the mid-70s, making for a picture-perfect event. An hour following graduation ceremonies in the campus stadium, where former US Vice-President Hubert Humphrey gave the commencement address, a small group gathered in the O'Shaughnessy Education Center for a more solemn ceremony. I raised my right hand on the auditorium stage, took the United States Uniformed Services Oath of Office, and received my commission as a USAF Reserve Officer. Moments later, with my brothers looking on, my mother proudly pinned on my second lieutenant bars. Commissioning was the culmination of years of hard work. No doubt more lay ahead of me. Nevertheless, to say it was a memorable day would be an understatement.

The following morning, with my car packed, a bachelor's degree, and an officer's commission in hand, I walked out of Dowling Hall for the last time, leaving Saint Thomas for a more significant challenge. With one major accomplishment behind me, completing UPT remained the last obstacle between me and earning my Air Force wings, which I had set as my goal many years ago. Memories of sitting in Mr. Liljegren's office almost exactly five years earlier seemed like a lifetime ago. Through determination, discipline, and hard work, I had overcome the hurdles he told me I would do better to avoid. Up to this point, I had beaten the odds.

What remained to be seen next was whether I would further defy the odds in what was sure to be a grueling test of mental and physical discipline over the intense 52-week pilot training course that lay in store for me. Months later, I would get the opportunity, one chance, to achieve my dream when I arrived at Vance AFB in Enid, Oklahoma, where my classmates and I would train with the goal of earning our Air Force wings and pursuing the career that followed. So far, just making it there had defied the odds. Completing UPT, much less finishing top of the class (which was comprised entirely of AFROTC distinguished graduates), were even longer odds.

But if I had learned only one thing over the past five years, it was to never bet against my ability to beat the odds.

4

Tweets and Talons

"Flying is more than a sport and more than a job; flying is pure passion and desire, which fill a lifetime."

GENERALLEUTNANT ADOLF GALLAND

December 22, 1977
25th FTS
"H" Flight Operations
Vance AFB, Enid, Oklahoma

"Hey, Zettel, it's your turn in the barrel. Get your butt in here," shouted Capt Art Schwall, his head sticking out from his office, nestled next to the entrance to "H" Flight's crew room. His request was obviously directed at me.

Schwall was the commander of "H" Flight, the latter being one of many making up the 25th Flying Training Squadron (FTS) of the 71st Flying Training Wing at Vance AFB in Enid, Oklahoma. The flights were responsible for teaching fledgling student pilots how to master the T-38 Talon. Learning to competently fly the twin-engined supersonic trainer was the final test prior to earning one's wings after the USAF's 52-week UPT course. Over that period, my class had lost a handful of individuals who had either washed out of the program (i.e., did not progress at a sufficient rate or lacked the necessary aptitude) or chose to voluntarily take the Self-Initiated Elimination (SIE) route and return to civilian life. Those who had made it this far were likely to graduate, although there were no guarantees until their last check ride was completed.

Fifteen weeks earlier, 31 of my UPT classmates and I had completed the Basic Phase of the pilot training curriculum, having finished flying the twin-engined T-37 Tweet, the USAF's primary jet trainer. With Tweet flying behind us, we literally just walked to the squadron building next door, and there, we prepared for the final seven-month push toward earning our wings. The Advanced Phase of UPT built upon what everyone had learned up to that point, and it did so by increasing the tempo, speed, and dynamics of training, all to produce a military pilot ready to move on to his next flying assignment.

And the "assignment" was what Capt Schwall was summoning me to discuss. As subjects go, no single topic was talked about more by UPT students than what they wanted to fly after getting their wings. It's what aspirations were made of. And there was often a big difference between what one desired to fly and what the USAF thought you were qualified for. And without it being said, more than likely, what airplane you received following a year of training would essentially decide your USAF career and where it would take you in terms of opportunities. This meeting with my flight commander would lay all the cards on the table, and it was his job to give me the best advice when making my preferences known on my assignment "dream sheet," which would essentially decide my future.

The appointed time for this meeting with Capt Schwall had been on the flight scheduling board since yesterday, and I had been waiting at the duty desk for the past half-hour, trying to appear disinterested and calm. Outwardly, I hoped I was. Hearing my name called, I went to his office door, where he waved me in and told me to have a seat.

"Okay, lieutenant, show me your left hand and open it wide. I want to see if you can hold eight throttles in it." His joking reference to the size of the throttle quadrant of the B-52 bomber initially caught me off guard. Noticing my surprised expression, he quickly broke into a hearty laugh and dismissively waved his hand, knowing the B-52 was close to the last assignment I'd ever want.

"Don't worry, Zettel. I don't foresee any bombers in your future. Unless you really want one, of course." He snickered. The look of relief on my face brought him back to the seriousness of this decision of mine and, indirectly, that of some faceless staff officer behind a desk at the USAF Military Personnel Center (MPC) at Randolph AFB in San Antonio, Texas. Art Schwall was a great flight commander, and the sort of guy all my classmates and I admired. Not only was he a great pilot and instructor, but he was also a straight shooter. You knew exactly where he stood and, by extension, where you stood in his eyes when being evaluated. Or, in this case, counseled.

As a way of background, Schwall was what many of us called "a frustrated fighter pilot." While he might have been awarded a C-130 out of pilot training years before, his attitude and bearing were all hallmarks of a fighter pilot. No doubt had the opportunity presented itself, he would've been an excellent fighter jock. But that was not the case, and right now, sitting before him was a young lieutenant who was about to make a career decision, and looking to him for advice. With the jokes aside, he got right to the matter at hand.

"So, tell me, Rob, what's at the top of your dream sheet? Where do you want to go?" This was more of a rhetorical question, as he clearly had a copy of my assignment preferences on his desk before him, which he looked at with a puzzled expression that I could only interpret as bewilderment. I hesitated.

"Well, I've got an F-4 as my number one choice, with an RF-4 as my second choice." I don't recall what was further down the list, but I wanted to be a fighter pilot, and nothing screamed fighter more than the venerable Phantom II.

"Yeah, I can see that. Where's the F-15?" Schwall asked without hesitation, his gaze now riveted on me.

Did he just say F-15? Seriously?

For the better part of the past nine months that I'd been at Vance, an F-15 assignment was a rarity, and it was typically reserved for the very top graduate of any UPT class. I can recall only three Eagles awarded to new graduates during that period. While I knew I was doing well compared to my classmates, I wasn't so presumptuous as to even think of such a lofty assignment for fear of wasting a choice should I not be a legitimate contender.

He looked at me with as serious an expression as I'd ever seen from him and, tapping the preference form with his index finger, said, "If I were you, I'd change this form and put the F-15 as your number one choice. If an Eagle is going to be awarded, I believe you're the guy to get it."

Is he telling me I'm at that level? Possible top graduate? Holy shit!

His directness took me aback even more. Right now, everything he was implying was that I was in the running to be one of, if not the top, graduate of my class. The implication of his statement wasn't lost on me.

When my classmates and I started UPT in March, we were given a questionnaire to complete. Quite simply, it asked us to list our assignment of preference upon earning our wings, which, at that time, still seemed like an eternity away. After all, we hadn't even had our first flight in a T-37, much less knew where we'd finish among our classmates if we didn't first wash out of the program. I'm not sure what the purpose of the exercise was, or what became of the forms.

Whatever the case, I remember listing the F-4, the T-38, and, as a fallback choice, a C-141 transport, in case I didn't burn up the program and finished in the lower half of the class. How about that for confidence? Or so went my reasoning. I honestly don't know if one was allowed to put more than the three aircraft I had listed on the questionnaire. But those were what I'd put down, partly because we all knew that to get a fighter, you had to be near the top of your class – in the top third for sure.

Comparing notes with my classmates later that night at the O'Club, I discovered that most of them had also listed a fighter as their top goal upon graduation. I don't recall anyone mentioning that they had written down an F-15, possibly for fear of seeming detached from reality. It quickly became clear that this whole year would be a 52-week competition to see who would garner the top spot and, with it, launch their career flying the fighter of their choice.

As a bit of background, due to the post-Vietnam War pilot drawdown, the projected number of USAF UPT graduates for 1977–78 was planned to be the lowest since the Korean War. Without the need for pilots, the USAF had been culling pilot candidates from its ROTC ranks for the past year or more. In my case, I was one of two out of 16 ROTC cadets who started my senior year at the College of Saint Thomas to receive orders for UPT. Fortunately, my classmates and I had only been accepted at UPT because we'd been among the top AFROTC graduates at our respective colleges and universities less than a year earlier. Hence, when comparing assignment aspirations, we silently knew it would be a long year, with little margin for error if we wanted to reach our goal. The competition was going to be stiff, with long odds to finish at the top of the class.

After taking it all in, I gave Capt Schwall my reply, "Yes, Sir. If you think I've got a shot at it, I'll rework my preferences and turn in the form to you by the end of the day."

He finished with, "I'm glad to hear it. I wouldn't tell you this unless I believed it. No one else in your class has aced both their Contact and Formation check rides as you have, and I understand you're likely to do the same on your upcoming Instrument check. So, unless you step in it big time, which I seriously doubt, you'd be foolish to pass up the opportunity to get an F-15 by not listing it as your number one preference."

With that, he stood up, which was my cue that this chat session was over. After thanking him for his advice, I left his office and went about reworking the form I was holding in my hand. In less than 30 minutes, my assignment preference form, now with an F-15 as my number one choice, was back in Art Schwall's hands. It would be another seven weeks of training before my classmates found out what direction our fledgling flying careers would go.

February 24, 1978
1800hrs
Officers' Club
Vance AFB, Enid, Oklahoma

The bar and lounge area of the O'Club was packed, the atmosphere heavy with anticipation. It was so busy that the crowd had spilled out into the foyer and games room of the club. For myself, and surely many of my classmates, there was a good measure of trepidation mixed in with the emotions associated with finishing UPT and awaiting the assignment announcements. Would the latter bring joy or disappointment? While I had reason to be hopeful, there was always a chance your hopes were about to be dashed by some quirk of fate that no one had expected.

Hours earlier, the word had quickly spread across the base that the assignments for Class 78-04 were to be announced at the O'Club that evening. It was an event like no other at every pilot training base throughout the USAF, occurring roughly every seven weeks as each successive UPT class approached graduation. Seated at tables throughout the lounge or at the stools along the bar itself were the 32 members of my class, as well as the wives of nine of my classmates. On the periphery of this crowd were anxious members of junior classes, clearly interested in what would become of the next class to earn their wings less than a month from tonight. I, along with several of my close buddies, were at the back of the room, leaning up against the bar, liquid courage already well in hand, with backups lined up to give comfort if necessary.

The protocol for announcing the assignments was simple, and followed a two-step process. First, in order of rank, and then alphabetically. Being a second lieutenant and a last name starting with "Z," I would be the very last assignment announced. With everyone in place, the event kicked off. As the two class commanders stood up to address the crowd, the din of conversation and laughter quickly subsided. Following opening remarks and a few jokes, most poking fun at a couple of boneheaded students, they got down to announcing each student pilot in order, and had them stand up to await their fate.

By this point in the program, while there was no formal class ranking list, almost everyone knew where they stood in the mix. For all but a few, long gone were the dreams of finishing in the top half of the class, much less the number one position. Throughout the past several months, for most, those aspirations had long faded, as the need for repeated flights, failed check rides, or performance that simply met the requirements for graduation, and nothing more, had distinguished them. That reality, in turn, by and large "fueled" what everyone had asked for in the way of assignment preferences weeks earlier. But there was cause for a foreboding sense of trepidation among a few others.

In years past, top graduates typically asked for, and mostly received, their choice of assignments. Those who finished high enough in the class often went with the few fighter slots made available. If no fighters were left, the next choice on the list was frequently a return assignment as a T-38 Instructor Pilot (IP), perhaps even volunteering for a "heavy" such as a C-5 or C-141 if there were no IP slots available. What was almost universally at the bottom of everyone's preference sheet was a desire to go to a B-52 bomber or KC-135 tanker as part of SAC. And here lay the source of concern and anxiety among the top performers. Just when you thought your hard work was about to pay off, like most things in the Air Force, it came with a caveat.

More recently, it had become increasingly evident to the SAC leadership that they were consistently getting the lowest-ranking graduates out of UPT, with its less-than-desirable consequences. Not only was it a cause of embarrassment for the command, but more concerning, it had long-term implications for the future leadership of their bomber and tanker squadrons years later. Something had to be done, and the top graduates were painfully aware of the "remedy" to this problem.

The solution implemented by the Air Force was a simple one, regardless of whether it was considered unfair to most of us awaiting our future assignments. It was decided that the long arm of SAC could reach out and grab one pilot destined to finish in the top ten percentile of their graduating class. In other words, no matter what the pilot's preferences might be, he would be going to SAC, where, most likely, he would have the misfortune of flying a B-52 bomber. Ouch!

The first two assignments handed out that evening were to the two senior-ranking officers of each section of the class. Right off the bat, both guys, who were former F-4 Weapon Systems Officers, were given assignments back to the Phantom II. Cheers and applause erupted following each announcement, accompanied by handshakes and congratulations from the officiating officers, as well as hugs from their respective wives once they returned to their seats at the tables.

Damn! Two Phantom IIs have gone right away. I hope there's at least one left or, just maybe, an Eagle!

While there were no certainties about what aircraft would be assigned, some weeks earlier, word had come from MPC that only a handful of fighters would be among the assignments. With two F-4s gone so soon and all of my classmates ahead of me waiting their turn, I was a bit concerned. The following eight assignments announced included an assortment of "heavies" – C-141s, KC-135s, a C-130, and a T-38 IP assignment.

About what I expected. No real surprises so far.

The next name was called. "Lt Dave Eichhorn." Dave was a solid student. An electrical engineering graduate from the University of Illinois, he'd aced most of the academic tests throughout the year, done well in both the T-37 and T-38, and, along with me, had most recently received an "Excellent" on his Formation Check Ride. He was expected to be among the few who would get a fighter. Like me, he'd asked for an F-15 as his first choice, followed by an F-4, etc. The place was abuzz with anticipation as Dave stood, and all eyes were on him. With the crowd quieting, the officiating officer briefly hesitated and then read the assignment.

"B-52, Dyess Air Force Base." In an instant, all the air was sucked out of the room, and what had been a lively crowd was suddenly still. One of our T-38 IPs, who was standing nearby along the bar, and annoyed with what he thought was a failed attempt at humor, yelled out over the quieted crowd, "Okay, now tell him what he really got."

The officiating officer, again, looked back at the sheet in his hands, appeared to double-check the list, and simply replied, "That's what it says. B-52 to Dyess."

What most had anticipated to be exciting news fell like a thunderclap, leaving the crowd in stunned silence. Dave, like the trooper he was, and with his jaw clenched, nodded, hesitated for a second or two, and then simply sat down. The look of utter disappointment on his face is hard to put into words. All the work, dreams, and high expectations were gone in an instant. There was to be no celebration, no ringing of the bell that hung off to the side of the bar, which typically would be rung by an excited student about to buy a round of drinks for the entire crowd.

Oh shit! You've got to be fucking kidding me!

While I was stunned by Dave's assignment, I'm ashamed to say another part of me selfishly felt relief thinking the long arm of SAC had reached out and grabbed its sole sacrificial lamb, and I would, just maybe, be spared a similar fate. It was an uneasy feeling taking some small sense of relief at another's misfortune. There was no time spared for people to come to Dave and say anything. What could one say? Words couldn't ease the disappointment that Dave was feeling. And as quickly as it happened, the next assignment and recipient were announced.

And on it went. The following 11 classmates all received a smattering of "heavies" along with a few First Assignment Instructor Pilot (FAIP) slots interspersed among them. But still no fighters.

My best friend at UPT, John Pasqual, was awarded a T-38 FAIP assignment to Reese AFB in Lubbock, Texas, where he and his wife, Elaine, would go on to excel and have a stellar career. The remaining numbers were dwindling, and still no fighters had been awarded save for the first two Phantom IIs at the very start of the program. Thus far, six B-52 and KC-135 assignments have been handed out, and I was hoping that was the end of it.

Another good friend, Dennis "D" Ward, had just been given a T-37 FAIP assignment back to Vance, and suddenly I was the last guy left.

"Lt Rob Zettel." All eyes shifted to where I was at the back of the room, now standing, beer bottle in hand, awaiting my fate.

Come on, please let it be a fighter. No Eagle had been announced yet, so perhaps there's a chance. But right now, a Phantom II would be absolutely fantastic!

Again, the officiating officer paused a moment, looked down at the last name and last assignment on his list, and read off the award.

"Lt Zettel, F-4 Phantom to Luke Air Force Base!"

The place erupted in applause and shouts of congratulations. I hesitated a second as relief poured over me, and then wasted no time making my way to where the bell was hanging and ringing it for a good five seconds. This round was on me for the entire bar, and I celebrated well into the night along with several of my classmates. On the following Monday, it was back to business.

The final four-week stretch of training before graduation focused on finishing Instrument check rides for everyone. On a cold gray Saturday morning two weeks later, I took off from Vance AFB in the back seat of a T-38 for Barksdale AFB, Louisiana, and my Instrument check – the final check ride in the program. In the front seat, and the check pilot that day, was Capt Doug "Disco" Dildy. The flights to and from Barksdale AFB, as well as the numerous approaches in between, were uneventful. Five hours later, with the flights behind me and a 90-minute oral evaluation now complete, Doug stood up, congratulated me on a stellar performance, and shook my hand. I had just finished the program with another "Excellent" on the ride, and became the only one in the class to ace every check ride in the T-38.

March 17, 1978
1400hrs
Base Theater
Vance AFB, Enid, Oklahoma

The assembled crowd of proud parents and relatives of the UPT Class 78-04 had taken their seats in the base theater at Vance AFB, with the 32 members of the class seated in the front two rows. Following the Pledge of Allegiance and opening remarks by wing commander Col Thomas Magner, who welcomed everyone to this important event, the day's proceedings centered on the presentation of awards to the honor graduates and, finally, the highly anticipated awarding of their USAF wings.

My mother, Harriet, along with brothers Chuck and Mark, had flown into Oklahoma City the previous afternoon and, along with more than 200 other guests, were among the crowd. Following some words of "inspiration" by a colonel whose name I've long since forgotten, the presentation of awards began. As the latter were described and the honorees' names called, each respectively made his way up and across the stage, where Col Magner presented each award and shook the recipient's hand.

The most significant awards were those of the Distinguished Graduates, the Academic award, and, finally, the Top Flyer award. Dave Eichhorn and I were presented with Distinguished Graduate honors, which are awarded to those who finished in the top ten percent of the class. Additionally, Dave garnered the Academic award for acing no less than eight of the 11 tests we'd been given over the previous year, covering a wide range of topics from weather to applied aerodynamics.

I was called next to receive the Top Flyer award. I didn't even know they handed out such an item, and I was a bit surprised to hear my name called again to come up to receive yet another award. With the honor awards portion of the ceremony over, it was time for the real point of the day — handing out each pilot's wings. While one would think receiving my wings would be the highlight of my day, that distinction came about 15 minutes after UPT Class 78-04 had been dismissed. That honor was left to my mom, who carefully pinned those silver wings upon my chest with my brothers looking on. It was the proudest moment of my life.

There was a graduation banquet at the O'Club that evening, where cigars and drinks were the order of the evening. I even remember my mom picking up a cigar for the "photo op." She and my brothers had never been to any sort of military installation, and the event they were witnessing, and very much a part of was something that left an impression on them. Not only was I a part of a tiny and highly skilled fraternity, but one that I had somehow managed to finish at the very top of. Having grown up in the shadow of my brothers, I could sense their pride that their "little brother" had finished at the top.

Within a couple of weeks, I received orders to attend Fighter Lead-In Training at Holloman AFB in Alamogordo, New Mexico, for a three-month stint. There, I was finally going to be introduced to the basics of what training in my follow-on assignment in the F-4 Phantom II was going to entail. Everything I was experiencing just kept getting better, seemingly with each passing day. What awaited me at Holloman AFB and, later, Luke AFB, in Arizona, I had no idea. I only knew I was on an incredible ride, and I had no intention of getting off anytime soon.

5

F-4 Phantom II – The Beast

"A man has only one virginity to lose in fighters, and if it is a lovely plane he loses it to, there his heart will ever be."

ERNEST HEMINGWAY

September 21, 1978
Gila Bend Air Force Auxiliary Field, Arizona
1510hrs
F-4C 64-0660

"'Winder Two-One', request closed." My radio call to the USAF airfield tower controller was one he had undoubtedly heard hundreds, perhaps thousands, of times before while handling the steady volume of traffic that used the Gila Bend Air Force Auxiliary Field (AAF) as a convenient place to practice landings for pilots new to their assigned fighters from nearby Luke AFB. This afternoon, I was the only fighter in the traffic pattern, and it must've been pretty relaxing duty in the tower.

"'WINDER Two-One', cleared left closed, Runway Three-Five, cleared for the touch and go," came the tower controllers' immediate reply, clearing me for yet another practice pattern in the venerable F-4 Phantom II.

The aircraft was legendary. As a young second lieutenant, my first introduction to the F-4 was a year earlier, while I was a student in UPT, during a cross-country flight in the T-37 "Tweet." My instructor and I had landed at Little Rock AFB, Arkansas, and were guided to the transient alert ramp, where a groundcrew member marshaled us to a parking spot beside a pair of US Marine Corps Phantom IIs. I remember stepping out of the diminutive "Tweet" and looking up in awe at these beasts parked next to us.

I couldn't get over their size. They were enormous, like a giant Tyrannosaurus rex ready to instantly gobble up my cute little twin-engined jet trainer. I remember tentatively venturing over to look at the one parked closest, almost embarrassed to do so in the presence of the Marine Corps pilots who were busy getting ready to start their engines and launch off for somewhere unbeknownst to me.

Everything about the Phantom II was huge and somewhat intimidating to me at the time. For starters, your eyes were immediately drawn to the two engine intakes that dominated either side of the fuselage. A grown man could easily crawl inside them. By comparison, the engine intakes on my T-37 trainer could be covered by one's outstretched hand. Similarly, the variable area exhaust nozzles of each of the F-4's General Electric J79-GE-15 engines were four feet in diameter. Those of my T-37 were mere inches across.

For the previous 15 years, the F-4 Phantom II had been the preeminent frontline fighter in the USAF. To say it was a warrior would be a gross understatement. The airplane I was flying today was a veteran of the previous air war in Vietnam, its crews having been credited with three MiG-17 kills just over a decade earlier in 1966–67. As I'd climbed up the ladder an hour earlier to enter the cockpit, I couldn't help noticing the distinctive red stars adorning the splitter plate in front of the left engine intake, with "MiG-17" stenciled beneath each. The F-4 was a warrior, a beast, and I was slowly learning to tame it.

Over the previous five flights in the Phantom II, I had become accustomed to its handling and was getting to know its nuances, both good and bad, which every fighter has. It was a brute compared to the T-38 I had flown most recently. Where the Talon was agile and light, the F-4 was all business. Today's gross weight at takeoff nearly an hour earlier was roughly 47,000lb, or four times that of the T-38. That said, it didn't disappoint you when it came to handling. It was just different. If the T-38 was a sexy little sports car, the F-4 was a muscle car. You knew, felt, and experienced it when you started its engines. It just came alive like you'd awakened a sleeping dragon.

My instructor, Maj Gene "Fud" Fudula, was in my back seat. This was my sixth hop in the airplane, and he had been my instructor since the first hop a week prior. While I'm sure "Fud" wasn't yet entirely trusting of my skills in the Phantom II, I did sense he was becoming reasonably comfortable with my flying abilities, such as they were with only 250 hours of total time in my logbook. I emphasize "reasonably comfortable" – I imagine that's about as much as you could be when you had a brand-new second lieutenant at the controls of your Phantom II.

Over the previous five hops in the airplane, I'd logged 7.5 hours and roughly 20 landings. Everything was starting to come together pretty well. After all, I had been flying overhead patterns in the T-38 for some time now. In the F-4, once you got accustomed to it, it wasn't too much different, just a lot bigger, a lot heavier, and not nearly as sporty as the T-38.

The Phantom II accelerated nicely with landing gear and flaps retracted and the throttles fully forward in their MIL power position. It was a solid-feeling aircraft. The controls responded to the slightest input to the stick and rudders. Within seconds of completing my third "touch and go" landing, I was approaching the runway's end with the airspeed needle passing a comfortable 200KIAS.

With the tower's clearance to commence my climbing left turn to downwind, I had just begun pulling back on the stick, getting ready to blend in the left rudder and aileron to start my climbing turn to downwind, when the Master Caution light at the top right-hand corner of the instrument panel suddenly illuminated, alerting me that something was wrong with my Phantom II. Despite being in the middle of the climbing turn, I glanced down at the cluster of warning and caution lights positioned at the forward part of the right instrument console. There, a single annunciator, the sixth light on the right row of caution lights, was lit up, black lettering against a bright yellow background – "BLC [Boundary Layer Control] malfunction."

What the fuck! BLC malfunction? Damn! What's the boldface? Oh yeah, Gear – Down, Tailhook – Down!

Without hesitation or a word to "Fud" in the back seat, my left hand came off the throttles as I reached for the gear handle and slammed it down, followed instantly by doing the same with the tailhook handle on the right side of the instrument panel.

Just like in the simulator . . . it's a lot louder, though!

In an instant, the landing gear doors opened and the gear dropped into the slipstream of the accelerating Phantom II, jolting "Fud" back from a sense of complacency about what had been looking like another routine pattern. Having no similar annunciator light in the rear cockpit to alert him of what I saw, he was somewhat at the mercy of this young, inexperienced lieutenant seated five feet in front of him who was in control of the airplane.

"What the fuck are you doing?" came his inquiry with an unmistakable tone of annoyance and surprise.

"Sir, I've got a BLC malfunction light. The gear is down, dropping the hook now." My response was brief and merely a recitation of the immediate action items, commonly referred to as "Boldface," to be performed from memory in this particular emergency.

There was a slight hesitation. After assessing the situation, "Fud," still a bit excited, replied, "Oh! Okay. Yeah . . . good job. Just continue your climb to pattern altitude, but roll out on downwind a bit wider. We'll be faster than normal and need more room for the final turn."

While bending the Phantom II around in a left-climbing turn, my next move was a call to the controller.

"Tower, 'Winder Two-One,' declaring an emergency. We've got a BLC malfunction indication and will be setting up for an approach-end barrier engagement."

Good. Be direct; let the controller know your intentions, and allow them to adjust accordingly. If, for some reason, there's a conflict, they'll tell you.

While I was in the climb to downwind, everything else looked perfectly fine with the Phantom II. In quick succession, I moved the flap control switch, located outboard of the throttle quadrant on the left sidewall, to the full-down position. Now fully configured, all that remained was to fly a pattern to ensure I'd land well before the BAK-9 barrier, giving myself the best probability of cable engagement.

Let me explain why a BLC malfunction was a big deal in the Phantom II. At the heart of the BLC system was incredibly hot air from each engine's 17th-stage compressor. Each wing's associated ducting and valves directed the high temperature and high-velocity laminar air over the wings and flaps, delaying flow separation which in turn reduced turbulence and drag. This is all a fancy way of saying it would lower your stall speed and, by extension, reduce your landing speed. It was a great design idea for a Phantom II on its landing approach to an aircraft carrier, where reducing airspeed and AOA were critically important. However, it was not necessary for USAF F-4s, which typically had least 9,000ft of runway available.

Nevertheless, the light was on, and it was a critical emergency – just months later, the USAF deactivated the BLC system on all remaining F-4C/Ds in service. With the BLC malfunction light on and the flaps up, it told me one or more of the four valves in the wings were in the open position. In layman's terms, I had uncontrolled hot air at more than 200°C (392°F) being ducted inside my wings and right next to things that liked to burn, like fuel and hydraulic fluid. If not remedied soon, issues such as external fuel tanks unexpectedly dropping off, hydraulic failure, and possibly an aircraft fire were likely to occur.

The F-4 Phantom II flight manual specified immediate action items as follows – lower the gear and tailhook and plan for a landing with an approach-end barrier engagement. That afternoon, the BAK-9 arresting system was located 1,000ft down from the approach end of Runway 35 at Gila Bend.

This is early in the qualification phase of our training, and thus far, neither my classmates nor I had ever taken an approach-end barrier. Moreover, it wasn't even called for in the syllabus, except for dropping the hook in the simulator as part of a hydraulic emergency procedure. The Air Force rationale was that if you're flying a Phantom II, you will eventually take a barrier, so don't sweat it – you'll experience it soon enough, with such an event essentially being seen as "on-the-job training."

While we were on downwind, "Fud" gave me a quick verbal briefing on how to take the barrier and not fuck it up. Basically, he told me "lieutenant, just do a normal landing, but be sure to put it down at least 500ft before the barrier, keep your feet off the brakes, and be sure to lock your shoulder harness. Oh, and if the hook misses the cable, don't panic. There's another one further down the runway at about the 3,000ft mark. If the hook misses both barriers, we'll go around and try it again." There was no panic in his voice whatsoever. Instead, there was concentration and focus.

Hey, no big deal. Right? This ought to be fun . . . or not!

Several minutes later, as "Fud" had briefed, I made sure I touched down well short of the BAK-9 barrier and, shortly after passing over the two-inch cable stretched across the runway, felt the tailhook snag it, bringing our stricken F-4 to a rapid stop within seconds. I had just logged my 21st landing in the Phantom II, and the first of what would prove to be several more barrier engagements over the next couple of years in the F-4. They were right; if you flew the Phantom II long enough, you would end up using the barrier. If you hadn't, then you never really flew a Phantom II. It was that simple.

With our F-4 in the barrier and no chance of it being repaired quickly, the only way back to Luke AFB was by car. Luckily, with Gila Bend AAF now closed for the afternoon, the Supervisor of Flying (SOF), his duty in the tower over, offered us a ride back to the base. With our helmets, G-suits, and ejection seat harnesses stowed in the trunk, we jumped in and, an hour later, were dropped off at the 311th Tactical Fighter Training Squadron (TFTS). The next day, I was back in the air, with "Fud" once again in my back seat. Such was the pace of training at Luke AFB. This time, luckily, there were no unplanned stops in Gila Bend.

Two weeks later, on October 5, I passed the initial qualification check ride in the F-4. Amazingly, exactly three years earlier, I had just completed only my seventh hour of solo flight in a Piper Cherokee as a fledgling student pilot in college, and now, as I climbed down the ladder of F-4C 63-7517, I was qualified in one of the most iconic fighters of our time. If this wasn't heady stuff, the sort that dreams were made of, then what was?

From that point on, the remainder of the course for myself and the other 14 members of F-4 Class 78-EBL was packed with academics, 21 simulator sessions, and roughly 70 sorties, all part of the syllabus designed to turn out a combat-capable Phantom II pilot in approximately four months. Notice I said, "combat-capable" pilot, which differs significantly from "mission-ready" (MR).

The mission of a Replacement Training Unit (RTU) such as the 311th TFTS was to provide an operational fighter squadron with a pilot thoroughly trained in the fundamentals of his assigned aircraft's primary mission. Everything related to preparing a raw F-4 pilot to be combat capable was done in a building-block approach, with the student progressing incrementally through all phases of what the Phantom II was required to do as a war-fighting machine. After initially qualifying in the airplane, the serious work began.

In our case, most of our training was focused on the ground attack role, with dozens of hours spent on the conventional and tactical gunnery ranges spread over thousands of square miles of desert in southern Arizona. These sorties involved dropping countless practice bombs and expending hundreds of 20mm cannon rounds in the strafe pattern. It may have seemed repetitive, but when finding your comfort zone in a new fighter, such flights were well worth the time and effort.

Additionally, two crucial elements of the F-4 mission were introduced at this point in training – low-level tactical navigation and air-to-air refueling. Once you experienced these, you knew you were in the big leagues of tactical aviation. And here, the Phantom II didn't disappoint; it excelled!

At the time, coming just years following the air war in Vietnam, low-altitude, high-speed ingress to any target area was the tactic of choice for F-4 strikers intent on both surprise and survivability – read anti-aircraft artillery (AAA) and surface-to-air missile (SAM) avoidance. For me, flying hundreds of miles at low altitude, at 420–480KIAS, just above the desert floor, and then pushing it up to 540KIAS from the initial point to the target was exhilarating. Additionally, the sense of accomplishment of arriving at the initial point, having flown below 500ft AGL for the previous 30–40 minutes and then popping up to deliver your bomb on time, on target, was addictive. For this 24-year-old, I couldn't get enough of it.

Mastering air-to-air refueling was an additional, yet no less important, element of our training. While often brushed off as a given, in reality, it's key to any successful fighter mission. While I was pumped up about being a fighter pilot and had, one could say, just a bit of an ego, a good friend of mine and stellar tanker pilot Lt Col Mark Hasara is fond of reminding me, "Nobody kicks ass without tanker gas . . . nobody!"

Truer words were never spoken, and it is the reason why tanker pilots never buy a round in a bar when fighter pilots are present. Figuratively speaking, while fighter pilots may be the ones who score the touchdowns, we don't get into the end zone without the help of our friends who pass the gas!

Up to this point, while we were all pretty good at formation flying in a four-ship of Phantom IIs, sidling up beneath a KC-135 Stratotanker and taking on thousands of pounds of jet fuel while maintaining a precise position was a unique skill set all of its own, and a crucial one to master if you ever hoped to be a mission-ready fighter pilot. Doing so in the weather at night was an altogether different experience, requiring focus and situational awareness (SA), whether you were the flight lead or number four in the formation. The learning curve was steep. Either you kept up or were left behind. And if my past performance had proven anything, I wasn't about to squander this opportunity and get left behind.

While the Phantom II was indeed a fighter, and fully capable of air combat operations, that mission had largely been taken over within the USAF by the recent arrival of the F-15 Eagle. The F-4 was jokingly labeled the "jack of all trades, master of none," and this pretty much summed up our training at Luke AFB for the air combat role. While we completed close to a dozen sorties dealing with intercepts, Basic Fighter Maneuvers (1-v-1), and Air Combat Maneuvers (2-v-1), it was all pretty basic, and never enough to master the air combat role. Moreover, it was all flown against other squadron F-4s, never against adversaries in dissimilar aircraft, nor was there any discussion remotely addressing tactics.

Overall, the air combat training we received seemed more of a "square filler" than a serious effort to have you learn the air-to-air mission. As such, with our minimal training, we weren't a credible threat to MiGs upon completing the course. After all, our primary mission was ground attack, which was what we concentrated on.

By early January 1979, with F-4 training approaching completion, my classmates and I were told to submit our preferences for our follow-on operational assignments. With dozens of F-4 bases spread out across the US, Europe, and the Pacific, there were plenty to choose from. Simply pick an area, and if available, you'd be sent there. Simple. Or so we were told. Never having been out of the country, and of German descent, I listed several F-4 bases there, followed by several others in Europe, fully expecting I'd be assigned to one of those. Near the bottom of my list were two bases in South Korea, followed by Okinawa, Japan. Two weeks later, when the assignment list arrived, not only was I not being sent to one of my preferences in Europe, but instead, my orders were sending me in the opposite direction, to Asia and the 18th Tactical Fighter Wing (TFW) at Kadena AB in Okinawa!

The rest of my classmates, except for myself and Larry "Murph" Murphy, had been assigned to various F-4 bases throughout the US and Europe. "Murph" and I were the only two with orders to Kadena AB and, ironically, the same unit – the 12th Tactical Fighter Squadron (TFS). It didn't take us long to realize that there wasn't a single F-4 IP in the 311th TFTS who'd been previously stationed at Kadena, which meant we struggled to gather any information on our future posting. All we were able to ascertain was that the 18th TFW was a massive Wing with four F-4 fighter squadrons and a single RF-4 reconnaissance unit assigned to it.

To our surprise, we soon discovered that the 18th was due to transition to the F-15 sometime later that year, and we were told it was probably a blessing we were headed there, as we'd surely get into the Eagle in no time. I was about to find out real soon.

Weeks later, with F-4 training behind us, "Murph" and I, aboard a Northwest Airlines 747, landed in Naha, the capital of Okinawa Prefecture, the southernmost prefecture in Japan. Our squadron sponsors, two lieutenants who had been in the 12th TFS for less than a year, were there to meet us and welcome us to Kadena. That evening, after dropping us off at our assigned officer's quarters and following a shower and a change of clothing, it was off to a local Japanese teppanyaki restaurant, where we met several of our new squadron mates. The beer flowed and the food was delicious. I don't remember buying a thing. It was a great way to get over jet lag.

Oh, and that promise of a transition to the F-15? It never happened. Shortly after our arrival and being welcomed to the squadron by the 12th TFS commander, Lt Col Gil Dunn, we were informed that we wouldn't be eligible for an F-15 training slot, as we were too new, and the cut-off for selection to the Eagle was 450 hours of F-4 experience. In fact, we were the very last Phantom II fighter pilots ever assigned to Kadena. So, we were welcomed into the squadron, but told not to get too comfortable, as we wouldn't be staying beyond our 18-month assignment period. Never one to worry about things I have no control over, I was determined to be the best I could in the intervening time, and let the rest sort itself out in the months ahead.

6

A Vector

"Obstacles are those frightful things you see when you take your eyes off your goal."

HENRY FORD

For a new squadron pilot without any previous experience in the Phantom II, a typical week's flying schedule consisted of between three and five sorties. Almost all of them were to either a tactical range located on one of the islands to the southwest of Okinawa or to the conventional gunnery range situated on the small island of Iejima, roughly 40 miles to the northwest of Kadena AB. Unfortunately, there was zero opportunity to train at low altitude over land. With Okinawa in the middle of the East China Sea, tactical low-altitude training was only available in the Philippines or South Korea, where the USAF had several fighter bases and ranges.

When it came to air-to-air training, what little we had was almost non-existent. For the first seven months at Kadena AB, I averaged less than two sorties per month dedicated to anything remotely resembling air-to-air training. It could be Basic Fighter Maneuvers (BFM) one day, and then a month later, it might be a single Advanced Combat Maneuvers sortie or intercept training. Consequently, without the benefit of consistency, you never became proficient. You could say we knew enough to be dangerous but not deadly, and certainly not a serious threat to MiGs if we'd ever gone into combat.

Consequently, seven months after my arrival, it was a big deal when the Pacific Air Forces (PACAF) Aggressors came to town for a dedicated deployment against the 12th TFS. This was mainly because it was the first dedicated air-to-air training I had ever done, aside from the minor exercises I had completed during my F-4 training course with the 311th TFTS at Luke. And that was almost nine months earlier.

To set the stage for what was about to happen, the 26th Tactical Fighter Training Aggressor Squadron (TFTAS), based at Clark AB, was PACAF's dedicated adversary unit flying the F-5E. The squadron's primary mission was to provide realistic air-to-air training to USAF fighter squadrons while emulating Soviet and North Korean tactics and aircraft. The unit had commenced flying the Aggressor mission from August 1975, when, as the 26th TFTS, it had received a handful of T-38s. By the time the squadron (which had been redesignated in November 1977) arrived for its two weeks of dedicated training with the 12th TFS, it had transitioned entirely to F-5Es, operating a dozen sleek fighters similar in both size and performance to the Soviet MiG-21.

The pilots assigned to the 26th TFTAS were all experienced fighter jocks capable of providing the most realistic dissimilar training possible, just short of real MiGs. To a young lieutenant who knew next to nothing about air-to-air tactics and three-dimensional "turning and burning," the Aggressors were at the top of their field, and I was about to get my introduction in a most humbling way.

September 11, 1979
W-173 Overwater Range
55 nautical miles east-northeast of Kadena AB, Japan
"Dirty Two-One" (F-4D 66-7549)

"Jink!" The mere mention of the word to any fighter pilot conjures up images, feelings, and memories – usually not good ones – of being on the defensive end of a gun attack by another fighter inside his cannon's lethal range and either already firing, or about to. For the uninitiated, a "jink," sometimes referred to as a "gun's jink," is a last-ditch and often violent maneuver by the defender to avoid being gunned. And this was just in training.

With my upper body and head cranked around and looking back left through the canopy, I was seeing exactly what my WSO in the back seat, Capt John "Sheek" Sheekly, was seeing – an attacking Aggressor F-5E closing inside of 2,000ft with his nose slightly in lead of our hard-turning F-4D and about to saddle up for a guns-tracking kill unless I could thwart his attack with some deft moves of my own.

Get out of sync with him ... become unpredictable ... move the airplane ... now!

Without hesitation, I aggressively moved the stick toward its forward stop. The Phantom II responded quickly, going from positive six to nearly zero Gs. The instant the plane unloaded, I applied full right rudder, rolling the big fighter 180° in the opposite direction, immediately followed by another hard pull back on the stick, right back into 6Gs again, all to force the attacker out of sync with us and to survive the gun attack. While the move likely wouldn't shake the Aggressor, it would force his nose off of us, momentarily ruining his tracking solution and buying us some precious seconds to re-acquire him and ready ourselves for what surely would be his reposition and subsequent reattack.

Get a tally on him . . . we're passing 15,000ft . . . hard deck at 10,000ft . . . never quit!

Now, in a nose-low, 5G, right-hand turn, I was straining hard against the Gs, my breathing hurried as I cranked my head around, this time looking up through the canopy over my right shoulder. Sheekly was doing the same thing as we desperately tried to get a tally on the bandit. A "gun's jink" could be a very disorienting maneuver, with the most significant factor for survival being the ability to re-acquire the attacker through all these gyrations. The one thing we knew for sure was where the attacker would turn up – high and inside our turn, setting up to pursue his gun attack.

Hampering my ability to defeat this attack was the fact that my Phantom II was losing energy with every turn and each onset of Gs. We had started the engagement, a canned setup with me defensive, less than a minute earlier at close to 420KIAS, with the Aggressor initiating his attack from our "seven to eight o'clock" and 9,000ft back.

Following a break-turn at more than 6Gs to defeat his simulated AA-2 "Atoll" (NATO reporting name for the Soviet Vympel K-13 short-range, infrared-homing air-to-air missile) attack and subsequent maneuvering, we were now down to less than 300KIAS. With the decreased airspeed, my turn rate had also diminished. With the Aggressor so close, there was little opportunity to unload the airplane for more than a few precious seconds to regain airspeed before his nose position warranted another series of defensive responses from me, all of which only served to bleed even more airspeed. And right now, airspeed, what was left of it, was all I had.

Unlike the attacking F-5E, which boasted a very slick and clean airframe, our energy management was further hampered by the two 370-gallon external wing tanks we carried. Had this been actual combat, I would've jettisoned those long ago with a simple push of the external stores' emergency release button on the lower-left instrument sub-panel. Regardless, even if our F-4 had been clean, at more than 40,000lb gross weight, our jet weighed in excess of three times as much as the F-5E, and at this airspeed simply wasn't as agile. Unless we could fend off the gun attack and make it to the "hard deck," today set at 10,000ft AGL above the dark blue waters of the Pacific Ocean, we would be hard-pressed to survive against such a skilled adversary.

With my nose 50° below the horizon in a 135° right bank, and using every bit of "God's G" available to help maneuver the Phantom II, I re-acquired the F-5E rolling to the inside of my turn, his nose beginning to stabilize on my now wallowing airplane and no more than 1,500ft behind me – well inside of his cannon's lethal range of 2,000ft.

"His nose is coming on, 'Z-Man'. We're passing 13,000ft . . . 280 knots." Sheekly's running narrative let me know I needed to throw in at least one more series of maneuvers before we had to recover above the hard deck. If we descended below 10,000ft AGL, it was effectively the same as a kill for the Aggressor, as we would have "hit the ground" in our attempt to evade our attacker.

Reduced airspeed . . . sluggish responsiveness . . . hold the control inputs longer . . . Now!

Once more, I shoved the stick forward, this time into a negative 1G unload, and held it there for what seemed like an eternity. In reality, it was two to three seconds. With the F-4 nearly inverted and at negative G-loads, our bodies were jammed against the canopies – only our harnesses, securely buckled to the ejection seats, kept us from being smashed against them. Besides our bodies, anything in the cockpit that was not secured was sent flying – dust, approach plates, water bottles, tape recorders, and so on.

Unloaded and hanging in the straps, I once again applied full right rudder and aileron, rolling through fully inverted before stopping at approximately 135° in a left-descending dive, the nose now 60° below the horizon. Sheekly, having been tossed around, was noticeably silent, his heavy breathing the only sound emanating from the rear cockpit over the intercom. The disorienting nature of the last jink maneuver was just too much to keep up with. Task saturation had set in. But flying the airplane, I was not about to give in, and I certainly wouldn't give the Aggressor the satisfaction of running us into the simulated ground looming before us.

Descending through 12,500ft . . . hard deck at 10,000ft . . . roll wings level and pull!

While the Aggressor was undoubtedly still in pursuit, my immediate concern was recovering my airplane before hitting the 10,000ft AGL hard deck. It was pointless defeating the attack, only to then subsequently "hit" the ground. With my airspeed hovering around 250KIAS, the Phantom II was sluggish, making a recovery from a 60° nose-low dive in the available room rather dicey.

Don't bury the stick . . . ease the pull-out . . . use every bit of altitude . . . don't stall!

I immediately kicked in full right rudder and aileron, rolled back upright, leveled the wings, and began the pull-out, gingerly easing the stick back and keeping no less than 250KIAS in the recovery. While the sink rate was tremendous, the stabilator dug into the airstream, and the big fighter slowly began its recovery, descending through precious altitude with every second.

"You got a tally on the bandit, 'Sheek'?" While concentrating on not hitting the deck, I was still cognizant of the other threat stuck to me for the previous 90 seconds, like a wet booger!

"Negative, 'Z-Man'." Sheekly's response wasn't reassuring. Being in our predictable state left me with a sick feeling in my stomach, knowing what was likely to follow. Seconds later, my hunch was answered.

"Gun tracking kill, F-4 descending through 11,000ft. 'Baron One-One,' knock it off."

"'Dirty Two-One,' knock it off." While the verbal KIO call was a mere formality dictated by the rules of engagement (ROE), for all practical purposes, the fight ended at the "gun tracking call," and we all knew it.

"Gun tracking kill." Few things are more disheartening for a fighter pilot to hear than those three words. In my position, some would perhaps take solace from the fact that air-to-air combat wasn't our squadron's primary mission, and we rarely dedicated any significant sorties to improving our skill set much beyond currency. Certainly, nothing approaching proficiency. Still, others would say that, considering the setup and the fact that it was my first time fighting against an Aggressor in his F-5E, I didn't do too badly. Nevertheless, it stung profoundly and left an indelible mark on my psyche.

We set it up again minutes later with enough fuel for one more engagement. The results weren't much better, as I struggled to fend off the Aggressor once he closed within 2,000ft.

You've got to be shitting me! A hard-wing F-4, with external wing tanks, starting defensive against an agile F-5E? It was like clubbing baby seals for him!

With the second engagement over, we recovered to Kadena AB, with me flying on the Aggressor's wing for the return flight home. On the way back, I had time to reflect on what I had just experienced in the previous two engagements. Moreover, where was I headed as a fighter pilot? I couldn't help but think that if I wanted to get better at air-to-air, it wouldn't happen while I was at Kadena AB, nor in any squadron focused solely on ground attack.

I can do better than this. At least, I could have if given the opportunity and proper training. There's got to be a better way.

Back at the squadron, the ensuing debrief, led by the Aggressor pilot, Capt Terry Venema, was thorough and to the point. In addition to Sheekly and I, Maj Pat "P.O.B." O'Brien, 12th TFS assistant operations officer, sat in on the debrief, no doubt to get a sense of how this young lieutenant did on his first Dissimilar Air Combat Training (DACT) sortie against an experienced Aggressor and the F-5E.

O'Brien had been assigned to Kadena AB shortly before my arrival eight months earlier, and we quickly bonded; he, an accomplished fighter pilot with several tours in the Phantom II behind him, and I, the "FNG" (fucking new guy) with some apparent talent but sorely in need of a vector. Having recently returned from a two-week *Cope Thunder* tactical training exercise at Clark AB, where I'd flown as his wingman, O'Brien had gotten to know both me and my flying abilities well. While it was readily apparent I hadn't mastered the air-to-air mission, I had proven to be quite skilled in the ground attack role, often taking my share of quarters from other flight members when returning from the gunnery range, where the best scores in the bombing and strafing events pocketed the wagers. O'Brien, perhaps purposely, had become a mentor, and his presence in the debrief was fortuitous.

With Venema leading the debrief at the dry-erase board, he wasted no time walking us through each engagement. With our respective tape recorders helping to replay segments of the engagements, it didn't take long to recreate each, dissecting moves and countermoves as the fights unfolded. It was a masterclass on how to debrief the intricacies of air combat; he drew each fighter's position on the board and what each was doing relative to the other as the engagement progressed, often pausing to discuss salient points of what each of us saw and, perhaps more importantly, how Sheekly and I had worked as a team.

Throughout the debrief, while we had obviously done some things well, especially for the first time fighting against the F-5E, my energy management while attempting to defeat the follow-on gun attacks needed work. The major takeaway that perhaps stung more than the other critiques was the lack of effective communication between Sheekly and me throughout the engagement. It wasn't good. No, to be brutally honest, it was embarrassing. It was so poor that it probably hindered our effectiveness more than if we had each just gone "cold mic!"

Ouch! I've got a long way to go before I can even begin to think about being a MiG killer.

With the debrief over, we broke up and headed out into the hallway. I turned right and was about to head to the duty desk to note any changes to the day's flying schedule when I heard O'Brien behind me clear his throat, subtly wanting to get my attention.

"'Z-Man,' wait up a minute," he said, lagging behind the rest and wanting to bend my ear a bit. He'd seen the disappointment on my face in the debrief, having wanted, perhaps expecting, me to have done better than I did. With just the two of us now alone at the far end of the hallway, he continued, "If you want to get better at this, you need to go somewhere where air-to-air is all you do. Unfortunately, they won't let you stay here and transition to the Eagle. That would've been ideal, and they'd be lucky to have you in the Wing. But, if you're willing to stay in PACAF following your current tour here, there may be an option worth pursuing."

Stay in PACAF? Where? The Philippines? Korea?

I was suddenly all ears, and more than a bit taken aback. I still had roughly another year before my 18-month assignment at Kadena AB would be up. As usual, focused on my more immediate challenges rather than what lay ahead, I hadn't thought about where I'd be headed a year from now, thinking it would somehow all work out. I soon discovered that if you left your career choices up to some staff officer in Assignments, you'd be hugely disappointed. It was quickly apparent that O'Brien wasn't about to let that happen. Not without some pushback.

He continued, "First off, what do you want to do? What direction do you want to go in as a fighter pilot? Do you want to be hauling iron or killing MiGs? Your next assignment out of here will largely define your career path." O'Brien's challenge had succinctly laid out the simple choice before me as no one had ever done before.

"Well, despite today's lackluster performance, I'd like to get into the air-to-air mission. Someday, I want to be that Aggressor leading the debrief. To be one of the best," came my unfiltered response. I suddenly had a flashback to that 16-year-old kid, sitting in Mr. Liljigren's office at Case High School and being asked questions about things I hadn't before given much thought to. "How can I get there from where I'm standing right now?" I blurted out as if to add context to my previous answer.

"I've got an idea, and there are some things you aren't even aware of, much less thought of them yet," O'Brien added.

Over the next few minutes, just standing in the hallway, he laid out the reality of the two stark choices before me: choose to stay in PACAF and shape my future, or return to the States, still in the F-4, and most likely get sent to yet another ground attack squadron, or worse, be sent back to Luke AFB to be an RTU instructor. Choosing to do either of the latter two choices, I could kiss away ever being in an air-to-air squadron, much less being chosen to be an Aggressor.

"But if you want to learn air-to-air, the simple answer is, you need to stay here in PACAF and get yourself assigned to Osan." I gave him a puzzled look, and he sensed it, adding, "Osan has the last remaining F-4E air-superiority squadron in the entire USAF. If you want to get good at this, that's where you've got to go. And from where you're standing, you can get there, and I think I can help."

O'Brien quickly pointed out that it wouldn't be as easy as saying I wanted to be assigned to the 36th TFS at Osan AB, one of three airfields in the Republic of Korea where the USAF then had Phantom IIs stationed. Firstly, according to O'Brien, you would have to get the staff officer handling F-4 assignments at PACAF HQ back at Hickam AFB in Hawaii on board with the idea. "Getting him to buy in would be no small feat, as he will want to send you to Kunsan AB and the 8th TFW, given that you're already flying the F-4D, are current in the ground attack mission, and are nuclear certified, among other qualifications. You'd be the easiest slot those assholes would fill all year. 'A face in a place,' as they're fond of saying. So, to get them on board, you will have to lead-turn the process, lay down a few markers, and get some help."

Markers? I don't know anyone in PACAF outside of here. I'm just a lieutenant in a Wing of F-4s, the numbers dwindling weekly with the arrival of each additional F-15.

O'Brien continued, "On our end here, we can help, and I'll make a few phone calls. Better still, perhaps get you a cross-country up to Osan and see their squadron commander, introduce yourself, and tell him you want to work for him. Nothing speaks louder to those assignment-weenies at PACAF than a squadron commander telling them he wants you in his squadron. So, there's work to do if your objective is someday becoming an Aggressor."

My head was spinning, trying to absorb everything he had just thrown my way. And then, as if it wasn't already in overload, he added one more telling piece that simply exploded my simpleton brain.

"And if you someday become an Aggressor, there's one more thing you should keep your eye on. Eventually, get back to Nellis and go fly 'types.'"

I looked at him, cockeyed and completely puzzled, and asked, "'Types', what are 'types'?" I added, perhaps a bit too loudly.

O'Brien made a shushing sound and looked around, ensuring no one else was nearby and possibly within earshot of what he would say next. He then looked at me and whispered, "MiGs! We've got fucking MiGs back at Nellis. Well, not at Nellis, but up at a very secret location north of there, up in the desert. Oh, one more thing – you've never heard this from me. This conversation never happened."

MiGs? We've got MiGs? You gotta be fucking shitting me!

I looked at him with wide eyes, my naivety about such things no doubt showing in my expression. The look he gave me told me not to ask any more questions and not to share this with anyone else, anywhere! For a guy who just got his ass handed to him by an Aggressor, the mere idea of qualifying to fly one of the USAF's top secret MiGs, which I had even less

A VECTOR

of a clue about, was so outside the realm of possibility that I dismissed the whole idea as soon as O'Brien had uttered it. Getting to Osan was one thing. Someday flying a MiG fighter was beyond comprehension and, in my view, only something attainable by the near god-like.

However, I had been given a vector, at least as far as a subsequent assignment was concerned, and that was all I needed to set a plan in motion. And now that I had it, I wasted no time in going after it. While I had no dreams of flying MiGs someday, I at least had an initial objective in mind and was laser-focused on getting to the 36th TFS at Osan. The first step would begin the following morning.

With a 19-hour time difference between Kadena AB and PACAF HQ in Honolulu, Hawaii, I was in the squadron at 0500hrs the next morning to ensure a higher probability of my phone call via the Automatic Voice Network (AUTOVON) communications system going through, as well as catching the staff officer in Fighter Assignments at his desk at 1000hrs. To say the reliability of AUTOVON was "spotty" would be a gross understatement. Still, despite its quirks, it was preferable to sending a letter 4,600 miles across the Pacific, expecting it to be acted upon with any sense of urgency. Then again, I had no guarantees that the same staff officer would take a young F-4 driver at Kadena AB seriously. With nothing to lose, and having rehearsed my rationale for asking to go to Osan, I dialed the number I'd been given for the Fighter Assignment desk at PACAF HQ.

As O'Brien had predicted, on my first call to the major handling F-4 assignments back at his comfortable desk in Hawaii, he almost laughed when I told him of my desire to go to Osan.

"Lieutenant, you're already qualified in the F-4D, a flight lead, nuclear certified, and all the rest. I can't send you to Osan. You're a qualified ground attack F-4 jock, and that's what I need at Kunsan. I've two squadrons there that rotate pilots every month. That's where I'll be sending you. I'll send others to Osan. But right now, if you want to stay in PACAF as an F-4 jock, I only have a slot for you in the 8th TFW at Kunsan AB." I've heard better sales pitches from used car salesmen. Over the next several minutes, he did his best to convince me. Or perhaps he was trying to convince himself. Whatever the case, I wasn't interested. Where others may have folded, I pushed back.

"Sorry, sir, but that's not the direction I want to go in. I want to join the 36th TFS, as they're primarily air-to-air. I appreciate your offer, but that's not in my best interest."

There was some grumbling on the other end of the line, accompanied by rationalizing why I'd be making a huge mistake trying to switch roles to the air-to-air mission, before he returned to his worn-out line of why he couldn't send me there. He added that it would still be several months before he'd work on my follow-up assignment, and that I should consider it. Otherwise, there wasn't much he could do for me. Another option, he added, would be to return to the States and all the rest that O'Brien had correctly predicted would be my "fate." With the discussion over, I politely thanked him and ended the call. It was apparent I'd have to work on this assignment from several angles to manage my future fighter career effectively.

Over the following months, I left no stone unturned in pursuit of the assignment to Osan. Taking O'Brien's advice, I coordinated a visit to see the 36th TFS commander and to make my case in person. But to do that, I needed a jet, and not just any jet, but one of my squadron's F-4s!

With a bit of luck, and no doubt O'Brien greasing the skids, the CO of the 12th TFS approved a weekend "cross-country" flight, enabling me to do just that. On December 7, 1979, I took off from Kadena in F-4D 66-7709 and made the 2.2-hour flight to Osan, where I met with Lt Col Joe Hurd, the 36th TFS commander, and explained to him why I wanted to join his squadron. I'm pretty sure he'd never had anyone show up personally to make their case before. It was a relatively low-risk gamble for him, as I was already in-theater and familiar with Korea, Kadena, and Clark AB. Essentially, achieving MR status would be relatively straightforward.

While it wasn't a long meeting, and I had no guarantees it would secure my orders to the 36th TFS, it certainly couldn't have hurt. I'd done my part, felt that I'd presented myself well, and would leave the rest to Hurd. I would never know whether he had interceded with the assignment process or not. Additionally, I later discovered that several of the Aggressors had also put in a good word for me, something to the effect of a young and determined F-4 lieutenant at Kadena who wants nothing more than to come and fly as a member of the "Flying Fiends" (the nickname of the 36th TFS). Oh, and if given the chance, he might someday make a good Aggressor.

Following months of phone calls to Fighter Assignments and pressing my desires to be assigned to Osan, in mid-May 1980, orders indeed arrived assigning me to the 36th TFS effective September 1. Somehow, with lots of help, I had managed to avoid being sent to Kunsan AB and the 8th TFW. While that probably would have worked out well, and I could have transitioned to the F-16, which was soon expected to arrive there, it wasn't what I wanted to do. I had cast my lot and was now headed to an air superiority squadron, where I would soon be flying the F-4E.

A VECTOR

On Monday, September 1, I boarded a C-130 aircraft bound for Osan and said goodbye to Kadena AB, touching down several hours later to a warm welcome at what would be my home for the next 12 months. Within two weeks, I'd made my first flight and, three months later, was signed off by Lt Col Hurd as a new flight lead. The pace and scope of the operations undertaken by the unit were precisely what I'd hoped for, and all focused on the air-superiority mission. Not only did we train for it daily, but the threat was real, with the border of North Korea just minutes away from Osan AB for our Phantom IIs in full afterburner, a pair of which, along with their crews, sat MiG alert 24/7. If the concept of engaging North Korean fighters wasn't enough to stimulate you, blasting off on the occasional practice scramble in an F-4E with its complement of live radar and IR missiles and fully loaded 20mm cannon certainly was.

I lived for this, with each day being another opportunity to build experience. Over the ensuing months, I participated in various tactical scenarios and air combat exercises, which further refined my air-to-air skills. Additionally, serving as the project officer for numerous Aggressor deployments provided me with exposure to and experience in their mission, as well as ready access to their pilots, many of whom I had become well acquainted with. Strangely, on only a year-long tour, within months of my arrival I was already thinking about the next assignment. The goal of becoming an Aggressor was still foremost in my mind. Very shortly, circumstances would force my hand and, with it, a decision that would, unbeknownst to me, shape my future as a fighter pilot.

7

The Fork in the Road

"Good luck is often with the man who doesn't include it in his plans."
                                                                ANONYMOUS

March 1981
36th TFS Operations
Osan AB, Republic of Korea

I remember standing at the duty desk that early spring afternoon, the large windows of the squadron's Operations room providing a panoramic view of the runway and adjacent taxiway from the second floor of the 36th TFS building on the immediate southern edge of the airfield. Osan AB, located just 34 miles south-southeast of the South Korean capital, Seoul, was the USAF's closest airfield to the border with North Korea and, without doubt, would be one of the first targeted should hostilities ever erupt with the volatile regime to the north. The blast walls surrounding the building, the hardened aircraft shelters, and the revetments for the squadron's 24 F-4Es were a subtle reminder lest you forget why you were there.

I was in the Operations room checking the following day's flying schedule when my flight commander came in and pulled me aside, saying he needed to talk with me for a minute. He nodded toward the back of the room and, following his lead, I joined him near the far wall adorned with photos of every pilot and WSO in the squadron, all neatly arranged by their respective flights, with the squadron commander's photo prominently displayed at the top.

He looked around, seemingly to ensure we were out of earshot of anyone else. Luckily, the room was already vacant, except for a lone NCO staffing the desk and us. Without the distraction or worry of anyone else hearing us, he began.

"Well, just to let you know, Lt Col Hurd has been very impressed, as I have, with the job you've been doing and your accomplishments since you arrived in the squadron. And, after some discussion, we both agree that you're ready for more. To take your game to the next level."

Okay . . . where's he going with this?

During the next couple of minutes, he rattled off several accomplishments over the past several months since my arrival, not the least of which was leading a three-ship of F-4s on a live-fire missile exercise the previous month. We had flown non-stop from Osan AB to Clark AB, splashing two drones with direct hits by AIM-7E Sparrow missiles while en route. The 3.5-hour mission was the first of its kind ever attempted by any squadron in the PACAF, and it had been completed without a hiccup.

Additional "atta-boys" included stints as project officer for the recent successful Aggressor deployments, *Pave Spike* laser-guided bomb (LGB) checkout, and mission commander qualification, among others. No doubt, all noteworthy achievements in the short seven months I'd been there. Cutting to the chase, he proceeded, "Here's what we're thinking. We'd like to fast-track you in the IP upgrade program and nominate you for Fighter Weapons School. The timing is perfect, and we'd have you spun up and ready for a class scheduled to begin this fall at Nellis."

Whoa! Fighter Weapons School nomination! I didn't see this coming.

To begin with, this was heady stuff, as being considered for nomination by the squadron commander – a 169-mission veteran of the Vietnam War and former F-4 FWS instructor himself – was quite an honor, especially considering he had a whole squadron of pilots to choose from, many with much more experience than I. What's more, I'd just pinned on the rank of captain not more than two months earlier.

At this point, I had but two years of operational experience in the F-4 and had just cracked the 600-hour mark in the jet. Perhaps more importantly, I hadn't seriously contemplated, at least in the short term, even pursuing an FWS slot. In my mind, an Aggressor assignment was what I was focused on, although I'd never shared that goal with my flight commander, who, right now, was offering me an incredible opportunity.

For the uninitiated, the FWIC, taught at Nellis AFB, is a graduate-level instructor course providing advanced instruction in weapons and tactics to the USAF's best fighter pilots. Since my earliest days going through F-4 training at Luke AFB, FWS graduates, easily identified by the distinctive and highly coveted patch they proudly wore on the left shoulders of their flight suits, were acknowledged as the USAF's best. Every year, fewer than two dozen USAF F-4 pilots worldwide were selected for this opportunity. And now I was being offered a chance to join their ranks. It, indeed, was quite an honor.

This caught me entirely off guard, but before I could answer, he continued, explaining my qualifications and the rationale behind the decision. "We think your selection is almost a guarantee. For starters, your timing and experience are all in your favor, and, coming from the Air Force's only F-4 air superiority squadron, your nomination will most certainly get the attention of the Weapons School selection board. So, what do you think, 'Z-Man'?"

To say I was surprised is an understatement. Previously, there had never been a hint from my flight commander, much less a discussion of what my interests were, and now, here I was, trying to digest all of it on the spot. It was a very tempting offer, and one that most anyone else would have jumped at. However, despite my surprise, I knew the objective I had set for myself, and my answer was short, quick, and seemingly without hesitation. Possibly too quick.

"Hey, thanks a lot. I appreciate the confidence you and Lt Col Hurd have in me, the opportunities I've been presented, and your consideration for the Weapons School slot. But, in all honesty, I think I'd rather pursue becoming an Aggressor at Clark following this assignment."

And there, in one quick gut reaction, perhaps spoken too soon and without thought, the words, forever irretrievable, had just burned a pretty significant bridge. The look on my flight commander's face was one of shock and surprise. Never in his mind had he thought anyone would pass up a chance to be selected for a FWS class slot. Without hesitation, he shot back, his ego a bit hurt that I didn't want to follow in his footsteps.

"Let me get this straight. We're offering you the chance to go to F-4 Fighter Weapons School, and you'd rather be an Aggressor? You've gotta be shitting me?!"

"Well, yeah, I mean, that's pretty much it," I replied. "I appreciate it, and I'm flattered, but attending F-4 Fighter Weapons School has never been a goal of mine. The reason I want to become an Aggressor is that I want to stay in the air-to-air game."

I then offered up my rationale as if in my defense, "If I go to F-4 Fighter Weapons School, upon graduating, odds are I'll be sent to some RTU squadron or perhaps George AFB [in California] in the *Wild Weasel* mission. No offense to those guys, but I don't want anything to do with either of those options. For someone who wants to stay in the air-to-air game, going to F-4 FWS is a dead end."

Left unsaid was the fact that, whether people chose to admit it or not, the F-4 was an aging weapons system, and it was being rapidly replaced by new F-16s worldwide. To get stuck in the Phantom II at this point would have been a bad move, as every F-4 squadron in the USAF, with the

THE FORK IN THE ROAD

sole exception of the 36th, was "hauling iron," not missiles. The direction I wanted to go in wouldn't lock me into any particular weapons system and would, instead, open up my options down the road should I desire to go to the F-15 or even the F-16 at some point. The good news was I didn't need to make those decisions just yet.

And with that, the conversation was over. Before my flight commander turned away, he asked if I'd already lined up an Aggressor assignment, to which I honestly replied I had not. It then dawned on me that perhaps I had answered much too quickly and should have sat on my answer and built one bridge before I'd burned another.

"Well, if that's what you want to do, I can't argue with you," he said. "That's a great assignment as well, and you'd make a good Aggressor. Let me know if there's anything I can do to help."

While he might've been disappointed with my answer, he was, after all, a great guy, and I took him at his word. And with that, he turned and left the room, leaving me having just thrown cold water on one potentially significant assignment, and with nothing tangible lined up – only the idea of what I wanted to do. There was only one way to turn that idea into reality, and this time it most definitely wasn't going to involve a call to a staff officer in Fighter Assignments at PACAF HQ. Instead, the next AUTOVON call I'd make would be to the Aggressor commander himself at Clark AB.

With yesterday's discussion behind me, I decided it would be best to contact the CO of the 26th TFTAS as quickly as possible, for, depending on the outcome of this next phone call, I might need to reconsider the offer of the FWS slot. However, it was pretty evident that I had pissed off my flight commander, who also happened to be the squadron's Weapons Officer, and revisiting that option was in serious jeopardy. In retrospect, it wasn't the most brilliant move I had made without already having something in my hip pocket to fall back on. No, that bridge had definitely been burned. There was no going back if I got shot down on this phone call.

Here goes. The Aggressor assignment is what you've had your sights on . . . don't fuck it up!

Once again, using AUTOVON, it wasn't easy to get a phone line through to Clark AB, 1,600 miles away on the Philippine island of Luzon, and located roughly 40 miles northwest of Manila. Eventually, on my third attempt, I reached the 26th TFTAS and asked to speak with its commander, Lt Col Nels Running.

As a bit of background, I'd first met Running when I was a lieutenant at Kadena, and he was a new lieutenant colonel, fresh from a staff tour at the Pentagon. Running was well-liked, especially amongst us junior officers, for not only was he a fun-loving and approachable guy, he had an enviable background that young fighter pilots like me found compelling – two tours and 274 combat missions in the F-105 during the Vietnam War, followed by two years flying the F-4E as left-wing while a member of the Thunderbirds.

This was why I figured he would be the one person with the answers to my self-made predicament. So, it wasn't as if I was making a blind call without him at least being familiar with me. Within a minute, he came to the phone, and I politely introduced myself, just in case he'd forgotten.

"'Z-Man', how the hell are you? Everything going well up at Osan?" Running, not missing a beat, jumped right in as if he'd just seen me yesterday. Luckily, I had crossed paths with him on several occasions while at Clark AB for a *Cope Thunder* exercise the previous month. He was familiar with my status in the 36th TFS and, more importantly, my interest in someday, perhaps, joining his unit. The timing, it seemed, couldn't have been better.

"Yeah, it's going well, but let me tell you what I've just done. I may have stepped on it here, and I'm calling for a bit of help and advice," I replied.

With that, I recounted the discussion I'd had the previous day with my flight commander, the offer to go to the F-4 FWS, and how, rather than sitting on my answer for at least a day, I proceeded to go with my gut instinct. I told him of my desire to be an Aggressor instead. Needless to say, I may have upset the apple cart in the process.

"So, that's what I'm calling about. What do I need to do to become an Aggressor and come work for you at Clark?"

There it is . . . Your cards are all on the table . . . You're either gonna be a hero or zero.

There was an uncomfortably long pause. For a moment, I thought my call and the sudden predicament of my own making might have put Running in an awkward position. Seconds later, he broke the silence by asking, "'Z-Man', how much time do you have in the F-4 right now?"

"Sir, I just broke 600 hours. I expect that by the time my tour is up I'll be pushing 700."

There is another pregnant pause on the phone line as the Aggressor commander thinks about it for a moment. After a few seconds, which to me seems like an eternity, he comes back with his answer.

"Okay, 'Z-Man,' you're hired. We'll take you."

You've got to be shitting me! That's it? I'm hired?

Having known Nels Running previously when we had both been at Kadena certainly hadn't hurt. Like many things in life, having a personal

THE FORK IN THE ROAD

connection was key. Without hesitation, I thanked him for placing his trust and confidence in me. He told me not to worry about it, and that he would be calling PACAF HQ the following day to inform the Assignment Desk that I would be a "by name" request to come to the 26th TFTAS. And if things went as expected, I could anticipate receiving orders within six to eight weeks.

And that was it. There was nothing more to it. Luckily, I had managed to secure my next assignment, one I had set my sights on two years earlier after just having my ass handed to me by the first Aggressor I'd flown against. As Running had predicted, approximately six weeks later, I received orders sending me to Clark AB and the 26th TFTAS via Nellis AFB and the five-month formal Aggressor course due to commence there in mid-September 1981.

On Thursday, August 20th, 1981 in F-4E 67-0351, I flew my final sortie as a member of the 36th TFS "Flying Fiends" and the last ever in the Phantom II with my WSO, Lt Tom Griffith, in the "pit" (rear cockpit). Weeks later, following my return to the States and a brief visit to Racine to see my mother, Harriet, I arrived at Nellis AFB and reported to the 65th Fighter Weapons Squadron, which became the 65th TFTAS at year end (and, eventually, the 65th AS in April 1983). There, as a member of Aggressor Class 82-AAN, I, along with nine other pilots, would spend the next five months going through the formal USAF Aggressor checkout program.

It was while there, one early November afternoon, that I was in-briefed on a program called *Constant Peg*. This gave me my first formal knowledge of the existence of the top secret MiGs the USAF operated at a remote airfield tucked away in the desert 120 miles northwest of Nellis AFB. Sitting in the 65th TFTAS main briefing room, I remember listening wide-eyed as Capt Mark Postai and Maj Chuck Corder, members of a unit called the 4477th TES, briefed me and my classmates on the MiG-21 and MiG-23, respectively. Both pilots, simply referred to as "Red Eagles," were actively flying these fighters, and we, as part of the syllabus, would soon get a chance to fly against them. Simply stated, I was floored. Once we left that room, there was to be no discussion, anywhere or to anyone, about what we had just heard.

So, this is what Pat O'Brien was talking about two years before in the hallway at Kadena!

At that moment, little did I know that almost two years later, to the date, I would be a "Red Eagle" myself. But in the meantime, I didn't even fathom such a prospect, as that seemed too remote a possibility. On February 10, 1982, I made my final flight at Nellis AFB as part of the checkout program, and one week later I arrived at Clark AB to begin my tour as the newest Aggressor in PACAF. The 26th TFTAS's new commander, who had recently replaced Lt Col Nels Running (who was responsible for my selection as an Aggressor), was there to greet me as I stepped off the military charter flight. It was the start of what would turn out to be yet another outstanding chapter in my fledgling career as a developing fighter pilot.

Just three years earlier, I'd arrived at Kadena AB as a "puppy" F-4 pilot. Since then, I'd progressed from possessing only rudimentary air-to-air combat skills to now being entrusted with providing the very best instruction to fighter pilots throughout PACAF. If I'd learned anything in those years, it was that there was always room for improvement in my air-to-air skill set. As I would soon find out, luck would once again land on my shoulders and pair me with a fighter pilot who would help take those skills to yet another level.

8

Sharpening the Edge

"If I have seen further, it is by standing on the shoulders of giants."
                                                    SIR ISAAC NEWTON

June 24, 1982
W-179 Air-to-Air Range 60 miles west-northwest of Kadena AB
F-5E 75-0612

"'Baron' flight, Knock it off. Knock it off. Control, knock it off," came the call from our GCI controller, Capt Steve "Mace" Mercer, signaling that the engagement with the pair of F-15s from the 67th TFS had come to an end, and, following the air-to-air training ROE, for all fighters to cease maneuvering.

In quick succession, my flight lead, Capt Clarke "Frog" Peele, and I, Aggressors from the 26th TFTAS, each flying an F-5E, acknowledged the KIO. With the two Eagles and their GCI controller on separate, discreet ultra-high frequency (UHF) radio, any information needed to be passed to us was relayed by each side's GCI controller, who sat just feet apart beside each other at their respective control scopes back on the ground at Kadena AB.

"'Baron' control, say the reason for the knock it off," queried Peele.

"Roger, 'Baron Two-One.' The Eagles are 'bingo' [minimum fuel limit for safe recovery] and RTB [return to base]. The range is clear to the west." Came Mercer's reply, his GCI counterpart controlling the Eagles informing him moments earlier that the F-15s had reached their recovery fuel state and would be departing the range space to the east and heading back to Kadena AB.

"Roger control. 'Baron Two-One' flight, fight's on, fight's on," came Peele's radio call that the air-to-air engagement between our two F-5Es was now on instead. At his call, I immediately selected full afterburner and began a hard turn to the right, in the direction of my last visual on my flight lead, in an attempt to obtain a "tally ho" on Peele, who, as previously briefed, would now be trying to gain positional advantage on me and, if possible, saddle up and gun me. While the air combat training ROE still applied, other than that, we were both cleared for unrestricted maneuvering.

Having just finished "scissoring" with the pair of Eagles just above the hard deck at 10,000ft AGL, I was wallowing at close to 200KIAS, doing my best to avoid descending below the hard deck and in not much of a position, energy-wise, to engage "Frog." To make matters worse, in all of my maneuvering over the past minute with the two F-15s, I'd lost my visual on "Frog," compounding my dilemma still further.

As a way of background, whenever "Frog" and I were out flying against a pair of fighters during 2-v-2 DACT, be it F-15s, F-16s, or F-4s, as soon as our "bingo'd" out and were headed for home, the fight between the two of us was on! This "auto-fight's on" was one of our "agreements" whenever we flew together, which we did with uncommon regularity.

Firstly, it taught each of us to maintain a visual on one another despite fighting with one, or in today's case, two opponents. By doing so, it built SA and was akin to juggling multiple balls without becoming fixated on any single one. Secondly, it made you aware of your energy state and your next best move to defend yourself should your adversaries suddenly call KIO and head for home, and your "buddy" was about to pounce. Today, I'd lost sight of "Frog" and was left vulnerable at the bottom of the area. Not where I wanted to be.

This is gonna suck! Where is that sneaky bastard?

"If you don't wanna get popped, you'd better break left," I heard "Frog" radio, an unmistakable giggle in his voice.

Damn! I don't see him back there.

The last time I'd had sight of "Frog," he was circling about 2,000ft above the fight, no doubt sensing an impending KIO, and was setting up to pounce on me.

Bastard! You could've come down here and helped me with those F-15s!

Not wishing to give "Frog" an easy shot, "tally ho" or no "tally ho," against my better judgment, I unloaded the airplane and rolled 180° to the left and came back in with nearly full-aft stick, the maneuvering flaps extended and trying to generate as many angles as possible to defeat his missile attack and, hopefully, pick up a tally on him. Now, in a hard left turn, with my head and torso twisted around as much as possible, I strained to find his attacking F-5. Nothing!

Oh shit! I've got a bad feeling about this.

"Atoll kill, on 'Baron Two-Two,' knock it off," came the call from "Frog" over the radio.

"'Baron Two-Two,' knock it off," I replied.

God damn! I can't believe he did that.

"Thanks for the turn back left, 'Z-Man'. I never would've gotten that shot if you'd kept coming right," he chuckled.

With both of us also near our "bingo" fuel for recovery, we rejoined and headed for Kadena AB. Once on the ground and out of our fighters, Peele was quick to come over to where I was standing next to my F-5E, filling out the aircraft logbook, and laughing about how I'd fallen for the oldest trick in the book. Such was any flight with "Frog." Every single one was a unique experience, and always an opportunity to hone my skills still further. On this occasion, cheating with a radio call was one I'd tuck away for future use. As a relatively new Aggressor, I had a lot to learn, and Peele wasted no time in ensuring that my learning curve was steep.

Having arrived at Clark AB at the beginning of March 1982, by June, I had quickly settled into the squadron. For a young aspiring fighter pilot whose objective was to continue to improve his air combat skills, the Aggressor assignment was near-perfect. For myself, coming from the F-4 community, where, other than at Osan AB, there was zero opportunity to continue in the air-to-air mission, there was no better posting.

Of the four Aggressor squadrons in the USAF (the 64th and 65th TFTASs at Nellis AFB, and the 527th TFTAS at RAF Alconbury, in England), the 26th TFTAS, in my opinion, was the place to be, especially as a young Aggressor. I realize that this is biased, but in my view, Clark AB was the best place to be, and I don't say that lightly. Allow me to explain.

Firstly, just from a flyer's standpoint, at Clark AB, with its tropical setting and a mean temperature of 88°F, you were blessed with great weather pretty much year-round. Next, our proximity and ease of access to operating airspace were perhaps the best of any USAF base worldwide. For instance, while Blue Force adversaries would fly more than 100 nautical miles to enter the *Cope Thunder* exercise airspace stretched out over thousands of square miles to the northwest of Clark AB, we Aggressors, immediately after takeoff, simply made a right turn out of traffic around Mount McDonald five nautical miles to the southwest of the airfield. Moments later, we were in the exercise area talking to our GCI controllers. In no other location could you maximize your training as you could at Clark AB.

Additionally, unlike the two squadrons back at Nellis AFB, we had no requirement to dedicate valuable sorties for pilots going through the formal Aggressor training course every few months. In contrast, in the 26th TFTAS, the vast majority of our sorties were devoted solely to training frontline operational fighter squadrons. Another huge benefit of flying out of Clark AB was it just wasn't as busy as Nellis AFB. While Clark AB had only a single runway, we shared it only with the two F-4 squadrons based there, in addition to the regular contingent of transient passenger and cargo transport traffic that routinely made its way in and out of the airfield.

As PACAF's single dedicated adversary squadron, we provided DACT for nine different fighter squadrons in the Western Pacific – two F-4 squadrons at Clark AB, three F-15 squadrons at Kadena AB, and four F-4/F-16 squadrons at three bases in South Korea. With the majority of our DACT tasking occurring in locations other than Clark AB, and with the sites in Okinawa and South Korea being only two to four hours' flying time away, we were often deployed to these locations on temporary duty, typically for two weeks at a time. For a young Aggressor eager to gain experience, it was the perfect fit, and I spent approximately 40 percent of my time away from Clark AB, loving every minute of it.

The last item that made the 26th TFTAS singularly unique from the other Aggressor units was that we had a secondary air defense mission in the event hostilities ever broke out in Korea. As a result, we had a legitimate requirement to maintain limited weapons currency and proficiency in the firing of both 20mm cannon and AIM-9 missiles. Consequently, we were the only Aggressor squadron that would routinely conduct live firing with the F-5E's pair of nose-mounted M39 cannons (I still have a chromed 20mm cannon barrel from one of our jets mounted and prominently hanging in my office) against a "Dart" aerial gunnery target towed by one of the F-4Es assigned to the 3rd TFW at Clark AB.

While all the above were reasons enough to choose to be an Aggressor at Clark AB, left unsaid was the fact that you couldn't help but gain a lot of experience very quickly. When I look back on the time I spent in the Philippines, I was flying, on average, approximately five to seven times per week. That made for incredible proficiency. With an average sortie duration of only 0.9 tenths of an hour, you didn't rack up a lot of time in your logbook. Still, we weren't looking to build hours to juice up a résumé to become airline pilots. Rather, in those 54 minutes you were airborne, you maximized every pound of JP-4 jet fuel you carried. Additionally, the types of sorties we flew varied daily in response to the training requirements or briefed scenarios of the host squadron.

The best DACT sorties we flew were at Kadena AB while providing adversary support for the F-15s of the 18th TFW. Whenever we deployed there, we were almost always scheduled to perform, at a minimum, 2-v-2 (two F-5Es versus two F-15s) sorties, with the majority of flights being 2-v-4 or 4-v-4 against the Eagles. So, you were flying against large packages all the time, consistently emulating Soviet advanced tactics and formations daily. Conversely, whenever we flew against PACAF F-4 squadrons, except for the 36th TFS at Osan AB, they generally were no larger than 2-v-2 scenarios.

When back home at Clark AB, if we weren't providing direct support for the F-4s of the 3rd TFW, we were flying as the primary adversaries in *Cope Thunder* exercises, held six to eight times a year. These two-week events were PACAF's version of *Red Flag*, the USAF's first large-scale tactical air exercise established at Nellis AFB in 1975, which continues to be regularly held to this day.

If you consider everything I've already mentioned that helped make my assignment as an Aggressor a hallmark event in my fledgling career as a fighter pilot, the single tangible thing that enabled me to develop more than anything else was who I ended up flying with and learning from. Within the flight I had been assigned to upon my arrival in the squadron was a collection of very experienced fighter pilots, all of whom had stellar backgrounds previously as either F-4 or F-15 pilots before becoming Aggressors. But the one aviator that stood out and had the most significant impact on my progression as a young fighter pilot was Capt Clarke "Frog" Peele.

Simply called and referred to as "Frog," Peele had established an enviable reputation for himself as a young and talented F-4 pilot at Eglin AFB, Florida, before receiving a by-name request to become an Aggressor at Nellis AFB as a member of the 65th Fighter Weapons Squadron. Fast forward a few years, and "Frog" arrived at Clark AB just weeks prior to me, where we just happened to be assigned to the same flight. That was most fortuitous, as had that not happened, I would not have had the opportunity to fly with him as regularly as I did.

I recall an early flight with "Frog" shortly after I arrived in the squadron, each of us in our respective F-5Es, which had us scheduled to conduct some 1-v-1 engagements. In a classic case of the most experienced Aggressor pilot in the squadron showing the "puppy" he had a lot to learn, I was sufficiently humbled by "Frog." It was the very first time we'd ever flown together. While I admittedly made several boneheaded mistakes, what I learned on that sortie, and the ones that followed, with "Frog" left a lasting impression on me. Moreover, it was the starting point for me to take my abilities, such as they were, to a much higher level. It didn't take me long to realize, despite my background before becoming an Aggressor, that I had so much more to learn. Fortunately for me, "Frog," for whatever reason, took me, figuratively, under his wing and challenged me at every opportunity.

Over the months, he and I would fly together regularly, almost as a paired crew, alternating lead and wingman roles. He was a role model on how to be the very best Aggressor possible, whether in the airplane or in the briefing room. He held high standards and expected those around him to do the same. Either you'd cut it, or you didn't. There was no slack in "Frog's" one-link chain. To this day, "Frog" remains one of the very best fighter pilots that I have ever flown with or against.

9

Inherent Risks and Cheating Death

"There are pilots, and there are pilots; with the good ones, it is inborn. You can't teach it. If you are a fighter pilot, you have to be willing to take risks."

BRIG GEN ROBIN OLDS

September 15, 1982
1135hrs, Philippine Standard Time
40 miles west of Clark AB, Philippines
20,000ft AGL over the South China Sea
F-5E 75-0612

"'Baron One-One,' 'Dice Two-One' flight is ready." The flight lead's call told me that his pair of Phantom IIs was at approximately 400KIAS, in their Combat Spread formation, and ready for me to begin the engagement. In anticipation of his call, I had already selected full afterburner and had accelerated to approximately 450KIAS. With position and energy to my advantage, I wasted little time in replying.

"'Baron One-One.' Fight's on, fight's on!"

With my call, I rolled into a 135° left-slicing turn toward the Phantom IIs several thousand feet below and one mile north of my sleek F-5E. They were headed eastward, spread 6,000ft to 9,000ft apart in line abreast formation, with the wingman stacked approximately 1,000ft above his leader. Seconds later, and established in a 45° dive, I rolled out and pointed the nose straight at the focus of my attack – the F-4E closest to me on the right side of the formation. Once established in the dive and nose-on, my pure pursuit conversion toward the wingman would be challenging to detect until inside 6,000ft. From the pilots' and WSOs' vantage points in the cockpits of the two Phantom IIs ahead of me, I would have appeared little more than a dot from the formation's "high four o'clock" out of the sun.

Two hours earlier, back in the briefing room within the confines of the 90th TFS, the flight leader had laid out the objectives of today's flight on the large dry-erase board before the members of his flight and me, who would be the sole supporting adversary. My role was simple. As the Aggressor (read "bad guy") in "Baron 11," I was to target the two-ship formation of F-4Es of "Dice 21" flight from outside the formation and within simulated "Atoll" range and force the pair of Phantom IIs to work in concert to first defeat the initial attack and then maneuver to kill me if possible. Simple.

More specifically, I was to engage "Dice 22," a relatively new and inexperienced wingman who had reported to the 90th TFS only months earlier and was presently undergoing extensive and dedicated exposure to DACT, today with me in the F-5E simulating the adversary during the ensuing engagements. My primary objective was to challenge the "FNG" to see if he could maneuver his F-4E to counter my simulated "Atoll" attack, regain his lost airspeed, maneuver to re-enter the fight in a position of advantage, and assist his flight lead in eliminating the lone bandit. He would fail to accomplish any of these tasks if he lost sight of his leader or, even worse, the bandit.

Today's lead – "Dice 21" – was Capt Wayne "Huggy" Hughes. Moments before I'd stepped into the briefing room, he'd pulled me aside and had privately given me the objectives of the flight, which was to include the first Dissimilar Air Combat Maneuvers (DACM) for his wingman, who needed to demonstrate proficiency in mutual support of his leader during a maneuvering fight against my F-5E, simulating a threat MiG-21. While he was proficient in similar scenarios against his fellow F-4E squadron mates in previous flights, today would be the first time the wingman had been pitted against the much smaller, more maneuverable F-5E fighter.

As briefed by Hughes, once in the area and when all players were ready, "Baron 11" (me) would make the "fight's on" call, signaling that we were all cleared to maneuver, and I was to attack at the time and place of my choosing. Hughes told me that he would ensure his wingman was on the right side of the formation, leaving me the choice of which direction I chose to attack from. The last thing he wanted was an Aggressor attacking him and wasting time and fuel.

Hughes had graduated from the F-4 FWS at Nellis AFB years earlier and was currently the Weapons Officer in the 90th TFS. With vast experience and thousands of hours in the Phantom II, his credentials weren't in doubt. Today's DACM training focused on the inexperienced wingman and his WSO, working in concert with his flight lead, to defeat and, hopefully, kill the attacking bandit. We were about to find out if he was up to the task.

INHERENT RISKS AND CHEATING DEATH

With four sets of eyeballs in the Phantom IIs' cockpits eagerly scanning the skies for my attack, I anticipated a "Break" call any second. Approaching 6,000ft and nose-on to "Dice 22," with my airspeed nearing 480KIAS, the radio came alive with the defensive directive, "'Dice Two-Two,' break right. Bandit 'four o'clock high!'"

At the call, I saw both Phantom IIs roll into hard right turns, with vapor trails emanating from their wingtips in the humid Philippine summer air, indicative of the 6Gs their pilots were generating during their turns. By now, both pilots had selected full afterburner, and the tell-tale signs of dark black engine smoke, typically trailing Phantom IIs whenever at any throttle setting less than afterburner, had suddenly disappeared. In their place, their GE J79 engines were now at full afterburner, each producing almost 18,000lb of thrust to help maintain as much energy as possible during their hard break turns.

With each Phantom II weighing close to 45,000lb with just its internal fuel, energy management was critical when maneuvering to defeat, much less kill, a small, agile fighter. USAF F-4 combat losses to similar slashing attacks by Vietnam People's Air Force (VPAF) MiG-21s were a testament to the challenge facing "Dice 21" flight. Had this been actual combat, the crews would have also jettisoned their external fuel tanks in the turn. Today, as this was simply training, they stayed with the aircraft.

Closing the distance rapidly, and approaching 4,000ft, I faced more angles than I could safely counter without jeopardizing my advantage. Moreover, out of my left-front windscreen, I noted Hughes bending his Phantom II around, his lift vector on me at "ten o'clock" and barely a mile away. If I continued my attack on the wingman, Hughes would shortly have me in his gun sight, and I'd have squandered my initial advantage and found myself maneuvering defensively.

With the hard turn by the wingman, my only option was to switch my attack to Hughes's F-4E. This "switch" was fully anticipated and somewhat by design to see if the wingman, who was now suddenly no longer under attack and threatened, could unload his aircraft, regain his depleted energy and airspeed, keep sight of the fight, and then re-enter the engagement to support his leader, who was very shortly going to be under attack by me.

I didn't waste any time making the switch. With few good options, I quickly rolled hard left to attempt a conversion on the remaining Phantom II. To counter the angles presented by Hughes in "Dice 21," I instinctively performed a loaded roll up and to the outside of his Phantom II to solve part of the angular closure problem I was faced with, plus hopefully align myself with his aircraft for a possible gun attack.

Completing my maneuver, I rolled out with Hughes about 3,000ft out in front of me. With my nose still in lag, I smoothly pulled to the inside of his turn to generate cutoff and further close the distance. A glance back over my right shoulder revealed that the wingman had regained his energy and was pitching back into the fight, but he was still a good 7,000–9,000ft outside our turn circle. I had time to pursue a possible gun attack on "Dice 21" before the wingman presented a credible threat.

Another 15–20 seconds, and I'll be able to gun the leader. There's no way the wingman will get back into a gun's position any sooner.

Having assured myself that I had time to concentrate on the leader, I did just that. From the initial attack point, we had gone around one full circle, with much of the last 180° of this turn occurring in the vertical and rapidly going downhill as "Dice 21" attempted to preserve the remaining energy in his F-4E. Hughes had suddenly found himself in a problematic defensive bind – an attacking F-5E had a positional and energy advantage, and his wingman was still well outside a position to bring his weapons to bear on the attacking bandit. Not expecting this, Hughes suddenly had to work to survive.

I'm sure when he set up the scenario, he hadn't expected to be in the state he was in. Unable to unload to regain his energy, he was quickly running out of options to thwart my attack, save for jinking if I closed another 1,000ft and got myself aligned on him within 2,000ft. The range was closing quickly.

I sneaked one last peek over my right shoulder while pursuing "Dice 21" and saw his wingman about 4,000–5,000ft back and high at my "four o'clock." I had about 10–15 seconds to try and complete a gun attack on his flight leader before I had to break off my pursuit and defend against his attack. At this short range, the angles to my F-5E would be too much for a valid AIM-9 attack. I estimated a gun attack was the wingman's only option, and I felt extremely confident I could defeat this and probably force an overshoot. With some luck, I might find myself with both Phantom IIs out in front and without the energy to defend against me.

Okay, now this is where things got strange and events aligned, allowing me to be here recounting this story. I was about 1,800ft behind Hughes in "Dice 21" and quickly approaching a range where I was about to settle the pipper of my gunsight on his fuselage and commence tracking him for a simulated gun kill. He was still in a right-hand descending turn, dark blue waters of the South China Sea about 15,000ft AGL below us, glistening brightly in the high morning sun, and coming through approximately 070–090° magnetic heading.

INHERENT RISKS AND CHEATING DEATH

As I previously mentioned, my aircraft's fuselage was aligned with his, with my nose ever so slightly in lag, but I was beginning to pull lead to settle on the gun kill. Undoubtedly, I had wrongly assessed the wingman's earlier position and energy state, and thought he wouldn't be back in the fight and a threat for some time. Events would soon prove me wrong – almost dead wrong.

I was just about to settle the pipper on Hughes's aircraft and squeeze the trigger on the control stick when the strangest thing I've ever experienced in all my years of flying, before or since, occurred. Despite a cloudless day and the sun high in the sky approaching midday, my cockpit suddenly darkened as if it were twilight!

Whoa! What the fuck?

It has been said that the time dimension slows when experiencing a life-threatening event, sometimes referred to as temporal distortion. And whether you've ever experienced such a phenomenon or not, I can attest that it's real. I sensed it, felt it, and experienced it.

SA is a topic that fighter pilots often discuss, whether they possess it or not, throughout an engagement. I assumed I had correctly assessed the position of each F-4E and their respective energy states in the seconds leading up to this point. In retrospect, it was readily apparent, in my focus on gunning Hughes in "Dice 21," that I'd lost it. This loss of SA, even for a few fleeting moments, ended up almost costing me my life. But in that instant, when the shadow enveloped my cockpit, I suddenly got it back. As you're about to discover, only my efforts in the next few seconds saved me, two aircraft, and most likely the lives of those aboard "Dice 22."

The mere presence of this shadow instantaneously told me an aircraft I'd previously thought I'd kept track of was now an immediate threat to us both in the form of an impending mid-air collision. Moreover, the shadow told me the pilot flying that aircraft had lost his SA and, by extension, his sight of me. Ironically, we had addressed such a possibility that very morning during a review of the air-to-air training ROE to be adhered to. Chief among them was never to lose sight of the adversary you're attacking and never break the 500ft safety bubble around any aircraft. If you did, and you hesitated to correct the error, it was a recipe for disaster. Cardinal rule No. 1 of air combat training had just been broken!

As soon as the cockpit went dark, my head instinctively jerked back in time to see the whole underbelly of "Dice 22's" F-4E less than 50ft from my canopy, and closing!

He's going to hit me . . . I'm dead!

Remember my earlier reference to time slowing down? In what had to be only a mere second, at most two, I could distinctly see, almost count, the rivets on the Phantom II's belly panels, the outline of the landing gear and auxiliary air doors, and the blinking white position lights below each air intake as the big fighter blotted out the sun mere feet from my canopy. It was so close I couldn't even see the painted shark's teeth that adorned the nose of each of the 48 F-4Es and F-4Gs in the 3rd TFW. All of this was taken in by my eyes and imprinted in my brain in a nanosecond.

Fuck!

Instinctively, my right hand jammed the stick forward until I swore it hit the instrument panel, and held it there. I braced myself for what was surely going to be the crush of two fighters disintegrating in a terrifying tangle of flame, smoke, debris, and body parts. Despite being tightly strapped into the ejection seat, my body was thrown to the top of the canopy, my head and neck contorted up against its frame and forward canopy bow, luckily protected by my helmet.

The force of -3Gs violently pitched my F-5E down and outside the arc it had previously carved in its descent while pursuing "Dice 21." My left hand and arm flailed upwards, yanked off the throttles by the violent force of the negative Gs. My right hand, inexplicably, still held onto the control stick in its fully forward position.

I next felt a powerful jolt as the aircraft was savagely tossed to the right.

God damn, he's hit the tail!

Oddly, the fact that I sensed this immediately told me that I was somehow still alive, but now had another problem. Instead of a collision, the violent jolt had been my aircraft going through the wake turbulence of "Dice 21's" jet wash at -3Gs and close to 300KIAS. The disturbed airflow I had just flown through had caused the right engine to flame out. The compressor section of the F-5E's GE J85 engine wasn't designed to handle such abuse. This jolt was immediately accompanied by the illumination of the Master Caution and Right Generator lights on the instrument panel.

Instinctively knowing I wasn't in further danger of a collision with either of the Phantom IIs, I relaxed the forward pressure on the stick and regained positive G forces on my airplane. While I was no longer pinned up against the canopy, with the left engine still at full afterburner, the aircraft now yawed awkwardly to the right. The odd sensation of being in uncoordinated flight while in a rapid descent with the ocean surface looming below was, in a sense, bizarre.

Sixty degrees nose-low . . . passing 11,000ft . . . recover this thing, "Z-Man"!

"Knock it off, knock it off. 'Baron One-One,' knock it off!" I radioed on the shared UHF, my voice tinged with more than a hint of excitement. The two members of "Dice" flight responded promptly.

"'Dice Two-One,' knock it off."

INHERENT RISKS AND CHEATING DEATH

"'Dice Two-Two,' knock it off."

In the moments following the avoidance of a catastrophic mid-air collision, I was focused on the status of my aircraft and whether I would be able to return to Clark AB – partly because I wasn't entirely convinced my airplane hadn't been hit.

How could we have been that close and not hit?

Surprisingly, the least of my concerns was that of "Dice 22," who had nearly killed us. As it turned out, in his attempt to re-enter the fight, he had not only lost sight of me but badly overshot my maneuvering F-5E. Making matters worse for him, he had flushed out slightly high and in front of me, and had no idea of where I'd gone. Laughably, had I not just avoided a mid-air collision by mere feet, and both engines been running, it wouldn't have been too much of an effort to have pulled some lead and gunned him.

Of immediate concern, however, was assessing the condition of my stricken fighter. The good news was that, despite a lifeless right engine, I was fortunate to have still windmilling RPM, and the oil pressure gauge was still alive with its indicator holding steady in the green band. Both gauges showing life told me that the engine hadn't seized, and there was a better than even chance of getting a restart while en route back to Clark AB. But right now, my focus was on whether my airplane was still intact.

"'Dice Two-One,' 'Baron One-One' is visual at your right, 'three o'clock,' slightly low," I radioed. "I will need you to rejoin and look me over."

"Roger 'Baron,' 'Dice Two-One' has a visual and will rejoin on you," said Hughes. "You've got the lead, 'Baron.'"

"'Dice Two-Two,' take it back to the field and make it a full stop. 'Dice Two-One' will escort 'Baron One-One' back." Hughes's vocal admonishment of his wingman left no doubt of the seriousness of what had just occurred. Only by the slimmest of margins had a catastrophic mid-air collision been avoided.

"'Baron One-One' is declaring an emergency and turning toward the field. I've lost my right engine and will attempt to get a restart shortly," I transmitted, letting Hughes know the seriousness of my situation.

"'Dice Two-One,' when you rejoin, give my airplane a good look-over and make sure everything's still where it's supposed to be. I'm not sure 'Dice Two-Two's' airplane didn't make contact with me." Two clicks over the radio by 'Dice 21' told me he understood the gravity of the situation and would rejoin on my crippled F-5E.

A minute later, Hughes joined up on my right wing while I was on a steady heading with the airfield straight ahead at a distance of 40 miles. While I went through the procedures to restart the failed engine, he inspected my aircraft for any apparent damage. Everything seemed in order despite the ordeal I'd just gone through. It's almost beyond human comprehension to understand how close we came to losing two fighters and three crew. Had my aircraft been anywhere else around that turn circle in pursuit of "Dice 21," the sun's position would not have aligned to enable the resulting shadow that saved my life. What were the odds? The question people often ask is, "What happened? How did you get into that predicament that you almost lost two jets?" While inexcusable, it was simple to explain.

In the wingman's attempt to get back into the fight, he had pulled too much lead, and did so in-plane with my aircraft, almost perfectly aligned with his. With that, I was below his belly during his whole conversion, rendering me invisible to him or his WSO. He assumed once he'd pulled lead that I'd "pop out" in front of his nose, and he'd simply saddle up for a gun kill. What he hadn't counted on, being inexperienced, was the ever-changing dynamics of the fight, which had made my turn circle much tighter, and he had both miscalculated and mistimed his entry to the engagement. Luckily, the sun's position was where it was during his re-entry, or you wouldn't be reading this.

The remainder of the single-engine approach and landing at Clark AB was uneventful. Despite repeated attempts to restart the right J85, none was successful. Following an extensive debrief with Maintenance on the conditions of the flight at the time of the engine failure and subsequent attempts to restart it, I proceeded to the 90th TFS for the debrief. With all that had just transpired, this was going to be a good one.

When I entered the room for the debriefing, it was apparent that Hughes was furious and had undoubtedly given his wingman and backseater a harsh berating minutes before my arrival. The wingman sat there absorbing a professional dressing down the likes of which I hadn't ever witnessed. While it was uncomfortable, the reality of almost losing two fighters and the mistakes made leading up to the event were apparent. Sensing this had gone on long enough, I subtly intervened and directed the remainder of the debrief to focus on what we'd learned and what each member would do differently to prevent a repeat of such an event. I do not doubt that the lessons learned by each crewman involved stayed with them for the remainder of their careers.

Those who fly fighters often refer to something we call the "Big-Sky Theory." Discussed over beers at any fighter bar in the world, it holds that despite the inherent dangers involved in air combat, the odds of being in an actual mid-air collision are infinitesimally small due to the sheer vastness of the sky. Still, it happens.

People often ask me, "What's the closest you've ever come to being killed?" I usually answer that in part with a question of my own, and only half-jokingly. "You mean the ones I know about, don't you?"

INHERENT RISKS AND CHEATING DEATH

We've all known friends or acquaintances for whom the "Big-Sky Theory" had broken down, and they never came back to share with us the one thing they would've done differently had they had the benefit of hindsight. Sadly, those lessons were never heard or learned.

As an Aggressor pilot, I had my share of "close calls." Several involved fighters from different squadrons that I was flying against, and on other occasions, with the ground itself. All those lessons and experiences helped make me a better pilot, whose ability to maintain SA in any number of demanding scenarios and situations was precisely what training was designed to achieve. Such experiences would save both my life and the lives of others I flew with and against in the months and years ahead.

Looking back on it, I beat the odds that day. Without the chance position of the sun at that exact moment during our engagement, there would not have been a "lucky shadow" to alert me to the presence of danger. Had our two aircraft hit, there would have been no wreckage to recover, save for some minor debris on the surface of the South China Sea 40 miles west of Clark AB. The pilot and WSO might have been able to eject. If so, they would have been the only ones.

I often wonder what Hughes and his WSO in "Dice 21" witnessed in the moments leading up to our near miss. Did it happen too fast for them to intervene with a simple "knock it off" on the radio? Fortunately, none of it was needed, as I had more than a bit of luck riding with me that day. As the saying goes, "I'd rather be lucky than good!"

The operational tempo of the squadron continued unabated for the next few months, with the usual temporary duty travel (TDY) deployments to Kadena AB and *Cope Thunder* exercises back home at Clark AB keeping me plenty busy. But it wasn't all work without any fun. Sometimes, as I was about to find out, there was perhaps a little too much of the latter.

A pleasant break from the usual routine was the arrival of Royal Australian Air Force pilots and their Mirage IIIO fighters of No 75 Sqn for a month-long TDY in November 1982. As you might imagine, there was never a dull moment either flying or afterward at the O'Club or the nightclubs in nearby Angeles City with our Aussie guests around. One memorable event was a party hosted by me and my roommate, Capt Mike "Action" Jackson, another Aggressor and fellow bachelor, poolside at our off-base home. It was quite the gathering, for on hand, in addition to our squadron mates and our Aussie guests, were F-15 and F-16 pilots from the 12th TFS at Kadena

AB and the 80th TFS at Kunsan AB, respectively, all of whom were at Clark AB while TDY for the ongoing two-week *Cope Thunder* exercise.

On this occasion, a few of our Aussie friends, upon returning from an emergency beer run I'd sent them into town on in my truck, came back with not only several cases of cold San Miguel but several young, lithe dancers from one of the local nightclubs, much to the chagrin, I might add, of a few of the Aggressor wives.

As one might imagine, it wasn't long before the dancers and their Aussie escorts were all in the pool, and in no time at all, our new guests had happily discarded their bras and tee-shirts and were adding a new measure of excitement to the party. Not one to miss an opportunity to join in on the fun, a few other pilots and I did so by jumping off the house rooftop into the pool. If the party hadn't already taken off, this certainly took it to another level. If memory serves, additionally, there were several "full moon" sightings that night over the rooftop. A measure of the party's success was a handful of wet T-shirts, bras, and even a few panties found poolside the following morning. All in all, in my view, the party was a huge success.

However, these apparent acts of debauchery earned me a closed-door meeting in the squadron commander's office the following Monday morning, where, while ordered to stand in a brace before his desk, I was told in no uncertain terms that his wife had not appreciated the lewd display of frivolity the previous Saturday evening. It should be noted that this wasn't a squadron party, but one to which he and the others had been invited. Nonetheless, it was a pretty good ass-chewing. While I wasn't officially reprimanded, in my view, this dressing down was underhanded and cowardly.

The key takeaway for me following this event was as follows. If in a leadership position, refrain from trying to be one of the guys while on the road TDY and then admonish them for similar behavior when back home, especially when you're in attendance and seen to be enjoying it. Worse yet, never use your wife as the excuse for calling one of your troops in on the carpet. Needless to say, that commander never again had my professional or personal respect, nor that of a good number of my squadron mates once word had gotten out about the closed-door meeting.

Two weeks later, in early December, I returned to the States on a trip I had planned for months, taking several weeks of leave to go back home to Wisconsin and spend the Christmas holiday with my mom and brothers. While en route home, I stopped in Las Vegas for a couple of days and paid a visit to the 65th TFTAS and spoke to the unit's commander, Lt Col Mike "Bat" Press, about a follow-on assignment nine months later when my 18-month Aggressor tour at Clark AB was up. I knew Press well, for he

INHERENT RISKS AND CHEATING DEATH

had been the 65th TFTAS CO when I had attended the formal Aggressor training course earlier that year. As expected, he supported my choice to return to Nellis, telling me I'd be a welcome addition to the squadron.

Just minutes later, after leaving his office and feeling good about having secured my next assignment, I ran into someone I'd known for years. As I stood there talking with him in the middle of the hallway, little did I know my career was about to take an unexpected turn. Timing is everything, and in this instance, the coincidence of meeting him there at that moment, with the message he was about to deliver, would have a profound influence on where my career as a fighter pilot would go. It was Las Vegas, baby, and Lady Luck was about to pay me a visit.

10

Right Place, Right Time

"It's not enough to be in the right place at the right time. You have to be the right person in the right place at the right time."

T. HARV EKER

December 13, 1982
65th TFTAS
Nellis AFB, Nevada

"'Z-Man,' what are you doing here?," asked my good friend and former Aggressor squadron mate Capt Jim "Meat" Day as we approached each other, meeting in the hallway at the north end of the 65th TFTAS building – Jim had just entered as I was about to depart following my talk with Lt Col Mike "Bat" Press.

"Hey, 'Meat', what's up? I'm just back from Clark for a few weeks for the holidays and decided to stop by and talk to 'Bat' about coming back here when I finish up my tour in another nine months." I replied, shaking hands firmly with Day.

Day and I went back several years to when I was a young F-4 pilot at Kadena AB and Jim was an Aggressor GCI Controller with the 26th TFTAS, regularly on Okinawa during Aggressor deployments. During that time, we came to know each other well while hanging out at the "Skoski KOOM" (Small Kadena Officers Open Mess) bar, along with several other members of the Aggressors, sharing stories, jokes, and tales of flying over an untold number of beers. We'd briefly been squadron mates at Clark AB when I first arrived earlier in the year, before Day's departure for his current assignment at Nellis. Jim was a standup guy and, along with his wife, Lucy, was one of the few Aggressors on hand to welcome me when I stepped off the military charter nine months earlier at Clark AB as the newest addition to the squadron. A better man you'll never meet.

After a minute or two of trading pleasantries and catching up on what was happening back at Clark AB, he asked me a question that took me aback and, for a moment, seemed odd.

"Do you happen to have your Class A uniform with you?" he asked.

"Well, yeah. Not with me at the moment, obviously, but back in my 'Q' room," I replied. As I'd traveled on "space available" status aboard USAF C-5 and C-141 transports across the Pacific to get to the West Coast, as was customary, I'd done so in uniform. As such, my more formal "Class A" uniform was back at my Visiting Officers' Quarters room there on base. "Why do you ask?" I added, more than a bit puzzled.

"Well, your name is on a short list of guys that my commander, Lt Col Gennin, is looking to hire at the 4477th TES within the next year, possibly. The squadron is expanding with the arrival of additional planes, and consequently, he's looking to hire a few more pilots. You're one of a handful of Aggressors outside of Nellis that Gennin is looking at," Day explained.

Me? My name is on a list of pilots the commander of the "Red Eagles" is considering hiring to fly top-secret MiGs? You gotta be shitting me!

The look of surprise on my face must have registered with Day, as he quickly explained how the two were related. It was only then that I noticed the "Red Eagles" squadron patch on the upper right sleeve of his flight suit. When Day had left Clark AB for Nellis AFB in early March, I'd just assumed it was to one of the Aggressor squadrons. Things were slowly starting to come together and make sense, but I was still in a bit of a fog. Jim quickly added that, as one of his additional duties in the 4477th, Gennin had assigned him the task of compiling a list of fighter pilot candidates who met the qualifications necessary to be a "Red Eagle." Somehow, unbeknownst to me, my name was on his list, and here I was, not 7,400 miles away in the Philippines, but unexpectedly standing right before Day.

"Since you're here, it might be the perfect opportunity to get you in for an interview with Gennin," he added. "Are you going to be around tomorrow?"

Whoa! Interview? 4477th? MiGs?

"Ahh, yeah. I'm going to be here until Wednesday, when I was planning on flying back to Chicago," I mumbled, still trying hard to absorb what Day had just told me.

With that, he told me he'd coordinate with Gennin later that afternoon to see if, the next day, after the "Red Eagles'" returned from Tonopah, it would be possible to schedule an interview for me. Day added that I could expect a call from him later today to confirm whether the interview would indeed be taking place, and he would also leave a message in my room if I was unavailable. I told him that if all else failed, he could probably find me at the O'Club bar that evening. Regardless, he left me his phone number at the squadron, telling me to call him in the morning if I hadn't yet heard from him.

Later that evening, I received a call from Day in my room, informing me that the interview was all set, and that I should plan on being at the 4477th TES building for a 1630hrs interview with Gennin. There wasn't much more than that: a location and time. Additionally, I was required to wear my Class A uniform to the interview. I didn't have much to go on to help prepare for my meeting with Gennin other than what I had been told during the *Constant Peg* in-brief a year earlier. I had to ask Day for the squadron's location at Nellis, as I'd never been there. The adventure was about to begin tomorrow, and in less than 24 hours, the commander of the "Red Eagles" would have his answer as to whether I was a genuine candidate for the job or not.

December 14, 1982
1630hrs Pacific Standard Time
4477th TES Building
Nellis AFB, Nevada

I arrived sufficiently early before the appointed time for my interview with the commander of the 4477th TES, Lt Col George Gennin. The "building" serving as the Nellis AFB location for the "Red Eagles" wasn't a building at all. Instead, it was a rather nondescript, desert-tan colored double-wide trailer located a block north of the far end of Fitzgerald Boulevard, just two blocks from Nellis AFB Operations, in a lot that looked as if it had just recently been reclaimed from the surrounding desert scrub. Hardly what I'd expected for a squadron cloaked in secrecy and, unknown to the majority of people anywhere, operating Soviet MiGs at a remote airfield 120 miles to the north-northwest of Nellis AFB. Or, just maybe, it was the perfect cover.

Regardless, there was no sign or designation indicating that this was the home of the "Red Eagles". It simply had a building number. After one last check to ensure my uniform was in order, I entered through a door on the flightline side of the trailer that looked anything but secure, and one that any petty burglar could open in seconds.

And these guys are a top secret outfit? I hope they don't store classified information in here.

Stepping through the doorway, I immediately encountered a beehive of activity. There were guys in flight suits milling about the hallway, only some of whom were sporting the 4477th TES patch, the remainder wearing squadron patches from different units, no doubt waiting their turn to debrief earlier training engagements. The one thing that immediately struck me was the fact that I was the only one in the entire trailer wearing a Class A uniform. As soon as I entered, those already in the hallway immediately stopped what they were doing and looked at me, no doubt asking themselves who the numb-nuts in the uniform was.

This has got to be a setup. There's nothing like being the only guy in an ice cream suit in a room full of fighter pilots in flight suits!

Luckily, Jim Day, who had been expecting my arrival, was soon there to escort me in and save me from an otherwise very awkward scene. Stepping into a flight room off the hallway, he introduced me to several "Red Eagles" pilots and GCI controllers seated there, none of whom I had met before, all of them eyeing this new guy standing there in his Dress Blues. He was quick to explain that I was back from Clark AB on holiday leave and, as was evident from my attire, there for an interview with Gennin. After a minute or two of introductions and discussing how the two of us had been squadron mates in the 26th TFTAS together, Day excused himself and left to check if Gennin was ready to conduct the interview, promising to return shortly.

In a few minutes, Day indeed returned to tell me that Gennin and the operations officer, Maj Burt "Buffalo" Myers, were ready to meet me. It was a short walk down the hallway to Gennin's office, where I was led in and introduced to the "Red Eagles'" commander and operations officer, neither of whom I'd ever met before. Gennin's office was small, consisting of little more than a desk, a couple of chairs, a bookcase, and a filing cabinet. The walls were bare. Nothing as much as a calendar in sight, adorning any wall. At least he had a window. With the introductions made, Day excused himself and left, closing the door behind him as he did so. Gennin gestured toward the chair before his desk, indicating for me to have a seat. With not so much as a single note on the two men there, I was pretty much going in blind as to what to expect.

Well, you're here, "Z-Man." I never expected this. Give it your best shot.

Gennin began by thanking me for taking the time to stop by while I was back in the States on leave to meet with them. While I'd never met Gennin before, it wasn't hard to take an immediate liking to him. He had a no-nonsense nature about him, but at the same time, he was easy-going and made one feel at ease.

Meanwhile, Myers stood the whole time off to the side, leaning against the wall, not saying a word. His callsign, "Buffalo," was perfect, as he was an immense man – the sort you'd want on your side in a bar fight or anchoring a National Football League (NFL) offensive line. Both men were wearing FWS patches on the left shoulder sleeves of their flight suits. These individuals were not only FWS graduates and instructors, but also, as I later discovered, veterans of multiple operational tours in the F-4 during the Vietnam War.

Contrastingly, I'm sitting there as a "slick-wing" captain, and the only one in "Blues!" If ever one could have been justified in feeling the least bit intimidated, it was then. I don't remember ever having a formal interview before, and while this wasn't exactly that, I knew if I tubed it, so too would my chances of ever setting foot in this squadron again.

Okay, here goes.

In all honesty, I was still somewhat dazzled even to be sitting here talking to the commander of America's "Secret MiG Squadron" about possibly coming to work for him. And flying actual MiGs, no less. For the next several minutes, he discussed the limited information he could share with me about the plans to grow the squadron and, consequently, the need for more pilots. He further explained that he was looking beyond Nellis for talent outside of the two Aggressor squadrons based there, and that was how my name came to be on the short list of qualified pilots he was interested in.

In essence, the "interview" was more of an explanation of "who we are, where we're going, and what my expectations are" – essentially a road map for any prospective squadron pilot. Throughout the 25–30 minute session, Gennin never once mentioned the word "MiG," instead referring to the MiG-21 as the F-5 and the MiG-23 as an F-4. The unclassified cover story, he explained, was simple: "The 4477th TES operates highly modified, unspecified, F-5 and F-4 test aircraft."

Gennin then addressed something that must have been personally difficult for him: the crash of a MiG-23 just seven weeks earlier, tragically killing its young pilot. He had been the commander for less than three months when the 4477th TES suffered the program's second fatality, the first having taken place three years earlier in a MiG-17, also killing its pilot.

"Let me be clear. While it may not be obvious, this is a risky job," he said. "While I have complete confidence in our maintenance troops and their expertise, we simply don't know everything about these aircraft like we do our fighters. I just want you to be fully aware of what you might be signing up for. We don't have any simulators, no two-seat trainers. In the cockpit, you'll only find a few instruments you're familiar with; all the rest are stock, as they were made in the Soviet Union.

"Should you be selected, I expect you to provide the best possible training to our frontline fighter pilots, including those from the Navy and Marines. To do that, I need you to be focused and ready. You'll be given an awful lot of responsibility, easily double that of any other fighter squadron in the USAF, and with it, the opportunity of a career. It doesn't get any better than this, 'Z-Man.' Are you interested?"

While on the outside, my demeanor was one of cool, calm, and collectedness, on the inside, my mind was in sensory overload, still trying to comprehend the fact that I was sitting in this chair discussing the real possibility of actually being asked to join, arguably, one of the most talented and select groups of American fighter pilots anywhere.

"Sir. I can't imagine wanting to do anything else at this point. I'm all in." I added after a measured pause.

With that, Gennin pushed his chair back from his desk and rose. This was my cue that the interview was over. I stood and shook his outstretched hand, thanking him for the opportunity to meet with both of them. Gennin, once again, thanked me for coming by and wished me a safe journey back to Clark AB in the New Year. Myers, following Gennin, did the same. As I was turning away and about to exit his office, Gennin said to me, "One more thing, 'Z-Man.' Don't call us, we'll call you."

"Yes, Sir. Thanks again." I nodded, having gotten the message. As I walked out of the trailer and headed back to my room, while I was happy with how the interview went, I told myself that it was doubtful I'd get such an assignment. But I told myself at least they now knew who I was, and perhaps, at some point down the road, another opportunity would present itself.

Over the next couple of weeks, I made the most of my remaining time back in the States on holiday, taking in the benefits of American culture that many people simply take for granted. The Washington Redskins had the best record of a strike-shortened season, finishing 8–1. At the box office, Steven Spielberg's new movie, *E.T.*, had just been released and was all the rage across America. Olivia Newton-John's hit, "Physical," was the No. 1 song in the land, while my personal favorite, "Down Under," by the Australian rock band Men at Work, had been climbing the charts in the USA since its debut in October.

There was a lot to celebrate come New Year's Eve when I rang in 1983, partying with my brother Mark in the New York City area at a nearby nightclub and enjoying just being out in a crowd, beautiful women everywhere. There's nothing better than returning to the States after being away for so long and suddenly being immersed in American culture. Is this a great country or what?

But all good things come to an end, and two days later, having made my way to the West Coast, I once again boarded a series of C-141s and KC-135 tankers for the trek across the Pacific, eventually landing back at Clark AB on Thursday, January 6. While I hadn't forgotten about the interview with Lt Col Gennin at Nellis weeks earlier, neither did I hold out hope that I'd be selected for such an assignment. Months would pass without a word or even a hint of a possible "Red Eagles" assignment until one fateful day in June, and it did so in a most unexpected way. Once again, good fortune would land on my shoulders.

11

"How'd You Get this Assignment?"

"I'd rather be lucky than good."

ANONYMOUS

June 10, 1983
26th AS
Clark AB, Republic of the Philippines

The crew van rolled to a stop in its assigned spot in front of the 26th AS. Sweaty from the 2-v-1 DACT sortie I'd just flown against a pair of Phantom IIs from the 3rd TFW, I was more than ready to seek out the air-conditioned comforts of the squadron building. So, I got up, parachute slung across my back, grabbed my helmet bag, and stepped out of the "bread van," so-called Air Force-wide due to their uncanny similarity to typical bread delivery trucks seen at local grocery stores everywhere. The midday sun and high humidity of the Philippine summer quickly rendered me a sweating mess as I strode the few steps to the entry door and quickly stepped inside.

What a relief. Back to air-conditioning.

I hadn't walked more than a few steps when the officer sitting at the duty desk, Capt Phil Gilbert, looked at me and summoned me with a hand gesture.

"Hey 'Z-Man,' I just got a call from the DO's office, and 'Brows' wants you down there as soon as you finish up your debrief."

"Brows," as most junior officers casually called Col Chuck Holden, was the Deputy Commander of Operations for the 3rd TFW at Clark AB. As such, he oversaw the flying operations of the Wing's two F-4 squadrons and the F-5Es of my squadron, the 26th AS. His callsign was a moniker bestowed upon him years earlier as a young lieutenant due to him possessing the bushiest set of eyebrows you were ever likely to see, anywhere! The callsign was perfect.

And although he was usually a great guy, this message was still like a bucket of cold water in the face because I figured I was about to get my ass chewed for something I had done while airborne for the past hour. It's like one's initial reaction when seeing flashing police lights in the rearview mirror. You almost assume you're guilty while knowing you're not, but there's a distinct possibility you are.

Ahh shit! Now what? I didn't screw up anything. The mission was a cakewalk. What could I have fucked up?

For a moment, I had a flashback of being back to my time at Saint Edward's grade school, when I was told to report to the principal's office. There, a strict Dominican nun was waiting to dole out corporal punishment for some infraction of school rules and an overall lack of discipline. It was a trip I'd made several times, and the empty feeling was the same each time.

Gilbert, seeing the look of exasperation on my face, which was familiar to any fighter pilot when told you were to report to the DO's office, was quick to ease my worries. "Hey, I think it's good news, 'Z-Man,'" he was quick to add.

Good news? What good news could possibly await me at the DO's office?

Then it dawned on me.

Could it be news of my next assignment? Nellis? The 4477th? MiGs?

A return to reality quickly followed this moment of delusional euphoria. I shot back, "Phil, are you fucking with me?" More than a hint of annoyance in my retort.

"No, 'Z-Man,' I think this is real – no shit," he replied, a bit defensively.

Hmmm, he must be serious to say he isn't bullshitting me.

The congratulatory expression on his face was reassuring. So, either he was suckering me in, or perhaps it was true. "Thanks, Phil. I'll likely find out soon enough," I added.

With that, I turned down the hallway to the Life Support shop to unload my flying gear, my head now filled with possibilities of what lay ahead. I hung up my parachute, turned in my helmet for the specialists to clean and inspect, and finally unzipped my G-Suit, hung it up, and began to look semi-normal again. I was a sweaty mess, but I didn't care. This was how we usually looked when we got in from a flight. But right now, there was more on my mind than the mild discomfort of a sweat-soaked flight suit.

This news can't possibly be real. Can it?

The ensuing debrief with the F-4 two-ship I'd flown against an hour earlier was over quickly. While I gave them a full accounting of how the 2-v-1 engagements went from my vantage point, I must admit I didn't spend extra time reviewing any "piss ants." Curiosity was getting the better of me, and I was ready to head out and see what fate awaited me at "Brows'" office.

"HOW'D YOU GET THIS ASSIGNMENT?"

With the debrief over, the drive to the HQ building of the 3rd TFW and Col Holden's office was a short one, just three blocks away. After giving myself a quick check to ensure I looked as presentable as possible, I walked into the colonel's outer office, introduced myself to his secretary, and quietly sat, waiting to hear what "Brows" had in store for me. Still, I had this lingering doubt in my head that told me there was a good chance I was about to get raked over the coals for something I had done but had already forgotten about.

There's confidence for you.

Now I must confess I wasn't too worried about this as, for one, I was confident I hadn't fucked up anything. Secondly, Holden was a big-picture guy. Having survived three combat tours flying the F-100 and F-4 in Vietnam, it wasn't his style to personally dress down one of his pilots for anything but the most egregious infractions.

No, I'm okay. This meeting has to be good news.

After a few anxious minutes, I heard the secretary answer her phone. "Yes, Colonel?" I could make out a muffled voice on the other end of the line, followed by the secretary's reply, "But of course, Sir. I'll send Capt Zettel right in." Hanging up the phone, she turned to me and said, "Captain, Col Holden will see you now."

Okay, here goes! Either Hero or Zero!

Upon entering, I saw Holden comfortably lounging back in a stuffed leather desk chair, boots up on his desktop, a cigarette dangling from one corner of his mouth, the sleeves of his flight suit bunched up around his elbows.

He's definitely laid back . . . doesn't look like an ass-chewing to me!

I walked forward, stopped at a position of attention in front of his desk, promptly saluted, and reported.

"Sir, Capt Zettel, reporting as ordered."

With that, Holden half-heartedly returned my salute while somehow managing not to tip over backwards in his chair, remove the cigarette and half-wave, while mumbling something I took for "stand at ease." In his left hand, I could see that he was holding a letter-sized piece of paper. As he pulled his feet off his desk, he leaned forward, elbows on his desk, looked at me over his glasses, and said, "'Z-Man,' how in the fuck did you get this assignment?"

After a long pause, a smile appeared on his face. It was good news, after all.

"Sir, what assignment would that be?" I asked, feigning surprise.

"Well, 'Z-Man,'" he added, "I've got a letter here signed by one each Lt Col George Gennin, Commander of the 4477th Test and Evaluation Squadron at Nellis AFB, addressed to Maj Corder [Commander, 3rd TFW], saying you've been selected to be a member of the 'Red Eagles.'"

So that's it. I'm heading to Nellis to fly MiGs. You've gotta be shitting me!

"Sir, I did have an interview for the job in December of last year, back at Nellis while on leave. Quite frankly, I didn't expect to be selected. At least not quite this soon. Sir, I honestly didn't think I could get there from here."

"Well, you sure did. Congratulations, 'Z-Man.' It's one helluva opportunity. Great assignment. Go there and make us proud. You've done well. You've got a few months of flying ahead of you before you report to Nellis. Don't fuck it up. See you at the bar tonight. You're buying!"

"Yes, Sir!"

With that, I took my cue to depart, assumed the position of attention again, and snapped off a brisk salute, which, in turn, Holden returned with the same half-assed effort as earlier. It took all I could to keep from cracking up at that. The epitome of Air Force customs and courtesies, he wasn't. "Brows" was at heart a fighter pilot first and, like many of us who counted ourselves amongst that brotherhood, saved the snappy salutes and starched appearance for change of command ceremonies. This most definitely was not one of those.

I left his office still in some disbelief at what had just happened. Before I drove away, I read and re-read the letter Holden had handed to me, still coming to grips with what it was telling me. During the short drive to the squadron, memories of how I came to receive this assignment flashed through my mind. How does one even start such a journey? A path so unlikely that no Hollywood writer would dare to script it. Even stranger, I had received my private pilot's license back in college, flying a Piper Cherokee 140, barely six years earlier. Now, I had landed arguably one of the top assignments for any US fighter pilot anywhere.

It would be another four months before I boarded the Flying Tigers Airlines 747 bound for the US and the new assignment waiting for me at Nellis. Following Holden's advice, I kept my nose clean and did nothing in terms of flying to draw undue attention to myself during that time. In retrospect, the assignment to the 26th AS at Clark AB, while somewhat predictable, was, in another sense, a turning point at that stage in my fledgling career as a fighter pilot. Perhaps it was simply fate that had me assigned to the same flight with Clarke Peele. Whatever one chooses to call it, without his mentorship, I never would have developed the flying skill set I had attained. And, as Peele had predicted, there was much more to learn. Once I had stepped into the 4477th TES building, the learning curve was about to take off nearly vertically.

12

Going Up North

"One of the greatest discoveries a man makes, one of his great surprises, is to find he can do what he was afraid he couldn't do."

HENRY FORD

October 26, 1983
0730hrs Pacific Standard Time
"Red Eagles" Operations
Tonopah Test Range

"Okay, 'Z-Man,' grab your jacket. Let's jump in my Jeep. Time for you to get the tour," said the squadron commander. With his coffee cup in hand, Lt Col George Gennin looked at me and nodded toward the door at the end of the hallway that led to the ramp where his Jeep was parked. It was my first day up at TTR, and I was about to get the grand tour by the squadron commander himself. We had just finished the unit's morning briefing, and as the 14 other pilots of the 4477th TES filed out of the large conference room, I picked up my flight jacket and followed "the boss" down the hall.

I had flown up to TTR from Nellis AFB with the others earlier on board two Mitsubishi MU-2 twin-turboprop aircraft, the flight lasting 45 minutes. As I would soon become accustomed, 0600hrs departures were the norm. And you didn't dare be late, for the airplanes departed on time, with or without you. The only exception was for "the Boss," rank, after all, having its privileges.

For my first trip "up North," Gennin had me scheduled to be on the same MU-2 as him, sitting directly across from "his seat," where he would spend the flight giving me the lowdown on what to expect when we arrived. Once airborne, most other pilots were soon fast asleep, having woken up at 0500hrs to arrive at the squadron in good time to catch the early takeoff. Not so with Gennin.

As I soon discovered over the following months, he never slept on these flights. Instead, he always had some paper or report before him, his seat light on, the only one in an otherwise dark cabin amidst snoring pilots, his trademark red pen in hand, editing something. There was no mistaking anything handed back to you if Gennin had already read it; it had his distinctive "red edits" all over it. To be handed back a report without any red marks on it was a significant accomplishment. So good was he at catching errors and correcting them that even the 57th Fighter Weapons Wing (FWW) Commander, Brig Gen Michael Kerby, wouldn't ask his staff to proofread anything that came to him bearing Gennin's initials. It was perfect!

An AFROTC product of Mississippi State University, George Gennin was already an extremely accomplished fighter pilot when he took command of the 4477th in August 1982. An F-4 FWS graduate who had completed three combat tours in Vietnam, Gennin was subsequently one of the earliest USAF pilots to check out in the F-16, eventually heading up the Multi-National Operational Test and Evaluation program at Hill AFB, Utah. Later, after being assigned to Nellis AFB and serving with the 57th FWW on F-16 test projects, he was tapped by the commander of Tactical Air Command (TAC), Gen Wilbur Creech, to take over as CO of the 4477th. Gennin thus became the first boss of the "Red Eagles" not to have had an Aggressor background. He was also the first pilot assigned to the 4477th with any significant F-16 experience.

"Oh, before we head outside, 'Z-Man,' you need to see this first," said Gennin. With that, he turned left, walked through the squadron lounge, and headed for a door in the back wall, behind which was the first of many surprises awaiting me that morning during my tour of the ultra-secure facility.

"This is our showpiece, our VIP hangar." He opened the door, and there inside were two immaculately clean aircraft, a MiG-21F-13 "Fishbed-C" and a MiG-23BN "Flogger-H," arrayed around a giant red star painted in the center of a glistening white hangar floor that you could literally eat off. Even the *Thunderbird* hangar was not as pristine. A giant American flag hung from the rafters behind the two aircraft, forming an awe-inspiring backdrop. As an American fighter pilot, if the sight of this didn't stir something profound inside, you weren't wired correctly.

"Welcome to the 'Red Eagles,' 'Z-Man.' This is what it's all about," he said.

I was awestruck. While I had imagined many things, this wasn't one of them.

"Throughout your assignment here, you'll fly both of these models and more. Wait until you see what's down in the big hangars," Gennin added.

GOING UP NORTH

Turning to leave, he motioned for me to follow. After exiting from the hangar and going through the lounge, he led me across the hall and past the duty desk area to the nerve center of "Red Eagles'" operations. There, mounted on the back wall, was a large Plexiglas panel displaying the day's flying schedule, complete with callsigns, assigned aircraft, pilots, scheduled range space, adversaries, and so on. It was typical of every fighter squadron I'd ever been in.

As with any squadron, a small core group of NCOs who are invaluable to its success is the constant element that keeps things running smoothly. The 4477th was no exception. Next, Gennin introduced me to someone I would come to know and hugely appreciate over the next several years. "'Z-Man,' meet TSgt Jerry Howell. Jerry, meet Capt Zettel, our newest 'Red Eagle.'" After shaking hands and exchanging pleasantries, Gennin was quick to add, "If you need anything, Jerry is our go-to guy. Thanks, Jerry." Something was familiar about Jerry. After a few moments, it dawned on me. If you've watched the 1970s television comedy series *M*A*S*H*, Jerry was the 4477th's equivalent to Sgt Walter "Radar" O'Reilly. He even slightly resembled "Radar," complete with round glasses and short stature.

With that, Gennin grasped the handle of yet another door, this one also at the rear and to the right of the scheduling board, and opened it. Not surprisingly, it was the entrance to another hangar, which, like the previous one, was adjacent to the squadron Operations area. Stepping inside, the hangar floor, while not as gleaming as the last, soon gave up its own surprise. In addition to two T-38 training aircraft, it also housed a fully operational MiG-17, with the Bort number "055" painted on its nose. Gennin told me its history, and that while the jet had served its purpose well in the early years of *Constant Peg* (this particular MiG-17 was originally part of the *Have Ferry* exploitation program) the aircraft was no longer flying. It was one of two MiG-17s previously operated by the "Red Eagles." Despite it being a challenging adversary, the jet was no longer considered representative of the current threat and had therefore been grounded, never to fly again.

"Okay, time to take a drive," said Gennin.

Once in his Jeep, which was parked immediately outside the west entry to the building, facing the runway, it was a short 100yd drive to the next hangar complex to the north, often referred to as "Phase II." At this hour, the aprons surrounding both hangar complexes were empty, although they were large enough to accommodate dozens of fighter-sized aircraft. The next complex was significantly larger than the one housing squadron Operations and two flanking hangars.

Gennin went on to explain, "This first hangar houses all of our MiG-21s. The next hangar houses our MiG-23s. Connecting the two are all our maintenance shops and workrooms."

Just as we were pulling up in front of the first hangar, its massive pocket doors slowly began to slide open from the center. Gennin stopped the Jeep just past the center of the hangar opening, looked at me, and added, "Show time, 'Z-Man.'" He then opened his door and stepped out. With this, my cue to follow, I was right behind him. He led the way to the center front of the hangar, revealing two rows of MiG-21s, four on each side, parked with noses pointed inward, the doors now almost half open. It was simply astounding.

Holy shit! God damn!

Whether Gennin had staged this purposely or not, the net effect was the same. It was an incredible, jaw-dropping way to be introduced to an operation that, heretofore, one could only have speculated about until then. You've got to understand that most USAF fighter pilots' only exposure to the MiG-21 was what they read in intelligence manuals, accompanied by mostly grainy photos. Now, right here before me, were eight of them.

After pausing to take it all in, Gennin waved for me to follow him. We walked into the hangar, where aircraft crew chiefs were busily attaching tow bars to a handful of MiG-21s about to be towed onto the ramp for the morning's flying schedule. Accompanying the din of activity was a distinctive smell – a combination of oil, hydraulic fluid, and jet fuel that evoked the scent of heavy aircraft maintenance. All around me were MiG-21s, some ready to fly, while others underwent various stages of maintenance. Several had their tail sections removed and were undergoing engine changes. Still others sat nearby with canopies off, their ejection seats undergoing inspection. It was a beehive of activity, about to grow ever louder, with the first takeoffs scheduled in just 15 minutes.

"Come over here, 'Z-Man,' and take a look at these. These are our two new ones," the commander said with a wink.

New ones? Where would we get new ones?

The MiG-21F-13s belonging to the 4477th were all Soviet-built models manufactured in the late 1960s, making them approximately 15 to 18 years old. Many of them had "hard miles" on them. The thought of any new MiGs was both puzzling and a welcome surprise. Farther ahead, parked on the right side of the hangar, were two light gray fighters, distinctly different in appearance from the others, which sported various camouflage paint schemes. There was something else different about them, but it was not immediately apparent.

"These are not MiG-21s," Gennin began, "Any clue as to what they are and where they're made?"

What? They most certainly are MiG-21s, aren't they?

"No, Sir. But they look brand new." I hesitantly replied, feeling I was being set up for something I should have known the answers to but didn't.

"They're Chinese. And technically, as I mentioned, they're not MiG-21s, but almost an exact copy of the Soviet MiG-21s we're flying. They're called F-7s," Gennin was quick to add.

By this time, we were walking around one of the F-7s, which had the large Bort number "44" painted on its nose and an unmistakable red star on its tail, as did all the others in the hangar. Gennin was, of course, correct. At first glance, the aircraft was indeed identical to the Soviet-built MiG-21F-13 parked next to it. He quickly pointed out some distinguishing features, including a different canopy, drag chute housing, and ejection seat. To the untrained eye, with identical paint schemes, you would have been hard-pressed to know the difference.

"This one was our first, but both are less than a year old and have fewer than 30 hours on them," he proudly added, patting the fuselage of "44," and filling me in on the squadron's plans to add at least six more over the following six to twelve months. With the aircraft's ladder in place, he motioned me to climb in and look at what I would soon be flying. I was not waiting for him to change his mind, and I climbed up the ladder quickly.

This has got to be staged, right?

The thing was immaculate! It was so clean that I hesitated to step on the seat cushion as I entered the cockpit. It even had that "new MiG" smell to it. Standing on the ladder and leaning into the cockpit, the "Red Eagles" commander gave me a quick orientation of the various displays and switches. Everything except a few instruments was "factory direct," meaning it was stock Chinese. However, to my surprise, unlike the Soviet models, which were marked in Russian, this F-7 was labeled in English. After a few minutes in the F-7, Gennin climbed down the ladder, indicating it was time to move on and see the rest of the complex.

Exiting the MiG-21 hangar, he led me through a maze of hallways and maintenance shops where dozens of technicians were already at work on various aircraft components, from hydraulic pumps to engine gearboxes, even repacking drag chutes. This middle portion of the North complex connected the two large hangars, which contained all the MiGs. Having left the MiG-21 hangar moments ago, we were about to enter the hangar that housed the squadron's MiG-23s.

As we entered, what immediately caught my attention were multiple airframes on jacks, with their tail sections removed and their engines missing. Gennin explained that while we had nine MiG-23s, only a handful were currently flyable, with many awaiting engines or repairs to recently discovered cracks in their wing boxes. As I would soon learn, while the more impressive of the two fighters operated by the 4477th, the

MiG-23 was, at best, challenging to keep operational. At worst, it was a maintenance nightmare.

As with the MiG-21 hangar I had just seen, when standing in the middle of this hangar, we were flanked by two rows of "Floggers." Even with their wings fully swept back, they were tightly packed in, not allowing for much space on either side of them. The sight was almost overwhelming, my senses flooded with what I could have only imagined previously. For the second time this morning, I was awestruck at the scope of the operation.

The 4477th flew both MiG-23MS "Flogger-E" and MiG-23BN "Flogger-H" variants, the fighter interceptor and ground attack models, respectively. A handful of each was parked before us, most of which were undergoing maintenance – only two of them were flyable. As before, Gennin led me to a MiG-23 with its ladder hanging on the cockpit side rail and invited me to climb up and take the seat. As with the MiG-21, it was the first time I had seen such an airplane in person. However, unlike the MiG-21, the first thing that stuck out was how big the MiG-23 looked on the ground. With the ladder in place, climbing up reminded me of the F-4 Phantom II and the seven rungs one had to scale to reach the cockpit. Once seated, Gennin, although not a MiG-23 pilot, pointed out a few of the features unique to the "Flogger," which, unknown to me at that moment, I would get to know all too well in the years to come.

Minutes later, once we had left the hangars and were back in his Jeep, Gennin drove out onto the flightline where the early scheduled jets had already started their engines and were beginning to taxi to the runway for the day's first takeoffs. It was simply exhilarating. The sight and sounds of both MiG-21s and MiG-23s operating right before me, heretofore only a distant dream, was something I'll never forget. Little did I know that just eight days later, I'd join this small fraternity with my first flight in a MiG-21F-13.

Once the early flyers were airborne and the ramp was quiet, it was a short drive back to the squadron, the whirlwind tour over. For the previous 45 minutes, I had been introduced to and met many faces that I wouldn't be able to associate with names for weeks to come. There were just too many. Only now did I understand the enormity of the operation, the scope of which I simply had no idea about. Aside from the MiGs, it was unlike any squadron I'd ever been in or had heard about. What I'd discover in the months to come was even more revealing.

Simply stated, Gennin's job as commander of the 4477th was way more complex than any other fighter or training squadron commander in the USAF. Where others would be solely responsible for just the flight operations side of things, Gennin, in effect, was responsible for everything, almost like a mini-wing commander. From flight operations to maintenance, including administrative personnel and GCI controllers, he had more than 150 officers and NCOs working for him. To ensure an efficient operation, the command structure of the 4477th was, and had to be, unique by design.

With the need for secrecy paramount, the fewer department heads reporting directly to Gennin, the better. In essence, the two major areas were operations and maintenance. What allowed such a unit to function without security breaches was testament to the quality of the people selected by Gennin and, by extension, his department heads. Such was the pride in being a part of this unique squadron that no one dared speak about what we flew.

To be sure, Gennin couldn't do this without a great deal of support from the four-star commander of TAC himself, Gen Wilbur Creech. As such, it wasn't uncommon for Creech to call Gennin direct, often daily, asking, "How's my squadron doing today?" Having unfettered access to Creech and his ability to run interference for the 4477th was unheard of for someone at the squadron commander level in TAC. However, this was no ordinary squadron. To his credit, Gennin leveraged the unit's unique status like a pro. No other squadron at Nellis enjoyed this sort of "top cover."

Of course, knowledge of Gennin's "direct access" to the TAC commander-in-chief was an endless source of irritation to both the Tactical Fighter Weapons Center (TFWC) commander, Maj Gen Eugene Fischer, and George's immediate boss at Nellis AFB, 57th FWW commander Brig Gen Michael Kerby. Gennin's ability to pull off this delicate balancing act while keeping his people out of harm's way was a testament to his leadership skills.

Luckily for me and the rest of the "Red Eagles" pilots, we, for the most part, were spared any knowledge of the political maneuvering occurring well above our pay grades. Instead, as the "new guy" at Tonopah, there was plenty for me to do as I went about settling into the squadron. My immediate focus, as outlined by our operations officer, Maj Monroe Watley, shortly after my return from my tour with Gennin, was to concentrate on my checkout in the MiG-21, which would start immediately – no additional duties, no other bullshit. I was there to fly MiGs, and weather and maintenance permitting, I'd do just that later next week.

Damn . . . this just keeps getting better!

Monroe, a career F-4 pilot, had been an FWS instructor in the Phantom II before coming to the 4477th. A gifted fighter pilot, he was one of only a handful currently flying the MiG-23. An easygoing and soft-spoken East Texan, he had an air about him that you couldn't help but immediately take a liking to. Watley would often give the morning's mass briefing, outlining the day's schedule, the squadrons we were flying with, any special duties, and visiting VIPs, among other details. Inevitably, he never failed to end the briefing with a joke that only he could deliver in his unique way, leaving the room in stitches. Even Gennin, a no-nonsense guy who wasn't given to joking, often wiped away tears of laughter following one of Watley's jokes. In short, he was a fighter pilot's fighter pilot, and I couldn't ask for a better guy to work for.

Wasting no time, Watley introduced me to Capt Mike "Mach" Roy, who would be my IP in the MiG-21 and would guide me through both the academics and flying portions of the training. I'd met Mike years before at Kadena AB when I was a new Phantom II pilot in the 12th TFS. Roy had been in a sister squadron, the 44th TFS, also flying the F-4, and later transitioned to the F-15 in 1979 when the Eagle first arrived in Okinawa. Following his tour at Kadena AB, Roy requested and received an assignment as an Aggressor pilot in the 64th Fighter Weapons Squadron at Nellis AFB. A mere 18 months later, George Gennin had selected Mike to join the "Red Eagles." Having flown the MiG-21 for nearly a year, and coupled with his extensive previous fighter experience to draw on, "Mach" would prove to be an outstanding IP. I had lucked out again.

The training footprint Watley had laid out would be a short and intense one. Where it would be customary in a "normal" squadron to take up to several weeks of academics and simulators before finally getting airborne in one's newly assigned fighter, here, it was just one week. Between now and the following Thursday, my time at Tonopah would be spent studying the MiG-21 flight manual and completing academic tasks. Having Mike Roy as an instructor was like having a private tutor. When he wasn't flying a MiG-21 as part of the regular schedule, Roy spent several hours each day with me, reviewing the MiG-21's systems, flight characteristics, and emergency procedures.

Without simulators or two-seat trainers for the MiGs in the 4477th, every bit of the hands-on training took place in an actual aircraft. We used the MiG-21 on static display in the VIP hangar for this. When not scheduled for a training period with Roy, I would often spend hours reviewing the flight manual and checklists, with the switchology associated with every normal and emergency procedure open. The time spent there was invaluable, as it took some adjustment for the brain to become accustomed to instruments and switches labeled in Russian, pressures measured in kilograms per square centimeter, and fuel quantities in liters. Sitting in the seat of this MiG-21 was "hangar flying" in its truest sense.

At the end of my first day at the TTR, the others and I again boarded the two MU-2s for the return flight to Nellis AFB, completing what for me had been a unique experience that would soon prove to be the norm as I became a MiG pilot in the 4477th. In retrospect, the day was one of surprise after surprise for me. To put this in perspective, what I've just experienced was an entire fighter squadron of secret MiG aircraft, hangared and out of view, away from prying eyes and satellites, at an air base most of the USAF knew nothing about, much less the American public. Without a doubt, this was perhaps America's best-kept Cold War secret, and little did I know at the time that it would remain part of "Black World" operations for another two decades to come. But right now, I still could not believe that I was going to be part of it. My first flight in the MiG-21 was just days away.

13

The Assets

"If you are looking for perfect safety, you will do well to sit on a fence and watch the birds. But if you really wish to learn, you must mount a machine and become acquainted with its tricks by actual trial."

WILBUR WRIGHT

Of all the questions I'm asked regarding my time in the "Red Eagles," the one most often asked is, "Where did we get the MiGs?" While there is no single-best answer, my most common reply is, "It depends on which MiGs you're referring to." Over the ten years the program existed, the 4477th TES operated MiG-17s, MiG-21s, and MiG-23s. I'll limit my discussion to the two I flew while in the "Red Eagles," namely the MiG-21 and MiG-23, as the MiG-17 had already been retired from the program by the time I arrived in October 1983.

Quite simply, all the MiG-21F-13s, bar one, were obtained from Indonesia. The exception was the same MiG-21 used by the USAF in the *Have Doughnut* exploitation program, which was flown between January and April 1968. This aircraft, incidentally, had come by way of Israel, the product of its Mossad-led Operation *Diamond*, which culminated in the defection of Iraqi Air Force (IrAF) officer Capt Munir Redfa on August 16, 1966. This same aircraft was used extensively as part of the *Have Idea* program from May 1973 until the formation of the 4477th in April 1977. Until then, under the mantle of *Have Idea*, the USAF's operation of MiGs had been a piecemeal affair, sporting only a handful of aircraft and seemingly without clear direction or endgame other than to provide a few exposures to a select few USAF and US Navy fighter pilots, but without any formal structure or regularity.

That changed with TAC now managing its own MiG program, known as *Constant Peg*. As with all DoD programs, formalization of the MiG operation saw *Constant Peg* receive the "lifeblood" it needed to operate and expand – consistent funding. With a steady stream of dollars now budgeted, the fledgling squadron began to add the staffing and resources necessary to make the concept of an operational MiG squadron a reality. At the core of this effort was an initial cadre of 11 maintenance technicians who were key to the program's success. To be sure, it began slowly, and it would be two years before they "turned a wheel" at TTR.

When the 4477th finally began operations at TTR on Tuesday, July 17, 1979, it did so with only a handful of aircraft – three MiG-21s and two MiG-17s, all of which had previously been part of the *Have Idea* program. With designs on expanding the program to expose more significant numbers of fighter pilots to current Soviet threat aircraft, the unit simply needed more jets and the parts to keep them flying. Having previously identified Indonesia as a source for two of the three MiG-21s currently flying, it was time to turn to the Southeast Asian country once again. With funding assured and maintenance expertise in place, by the fall of 1979, things began to take off like a house on fire. It was time for the "Red Eagles" to go hunting for MiGs!

November 30, 1979
US Embassy
Jakarta, Indonesia

The two men, dressed in blue jeans and t-shirts, could easily have been mistaken for visiting tourists when they entered the lobby of the US Embassy in Jakarta. The only giveaways were the olive-drab canvas parachute cargo bags they carried, along with two boxes of personal tools and a couple of cases of WD-40, which they guarded like gold. The pair had US military personnel written all over them.

One week earlier, MSgt Don Lyon and TSgt Jerry Baker had left Las Vegas for Honolulu on the first leg of their trip to Indonesia. While they didn't have official travel orders yet, they'd been told by their boss, 4477th TES Non-Commissioned Officer In Charge (NCOIC) CMSgt Bobby "Daddy" Ellis, to pack up and expect to head abroad at any moment. Having been ready to go for two weeks and growing tired of waiting, the two "Red Eagles" maintenance technicians decided to "take leave" and go on their own to Hawaii, and remain there until they received the green light from the US Air Attaché to board their flight to Jakarta. After all, sitting on Waikiki Beach drinking beers, soaking up the rays, and enjoying the attractive two-legged scenery was much more enticing than being at TTR all week waiting for the phone to ring and being told to get going.

As members of the "Red Eagles" advance team, they were prepped to help with the acquisition of additional MiG-21s from America's new ally. The price? Brand new F-5Es for the Indonesian Air Force in exchange for older and mostly unflyable MiG-21s, spare parts, and engines. Lyon, Baker, and Maj Dave "Marshall" McCloud were tasked with traveling to Jakarta, meeting with the US Air Attaché, and initiating the process before the rest of the "Red Eagles" maintenance team arrived days later.

By November 1979, Don Lyon had already spent 19 years in the USAF, having dedicated his entire career to aircraft maintenance. During that time, he had worked on a wide range of aircraft, from T-33s to SR-71s. If it flew, he knew how. If it didn't, he could tell you why. For the past two years, since volunteering to join the 4477th as part of the initial cadre of maintenance technicians, Lyon had become well-versed in everything related to the MiG-21, making him the perfect person to coordinate efforts on the ground in Jakarta. After finally meeting with the Air Attaché, they were informed that they would be driven to the airport the following day, where they would meet with members of the Indonesian Air Force. The Air Attaché quickly pointed out that he would not be allowed to accompany them onto the base. Furthermore, once his driver dropped them off, they would be on their own.

The next day, the three of them were driven to the air force side of Jakarta airport. After being introduced to a couple of Indonesian "handlers," they were taken on a tour. There wasn't much to see, and definitely no MiG-21s on the base. Those, they were told, awaited them at Iswahjudi AB, in East Java (an hour away by air), and they'd be flown there in the days ahead. The only aircraft at the base was an old MiG-19S on static display, which clearly hadn't flown in years. Although they were there to get MiG-21s, McCloud insisted they needed to find a way to take the MiG-19 with them. There was never a mention of adding a MiG-19 to the mix, an aircraft that the 4477th wasn't even operating.

With little else to do, the three brainstormed how to abscond with a fighter that wasn't on the list of aircraft they were authorized to pick up. McCloud soon struck a deal with someone, unbeknownst to either Lyon or Baker, for the trio were told shortly thereafter that they could also take the MiG-19. An inspection of what had been "given" to them was then carried out, with no further questions asked. Additionally, while a disassembled MiG-19 wouldn't be that big, they weren't sure there'd be room in the C-5A Galaxy assigned to transport the ex-Indonesian fighters to the States. Regardless, figuring it was better to ask for forgiveness than permission, they went about their work.

THE ASSETS

Despite not having flown in quite some time, the MiG-19 was intact, complete with external wing tanks and engines installed. In fact, it was a bit too complete. As Lyon soon discovered, the ejection seat had never been disarmed! It was a pitiful sight, but nothing the "Red Eagles" maintainers couldn't remedy and get back to flying condition if warranted. Two days later, SSgts Tom Burzynski, Dave Hollingsworth, and Mike Beverlin, and TSgt Chico Noriega arrived in Jakarta, rounding out the "Red Eagles'" "extraction" team. With the six maintainers ready to get started and Dave McCloud running interference for them, they found an old farm tractor and pulled the MiG-19 to a nearby hangar, where they soon got to work disassembling it. The fighter was in such sorry shape that the tires shredded right off the rims as they towed it.

While the Jakarta team was busy dealing with the MiG-19, Don Lyon received a message from CMSgt Bobby Ellis, who was also in-country at Iswahjudi AB. His instructions to Lyon were for him and Jerry Baker to get on a USAF C-130 that was arriving at Jakarta later that morning and join him at Iswahjudi AB to begin surveying the three MiG-21s he had located, and discuss how they were going to disassemble and crate them up in preparation for a C-5A to fly them back to TTR.

Soon enough, Lyon and Baker were on a USAF special mission C-130 headed for Iswahjudi AB, where, upon landing, they met up with Ellis. Together, the three of them began to assess the MiG-21s on base. The following evening, Don received a frantic call from Tom Burzynski back in Jakarta, who informed him that earlier that afternoon, an Indonesian national had come by with a piece of paper that listed each of the "Red Eagles" by name, rank, and serial number. Additionally, they were told to get the MiG-19 off base within 24 hours, or it would be buried along with all of them.

Their attempt at being low key and incognito hadn't fooled anyone. With their cover blown and a not-so-subtle threat made on their lives, it was time to get the team out of Jakarta. Bobby Ellis arranged to send the C-130 back to the Indonesian capital the following morning, load everyone, along with the now-disassembled and crated MiG-19, and fly them to Iswahjudi AB.

Once the entire "Red Eagles" team was safely out of Jakarta and at Iswahjudi AB, little time was wasted getting to work on disassembling and crating the three MiG-21s the Indonesians had agreed to hand over to the USAF. While the majority of the team was working on the aircraft, Ellis made a three-hour drive to Abdul Rachman Saleh AB, near Malang in East Java, to scour a parts warehouse for anything and everything that could help support MiG-21 operations. Two days later, he returned with a smile on his face and a truckload of "goodies." With everything packed and ready, it was time to head back to Tonopah.

As planned, a C-5A landed at Iswahjudi AB to pick up the disassembled MiGs, parts, and support equipment pallets the following morning. Among the first to step off the Galaxy was the 4477th commander, Lt Col Earl Henderson, who had brought with him some "sweet gifts" for their Indonesian friends. Once the C-5A's massive front cargo door was open, off rolled four brand-new F-5Es for the Indonesian Air Force. In their place, the four MiGs were loaded, along with the rest of the pallets and gear. Within hours, the C-5A was back in the air for the return flight to Clark AB. Two days later, following stops at Clark AB and Hickam AFB for refueling and change of crews, the same C-5A, along with its top secret cargo, landed at TTR under the cover of darkness and unloaded. The "Red Eagles" now had six MiG-21s.

Following the departure of the Galaxy from Iswahjudi AB, Don Lyon and the rest of the "Red Eagles" maintenance team returned to Jakarta the following day, flying with Garuda Indonesian Airways to Tokyo and then on to the US. Arriving back in Las Vegas one week before Christmas, Lyon had been on the road for 26 days.

So, you may ask, what became of the mysterious MiG-19 that the "Red Eagles" absconded with from Jakarta? For starters, it never flew. Moreover, two months after the MiGs were offloaded at TTR, Mike Beverlin, Jerry Baker, and Tom Burzynski secretly transported and assembled the MiG-19 in the Threat Training Facility at Nellis AFB, where it remained on display for years before being passed on to the National Museum of the US Air Force in the early 1990s. The fighter has been on display in the museum at Wright-Patterson AFB, Ohio, since October 1994.

With the addition of the three MiG-21s, the operational tempo slowly increased, affording more exposure to an actual threat aircraft. However, the goal had always been to intensify this effort still further. But, to do that and still allow Maintenance ample time to inspect, fix, and overhaul the aircraft meant there would be only a finite number of sorties available to fly with just six "Fishbeds" on the ramp. The only solution was to obtain more MiG-21s. And if you were going to do that, it made sense to go out and acquire the newest models possible. Where the "Red Eagles" went next to source their needed MiGs was about to shock everyone.

THE ASSETS

November 1982
1905hrs, China Standard Time
28,000ft over the East China Sea approaching Chinese airspace
C-5A

"Hey guys, you might want to come to the cockpit and have a look at this. It's something you'll probably never witness again. We're about to get some interesting company going into Beijing." The pilot's voice on the aircraft's intercom sounded distant, despite the sole occupants in the passenger section being only 20ft aft of the giant airplane's flight deck.

Sitting in one of the first rows of the passenger section on the upper deck and separated from the cargo hold below, TSgt Jim "J. B." Bell sat up, unbuckled his seat belt, and slowly made his way toward the cockpit. He and five other senior enlisted men, four from the 4477th TES and two from the 6513th TS, nicknamed the "Red Hats," had been spread out and relaxing comfortably in the mostly empty passenger area since their takeoff an hour earlier from Kadena AB. They were on a unique operation, and Bell and the others had no idea what to expect upon landing.

All they had been told weeks earlier, back in Nevada, in preparation for this trip was that they would be picking up some aircraft in China and flying back with them to TTR. Where in China were they going? They had no idea. Nor had they been briefed on their destination. Likewise, there had been no mention of the type or number of aircraft being collected. Again, as was the case with most things surrounding the "Red Eagles" and our MiG assets, the less information disseminated, the better. But, since the mission of the 4477th was to expose US fighter pilots to actual threat aircraft, Bell was pretty sure he'd be returning to TTR in a few days with some variant of the MiGs he and his traveling companions had already become accustomed to working on.

Jim was a 13-year veteran mechanic who had worked on every model of the F-4 in the USAF inventory, although he was then a MiG-23 crew chief. He had been with the "Red Eagles" for more than two years, being the 27th hire among this select group of maintenance professionals. Hired as a crew chief, when Bell asked what aircraft he would be assigned, MSgt Bill Wright pointed to a fully dismantled MiG-23BN sitting in the corner of a hangar and told him to get to work. Six months later, "Flogger" Bort number "32" was flying. Most recently, however, the MiG-23s had not been flying much due to engine issues. With his aircraft temporarily sidelined and plenty of time on his hands, when the Maintenance Chief asked who would like to go on "a trip abroad" to fetch some airplanes, Bell jumped at the opportunity.

Stepping inside the cockpit of the C-5A, Bell could barely make out the outlines of the two pilots at the controls, their faces only dimly lit by the incandescent glow from the instrument panel. As his eyes slowly adjusted from the much brighter lights of the passenger cabin, he soon took in the rest of the flight deck and, after pausing briefly, approached the pilots.

"What's going on?" he asked, looking outside into the darkness in both directions. No response. After a couple of awkward seconds, Jim felt a tap on his right arm. He noticed a set of headphones with a boom mic attached, which the flight engineer held out to him and then tapped his headset, pointing at Bell, indicating that he should put them on. He then realized that they couldn't hear what he was saying. Within a few seconds, Bell had the headset on and was talking to the aircraft commander at the controls in the left seat. He was quick to give Jim the lowdown on what was happening.

"We just entered the Chinese ADIZ [Air Defense Identification Zone]. Shanghai Center tells us to expect fighters to join up on us shortly. I have no idea what type. They must be on a discreet frequency, as we haven't heard a thing. But then again, they're probably speaking Chinese anyway, so it would be of little good to have them here with us. Let's keep a sharp lookout regardless. This ought to be interesting."

They didn't have to wait long. Soon, the Shanghai Center controller instructed the C-5A crew to maintain their current heading and altitude, and to expect PLAAF [People's Liberation Army Air Force] fighters to join them momentarily. Moments later, with the lights of Shanghai now visible ahead on the horizon, Bell noticed the aircraft commander motioning with an extended thumb toward the left side window. Leaning forward, Jim could just make out what appeared to be a pair of fighters, what type he wasn't sure, loosely flying alongside the giant transport, the two aircraft barely visible in the soft red glow from the C-5A's upper and lower rotating anti-collision lights. The Chinese fighters' wingtip position lights were, however, distinctly visible against an otherwise black night sky. A casual look to the right revealed nothing but darkness.

Bell had been around fighters for the entirety of his 13 years in the USAF and the "Red Eagles'" MiGs for the past two years. Still, he'd never witnessed anything like this. Then, surprisingly, almost as soon as they had appeared, the fighters seemingly vanished just minutes after their arrival, without Shanghai Center uttering a word. Bell knew that the fighters would have been limited on fuel, but that was a short visit!

Searching outside the C-5A's cockpit windows showed no trace of further PLAAF fighters. With the bright lights of Shanghai now beneath them, it was time to return to his seat and settle in for what promised to be a long night. Ninety minutes later, Jim felt the aircraft slowing, accompanied shortly after by the familiar sounds of first flaps and, eventually, the landing gear being lowered. They were on approach to Runway 36L at Beijing Capital International Airport. All he and his team were told was that a representative of the US Consulate would meet them once on the ground and coordinate loading their cargo. Bell sure hoped so because, to his knowledge, no one aboard the C-5A spoke Mandarin.

Having touched down and then cleared the runway, the C-5A crew was instructed to follow a vehicle to the parking apron. After the huge transport was stationary and its four General Electric TF39-GE-1C engines had been shut down, the massive nose of the Galaxy began to open, revealing its cavernous, but empty, cargo hold.

One can only imagine what was going through the minds of the two dozen Chinese workers who were on hand to help as they witnessed this sight. Despite US President Richard Nixon's historic visit to Beijing just ten years earlier, which marked the beginning of a new era in US–Chinese relations, Western air traffic to Beijing remained a rarity – the presence of an enormous, unmarked USAF C-5A on their ramp even more so. Its arrival under the cover of darkness was an indicator of how sensitive relations still were between the two countries. Whatever Bell and his team were about to load up, both countries wanted it kept a secret.

It was now just past 2200hrs, and the personnel from the 4477th, with the help of the assembled Chinese, had just seven hours before the C-5A needed to be airborne and on its way to Clark AB. The aircraft had been fueled at Kadena AB for the trip to Beijing and then on to Clark AB, and it wouldn't need additional fueling in Beijing – one less thing to coordinate and screw up.

As soon as they had parked, Bell, the rest of his team, and the entire C-5 crew all changed into civilian attire. Minutes later, outfitted in blue jeans and a variety of jackets, they exited the comfort of the C-5A and stepped out onto the ramp. It soon became apparent he'd packed too lightly!

Nearby, one of the Chinese workers noticed Bell's discomfort with the frigid temperature and offered him his gloves. Knowing there was no way the worker's tiny gloves could fit his huge hands, Jim politely shook his head, conveying with non-verbal gestures that he was okay. The US Consulate representative, standing nearby and witnessing this, caught Jim's attention and, after a couple of seconds, tilted his head toward the Chinese worker, encouraging him to accept the offer. To do otherwise would be disrespectful. Bell nodded and accepted the gloves from his newfound Chinese pal. After futilely trying to squeeze his hands into them, he simply stuffed them in his jacket pockets. He was still cold.

Neatly assembled on the otherwise vacant ramp in front of the C-5A were crated fuselages and wing cradles – the precious cargo. From the outlines of the wings, it was apparent that the aircraft were MiG-21s. However, these aircraft were not what Bell had expected. They were brand new and devoid of any markings. Indeed, the jets were so new there wasn't even dirt on the tire treads.

Bell knew nothing about the Chinese production of MiG-21s, nor even where these examples might have been made. All he and his team knew was that they were about to load and fly back with whatever was there. Four sets of wings in freight cradles and several engine crates told him that they would be returning with four brand-new fighters. As it turned out, these weren't MiG-21s at all, but new F-7Bs manufactured by the Chengdu Aircraft Industry Group in Chengdu, China, approximately 840 nautical miles south-southwest of Beijing.

Jim had no idea whether the new aircraft had been first flown to Beijing and then disassembled and crated or shipped directly from Chengdu. He suspected the latter, as they were immaculate. What was known was that everything was there for four complete Chengdu F-7s, including their engines. This was the first of three trips Jim Bell would make to Beijing. In total, he would be present for the acquisition of nine brand-new F-7s over the next 18 months.

With no time to waste, Bell and the rest of the maintenance personnel got to work. There were no USAF standard "K-Loaders" at the airfield to help ease the cargo onto the elevated cargo deck of the C-5A, so the "Red Eagles" team, as they always had before, simply improvised. After conferring with the loadmaster, they devised a plan and the order in which the F-7s would be loaded. With the "Red Eagles" operating the forklifts the Chinese had provided, and some ingenious use of plywood sheeting to line the C-5A's cargo deck, the last crate was onboard just past 0400hrs. Forty minutes later, with the cargo secured, everyone back on board, doors closed, and engines running, the C-5A taxied to Runway 35L. With clearance to take off, they were airborne minutes later, bound for Clark AB with their top secret cargo. Bell and his "Red Eagles" team had been on the ramp in Beijing for just under seven hours.

Six days later, following layovers at Clark AB and Hickam AFB, the same C-5A touched down at TTR under the cover of darkness late on a Saturday night to ensure complete secrecy. Once there, three of the four F-7Bs were offloaded and quickly moved into the Phase hangar for assembly in the ensuing months. Two hours later, the C-5A, with one airplane still aboard, lifted off at TTR for the 15-minute flight to Area 51. Like the 4477th, the 6513th TS was about to receive its first F-7B.

THE ASSETS

When the C-5A had landed at TTR hours earlier, 4477th CO, Lt Col George Gennin, the unit's maintenance officer, Capt George Tittle, and a handful of groundcrew were on hand to welcome them. The arrival of F-7s was a momentous accomplishment and a huge milestone in the history of the *Constant Peg* program. The eventual addition of eight F-7s would lead to even greater sortie production, resulting in increased exposure for USAF, US Navy, and US Marine Corps fighter pilots to real-world threat aircraft. It was this planned growth in sortie levels that necessitated an enlargement of the squadron and the addition of more pilots. Indirectly, the addition of F-7s led to my hiring by Gennin in June of the following year.

Upon my arrival at TTR in October 1983, only two F-7s were flying, Bort numbers "44" and "45." Over the next year, six additional F-7s were added to the growing fleet of MiG-21s, seemingly one every other month. I distinctly recall going out to a newly added F-7 one morning and noting that only 3.5 hours had been logged in the aircraft's logbook. It even had that "new MiG smell" to it.

Aircraft Bort number "44," the first F-7B operated by the 4477th, sported Lt Col George Gennin's name on the left fuselage just below the canopy frame. My name was added to Bort Number "45" shortly after I qualified on the MiG-21 in November 1983. Ironically, F-7B Bort number "45" was destroyed in June 1987 following an engine failure and unsuccessful flameout approach. Fortunately, the pilot successfully ejected and sustained no injuries. It was the only loss of a MiG-21/F-7 in the program's history.

The two aircraft, the Soviet MiG-21F-13 and the Chinese F-7B, were virtually identical, both in appearance and performance, save for minor differences that only a pilot who had flown both could appreciate. As such, we referred to both simply as a single fleet of MiG-21s. For flight records purposes, the Soviet models were designated as YF-110Bs, while the F-7Bs were logged as YF-110Cs. While some may have preferred the Soviet model, there was much to be said for flying a brand-new aircraft and the reliability that came with it. Throughout more than two years of flying both models, I never had a single maintenance issue with either. They were that reliable.

The acquisition of the MiG-23 was much more straightforward for the 4477th, the Central Intelligence Agency (CIA) having done the hard work for the USAF. Following years of preparatory work, on September 21, 1977, the US gained possession of its first "Flogger," a MiG-23MS from Egypt. Under the cover of darkness, the fighter was secretly loaded onto a C-5A and whisked off to Area 51. This MiG-23 was the same "Flogger" exploited in the *Have Pad* program in early 1978. In the following months, 17 additional Egyptian jets – a mix of both MiG-23MS and MiG-23BN models – would be secretly flown to Area 51 and delivered to the 6513th TS.

With the 4477th's formation in early 1977, the initial concept for *Constant Peg* centered around just a handful of MiG-17s and MiG-21s, although a desire had always existed to acquire more. The sudden availability of the MiG-23, which wasn't on anyone's radar in the 4477th's infancy, made that a reality. However, it would be two full years following the completion of *Have Pad* before the "Red Eagles" flew their first MiG-23 on November 1, 1980. The rest of the "Floggers" that would eventually fly as part of *Constant Peg* arrived shortly thereafter.

During my time in the 4477th, we had a total of nine "Floggers," comprising five MiG-23MSs and four MiG-23BNs. Like the MiG-21s and F-7s, they had unique USAF aircraft codes for each variant – YF-113E for the MiG-23MS and YF-113B for the MiG-23BN. Unlike the forgiving and easy-to-maintain MiG-21, the MiG-23 presented a significantly different learning curve for pilots and maintainers alike. When my turn came to strap on the "Flogger," I had heard all the stories about performance and "close calls." Little did I know I would soon add a few tales of my own.

14

Light the Rocket

"Great moments are born from great opportunities."
                                    HERB BROOKS, 1980 USA OLYMPIC
                                                MEN'S HOCKEY COACH

Thursday, November 3, 1983
0935hrs Pacific Standard Time
Tonopah Test Range

"'Bandit Three-One' requesting closed for the Clean and Dry," came the request by the pilot of the fast-accelerating T-38.

"Roger 'Three-One,' cleared for the closed, cleared Clean and Dry. The pattern is yours," came the crisp response from the tower controller, giving clearance for the chase maneuver to begin.

The supersonic T-38 we used for our chase duties had just moments before released its brakes on the runway alongside my MiG-21 and vanished. It had disappeared beyond the light wave-bending heat shimmer produced by the exhaust of its twin afterburners as it accelerated down the runway away from me. Seconds later, I watched the jet reappear at the distant end of the runway, seemingly like a mirage. It began a tight left climbing turn to downwind, the aircraft's glossy camouflage gleaming in the bright sunlight on this crisp November morning.

Thirty seconds after its brake release, the high-performance jet was level at 1,000ft AGL, above and abeam the airfield on a reciprocal heading to today's active runway, RWY 32. Now throttled back and maintaining 250KIAS, its pilot, Capt Mike "Mach" Roy, was poised to swoop down to rejoin my fast-accelerating MiG-21 shortly after I had left the runway following my takeoff.

"'Bandit Three-One' ready," Roy radioed.

This radio call was my cue to throttle up my MiG-21 and commence my takeoff roll. I smoothly advanced the throttle to the "Military Power" (MIL) setting just shy of the full afterburner detent, commanding full, non-afterburner power from the MiG's single Tumansky R-11F-300 engine. My right hand had fully depressed the pneumatic brake lever on the lower portion of the control stick, holding the brakes.

My MiG-21 reacted like a thoroughbred chomping at the bit, anxious to be freed from the starting gate, the aircraft's brakes – the reins – holding it against its will. An audible "creak" emanated from each main gear brake pad as it strained to keep this steed from running. My eyes darted over the engine instruments located in the lower right portion of the instrument panel. The RPM and oil pressure gauges both indicated that everything was functioning correctly, with no warning or caution lights illuminated. It was time to get this show on the road!

This is it, "Z-Man." Don't fuck it up!

With everything looking in order, I released the brake lever. I could hear, almost feel, the air escaping through the valves of the pneumatic brake system. My mount leaped forward as if suddenly spurred by its rider.

My feet were resting lightly on the rudder pedals. The lower fingers of my right hand added just a light tap or two to the brake lever to ensure the MiG was tracking straight down the runway, the stick was centered, and the ailerons were neutral. Now came more fun and excitement. With my left hand lightly gripping the throttle, I depressed the throttle lock with my middle finger and smoothly advanced the throttle past the MIL power stop to the afterburner detent.

At my command, raw jet fuel was injected into the spray nozzles located 25ft behind me in the afterburner section of the Soviet engine. I both felt and heard the resulting afterburner ignition. As if I needed a reminder, the instantaneous addition of 5,000lb of thrust pushed my torso farther into the ejection seat. A bright, fiery-orange afterburner plume, easily 20ft long, trailed my MiG and was visible to even those in the airfield control tower nearly a mile away. If the T-38's afterburner takeoff had broken the morning calm, the MiG's had just destroyed it.

I focused on keeping the aircraft tracking straight down the runway. The big rudder was effective in this effort, beginning at about 30KIAS, and the brake lever was now an afterthought and unnecessary. The airspeed indicator seems to leap through 100KIAS. At 130KIAS, I eased the stick back slightly and began to feel the nose lighten, quickly lifting off. Mere seconds later, I was through 170KIAS and airborne, the runway quickly disappearing below my nose as I pulled back the stick farther and established a 25° climb.

The stick forces were light, with the aircraft's roll response being incredibly effective at the mere hint of aileron in either direction. In short order, my left hand momentarily came off the throttle for the landing gear control handle, inches away on the left side of the instrument panel, raising it to its uppermost position. Immediately, I felt and heard the surge of hydraulic fluid through the system as the landing gear was retracted into the fuselage, followed in sequence by the gear doors. Their audible and welcome "thump" told me everything was in order.

All aircraft make distinctive sounds when their landing gear and flaps are in transition, whether retracting or extending, especially under the high pressures of their associated hydraulic systems. This one was no different, albeit unique, from those I'd previously become accustomed to on both the F-4 and F-5. Over time, the best pilots can quickly tell if something is amiss with their aircraft by the subtlest absence or change in these sounds and vibrations. It's something you feel, hear, and almost sense.

I next retracted the flaps while accelerating through 230KIAS, and the MiG-21, freed from this additional drag, was rocketing skyward. I was barely past the airfield boundary, with the airspeed needle approaching 300KIAS. For a moment, all was quiet except for the distinctive roar of the engine still in afterburner and, noticeably, my own hurried breathing.

"'Three-Two,' clean and dry. Button Three, go!" radioed Mike Roy.

"Two!" I instinctively replied.

Roy's radio call informed me, as my cockpit indicators showed, that all was well with my aircraft; all landing gear and doors were fully retracted, and no hydraulic fluid or fuel was leaking from the jet. It also snapped me back to the task at hand. After my quick reply, I reached down to the UHF radio control head on the center console in front of me and switched to channel three, the preset frequency for our training sortie.

During my acceleration and initial climb out, Roy completed a picture-perfect rejoin on my accelerating MiG from his previous position, 1,000ft higher and abeam, on downwind, heading in the opposite direction. While I'd been glued to what was happening in my cockpit, he'd swooped down in a 180° descending turn in his T-38 to momentarily rejoin off my right wing. Within seconds of his rejoin, he wasted no time crossing under my MiG-21 to visually confirm the fighter was airworthy, while cutting to the inside of my climbing left turn and taking up a loose position off my left wing. Thunderbirds or Blue Angels pilots would have been hard-pressed to do it any better. It was beautiful, and Mike had made it look effortless. Trust me, it wasn't.

This training mission was a definite "Go" as I climbed out in full afterburner at 300KIAS and soon rolled out on a southwesterly heading. I had been airborne for less than a minute, but already I had come to like this airplane. There was no time for daydreaming, though. There was work to be done, and I had a lot to get used to flying this single-engined Soviet fighter.

Where's "Mach"? He was just off my left wing.

A glance out the left side of the canopy, past the wing, revealed nothing but the ever-shrinking airfield below and the empty sky beyond. I gently banked the aircraft into an easy ten-degree left turn, and with a good twist of my head, I picked up Roy's T-38. Slowly dropping back low and behind me, it was readily apparent that its twin J85 engines were no match for the MiG-21's climb performance in full afterburner.

He'll catch up when I pull this thing out of afterburner. Man, this airplane can climb!

The squadron's operating procedures required us to maintain a minimum afterburner setting until we passed through 12,500ft Mean Sea Level (MSL), approximately 7,000ft AGL. At this point, so the logic went, if you came out of afterburner and your engine quit, you'd have enough altitude to perform a flameout approach to the same runway you just took off from and successfully recover the aircraft. Right!

However, with only a minute of single-engined fighter experience to my credit, I wasn't in any position to question that logic. Even though no one in the squadron had ever experienced an engine failure at this point in a flight, I certainly didn't want to become the first to prove the flameout recovery scenario was possible. I didn't dare touch the throttle and stayed at full afterburner until I passed 12,500ft MSL!

Roy checked us in on the assigned frequency and called Bandit Control, our GCI controller, to ensure he was up on frequency and monitoring us on his radar scope, located 120 miles away in the Range Control Center at Nellis. Our controller, this morning, Capt Billy Bayer, acknowledged Mike's radio call and informed us he had a radar contact on us seven miles west of the airfield, and our assigned area, Range 71, was clear of traffic. Without it being said, if we needed any assistance, he would be there to help us as necessary.

For Bayer and our other controllers, these missions were quite dull, as they had little to do other than listen to us discuss our actions and watch the tiny radar returns on their scopes move in varying directions within the airspace we were working. In contrast, what I was doing was anything but dull. My senses were alive to every vibration of the airframe, every subtle sound being both new and different, and registered in my brain as to what I would soon become accustomed to as my new "normal."

"'Bandit Three-Two's' throttling back," I radioed Roy.

My courtesy call informed him that I was deselecting afterburner as we had pre-briefed before takeoff. The two microphone clicks I heard over the radio through my helmet earphones signaled his reply and confirmed that he had copied. I slowly pulled back the throttle to the aft afterburner stop, and, once again, by simply depressing the throttle lock, the engine gently came out of afterburner, accompanied by the predictable reduction in thrust. As I did this, my eyes were on the engine instruments, with both needles of the RPM gauge showing standard indications for the twin-spool turbojet engine.

No need for a flameout approach for me today – I hope!

I eased the throttle back slightly to just below the MIL power setting, which would still provide excellent climb performance while allowing Roy to regain his lost ground on me with his T-38 still in full afterburner. He had briefed me to level off at 20,000ft, where I'd begin a series of maneuvers designed to get the feel of the airplane, just as I would with any fighter into which I was first becoming familiar. So, as briefed, I leveled off at altitude and set a course for the middle of Range 71, from where I'd shortly commence maneuvering.

This part of the Nellis AFB range airspace was as convenient as possible for checking out a new pilot. A short hop over the Cactus Peak mountain ridge, five miles west of the airfield, and you were in the area. Three minutes after becoming airborne, we were in Range 71, leveled off, and Mike had rejoined to a comfortable "chase position" slightly wide and aft of my wing line.

"'Bandit Three-Two' fuel check," he radioed. Roy's query about my fuel state was good, as I had significantly less endurance than his airplane, and it was a good habit to stay informed about my options.

"'Bandit Three-Two', Two point Three," came my response. The fuel gauge of this Soviet fighter read in liters, and that's what I had read off. My fuel quantity was 2,300 liters. In pounds, the metric used in most Western-designed fighters, I had the equivalent of 4,100lb of fuel remaining. Only a little compared, for example, with an F-5 fighter. "Short legs," as we called them, were one of the most significant drawbacks of the MiG-21's design. But presently, I was more interested in how it maneuvered and anxious to get a feel for it.

For the next ten minutes, I slowly got accustomed to what would be my "mount" for the next couple of years. A set of lazy turns and climbs followed by progressively more aggressive rolls, loops, hard turns, and stalls gave me a good appreciation of the airplane's handling characteristics. Its incredible rudder authority at slow speeds and high AOA immediately stood out to me as a superb characteristic of the MiG-21. Another feature that caught my attention was the jet's impressive turn rate near its designed cornering velocity, which was roughly 380KIAS. This, however, came at the cost of tremendous airspeed bleed-off in generating that same turn.

One feature that didn't concern me, and one that Western intelligence sources had been criticizing the MiG-21 for years about, was the reportedly poor visibility from the cockpit. While not comparable to the seemingly panoramic views from our newest fighters, such as the F-15, F-16, and F/A-18, what the aircraft lacked in cockpit visibility was quickly made up for by its superb agility and handling qualities. Right now, I liked it.

After completing the sequence of confidence maneuvers, it was time for recovery and my return to the airfield. One last check of my fuel showed approximately 1,300 liters remaining – enough to return to the field, perform a simulated flameout approach, and perhaps a single circuit in the landing pattern before reaching the minimum landing fuel of 500 liters. I had only been airborne for 15 minutes, in the practice area for 12, and I was already heading home.

No wonder the VPAF pilots who flew these against our USAF and US Navy fighter jocks during the air war in Vietnam didn't have much time to fight.

"Bandit Control, 'Bandit Three-Two's' RTB."

"Roger 'Three-Two,' the field is Zero-Four-Zero for 20," came the quick reply from Bayer.

When I told Bandit Control we were RTB, he gave me a vector to the airfield and its distance. While not necessary with the superb visibility we typically had, it was a common practice with practical application. Our MiGs lacked modern US instrumentation that could display our range from the airfield, and we'd seldom fly with a chase aircraft that could.

In an emergency with degraded engine performance or perhaps the complete loss of my only engine, knowing my distance from the field, along with my altitude, was critical for a safe recovery. It all came down to the aircraft's glide ratio. How far could my powerless aircraft fly for a given amount of altitude lost? I would soon learn to crunch the numbers in my head every time I returned to the field. This squadron practice would help pilots know whether they could make the field or not, and would later prove invaluable in the safe recovery of two of our assets in the months to follow.

The above scenario was a major topic of discussion at any "Red Eagles'" checkout, and mine was no exception. Mike's briefings over the past several days, in preparation for this flight, had outlined precisely what our procedures would be in the event of such an occurrence. What we were about to do next was apply this lesson and have the opportunity to experience firsthand how to recover my aircraft with a degraded engine.

I was going to fly a Simulated Flame Out (SFO) approach from a controlled position 15,000ft above the field referred to as "High Key." From this spot, literally "over the numbers" painted on the runway below, I'd pull my throttle back to idle, select full-speed brakes, and spiral down while holding 250KIAS – the aircraft's best minimum drag airspeed. When in a position where landing was assured, I'd put the landing gear down in time to do just that.

Let's consider this briefly and put it all into perspective. I was brand new in this airplane. I had never yet put the landing gear down, much less actually landed the jet, and now I was about to pull the throttle back and make a spiraling descent from 15,000ft AGL above the field, and this whole event would take less than a minute. Piece of cake. Right again!

We signed off with Bandit Control, switched to the tower frequency, and checked in. I requested clearance for the SFO, and I was immediately cleared. I made for a point just off the approach end of RWY 32 and descended to arrive there at 15,000ft AGL while slowing to the prescribed airspeed of 250KIAS to begin the maneuver.

The rationale for introducing this procedure to a new squadron pilot early on was to instill the necessary practices required to deal with an actual engine emergency in the months ahead, as well as to build their confidence. For instance, if you were out in an area flying a mission and suddenly had engine trouble, you would immediately turn toward the field and climb, trading off any excess airspeed above 250KIAS for every bit of altitude the airplane could muster.

Once there, you'd establish yourself in a descent toward the field at 250KIAS while attempting to restart your engine. Assuming the engine wouldn't restart, you'd assess whether your altitude was sufficient to make it back to the field and even attempt a flameout approach and landing. If the airfield was moving below your nose, you had excess altitude and were in pretty good shape. "Pretty good shape," of course, being a relative term. You still had no engine, but at least you could make it to the airfield. It was much better than having no engine and no chance of making the field. Lastly, all bets were off as to whether you'd "plumber" the landing or not!

That said, we "Red Eagles" pilots, as a group, were confident that on any given day, if we could zoom the MiG-21 to 30,000ft, we could reach the airfield from almost anywhere in our everyday working airspace, assuming there were no adverse winds, of course. Hence, GCI's help in establishing a bearing and range for us was essential, and it was practiced daily upon every RTB when initially checking out.

"'Bandit Three-Two,' 'High Key' for the SFO," I radioed the Tower.

One last glance outside the cockpit showed Roy's T-38 hanging loosely aft off my right wing on what would be the outside of the turn, keeping a close eye on the rookie – me.

"'Roger Bandit Three-Two,' cleared for the SFO. Winds are Three-Zero-Zero at ten," came the clearance, informing me that the surface winds at the runway threshold were 20 degrees left of the centerline at ten knots.

It's an ever-so-slight left crosswind. Easy on the initial turn, or you'll be tight on the runway coming around the base turn to final.

Cleared for the approach, I pulled the throttle to idle, simultaneously thumbed the speed brake switch on the throttle aft, and immediately rolled into a descending left turn high above the airfield. Directly below me, I made out the runway threshold, with the number "32" painted at the approach end, distinctly outlined against the surrounding sparse desert below me. At more than two miles above the airfield, it would have been next to impossible for the tower controllers or anyone else on the field to spot us. With our throttles at idle, we were nothing more than a pair of silent dots high above the airfield, spiraling down out of the azure morning sky.

With the engine back at idle and the speed brakes extended, I felt the airplane slow instantly, accompanied by a muffled rumble and distinct airframe vibration. This was caused by the disturbed airflow on the lower surface of the fuselage, where the speed brakes were housed, that had suddenly been hydraulically extended into the airstream. I was in a 45° bank, with the nose 15° below the horizon, and the aircraft had already slowed more than I wanted; the needle was now hovering near the 245KIAS mark and slowly dropping.

Damn, this thing bleeds airspeed fast! Get the nose down a bit.

With a couple of clicks forward on the stabilator trim switch atop the stick, the MiGs' nose lowered by a few degrees – it was now approaching -20° below the horizon, and the airspeed needle crept back toward the 250KIAS mark. With the aircraft properly trimmed, I managed to maintain position by making ever-so-slight adjustments to the pitch angle with the stick. While cross-checking my airspeed and bank angle, most of my focus was outside the aircraft. I was trying to meet the altitude "gates" throughout the maneuver to help ensure I'd have a chance of making the runway.

The first "gate," referred to as "Low Key," was located abeam the touchdown point on the runway. If I'd managed my descent correctly, I'd pass this "gate" at 12,000ft AGL, 180° degrees through the turn. I was at 11,400ft AGL – 600ft too low.

It's a bit low. Harden up your turn, Z!

Seconds later, now on the base-to-final turn, things were looking a bit better. A sneak peek at the altimeter showed it winding down through 7,700ft AGL with the runway now plainly in view high on my canopy at "11 o'clock." Making the turn onto final, I was quickly approaching the decision point of exactly when to select the undercarriage in preparation for landing. If I lowered it too soon, the additional drag would prevent me from making the runway. If chosen too late, I'd touchdown so far down the runway that it would be impossible to stop on what little runway remained.

I reached for the gear handle and lowered the undercarriage just as I was lining up for the final approach to the runway, 1.5 miles out and 4,000ft AGL above the runway elevation. The added drag of the landing gear forced me to lower the nose further to maintain my precious airspeed. With the nose down by another couple of degrees, it was questionable whether or not I'd make the runway if this were an actual engine-out emergency. I was about half-a-mile out and approaching 1,000ft AGL above the desert below when the radio came alive.

"'Bandit Three-Two,' go around," radioed Roy, who this whole time has been dutifully following me through the maneuver in a loose formation off my right wing. His call told me that it was close enough for today's practice, and I was to throttle up, clean up, and take it around for a normal landing, as we had pre-briefed.

"'Bandit Three-Two,' on the go," I radioed in response.

I smoothly advanced the throttle to the MIL power setting while thumbing the speed brakes switch forward. Even though the engine was slow to spool up and accelerate, which was characteristic and entirely expected for this type of engine, it did catch my attention. After a seemingly long ten seconds, during which I was still descending, the engine finally spooled up to full MIL power, arresting my descent toward the runway. Seconds later, with the landing gear and flaps retracted, my MiG-21 was accelerating toward 300KIAS at 200ft AGL above the runway and fast approaching the departure end of the field.

"'Bandit Three-Two,' request closed," I radioed the tower.

"'Bandit Three-Two' closed approved."

At the departure end of the runway, I pulled the aircraft up into a tight left climbing turn and rolled out onto downwind, abeam the runway, at 1,000ft AGL above the airfield, throttling back to slow in preparation for lowering the gear and flaps for landing. A quick check of the fuel gauge showed a mere 900 liters remaining. Enough to finish this pattern, land, and taxi it back to the ramp.

With the throttle back in idle, I was soon below the 270KIAS limiting speed for the gear, and with a quick pull on the handle, I heard and felt them extend. Three green lights below the landing gear control panel told me they were down and locked into place. With the additional drag of the gear aiding me in slowing the aircraft, I was soon below the allowable speed to select the landing flaps.

With a simple push of the flap control button, located just aft of the throttle, the two-position Fowler flaps extended into the landing position. As the flaps extended, I felt the airplane slightly porpoise and then stabilize – the stick pressure was ever so slightly lighter in feel, and the level flight attitude was about one to two degrees lower than in the "clean" configuration. It was a very stable aircraft, comparable to the F-5E I had been flying for the previous two years.

I continued to slow to 215KIAS until starting my descending base turn toward the runway, which was now back at my "eight o'clock" position. After confirming that the landing checklist was complete, I extended the speed brakes, began my turn, and contacted the tower to report my intentions.

"'Bandit Three-Two,' gear down, full stop, Runway Three-Two."

"'Bandit Three-Two.' The wind is Three-Three-Zero at 12, cleared to land, Runway Three-Two."

The base turn to final approach was uneventful and without surprises. I held 190–195KIAS around the final turn, rolling out about 1.5 miles at 180KIAS. The only noteworthy item was the somewhat limited visibility immediately out the front of the aircraft. Handling-wise, it was solid and honest. I flew it just like I would the F-5E.

In seconds, the runway threshold disappeared below the nose, and as I approached the touchdown point, I began easing the throttle back, maintaining 170KIAS to the flare. With the runway environment beginning to fill my peripheral vision, I brought the throttle back to idle and slowly eased the stick back, gently flaring the aircraft. The fighter smoothly touched down at 145KIAS, and I maintained slight aft pressure on the control stick, aerobraking until around 120KIAS, where I gently lowered the nose wheel onto the runway.

Seconds later, after pushing the drag chute button, I was rewarded with a noticeable tug on the airplane, slowing the jet further. A blur flew by 100ft above and to my right with a deafening roar, the distinctive, bluish-colored afterburners of a T-38 bright and alight. Roy accelerated in full afterburner toward the departure end of the runway to begin his pull-up at the start of his landing sequence.

Exiting the runway, not surprisingly, I snuck a glance at the all-important pneumatic pressure gauge. There were 60 kilograms of pressure left!

Whew! Enough pressure that I'll be able to taxi back. No need to be towed in on your first flight! How embarrassing that'd be.

Once clear of the runway, I quickly jettisoned the drag chute onto the desert infield between the runway and the main taxiway and ran through my after-landing checklist. It was a long taxi back to the ramp, where my crew chief marshaled me in and signaled me to stop. He then chocked the aircraft and gave me a right-hand, fingers extended, neck-slashing signal to shut it down. My first sortie as a "Red Eagles" pilot was complete.

My crew chief quickly attached the ladder to the side of the airplane and hopped up, extending his hand to congratulate me. I took it in my gloved hand and gave him a hearty shake.

"Congrats, Sir, you're America's newest MiG pilot," he said excitedly. I was unsure whether he was excited about my achievement or just pleased I had brought his airplane back without a scratch. Just before stepping out of the cockpit, I glanced at my watch with more than a bit of astonishment. The sortie I had just completed lasted only 24 minutes.

A few hours later, following a debrief of the sortie and a break for lunch, Mike Roy and I would again take to the skies for my second flight of the day in the very same MiG. I'd soon find this a typical routine here in the 4477th.

For me, my journey as an American MiG pilot had just begun. I walked away from the MiG-21 that morning wearing a big smile, while silently wondering what surprises lay in store for me flying these mysterious Soviet fighters over the next few years. Whatever they might be, I was excited about it and couldn't wait to get airborne again in just a couple of hours from now.

15

"I'm Not Him"

"Be yourself; everyone else is already taken."

OSCAR WILDE

December 12, 1983
HQ, TFWC
Nellis AFB, Nevada

The interview that awaited me had been scheduled and canceled several times over the past six weeks. As was part of the TFWC commander's policy, if at all possible, he wanted to have every new member of the 4477th TES meet with him before they started their checkout in the MiG-21. Hence, I found myself this Monday afternoon sitting in the waiting room outside of Maj Gen Eugene Fischer's office, waiting for my appointed meeting with him.

Five weeks earlier and just days before I made my first flight in the MiG-21, I'd had another interview, this one with the one-star commander of the 57th FWW, Brig Gen Michael Kerby. That meeting, much like this, I assumed, was more of a square-filling meeting where the general would have an opportunity to place a face with the name of the newest pilot selected to check out in one of the USAF's top secret MiGs. And now, here I was, already having checked out in the MiG-21, awaiting yet another interview. Ironically, it was almost exactly one year to the day that I had been sitting in Lt Col Gennin's office for my initial interview as a possible candidate for an assignment to the "Red Eagles." Once again, as with the others before, I was in my Dress Blues.

These guys sure like people to come in their dress uniform! I'm sure if they ever ran into me at the O'Club bar in my flight suit, they wouldn't recognize me.

After waiting about ten minutes, the general's secretary answered the phone, confirming with him that he was ready to see me. With that, she looked at me and nodded, saying the general would see me now. She got up, walked to the door to the general's office, and gently knocked.

"I'm not him"

There was a muffled reply on the other side, which I took for something vaguely like, "Send him in."

She opened the door and announced, "Sir, Capt Zettel, here for his interview." She turned to me and gave me a wink that I interpreted to mean the general was in a good mood, before gesturing for me to go on in. Once I was through the door, she left, closing the door behind her. I took a few steps forward to the desk where the general was sitting and came to attention, saluting him, and saying, "Sir, Capt Zettel, reporting as ordered."

He didn't rise from his seat as he returned the salute half-heartedly, motioning to a chair before his desk, indicating for me to be seated. With no hint of a handshake forthcoming, I sat down, quickly sizing up the general whom I'd never met before.

On the desk before him, I saw my latest USAF official photo, copies of what appeared to be my six latest Officer Efficiency Reports, and from the letterheads on several other items, letters of recommendation, all arranged in precise order. No doubt, he had had someone on his staff put together a pretty complete dossier on me for his benefit. He knew of my every assignment since I received my wings five years earlier and every squadron commander I'd worked for. In short, the general was holding all the cards and, as I was soon to discover, had a joker up his sleeve as well.

No bullshitting today, Z-Man. Smile. Nod. Yes, Sir!

After the standard "Welcome to Nellis, Captain" opening and several minutes of small talk, discussing my move there and asking if I was enjoying the assignment so far, he wasted little time cutting right to the chase.

"Captain, from what I can see in front of me, you've got an impressive record. And while I should be relieved at having a pilot with your experience as a "Red Eagle," there's something here that concerns me."

Uh, oh? What's this?

"Just recently – in fact, just over two months ago, we had an Aggressor with an almost identical background as you, F-4s in PACAF and Aggressors at Clark AB, jump out of a perfectly good F-5E up in the Alamo South range. I'm sure you're well aware of the accident I'm referring to." This opening salvo caught me a bit off-guard. This wasn't the usual pep-talk sort of "interview" I had been anticipating. I should have known at the outset, when he didn't address me by my callsign, "Z-Man," that it wasn't going to be the cordial experience I had expected. He wasn't finished. Fischer then, figuratively, pulled out a joker he'd been hiding and laid it on the table.

He continued, "You're in an even more high-profile position, a top secret program at that, flying what many consider to be national assets. Why should I think you're not the same? To go and fly an airplane beyond its limits and lose it!"

Whoa! There's a curveball. Take a moment and collect your thoughts. Don't fuck this up!

Maj Gen Fischer was correct. A former Aggressor squadron mate of mine, who had left Clark months before me and had been assigned to the 65th AS here at Nellis AFB, had lost control of an otherwise perfectly good F-5E and ended up ejecting from the ensuing spin, luckily sustaining only minor injuries. Within a day of the accident, the word had gotten back to us across the Pacific at Clark AB of what, in broad terms, had happened. Moreover, the accident had occurred just two weeks before my departure back to Nellis AFB. It was still fresh in my mind and a regular topic at the O'Club bar, especially amongst the Aggressors and anyone interested in listening.

Needless to say, whenever an aircraft was lost at any of the four Aggressor squadrons worldwide, it was a big deal and garnered a lot of attention. While it would be months before the accident investigation board issued its final report, the preliminary "unofficial" facts surrounding the accident all pointed to one thing – pilot error. The bottom line was this: the F-5E was a very forgiving aircraft and didn't spin unless the pilot pushed the jet beyond its designed flight parameters and/or, perhaps, his own. Additionally, there were other contributing factors that, while they weren't causal, were less than flattering to the incident pilot.

After the general finished, there was a long, somewhat awkward moment of silence, no doubt caused by my being unsure whether it was a serious question he expected a response to or more of a rhetorical one. Sensing he was waiting for an answer, I remember sitting a bit straighter in the chair, replying, "Sir, with all due respect, I'm not him. That's not saying I'm better, just that I'm charting my own course. Right now, that has me flying in perhaps the best program in the Air Force. I'm not about to jeopardize that opportunity or the program."

Fischer paused a moment, seemingly to think of his own response. Slowly, a smile appeared on his face, followed by his reply, "Good answer, Zettel. That's what I wanted to hear. I know you'll do a fine job. Be safe, okay?" With that more friendly tone to finish on, the interview was over. The general stood and reached out to shake my hand, adding, "Congratulations, 'Z-Man.' Before you go, tell me, what is the MiG-21 like to fly?" Fischer's sudden change in tone caught me a bit off-guard, but it was a welcome one.

Callsign use? I suppose it must have gone okay.

"Sir, as you can imagine, it's quite the experience. The engine response takes some getting used to, but overall, it's a real joy to fly. Very similar to the F-5E," I replied, following a respectful handshake with the general. A minute later, following a salute from him, I was outside and heading back

"I'M NOT HIM"

to the squadron, having quickly changed out of my Dress Blues and back into my flight suit, of course!

While no one could have predicted it, less than nine months later, circumstances would change considerably, and the Nellis-based Aggressors would be feeling Brig Gen Fischer's ire following the loss of a fifth Aggressor aircraft in less than a year, two of them claiming the lives of their pilots. I often wonder how different the interview would have gone had I met with him following those mishaps. I have a feeling it would have gone a lot differently, or maybe I never would have been considered for the assignment to begin with.

Perhaps it was just a coincidence. Still, following the hire of Capt Gary "Goldie" Craig, who came from the 64th AS in the spring of 1984, it would be almost two years before the "Red Eagles" hired another Aggressor from either of the Nellis-based squadrons. Times were changing, and with it, the complexion and make-up of the 4477th. Where it had once been the domain of pilots who were essentially all former Aggressors, that was no longer the case, just as George Gennin had intended.

That Friday, December 16, we concluded the year by flying our last MiG sorties, then stood down for the following three weeks over the holidays to give everyone, especially our maintenance troops, a much-deserved break and some extended time at home. As the hangar doors closed for one final time in 1983, hidden behind them were nine MiG-21s and six flyable MiG-23s. For the year, the "Red Eagles" had flown close to 1,200 MiG sorties while exposing 666 American fighter pilots to the threat aircraft, all while operating with just 16 squadron pilots.

In the coming months, as Gennin had anticipated and planned for a year earlier, the squadron would grow, adding seven new pilots, two GCI controllers, and nine additional MiGs. With the increase in pilots, controllers, and aircraft, as well as a rapid rise in the number of maintenance personnel, the volume of sorties generated increased exponentially. These additional flights, soon double the number from just two years earlier, would provide a significant improvement in the effectiveness of realistic training for an ever-increasing number of fighter pilots. For me, it was still mind-boggling to even be here. The 4477th was entering what would prove to be the best period of the program's existence, and I had three years ahead of me to "ride that wave." From here on out, it only got better.

16

Behind the "Black Curtain"

"The backbone of surprise is fusing speed with secrecy."
CARL VON CLAUSEWITZ

Spring 1984
0645hrs Pacific Standard Time
4477th TES MU-2 parking ramp
Tonopah Test Range

"Hey, 'Z-Man,' check this out. You gotta see this. Look, look!"

It was the whispered voice of Lt Cdr Jim "Rookie" Robb, US Navy, who at the same time was gently nudging me in the ribs with his elbow to ensure I didn't miss this event outside the van and at the top of the air-stairs of the MU-2 turboprop aircraft we'd just exited. I'd barely sat down beside him on one of the bench seats in the squadron van for the short drive to the squadron when he got my attention. I, like many of the other seven pilots aboard, was still a bit groggy following an "O'dark-30" wake-up back home in Las Vegas to make the 0600hrs flight up to TTR.

Jim Robb was one of three Navy pilots permanently assigned to the 4477th TES. "Rookie," as Robb was more commonly called, even by the junior officers, had joined the squadron just a week before me. As such, we spent a considerable amount of time together as we both went through our qualifications in the MiG-21, and had become good friends along the way.

Robb had gotten his callsign, "Rookie," after being the very first Naval Aviator to receive an F-14 Tomcat straight out of flight training nearly ten years earlier. Since then, he had amassed an enviable amount of experience as a fighter pilot, most recently serving as an instructor at the US Navy Fighter Weapons School before being assigned to the "Red Eagles." But fighter qualifications aside, at this moment, "Rookie," like the rest of us, was enjoying the prank at hand that seemingly was a constant here in the 4477th. Even at this early hour, today was proving to be no different.

Typically, once aboard the airplane for the 45-minute flight, most pilots would simply doze off and slowly recalibrate their gyros once on the ground at Tonopah. Nonetheless, even at this hour, "Rookie" was aware of some prank in the offing, and he wanted to make sure I didn't miss out on it. That's what good friends do, right?

Today's unlucky soul was none other than Maj George "Cajun" Tullos, US Marine Corps, the "Red Eagles" "token Marine," who was somehow still aboard the MU-2 and sitting inside the airplane at the top of its "air-stairs," frantically working on something before him on the floor. Minutes earlier, the other pilots and I had slowly exited the airplane, flashing our TTR security badges to the senior airman from the Security Police (SP) force positioned at the base of the stairs, complete with a loaded M16 assault rifle slung over his shoulder, to ensure no one arrived at TTR without the proper credentials. Without those, it would've made for an embarrassing trip to the base security office and detention until one's identity and clearance were validated. And the whole time, the rest of the group would be needling you mercilessly.

It might've been a bit before 0700hrs, and while I was still not fully alert, I quickly figured out what was happening and who the subject of the practical joke was.

Here's some background. Since we were often carrying classified material back and forth to TTR from Nellis AFB, the squadron commander had wisely chosen, months earlier, to issue every pilot with a briefcase to transport this material securely. Even better, these briefcases had programmable locks, allowing each pilot to set his unique passcode to access the contents, or more importantly, keep others out of his business.

A few "Red Eagles" pilots were in the habit of tossing their security badge into their briefcase at their desk back at Nellis before they left for home, quite confident it'd be there for them when they grabbed it on the way to the MU-2 for the flight back up to Tonopah the following morning. I think you can see where this is headed, as the rest of the van, which by now was filled with pilots and our enlisted driver, looked on at the lone pilot, Tullos, struggling to open his briefcase and retrieve his security badge.

Meanwhile, several of the guys in the van, who were in on the joke, only added to Tullos's woes, heckling him to get his shit together and hurry up.

"'Cajun,' what the fuck. Over?" and "How fucking old are we going to be?" were some of the more polite calls from the now fully alert and engaged kangaroo court aboard the van. All eyes were firmly on the struggling Marine.

Sometimes there's nothing worse than knowing you've been hoodwinked, and worse yet, having a gallery of your peers laughing at your expense amid that light bulb coming on. To make matters worse, the SP senior airman was still there, waiting for Tullos to produce his badge and not about to let him pass without first seeing it. The rules were simple – no security badge, no access to the TTR facility. This went on for about a minute as Tullos, with his US Marine Corps-standard "high and tight" haircut, became increasingly irritated and quickly turned beet red, as every single attempt to open his briefcase with his last known combination code proved unsuccessful.

What was now apparent to Tullos and the van-full of raucous pilots was that someone had secretly changed the code to his briefcase shortly after he had left the squadron building. The joker, knowing full well that Tullos had simply grabbed his briefcase in the morning as he headed to the MU-2, knew the odds were excellent that this practical joke would be one to remember.

To this day, I still don't know with certainty who changed the combination. "Rookie"? Possibly, but this seemed more the work of either Maj "Paco" Geisler or perhaps Maj Paul Stucky. My money was on Stucky, as he was already on board the van and adding to the calls for "Cajun" to move it so we wouldn't be late for the morning briefing. Whatever the case, with seven pilots giving him an earful, it wasn't long before Tullos had had enough of it.

Seconds later, he picked up the briefcase and hurled it out of the airplane for it to land at the feet of the SP, still dutifully awaiting the lone pilot to exit the MU-2. Immediately, Tullos bounded down the steps after it, grabbed the briefcase, and set it upright on the tarmac before the airman. With one quick motion, Tullos raised his right leg and brought his size 12 flying boot down on the briefcase. With a distinct "crack," in an instant, the briefcase was split open before the startled SP, who took a step back, unsure what this crazed Marine would do next.

Tullos reached in, found his security badge, and with a scowl on his now thoroughly flushed face, flashed it at the startled airman. By now, the passengers in the van were howling with laughter and making yet more calls to Tullos. "About fucking time, 'Cajun'!" followed by, "Come on already, the briefing's about to start! Damn 'Cajun,' let's get fucking going!"

The finale to these early morning shenanigans was an unfazed airman thanking the tall Marine for his security badge and rendering him a sharp salute, which Tullos returned with the same scowl on an even brighter, redder face. A few moments later, "Cajun" boarded the van, a busted and mangled briefcase in his arms held together only by a single hinge, looking like he could chew through a 16-penny nail. The guys were still ribbing him, but quickly, he broke out into a huge smile and laughed at the whole ordeal, vowing to get even with the bastard who set him up.

The couple of minutes it took to drive to the squadron were filled with laughter and back-slapping as someone had pulled yet another "fast one"

BEHIND THE "BLACK CURTAIN"

over on one of our own. Right then, Jim "Rookie" Robb, with perfect timing and deadpan delivery, simply added the final touch, "Hey 'Cajun,' nice fucking briefcase! You Marines really ought to take better care of your gear!"

The van erupted in one final round of laughter as we stopped outside the squadron building and piled out for the morning briefing, scheduled to begin in moments. It was the start of just another day for the pilots of America's MiG squadron.

To be sure, not all was fun and games, or practical jokes, up at TTR. To begin with, before a new pilot could even be granted access to the test site, you had to have undergone an even more thorough background investigation, which went well beyond that required for the secret clearances typically held by most pilots. Due to the sources involved in the acquisition of our aircraft and their exploitation, all 4477th TES pilots required and received Top Secret/Sensitive Compartmented Information (TS/SCI) clearances. Without such, we would not have been allowed to fly in the program. Needless to say, authorization for such a clearance was tightly controlled. Having an entire squadron of pilots with such a clearance was simply unheard of.

Moreover, as you might imagine, given the sensitivity of the *Constant Peg* program, almost everything that impacted our operations was cloaked in secrecy or subdued to draw less attention to our unit. From our remote operating location, off-limits to any aircraft without specific authorization, to clearing the ramp of any parked MiGs during known overflights of Soviet or Chinese spy satellites, to our cover story which alluded only to flying "highly modified, unspecified test aircraft" – everything was carefully crafted to keep our mission well-hidden from anyone without the need to know, which was pretty much everyone unless they were actively flying against our MiGs.

Even the T-38s we operated for chase purposes and regularly took on the road during cross-country "training flights" purposely lacked the typical large "WA" lettering on their tails or the black and yellow checkerboard fin flash standard on all other fighter aircraft assigned to the 57th FWW. It wasn't uncommon, wherever we landed to refuel, to be asked where we were from. When we told them Nellis AFB, they looked at us, shaking their heads, saying they'd never seen any T-38s like these before, and enquired where we were really from. Tossing them a 4477th TES patch usually served to keep further questions and speculation at bay. I never left TTR without at least a dozen "Red Eagles" patches tucked away in my G-suit pockets, just in case. Not surprisingly, I don't remember ever returning with a single one.

Despite the frequent practical jokes, if one had any doubt as to the seriousness of the nature of our mission, or of the armed SPs that routinely patrolled the area, one only needed to read the signs placed at regular intervals on the outside of each of the 4477th TES hangars:

WARNING
Highly Restricted Area
Special Access Required
Use of deadly force is authorized

Not only was one's access tightly controlled, but the mere possession of any sort of camera was as well. Luckily, this was well before the era of personal cell phones with cameras. That, in turn, is one of the reasons so few photographs exist of the aircraft and personnel in and around TTR. When we needed to photograph anything, generally for training purposes, authorization from the squadron commander was required. This letter of approval was carried with the photographer while on-site, and the film was tightly controlled and developed by select technicians at Nellis AFB, who had special clearance to do so.

Meanwhile, out of sight of even those briefed on *Constant Peg* were projects and programs that the squadron was occasionally asked to support by higher headquarters at the Pentagon or TAC, which lay well outside the realm of providing the most realistic air combat training to our frontline fighter crews. These requests were screened by a select group of senior staff officers tasked with overseeing the "Red Eagles" program, ensuring that our cover wasn't compromised in the process. When the requests reached the 4477th, our operations officer would brief us on the task to be supported and ask for volunteers. One such opportunity presented itself in the spring of 1985, and I immediately raised my hand and volunteered.

In this instance, the US State Department had made a request, on behalf of a North African country that will here remain nameless, seeking Pentagon assistance in providing enhanced air combat training for a select number of its fighter pilots. Oh, and by the way, their entire air force was comprised of nothing but Soviet-built MiG and Sukhoi fighters. In all likelihood, the State Department had no idea that the USAF had a squadron of top secret Soviet MiGs of its own, and would never know their request couldn't have landed in a better spot. Instead, it had simply forwarded the request via official channels to the DoD and left it for them to handle. Over the next few weeks, this request had made its way through the maze of directorates within the Pentagon before a call was made to the 4477th, asking if we could support it and, if so, by what means.

Then, one morning, at the end of a daily squadron operations briefing in early spring 1985, Maj Dave Bland, our operations officer, outlined the request, the host country, the timeframe and extent of the trip, and what he was looking for: preferably a MiG-21 instructor pilot who might be interested. As one of only a handful of MiG-21 IPs, and a bachelor at that, I didn't need to discuss such an absence with a spouse, so I was immediately on board. I told Bland I wanted in on the project. From there, things progressed quickly.

Within weeks, the State Department expedited the issuance of my official passport, which arrived via registered mail shortly thereafter. At the same time, it provided me with essential points of contact within the US and the host country. Additionally, travel plans were tentatively made, with the most convenient route being from New York's John F. Kennedy International Airport to Paris, followed by a connection to an Air France flight to the host country's capital city.

In the meantime, intrigued by the prospect of this next adventure, I had researched everything our intelligence officer could find regarding the country in question, including its inventory, particularly the MiG-21s currently in operation and their locations. It didn't take long to discover they were operating hundreds of MiGs, most of which were later models, such as the MiG-21MF, better known by its NATO reporting name, "Fishbed-J."

The idea of flying with foreign fighter pilots would be both exciting and revealing, not to mention perhaps a bit risky, given the uncertainty of their experience, proficiency, and the condition of their aircraft. Did I mention a probable language barrier? There was, without doubt, a particular element of risk associated with the whole plan. But I have thrived on measured risk and adventure my entire life. Flying another variant of the MiG-21 with pilots I'd yet to meet was just another step along a path I'd willingly chosen to travel years earlier.

And then, just weeks before I was expected to depart, the trip was canceled. By whom or why, I never found out. Only that there were rumors from the Pentagon of an undue element of risk associated with where I'd be operating from, and no clear means of contact. Basically, on the State Department's end, they had not worked out all of the logistics needed to satisfy the Pentagon before they sent one of their own on such a venture. What had looked promising and would've been a bit of an intelligence boon was over. I can only speculate about the insights I would have gained from flying yet another model of the MiG-21.

With that opportunity now gone, in a few short weeks, a few other squadron pilots and I would fly a handful of our MiGs to an even more remote and storied location for the balance of the summer. Welcome to Area 51!

Thursday, June 20, 1985
1740hrs Pacific Daylight Time
30 nautical miles north-northwest of Groom Lake, Nevada
"Bandit 11," MiG-21F-13

Our two MiG-21s, spaced 6,000ft apart in line abreast formation at 200ft AGL above the barren desert below us, streaked over the highway headed northbound, at 420KIAS, seven miles northwest of Rachel, Nevada. As we crossed Nevada State Highway 375, I couldn't miss noticing several 18-wheelers and RVs making their way west along this stretch of road, commonly called the "Extraterrestrial Highway," no doubt heading for the town of Tonopah, a further 100 miles to the northwest. They were the only vehicles visible on this otherwise desolate ribbon of asphalt that lay beneath the airspace of the Nellis ranges, 30 miles north of the mysterious Area 51.

If they were expecting to see aliens, they would be disappointed. Instead, if they just happened to have looked up in time, they might've noticed a sight perhaps as rare and mysterious as a foreign spacecraft. For they would have spotted what appeared to be two MiG-21s, bright red stars adorning our tails, flash past them and then seemingly disappear just as quickly. What were the odds of that happening, here in America, in broad daylight, no less?

Just seven minutes earlier, my wingman for this late afternoon's flight, Maj Paul Stucky, and I had taken off from Area 51's Runway 32 at Groom Lake, Nevada, and were making our way toward the northern edge of the ranges. Right now, with no scheduled adversaries or specific mission objectives at hand other than flying to maintain proficiency, we were out "joyriding" and seeing the sights. Better yet, we had the entire Nellis range complex, thousands of square miles, at our disposal for just our two sleek fighters.

For the next 40 minutes, Stucky and I covered hundreds of miles, crossing dozens of ridgelines in this high desert playground of ours, before returning to land at "Dreamland" (Area 51) and calling it a day. The next evening, we'd swap the lead and do much the same thing, this time with Stucky throwing in a high-speed aerial tour of the Nevada Test Site (now called

BEHIND THE "BLACK CURTAIN"

the Nevada National Security Site) and the hundreds of craters there in the Yucca Flat area, the visible remnants of underground nuclear explosions decades before. Such was our flying schedule for the period TTR was closed, and we were away at "Dreamland" for what Maj Ted Drake had coined "Exercise Summer Fun!"

Exactly one week earlier, my wingman and I for that afternoon's flight, Capt Gary Craig, had taken off from TTR and ferried our pair of MiG-21s to "Dreamland," which was to be our operating location until mid-August. During that period, the airfield at TTR would be closed, and its runway would be extended to 12,000ft.

When I taxied into the ramp area in front of the 6513th TS's hangar at "Dreamland," an oddly dressed character met me, apparently a crew chief, who marshaled me to my assigned parking spot and then crossed his arms high above his head, signaling me to stop. Seconds later, with clenched fists raised to eye level, thumbs pointed inward, indicating my MiG was chocked, he made a repeated slicing motion with his right hand across his throat, signaling me to shut down my MiG-21F-13. I had just arrived at Area 51, the infamous "Dreamland."

While the airfield within Area 51 was a scant 55 miles away from TTR, Craig and I had done a bit of "sightseeing" along the way. We managed to turn an otherwise ten-minute flight into a half-hour joyride. In my view, never let a full fuel load go to waste!

Thirty seconds after shutting down, the crew chief was up the aircraft's ladder to the cockpit, taking my helmet and welcoming me to our temporary home away from TTR for the next nine weeks. I did a double-take when I realized it was one of our 4477th crew chiefs, who had met my MiG-21 dozens of times before at TTR, but his attire today had completely thrown me off. Instead of the USAF standard fatigues worn by maintenance troops when working the flightline, there was nothing standard about him, except for his black boots. Instead, he was wearing cut-off blue jean shorts, a tee-shirt adorned with a beer logo on the front, a ball cap hawking Red Man chewing tobacco, and mirrored sunglasses. Other than the boots, he looked like he'd just come off of Lake Mead following a day of bass fishing and serious beer drinking!

Area 51 and the 6513th TS were the domain of Air Force Systems Command (AFSC). Apparently, they did things a bit differently here, including an apparent lack of adherence to USAF dress codes. It hadn't taken our maintenance guys even a day to "go native" and fit right in with the other technicians assigned there. As I was soon to discover, this was a relatively laid-back operation AFSC had going here. And, as the saying goes, "When in Rome, do as the Romans do."

With that said, as I climbed out of the MiG-21 and began to look around, my initial impression of the place was, in a word, disappointing. Perhaps I had been expecting more. Mind you, I had just come from an air base that had sprung up from almost nothing in the previous decade, where there were hardly any buildings more than seven years old, the troops were in uniform, and a sense of mission and excitement filled the air. All that was missing here.

To be sure, "Dreamland" had been in existence since 1955, serving both the USAF and CIA, and it showed. Where almost every building at both TTR and Nellis all sported uniform colors and even landscaping, in contrast, there was virtually none of that at "Dreamland." What a difference between TAC and AFSC. The former was a combat command, while the latter was a test outfit. Appearances notwithstanding, we were happy to be here, and the "Red Hats" of the 6513th TS would prove to be great hosts.

Given the nature of the programs conducted here, being granted access to the highly restricted Area 51 wasn't automatic, even for "Red Eagles" pilots already holding TS/SCI clearances. We had to overcome a few additional hurdles before we were allowed access. While none of them were show-stoppers, they did require strict compliance due to the presence of several ongoing, highly classified programs. In the weeks before we began operating out of Area 51, the one requirement we all had to submit to and pass was a lie detector test. The test itself was administered not by someone in an Air Force uniform, but by an individual wearing a sports coat and tie in a nondescript office on base at Nellis. Who they worked for, I never knew.

While none of us had any problem passing the test, Capt Jim Matheny did give the people conducting the test cause to briefly stop the questioning. When asked if he'd ever been convicted of a crime, Jim, with an impish grin on his face, simply asked, "Does stealing cars when I was a kid count?" The person administering the test, apparently not amused with Matheny's attempt at humor, and looking cross, blurted back, "No. Now quit fucking around and take this seriously!" Matheny, satisfied he'd pushed their buttons about as far as he dared, simply answered "yes" or "no" to the remaining battery of questions and 30 minutes later, having passed the test, was out the door, chuckling as he walked away.

All of us, already having been briefed on *Senior Trend* – TAC's F-117 stealth program – knew that Area 51 was where newly assigned pilots of the 4450th TG did their transition training for the aircraft. But that was it. What other programs the USAF had going there, I never knew, nor did I dare ask.

Regardless, by the time we would arrive late each afternoon, virtually every hangar door on this sprawling base was shuttered, and whatever was behind them, for whatever program we weren't meant to see, was well out of sight. So, while I had visions of perhaps observing operations of mysterious aircraft that the public wouldn't see for years, that was not the case.

For the next nine weeks, we conducted limited flight operations, launching only six to eight aircraft during a short two-hour period, primarily to maintain currency for our pilots. By mid-August, we had concluded our operations at "Dreamland." On the 20th of that month, flying resumed in full swing at TTR. "Summer Fun" was over.

17

"Stink Bugs"

"Security is paramount. I doubt there are ten people in Washington aware of this project. Maintaining secrecy must be your number one priority."
BEN RICH, "FATHER OF STEALTH"

April 1984
Late Evening
4450th TG Conference Room
Tonopah Test Range

Myself, along with three other "Red Eagles" pilots, Lt Cdr Jim "Rookie" Robb, Maj John "Skid" Skidmore, and Maj Paul "Stook" Stucky, were seated around the large conference table nestled within the confines of the 4450th TG's operating facilities at the north end of the TTR airfield. Located less than a half-mile from where we operated our MiGs, the rapidly growing ramp, operations, and support areas of the 4450th were a testament to the massive investment by the USAF in a program that was purposely well hidden at this remote site from anyone outside of those briefed in on it.

That evening, at the direction of our squadron commander, Lt Col George Gennin, and in coordination with the 4450th commander, those of us seated there were to be told what all this effort and investment was about. Ironically, the in-briefing of "Red Eagles" on the F-117 program was the result of Gennin refusing the 4450th's request to have its pilots in-briefed on our MiGs based at TTR.

Gennin's position was simple and supported by Gen Wilbur Creech at TAC HQ. 4450th TG pilots would not be in-briefed on the *Constant Peg* program unless all "Red Eagles" pilots were in-briefed on *Senior Trend* – the official name for the operational F-117 program managed by TAC. After some back and forth at higher headquarters, Gennin's position won out. Hence, over the previous several months, more than a dozen "Red

"STINK BUGS"

Eagles" had received the very briefing that the four of us were about to hear that evening.

With the security portion of the briefing completed and the accompanying non-disclosure statements signed, the commander of the 4450th, a full colonel, stepped to the podium to present the main event. Following a few minutes of introductory remarks and welcoming us to the 4450th, he cut to the chase – what we were here to see.

"Gentlemen, what you are about to see tonight is America's newest weapon system that will give our pilots the ability to hit an enemy target anytime, anywhere, virtually undetected. It's called the F-117A Nighthawk stealth fighter, designed and built by Lockheed, and in a short while, I'll take you down to one of the hangars where you'll be free to crawl all over one, sit in the cockpit, and talk to a couple of our pilots who have been flying the Nighthawk for some time. But for now, I think you'll enjoy this short video."

With the introduction over, the colonel nodded to a young lieutenant at the rear of the conference room. On cue, the lights in the room were dimmed, and the faint sound of a remotely located video projector's cooling fan could be heard humming away. A few seconds later, the large screen at the front of the room came alive. At first faint and dark, the subject, which was still to be revealed, was filmed under the cover of darkness. As my eyes adjusted to the dim view before me, I could make out the faint outline of a hangar and a mere sliver of light emanating from behind its massive doors. Slowly, the trickle of light steadily grew larger and brighter as it became apparent that the hangar doors were sliding open.

As the opening continued to widen, at the center of the brightly lit hangar was a single, odd-shaped, black aircraft that stood out against the dazzling white floor and surrounding hangar walls. As the doors neared the full extent of their travel, the video panned in closer, allowing the four of us a better view of this mysterious-looking airplane. Directly above the plane, hanging down from the rafters, was a giant US flag.

No doubt, Lockheed, knowing the value of properly marketing its latest technological marvel and the military contracts that hung in the balance, spared no expense to ensure the optics were perfect. Along with stirring music, it was a masterful attention getter, one that had all of us seated there leaning forward just a bit closer, intent on making sense of what we were seeing for the first time.

You gotta be shitting me! What the fuck is that? That's a fighter?

As I'm sure happened every time that video was shown, there was pure silence in the room, certainly from the four of us seated there. While nothing specific had ever been mentioned in the hallways of the 4477th by those already briefed into *Senior Trend*, there were occasional snickers and eye rolls regarding whatever was hidden within the 24 hangars on the north ramp. These were often accompanied by the use of the term "Stink Bug," apparently due to this aircraft's reportedly ungainly appearance, whispered to operate under the cover of darkness here at TTR after most of us were already asleep back home in Las Vegas.

Whatever name it went by, there it was, in plain view, at least on the screen before us. The video continued for a few minutes, with varying camera angles showing close-ups of various parts of the aircraft, all of which left me more amazed. Without a doubt, it was the strangest fighter, no, make that airplane I'd ever seen. When the video finished, the 4450th commander stepped to the podium once again to add a few comments, and then he opened it up for questions.

What he was allowed to share with us were the bare minimums. While those of us seated around the table all held TS/SCI security clearances and fully understood the sensitivity of such programs, we were well aware of the limitations of what would be shared with us. What he did brief us on, nonetheless, was eye-opening in its own right.

The biggest surprise, other than the aircraft itself, was that the 4450th Test Squadron (TS) had reached Initial Operational Capability just a few months earlier, on October 28, 1983, with the arrival of the 14th production aircraft at TTR. As such, it was currently fully combat-capable. He also didn't reveal how many F-117s they currently had hangared, or were expected to have. Still, it didn't take a mental giant to figure out from the two dozen hangars already built, and ongoing ground clearing farther to the north of the existing hangars, that it was going to be a lot more than just a squadron's worth.

Following another ten to fifteen minutes of questions and answers, the colonel signaled that it was time to head over to one of the hangars and see the F-117A Nighthawk for real. It was a short walk to what I figured was their equivalent of our VIP hangar reserved for just such occasions. As we entered from the right rear corner, there, positioned in the center of a gleaming white floor, was the aircraft that was the subject of all the secrecy. And although it looked, in my opinion, odd, it was nonetheless impressive. If nothing else, what dawned on me, and I'm sure the others, was that before us was the world's first operational stealth fighter, and from the looks of the level of construction ongoing at TTR, it would soon be joined by many, many more.

All these years, it's been kept a secret. The world has no fucking clue! How?

Over the next hour, two F-117 pilots gave the four of us an up-close look at the Nighthawk, stopping to point out many of its innovative design

"STINK BUGS"

characteristics, from the four multi-faceted pitot tubes at the nose of the fighter to the heat-dispersing dual-engine exhaust design that went into this technological marvel before us. Later, sitting in the cockpit, the three large cathode ray tubes used for primary flight information, navigation data, and imagery from its forward-looking infrared system cast an eerie, soft-green glow over me and the surrounding side consoles. The cockpit was not only spacious, but when compared to the MiG-21 I was flying, designed 30 years earlier and at the time considered one of the best fighters in the world, this aircraft was simply light years ahead. However, as I would soon find out, it was designed for a different role entirely.

The MiG-21 was, from its inception, intended to be a point defense interceptor – fast, agile, and lethal in the air combat arena. The F-117, as I was discovering, was just the opposite – subsonic, anything but agile, carried no missiles or guns, but a lethal and virtually undetectable bombing platform that could place its two 2,000lb GBU-10 LGBs in a bushel basket from 20,000ft above it. In essence, it was a fighter in name only. The two aircraft were simply worlds apart.

The presence of both top-secret programs at TTR wasn't a fluke, but rather a years-in-the-making symbiotic relationship, each somewhat co-dependent on the other, that allowed both programs to grow and flourish behind a veil of secrecy and cover stories, and separated from Nellis AFB and nearby Las Vegas by a 120-mile buffer.

In its infancy, the 4477th required a secure location to operate its top secret MiGs. At the same time, a tiny group of planners at HQ USAF with access to the *Have Blue* project, Lockheed's proof of concept demonstrator for a stealth fighter, knew it, too, would need a secure operating location if the aircraft was to remain a secret once handed off to TAC to become operational. The choice of TTR to bed down both programs was selected as the best of several different sites located throughout the southwestern US.

In the short term, the 4477th gained an operating location and funding to launch its fledgling program. With the "Red Eagles" already established at TTR, it wasn't a giant leap for USAF and DoD planners to design and fund an expansion of the once-narrow 9,000ft strip of asphalt and a handful of hangars into a huge modern air base to support the burgeoning F-117 program. By the time construction was finished, it rivaled anything the USAF had anywhere in the world. And all of this had come together and been built in just a few short years before my arrival.

During the early 1980s, with President Ronald Reagan in the White House, defense dollars flowed into both programs, allowing them to take off like a house on fire. For the 4477th, this translated into additional aircraft, personnel, and facilities. For the 4450th, it meant more than 50 stealth fighters, the hangars to shelter them, hundreds of maintenance and support personnel, and enough pilots to form two entire squadrons.

Both programs, with combined budgets in the hundreds of millions of dollars, were hidden and kept secret from the rest of the USAF and the US public until nearly five years later, when the F-117 made its operational debut during Operation *Just Cause* on December 20, 1989, over the skies of Panama. Ironically, despite the F-117's emergence from behind the "black curtain" of secrecy and becoming public, the USAF's possession and operation of MiGs by the 4477th would remain a secret for a further 15 years before its existence was officially revealed on November 13, 2006.

Following my initial introduction to the F-117 on that early spring evening, I never again visited the 4450th or even saw a stealth fighter fly during my remaining years at TTR, primarily because our respective units' flight operations were on opposite sides of the clock. For "Red Eagles," there was almost zero contact with our counterparts at the north end of the airfield, save for the rare crossing of paths at the Nellis O'Club on a Friday evening.

The reason was simple. We flew our MiGs strictly during daylight hours and had generally finished our daily schedule by 1500hrs, then headed back to Nellis AFB and our homes in Las Vegas. Conversely, the 4450th, for security reasons, only conducted F-117 flight operations after darkness fell and often well into the wee morning hours, ensuring all Nighthawks were back in their hangars with their doors closed hours before sunrise. As F-117 pilots were on opposite sides of the clock from family and friends back home in Las Vegas, 4450th pilots remained at TTR the entire week, arriving on Monday afternoon and not returning until the following Friday. Those of us in the 4477th, on the other hand, made the round-trip from Nellis AFB to TTR and back daily, rarely spending a night at the test site – bankers' hours when compared to our stealth fighter counterparts.

Consequently, as you might imagine, when the pilots of the 4450th were asleep in their rooms up at Tonopah, we "Red Eagles" were busy flying a full schedule. And being the pranksters fighter pilots tended to be, my fellow squadron mates and I would occasionally drop our buddies in the 4450th, who were soundly asleep, a sonic boom reminder of who flew real supersonic fighters and who didn't. When we did so, we jokingly referred to them as "Boom Arrivals." Our maintenance troops loved the

"STINK BUGS"

"sound of freedom," which was a fairly common occurrence at TTR. Beyond being the source of a lot of laughs, they were a great morale booster for all "Red Eagles," as you could both feel and hear the sonic booms throughout the entire complex. There was no other place like it anywhere in the USAF.

However, those instances aside, for the majority of the "Red Eagles," there was minimal direct contact with our stealth brethren on the north side of TTR. I, on the other hand, had a more direct connection with the 4450th through a good friend and roommate, Capt Dick "Tooey" Hoey, with whom I shared a house off-base in Las Vegas for more than two-and-a-half years while he was an F-117 pilot. My friendship with Hoey dated back several years to when he had been the weapons officer in the 12th TFS when I first arrived in the squadron as a brand-new F-4 jock. I had taken my first hop from Kadena AB with "Tooey" in the back seat on a rainy day in March 1979. Over the years, throughout several assignments each, we had stayed in contact and remained good friends.

You can imagine my surprise when I received a call from Dick one evening in late April, telling me he had been assigned to the 4450th and expected to arrive at Nellis in a few weeks. Oh, and by the way, would I be okay with him being my roommate until he found himself a place? Upon his arrival in Las Vegas, he promptly moved into one of the spare rooms and never left! Dick was a model roommate: paid rent on time, kept the refrigerator stocked with beer, had a boat we used regularly on nearby Lake Mead, and was never there throughout the week. Perfect!

All jest aside, by the time Hoey reported to Nellis AFB, he already had an enviable career in fighters. Following multiple tours in the Phantom II, as well as being a graduate of the F-4 FWIC, Dick had transitioned to the F-15 while at Kadena AB, before returning to Eglin AFB. There, he was assigned to the 3246th Test Wing, which he described as the best tour of his USAF career. Oddly enough, Hoey never shared with me exactly what he did while in Florida, only that it involved several top-secret weapons development programs that exposed him to the test side of fighter operations within the USAF.

It was no fluke, then, approaching the end of his tour, that Dick was recommended by his wing commander for a top secret program and assignment to Nellis AFB, the nature of which he couldn't be told, only that he would be "flying fighters in a high-profile program of national importance." He wasn't given any time to think about it – either he was in or not. Once he walked out the door, the offer was no longer valid. Needless to say, he signed up for an assignment, not knowing where it would lead.

Just weeks later, Hoey received orders to the 4450th TG at Nellis AFB via a checkout in the A-7 Corsair II with the Arizona ANG in Tucson, Arizona, eventually arriving at Nellis AFB in late spring 1984. Ironically, having just been briefed on the F-117 program, I knew exactly what Hoey would soon be flying before he did. Nevertheless, I never mentioned my access to *Senior Trend* and what lay ahead for him. All Hoey was told about what was going on within the 4450th TG was that his checkout in the A-7 was critical to the success of the program he was about to join. He couldn't wait to get started.

Just two months later, another new pilot assigned to the 4450th moved into the neighborhood with his family directly across the street from my house in Las Vegas. The individual was Capt Greg "Curly" Nicholl, whom I'd also known from Kadena AB, where he had been an F-4 pilot in the 25th TFS and subsequently, like Dick Hoey, transitioned to the F-15. Several years later, approaching the end of his assignment as an F-15 IP at Luke AFB, Nicholl, like Hoey, was contacted and interviewed for a top secret assignment with the 4450th TG at Nellis.

As with Hoey before and, no doubt, dozens of other pilots recruited for the job, Nicholl was only told that he would be flying fighters in a high-profile program of national importance. Again, the colonel conducting the interview needed an answer immediately. Once he left the room, so too would the offer. Nicholl, faced with a decision and unable even to phone his wife, hesitated for a moment and agreed. For a brief instant, Greg silently speculated that the mysterious assignment might be flying a MiG-25. That illusion immediately vanished when told he would first be checking out in the A-7 before heading to Nellis AFB!

Later that evening, Greg told his wife, Marcie, they would soon be headed to Las Vegas and Nellis AFB, as he had accepted an assignment that afternoon to a unit he had never heard of and did not exactly know what he would be doing. All he knew was that it was something of national importance and that it would entail a checkout in the A-7 down in Tucson, before reporting to Nellis AFB. Unsurprisingly, Marcie, ever the team player, was on board. Later that summer, the Nicholl family – Greg, Marcie, and their three children – moved into 682 North Straight Street. Without immediately knowing it, I'd gained not only another soon-to-be F-117 pilot for a neighbor, but, it turned out dear friends I'd stay connected with for a lifetime.

The following year, in June 1985, both Hoey and Nicholl would check out in the F-117, becoming "Bandits 176" and "179," respectively. During the intervening months, and throughout our entire association, while we were all assigned to Nellis AFB, we never once discussed what any of us

"STINK BUGS"

did, even within the confines of our own homes. Perhaps even stranger still, neither Hoey nor Nicholl ever saw any of our MiGs while up at TTR. Although both programs shared the same airfield, they might as well have been in different states, given the isolation of their operations.

In retrospect, while the F-117 stealth fighter was indeed a technological marvel, the success of the entire program was only made possible by the talent and dedication of two of the finest fighter pilots I've ever known, and others like them. I count myself fortunate to have been a witness to history in the making. Yet another case of right place, right time.

18

The Aggressors

"The aggressive spirit, the offensive, is the chief thing everywhere in war, and the air is no exception."

RITTMEISTER MANFRED VON RICHTHOFEN

August 23, 1984
1244hrs Pacific Daylight Time
38 nautical miles north-northeast of Nellis AFB
"Mig 11" flight

"Turn in, the fight's on," came the call over the assigned UHF working frequency for "Mig 11" flight, a pair of F-5Es from the 65th AS based at Nellis AFB and part of the 57th FWW.

At his "three o'clock" position, Maj Aric "Redeye" Johnson noted the planform shape of his wingman's F-5E silhouetted against the bright midday sky, clearly in a hard left turn towards him – the neutral air-to-air engagement setup from 12,000ft line abreast was now fully underway. Johnson responded in kind, reeling his nearly identical fighter into a hard, slightly descending right turn and rolling out on a reciprocal heading of south-southwest to that of his opponent.

At the initiation of the engagement, he'd instinctively pushed both throttles to the full forward detent, commanding the fighter's two J85-GE-21A engines to full afterburner. Almost instantaneously, he felt a subtle and reassuring nudge emanating from 28ft behind his ejection seat as raw fuel ignited each engine's afterburner section, generating a combined 10,000lb of thrust. His eyes, rather than inside the cockpit looking at the engine instruments, were outside, fixated on his opponent for this fourth and what would turn out to be the final engagement of his career.

The previous three hadn't gone particularly well for his wingman. Johnson had saddled up for a "guns-tracking" position during the second engagement, and "Mig 12" had failed to attain an offensive advantage on the other two. Regardless of Johnson's years of experience and status as an IP in the 65th AS, his wingman should have been doing better. And therein lay the reason for this "continuation training" sortie for his squadron mate – a rarity within any Aggressor squadron unless one of its pilots needed help honing his skills. From the outcome of the previous engagements, it was apparent that the "light bulb" hadn't yet fully illuminated for the Aggressor pilot at the controls of "Mig 12" when confronted with the three-dimensional dynamics of air combat.

As Aric rolled out wings level, he unloaded the aircraft to zero Gs. The familiar "light-in-the-seat" feeling told him he had eased the control stick just far enough forward to allow the sleek fighter to accelerate as much as possible before the merge. The feel of the control stick instinctively told him he had good energy on the jet. A quick glance at the airspeed indicator on the upper left side of the instrument panel confirmed it – 430KIAS and still accelerating.

Meanwhile, his opponent had turned a bit harder at the onset of the fight and was now slightly inside of Johnson and just above and to the right of his canopy bow. This engagement would be a right-to-right head-on pass, with Johnson's aircraft offset a few hundred feet south and nearly 500ft lower. The two fighters closed the two-nautical-mile gap at 1,500ft per second.

Approaching the merge, Aric noted his opponent beginning a right-slicing high-G turn down and into him. This lead-turn maneuver was intended to deny precious turning room to Johnson and his still-accelerating aircraft precious turning room. It appeared to be a good maneuver, and against a lesser opponent, it would have been a decent first move in the chess game of aerial combat. In a blur, the two fighters flashed past each other a second later, barely 300ft apart.

Man, he's laying some Gs on that thing. Better not piss away all your airspeed.

Rather than counter his wingman's move with a predictably similar turn up and into him, Johnson had continued straight ahead, still unloaded, the airspeed needle now hovering just below the 510KIAS mark.

Okay, it's time to see how he handles this.

With a smooth but steady aft pull on the control stick, the F-5E rocketed toward the heavens, the maneuver taking Aric almost into the pure vertical. With his jet carving a smooth turn upwards, he strained to get his eyeballs on his opponent from within the tight confines of the cockpit. His shoulders and head were twisted around fully to his right and rearward, his left hand, now entirely off the throttles, pushing hard against the left canopy frame to help turn his upper torso as far to his right as he could manage. This was an all-too-common contortion for a fighter pilot amidst a gut-wrenching pitched air-to-air engagement.

Once established in the climb, Johnson had eased off the Gs, allowing the fighter to zoom nearly 6,000ft above his starting altitude of 17,000ft MSL. This zoom, while neither a classic two-circle nor one-circle fight, was intended as a "curveball" to see if Aric's adversary could solve the three-dimensional problem of fighting in the pure vertical. By doing so, Johnson had traded almost 300KIAS of excess airspeed for altitude and, potentially, an advantage.

Deftly floating his fighter over the top of his vertical arc, and having pirouetted to a south-southeast heading, Aric noted that his opponent's aircraft had eased off the hard turn and, surprisingly, was still in a very nose-low descending attitude, with the underside of his aircraft strangely visible well below him. Something didn't seem right as Johnson began pulling his nose below the horizon to pursue his opponent. Where he'd expected to see "Mig 12's" nose pulling up and into him, it continued toward the desert floor below, the jet's afterburner aglow and visible even with the high sun now just past midday.

Come on, man, you've got plenty of airspeed. Pull up and into me. What are you doing?

For a moment, he thought he detected a sudden change in the aircraft's attitude, the entire planform of the fighter, now more than three miles below him, suddenly visible against the mottled desert beyond. And that's when it happened. A bright flash, followed by billowing smoke and debris strewn about on "Mig 12's" last heading. There was no hope of anyone surviving such an impact.

Instinctively, he keyed the mic button on the right throttle with his left thumb, and the words he'd uttered hundreds of times during his career came out yet again.

"Knock it off, knock it off," Aric shouted into his oxygen mask, the words unheard by anyone except him. There was no response from his wingman, nor did he expect any. His squadron mate was dead, a victim, the accident investigation board would later find, of a "G-induced loss of consciousness" incident. It is more commonly referred to simply as G-LOC.

Well, that's the end of this shit!

Over the past year, the Aggressors at Nellis AFB had lost no less than four F-5s. This crash made it five. Four of those five were from a single squadron, the 65th AS. Worse yet, Johnson had, ironically, been the IP for three of those four accidents that had resulted in the loss of two squadron mates. To say that the heat had been on for some time, from the two-star commander (Maj Gen Eugene Fischer) of the TFWC on down, was an understatement. The loss of so many aircraft was statistically untenable, given the hours flown compared to all other units in the USAF. Johnson had heard the rumors in the squadron hallways and at the O'Club over beers with his contemporaries. Pilots essentially told each other, "Don't be the next guy to fuck up, or you're toast!"

Johnson's recovery back to Nellis AFB was a haunting one. A wingman of his had failed to return with him for the second time in less than a year. As Aric touched down on Runway 22R, he instinctively knew he had just flown the last sortie of his career.

Before Johnson had even landed, word had spread that yet another F-5E had been lost, this time along with its pilot. The Aggressor community at Nellis AFB was stunned – not another one! In the ensuing days, while the squadron closed ranks around the grieving widow and the children left behind, and paid tribute to yet another fallen comrade, left unspoken was the sense of foreboding, knowing that the fallout from the accident would soon follow. Two weeks later, it did.

September 7, 1984
1400hrs
64th AS
Main Briefing Room

The ass-chewing every Aggressor pilot at Nellis AFB had anticipated was at hand. In the two weeks following the crash of Johnson's wingman, Maj Gen Gene Fischer was furious, and his wrath at a certain contingent of Aggressor pilots and the overall program would soon be felt.

The preliminary reports from the accident investigation team would antiseptically answer what any seasoned fighter pilot already knew – a seemingly accomplished fighter pilot had blacked out while in a descending hard turn during a grueling air-to-air combat training engagement and never regained consciousness in time to learn from his mistake. The accident board estimated the incident aircraft had hit the desert floor at close to 560KIAS, a nanosecond after registering a 12G airframe spike, undoubtedly caused by an impulsive "snatch of the stick." This last event, they further concluded, was clear evidence that the pilot had momentarily regained consciousness just long enough to pull back in a vain attempt to avoid the rocks looming before his windscreen in the final few seconds of his life.

The 12G "snatch," a panicked attempt to save his life, would have rendered the pilot unconscious for a second time, and mercifully, he most likely never saw his aircraft impact the terrain and disintegrate into thousands of fragments. The wreckage of the fighter was strewn across the desert floor for two miles, the most significant piece no larger than two feet across. The latter was part of the compressor section from one of the engines, still operating at full afterburner at the moment of impact.

The word had gone out the week following the accident that all scheduled Aggressor deployments for the next couple of weeks were canceled. Those pilots already on the road were recalled and instructed to return to Nellis AFB with their aircraft within 48 hours. Anyone on leave was phoned and told to return to base as soon as possible. This was serious, and the Air Force brass, from the four-star commander of TAC to the respective Aggressor squadron commanders, wanted to ensure everyone got the message – all 64th and 65th AS pilots were to assemble in the 64th's main briefing room at 1400hrs for an address by Maj Gen Fischer. Oh, and don't dare be late!

"Ahh . . . ten . . hut!" Shouted the 64th AS commander just inside the doorway to the briefing room as Maj Gen Fischer, followed by the 57th FWW's commander, Brig Gen Joe Ashy, entered. More than 70 assembled pilots from both Aggressor squadrons jumped to attention and stood motionless as Fischer made his way to the podium. The tension in the air was palpable. It was dead silent. Not a person breathed, much less moved, until, with a wave of his hand, Fischer motioned them to be seated. The assembled pilots quickly took their seats, steeling themselves for what was about to unfold.

As they sat, no fewer than six Aggressor pilots pressed the "Record" buttons on their handheld tape recorders, conveniently tucked out of sight in their flight suit pockets. What they were about to capture was epic. (*Note – the following remarks by him are unedited and as they were transcribed directly from the recordings mentioned above. They are presented in their entirety for contextual purposes*). Fischer began in earnest:

"Well, I asked Gen Ashy to get you all together, as you know by now, and bring you home from where you were at and keep you from going anywhere next week so that we might have a heart-to-heart talk on where we are at in the Aggressor business.

"To begin, I no longer have a warm feeling about the Aggressors. In fact, I've got an uneasy feeling about the Aggressors, and I don't like uneasy feelings, and I'm not gonna have that at Nellis, so we'll do whatever is necessary to correct it. That doesn't mean the Aggressors are bad, but I can tell you we won't be able to survive with the Aggressor program with the way we're going. And I'll be the first one to cut it out.

"The TAC accident rate this year is 3.2 [3.2 aircraft losses per 100,000 hours]. Without Nellis, it would be 1.9 for the entire Command. The 57th's accident rate is 10.8. Mind you, that's with the rest of TAC being 1.9. You can guess what the Aggressor rate is. The Aggressor rate is 22.9! And you don't have to be a mental goddamned giant to know that something's sick here. Something's terribly sick and terribly wrong. I look at the . . . at the accidents that we've had in the Aggressors over the last four or five years . . . it's a horror story."

No matter who you were, any objective look at the five Aggressor accidents in the previous 12 months couldn't have been more revealing of a program that had gone off the rails. Two accidents were due to loss of control, where the pilots flew excellent airplanes beyond their capabilities. A "win at all costs" attitude supplanted good judgment, resulting in the loss of both F-5s. Fortunately, both pilots safely ejected from the ensuing spins. Another loss was simply due to bad luck and not attributable to pilot error, as evidenced by dual engine fires followed by another safe ejection.

The last two losses, unfortunately, resulted in fatalities for both pilots. The first was a mid-air collision involving a 65th AS F-5E and an Eglin AFB F-15 during a *Maple Flag* exercise in Cold Lake, Canada. Luckily, the Eagle pilot safely ejected. The accident board couldn't definitively attribute pilot error to this accident. However, if one were to read between the lines of their report, it seemed to be a classic case of the "Big-Sky Theory" breaking down. In fighter pilot terms, at some point, two airplanes will inevitably collide with each other during actual or simulated combat. There is always a measure of inherent risk involved in these operations, and luck just ran out that day.

The second fatal incident was the most recent G-LOC accident, the proverbial straw that drove Maj Gen Fischer to address all the Aggressors today. Ironically, Aric Johnson had been the IP of record in the last three losses, where he'd ejected from a burning F-5E and had returned alone after losing two wingmen in the others. His flying days were over, and he knew it.

Fischer continued:

"Not a shiny record by any means. It's dumb-shit things; it's non-professionals flying airplanes that either exceed the airplane's capability or their own . . . or both . . . and leave wreckage all around TAC. Even during the good years of the Aggressors, when the accident rate in the Aggressor organization was low . . . they've left wrecks all over TAC . . . or with people that have been involved in flying with the Aggressors. We have cut most of that out and no longer have people killing themselves all around TAC while trying to fly with the Aggressors."

The USAF accident rate metric measures aircraft losses per 100,000 flying hours. While the overall loss rate for fighter aircraft within TAC in 1984 was 3.2 aircraft for that same sample size, the Aggressors at Nellis AFB were on track to lose the equivalent of an entire squadron of F-5s every five years. Extrapolating that rate further would result in the deaths of ten highly trained pilots. So, you could begin to sense the enormity of the problem facing Fischer:

"I can tell you two years ago, as a wing commander, the TAC commander stood up in front of every TAC wing commander at a commander's conference and said, 'When the Aggressors arrive at your squadron, you ought to treat it, at your Wing, you ought to treat it like the plague.' Boy, that's a hell of an indictment for a group of so-called professionals, for a group of people who are supposed to be able to fly airplanes better than anybody else in the Air Force. For a group of people who are supposed to be setting the standards and getting their command's air-to-air proficiency up and knowledge of enemy tactics high.

"That was a sad commentary on the Aggressors, and it was a sad commentary on Nellis, and I happened to be a wing commander in Florida at that time, and I thought, Jesus Christ, when the TAC commander has to stand up and say that something's sick in the Aggressors and somebody ought to fix that. But it never got fixed, and it ain't fixed today. And if I was the wing commander, I'd treat the Aggressors like the plague, and I'm beginning to feel that you're a plague here at Nellis. And I don't like it, and you shouldn't. It should make every one of you sick. A 22.9 accident rate. It ought to make you ashamed of yourselves."

So, there it was. Everyone in the room knew Maj Gen Gene Fischer was just warming up, and this ass-chewing would set a new level in the annals of USAF fighter pilot lore:

"And we brief all the VIPs that come in here that here's our Aggressor force. And we bring in only the most qualified people. Right, Kerry [Col Kerry Herron, 57th FWW Deputy Commander for Adversary Tactics]? You stand at this very podium and say, 'Only the best-qualified aviators do we allow in the Aggressors.' That's bullshit! The best-qualified people don't jump out of airplanes or run into the ground. Our problem is we don't have the best qualified. That's our problem. And we're going to change that. We're going to make some drastic changes. Some of you sitting in this room are gonna go, I guarantee you that. And we're gonna be goddamned careful who replaces you."

Even though many wanted to, no pilot in attendance dared look around the room at their colleagues for fear of being singled out for a verbal dressing down by the irate major general. Some already knew that their days as an Aggressor at Nellis or anywhere were over. They were likely among the first to be grounded and told to look for another assignment. That, or leave the Air Force. The options weren't good ones. Fischer continued:

"You lose control of an airplane in this business, and you might as well be thinking about what you're gonna do in your next job. It sure as hell isn't

The author is seen seated here in a Christmas 1958 photograph with his two older brothers, Mark (left) and Chuck (right), and our mother, Harriet. I was four years old at the time, and I had already seen my first aircraft, which had left a lasting impression on me. (*Rob Zettel collection*)

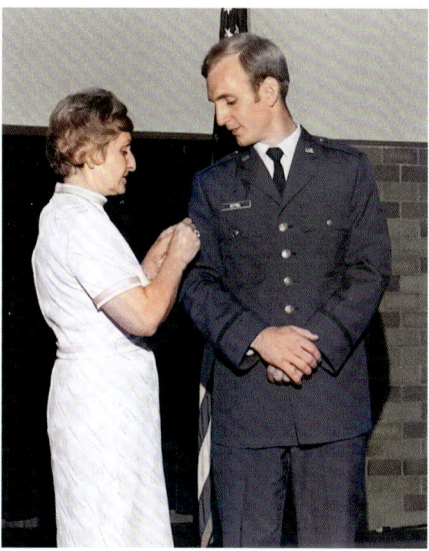

My mother does the honors of pinning on my second lieutenant bars following my USAF commissioning at the College of Saint Thomas, in Saint Paul, Minnesota, on May 22, 1976. (*Rob Zettel collection*)

On the flight line at Vance AFB, Oklahoma, next to a T-38 Talon "White Rocket." The first time I sat in the aircraft, I knew this was where I belonged. I would solo in the T-38 on November 18, 1977. (*Rob Zettel collection*)

With brothers Mark (left) and Chuck (right) at the UPT graduation banquet at the Vance AFB O'Club in Enid, Oklahoma. (*Rob Zettel collection*)

My mother pins on my wings following graduation from USAF UPT at Vance AFB on March 17, 1978. (*Rob Zettel collection*)

311th TFTS, Luke AFB, Arizona, January 1979. I'm seated atop the F-4C's left intake, fifth from the left. Our class comprised all pilots, no WSOs. Lt Larry "Murph" Murphy (top row, far left) and I were the only two assigned to PACAF and the 18th TFW at Kadena AB, Okinawa. (*Rob Zettel collection*)

Standing before a 12th TFS F-4D at Kadena AB in July 1979, I'm posing here with my WSO, Capt John Sheekly. We were about to take off for Clark AB, in the Philippines, for two weeks of TDY, participating in *Cope Thunder* 79-8. (*Rob Zettel collection*)

Seen standing atop my F-4E in the revetments at Osan AB, Republic of Korea, after joining the 36th TFS "Flying Fiends." This photograph was taken in spring 1981. I had just made captain a couple of months earlier. (*Rob Zettel collection*)

After making my final flight in the F-4E with the 36th TFS on August 20, 1981, at Osan AB, I shared a traditional bottle of "bubbly" with my WSO, Lt Tom "Mayberry" Griffith. Ten years later, then Maj Griffith spent 42 days as a PoW following the downing of his F-15E on January 17, 1991, during *Operation Desert Storm*. Tom was among the best WSOs I ever flew with. (*Rob Zettel collection*)

When I posed in my aircraft, F-5E 75-0612, at Clark AB in November 1982, little did I know that just weeks later, while back at Nellis AFB on holiday leave, I would be asked to interview for a position as a member of the 4477th TES. (*Rob Zettel collection*)

F-5E 75-0612 was photographed on short final approach at Kadena AB, Japan, in its distinctive "Lizard" camouflage. I was at the controls when this shot was taken. (*Rob Zettel collection*)

Capt Clarke "Frog" Peele, next to his Aggressor F-5E at Kadena AB in June 1983. The "Frog" was both a best friend and mentor. I owe much of my skills as a fighter pilot to his patience in molding me to his high standards. He was, without a doubt, one of the very best fighter pilots I ever flew with. (*Rob Zettel collection*)

Unbeknownst to me at the time, this USAF photograph was part of a package forwarded by the commanding officer of the 3rd TFW to his equivalent at the 57th FWW, recommending this young Aggressor to be part of the 4477th TES. (*Rob Zettel collection*)

NELLIS AFB   LAS VEGAS, NEVADA 89191   AV 682-5495/7/8

1 June 1983

Colonel John T. Corder
Commander
3rd Tactical Fighter Wing
APO San Francisco 96288

Dear Colonel Corder

Captain Rob Zettel has been selected for reassignment to the 4477 Test and Evaluation Squadron effective October 1983. As you know, the opportunity to be assigned to the 4477 TES is a unique opportunity--and normally occurs only once in a fighter pilot's career. We select only the best--Captain Zettel's selection and approval verifies he passed the test as the "Best of the Best." I am looking forward to working with Captain Zettel and I know he will contribute significantly to the 4477 TES mission.

Please convey my congratulations to Captain Zettel on his assignment to the 4477 TES.

GEORGE S. GENNIN
Lieutenant Colonel, USAF
Commander

The Ultimate In Air Combat

This was the letter handed to me when I was called to report to Col Chuck "Brows" Holden, the Deputy Commander of Operations for the 3rd TFW. Thinking I was about to be called on the carpet for some flying infraction, I was instead told I'd been selected to be a "Red Eagle."
(*Rob Zettel collection*)

4477th TES "Red Eagles" in June 1984, in a photograph featured in a slideshow for the farewell party of squadron commander, Lt Col George Gennin. These pilots are, from left to right, Capt Gary "Goldie" Craig, Maj John "Skid" Skidmore, Capt Jim "Wiley" Green, Capt Steve "Brownie" Brown, Lt Cdr Orville "Orv" Prins, Capt Rob "Z-Man" Zettel, Lt Cdr Jim "Rookie" Robb, Capt Paul "Stook" Stucky, Maj Dave "Blazo" Bland, Maj Larry "Shy" Shervanick, Maj Ted "Gabby" Drake, and Maj Frank "Paco" Geisler. (*Rob Zettel collection*)

Above The cockpit of the MiG-21F-13 was a less than stellar example of human engineering. Being used to Western-designed fighters, new "Red Eagles" found it a shock. Except for a different altimeter, airspeed indicator, transponder, G-suit fitting, and radio, the aircraft was vintage Soviet. (*USAF*)

Right The MiG-21F-13 was simply a pleasure to fly, excelling in the vertical. The large rudder allowed for superb high AOA control. Oddly enough, handling the aircraft on the ground was just the opposite, for its pneumatic brakes proved quite a challenge for new "Red Eagles" to become accustomed to. (*USAF*)

4477th TES commander Lt Col George Gennin leads a tour of the "Red Eagles'" VIP hangar for US Secretary of Defense Caspar Weinberger (right), with Assistant Secretary of Defense Frank Carlucci (far left) and TAC vice commander Lt Gen Bob Russ looking on. (Photo courtesy of Laureen Gennin)

Maj "Paco" Geisler, Lt Cdr "Orv" Prins, and Capt Billy Bayer of the "Red Eagles" are seen here with Laureen Gennin, wife of 4477th TES commander Lt Col George Gennin, at one of many parties hosted by the couple. (Photo courtesy of Laureen Gennin)

A 4477th TES MiG-21F-13 on a low-altitude run over the Nellis AFB ranges. (*USAF*)

Chinese-built F-7B Bort number "96" on the flight line at TTR. The 4477th TES would end up operating eight F-7Bs as part of *Constant Peg*, all of them brand new. I once opened the logbook for one I'd never seen before, and it revealed a total flight time of only 3.5 hours. (*USAF*)

Lt Cdr Guy "Brudog" Brubaker flies an immaculate T-38 over Cactus Peak, returning to TTR from one of many cross-country flights he and I made – I was flying the lead jet here. Note the absence of any identifying tail letters or fin flash. (*Rob Zettel collection*)

This US Navy Fighter Weapons School A-4E "Mongoose," complete with the famous TOPGUN insignia on its fin, is an example of the aircraft Lt Cdr Greg "Hollywood" Dishart was flying when he and I knocked heads (I was flying a MiG-21F-13 at the time) over Range 76 in the Nellis AFB Range Complex in the fall of 1985. (*US Navy*)

A rare photograph of a "Red Eagles" pilot and a squadron MiG-23, in this case a "Flogger-E." It was taken one spring day in 1986 while I was checking out as an FCF in the MiG-23MS. (Rob Zettel collection)

Maj Ted "Gabby" Drake, "Bandit 42," was instrumental in turning the MiG-23 program into the success it was, and many "Flogger" pilots who flew the aircraft with the "Red Eagles" owe him a debt of gratitude for making it safer by doing so. (*Ted Drake collection*)

The only thing that made the transition from the MiG-21 to the MiG-23 a bit easier was the general placement of the engine and flight instruments. The visibility hadn't improved, and there were a few new items, namely radar, wing-sweep controls/indicator, stick grip, INS, and a throttle that slid along a rail. (*National Museum of the Air Force*)

Learning and mastering this complicated cockpit presented another challenge for those who flew the MiG-23. It was but one week from my last flight in the MiG-21 until the first in the "Flogger," and the transition was made without the benefit of a simulator or two-seat trainer. (*National Museum of the Air Force*)

The AOA gauge in the MiG-23 was indispensable in helping the pilot get maximum performance out of his airplane. Starting at 18 units of AOA, the "knuckle-rapper" on the control stick would begin rhythmic tapping on your knuckles, tactily making the pilot aware he was entering the high AOA region. (*Rob Zettel collection*)

MiG-23 flap and wing sweep controls. The three-position flap control buttons (left to right, down–half–up) are just outboard of the wing sweep control handle. Wing sweep was manual, with detents at the 72°, 45°, and 16° settings. The standard wing sweep rate was 3.1° per second. The actual wing sweep position was verified by an indicator.
(*Rob Zettel collection*)

MiG-23MS "Flogger-E" Bort number "39" on final approach to land. It was one of several MiG-23s I flew while a member of the 4477th TES. Here, you can see the ventral fin retracted for landing. It retracted whenever the landing gear handle was placed in the down position. (*USAF*)

Best party ever! I am seen here (center) in the O'Club at NAS Miramar at the Second Annual Toga Party, held on August 9, 1986. I'm flanked by "Red Eagles" Lt Cdr Marty "Streak" Chanik (second from left) and Capt "Hawk" Carlisle (second from right). Entertainment was provided by Otis Day and the Knights from the 1978 movie *National Lampoon's Animal House*.
(*Rob Zettel collection*)

Just weeks following my last sortie in the MiG-23, I am seen here in the cockpit of an F-15 during transition training at Luke AFB, Arizona, as a member of the 426th TFTS in January 1987. (*Rob Zettel collection*)

The author in the 94th TFS's flagship F-15C over Jordan during Exercise *Coronet Archer* in July 1988. This was just months after the 94th had participated in one of the last *Constant Peg* deployments by any squadron before the 4477th flew its final official MiG sorties on March 4, 1988. (*Rob Zettel collection*)

The author poses with the commander of Air Combat Command, Gen "Hawk" Carlisle, while attending the October 2016 "Red Eagles" reunion at the National Museum of the USAF in Dayton. (*Rob Zettel collection*)

Rich Hofman, neighbor, coach, friend. He didn't know it at the time, but as the "big kid" next door, when Rich taught me how to play baseball, he instilled in me much more than how to just throw a ball and swing a bat. Discipline, hard work, and teamwork were values he imparted that helped shape me throughout my entire life.
(*Rob Zettel collection*)

The author stands next to a MiG-23MS in the National Museum of the USAF in Dayton. This was one of many "Fishbeds" and "Floggers" the author flew during Project Constant Peg while a pilot with the 4477th TES. Lt Col Zettel would finish his assignment with the unit having completed a combined total of 476 sorties in both MiG aircraft. (*Rob Zettel collection*)

gonna be flying fighters in the Air Force. Is that a threat? You're goddamned right it is. I'm sick and tired of so-called professionals. And please believe me, I'm only talking to a handful of you out there, because the vast majority go out day in and day out and do a tremendous job. You do it professionally. TAC's better off because of you. I'm very proud of you. But there are a few that can't get that through their goddamned heads, and they're not going to be with us any longer.

"You know it's absolutely asinine that we have lost five F-5s in the last year. There's not a goddamned wing in TAC that's lost five airplanes in the last year. And we're losing it with a simple airplane and highly skilled aviators. Now, how in the hell do you explain that? Is it because we got our heads up our asses? You tell me. I don't know what the answer is anymore. But five goddamned major aircraft accidents and loss of life in one of the world's simplest airplanes? Something is drastically wrong with the attitude of either the leadership or the aircrews that fly in the Aggressors, or both.

"My boss reminded me after the last one that the Russians have 60 wings of airplanes. In the last two years, they haven't had one out-of-control accident. So, who in the hell are we trying to emulate? What are we trying to prove in the Aggressors? Why is it we can't know when we've gone beyond reasonable prudent stops?

"Again, supposedly the most highly qualified aircrews, and we do the most dumb shit things in the world. We do things you wouldn't expect an RTU student to do. So, there's something in our software, in the Aggressors, that's sick. It's rotten. That needs to be cut out. Believe me, we're gonna get to it. If it kills me, we're gonna get to it. If it means doing away with the Aggressors, then I have no problem with that at all, because we're not doing TAC a service right now. We're a cancer on the side of TAC. They don't need us, and we don't need us."

Disbelief was on just about every face in the crowd. If it wasn't, then it was just an emotionless look of shock. But without doubt, the major general's last few words had everyone thinking the same thing.

Do away with the Aggressors? Seriously? But we're unique, indispensable. There's no way he'd do that! Or would he?

"We've thought of restrictions. That didn't work. As they never do. The restriction of not going out and teaching BFM to other units of TAC makes sense because we're not the teachers of BFM. We're the teachers of Soviet tactics, and we were doing that for a while, and while we were doing that, we were leaving wreckage all over the goddamned country. So, we quit that. And that makes sense; that's not our job. That's the wing commander's job, the DO's job, to teach BFM to his people, not ours.

"We even got so bad that we stopped BFM for the Aggressors. And if you stop and think about that, that's sick! That's absolutely sick! We let the newest RTU students fly BFM. And here, for our quote, "experts" in the air-to-air world, we have to stop BFM because we can't trust them. That's sick! So, we're not gonna have restrictions. That's not the way to do it, to attack the problem.

"The way to attack the problem is to get rid of the people who don't understand their own capabilities or their airplane's capabilities. Professional pilots don't jump out of good airplanes. Dumb-shit pilots jump out of good airplanes. And we've got dumb-shit pilots in the Aggressors. Dumb-shit professional pilots don't exceed their own capabilities. Or, if they're in their flight, they don't allow them to be exceeded by others. And we've got dumb-shit flight leaders, and we've got dumb-shit instructors. You name it, we've got it. There's our problem. That's our problem. It's not that we shouldn't fly BFM. That's crazy.

"The problem is that we've got people that don't, that aren't professional enough that they can handle flying an airplane, a simple, simple little airplane, in a simple goddamned mission. As I said, it doesn't pertain to all of you. But there's a goodly number of you that it does. We exceed prudent stops in the Aggressors. And I don't know whether you think being an Aggressor gives you a license to do that or not. Apparently, it does for some. Well, it doesn't. There are reasonable prudent stops in flying an airplane, keeping it under control, keeping your flight under control, worrying about your other flight members.

"Every accident we've had has been a horror story in one way or another. Everyone, except one, I think, where the goddamned thing caught fire. But every other one could've been prevented. There was absolutely no reason to lose the airplane, except somebody decided that the rules didn't apply to him, and he could do anything he wanted to, and he lost the airplane. And we've looked at some lifestyles, and they aren't very shiny for people involved in accidents. In fact, they make you sick.

"So, once again, do we have professionals across the board in the Aggressors? Hell no! Do we have the best aviators in the Aggressors? Hell no! Should we have? Yes! Are we gonna have? Yes! And we're gonna weed some of you out. And you know, sitting there, who you are. Believe me, you know. You know better than anybody else.

"The last accident we had, where we ran a kid into the ground [on his] fourth engagement. The third one was a long, extensive engagement, late in the afternoon, hot, tired, and we killed a young captain. Should we have stopped before we got to that point? Hell, yes, we should have stopped. Should somebody have known where to stop? Hell, yes, they should have known. There was a flight leader there. Did they? No. What happened? We ran an airplane into the ground. You've gotta stop that, gents. You've just gotta stop that.

"There are limits, prudent goddamned limits. You're being paid as mature, senior experts in air-to-air. That doesn't mean that every goddamned flight is grab your ass and go for everything you can get. There are rules. There are objectives. When they're not met, you knock it off and set it up again. When you look at the last accident we had, where we killed a young kid, that should've been stopped after the first engagement. Shit, he hadn't achieved the objectives on the first . . . the first exercise, but yet they went on . . . and on . . . and on until he finally went in.

"There's something sick in the Aggressors. You're gonna hear a lot more from other people. I just wanted to let you know where I stand. I've lost my patience, I've lost my sympathy, and as you well know, it doesn't apply to all of you. Some of you are doing an absolutely superb job, and I couldn't be prouder of you. But as a group, you stink. And you gotta crawl out of the shit so you don't smell anymore. Is that unmistakably clear? And whatever it takes, goddamn it, I want you to do it.

"I don't want any more business as usual. Every goddamn time we get you together, it's right back to business as usual the next day. I don't want that. I want every goddamned one of you to think about what you're gonna do to stop it. Climb out of the smell that's around ya. Good guys know how to do that. If all of you don't, we'll help you. But I'm not gonna lose any more F-5s. Now, I'm not gonna have any more F-5s go out of control. And if you do, you'd better have a goddamned career planned because it's not gonna be part of the Air Force. I'll do everything I can to run you out on a goddamned rail. That's not an idle threat. I'll worry about your morale when you get your professionalism up to where you deserve some . . . concern. Right now, you're not there. Okay, carry on."

As Maj Gen Fischer turned from the podium, the room was on its feet instantly and at attention, its pilots processing what they'd just heard, and how, for many, their career plans had just taken a sudden and unexpected turn. The phrase, "cancer on the side of TAC," spread like wildfire throughout the fighter community at Nellis AFB and the broader USAF fighter community worldwide. Those Aggressors who were the focus of Fischer's rage wore it like a badge of honor. The fallout was swift and widespread in the following weeks, just as the major general had promised. In the ensuing months, dozens of those seated in the room left the Air Force for careers elsewhere.

But that's a topic for another time, perhaps someone else's book. The intent here isn't an indictment of the Aggressors at Nellis, but rather to give context to the environment that all fighter pilots of the 57th FWW found themselves in, which had been percolating for years. It was a time of fierce competitiveness, with men pushing their machines and themselves to their limits – and in many cases, beyond those limits – with often predictable and tragic consequences.

We in the "Red Eagles" were insulated from the immediate fallout, given the nature of our mission and our operating location, 120 nautical miles northwest of Nellis. Operating out of TTR definitely had its advantages.

Ironically, just two months earlier, in what may have been a blessing in disguise, Brig Gen Joe Ashy had decided that no "Red Eagles" would be dual-qualified and fly with their previously attached squadrons at Nellis. While that hit home hardest to us who regularly flew F-5Es with the 64th and 65th ASs, it was consequential well beyond the Aggressor units. This decision, which seemingly came out of nowhere, would also impact the smaller contingent of "Red Eagles" who routinely flew F-15s, F-16s, and F-4s at Nellis.

Those of us who, up until just recently, had routinely been flying with the two Aggressor squadrons were now just outside casual observers. Nonetheless, I vividly remember getting the word that Friday afternoon up at Tonopah that shit had hit the proverbial fan down at Nellis hours earlier. When I walked into the O'Club later that evening, Fischer's tirade and what it meant for the Aggressors going forward were the hot topics at the bar. It was a memorable night, to be sure.

The 4477th had been closely related to the Aggressor mission since its formation. To say the "Red Eagles" and the Aggressors were joined at the hip would not be an exaggeration. Given the nature of the mission and flying the very aircraft the Aggressors were tasked to emulate, this made perfect sense. For those of us who had been flying the F-5E, it made for an easy transition to the MiG-21. Moreover, during the program's history, most USAF "Red Eagles" pilots had come directly from the Aggressor ranks. Until then, all but two Aggressor pilots, Mike Scott and I, had come solely from the two Aggressor squadrons based at Nellis. Scott, followed by me several years later, had been assigned to the "Red Eagles" directly from the 26th TFTAS at Clark AB.

The closeness of the roles of the two units made for a perfect cover story used throughout the period the 4477th was active. "Red Eagles" pilots flew "highly modified/unspecified" F-5 and F-4 test aircraft, so the cover story went. As mentioned earlier, each "Red Eagles" pilot who had previously been an Aggressor was attached to either the 64th or 65th AS. This was also true for our US Navy and US Marine Corps-assigned "Red Eagles," who maintained F-5E qualifications. Once assigned to the 4477th, all Naval Aviators attended the USAF Aggressor course regardless of whether they were already qualified in the F-5E or not.

Of the 20 currently assigned pilots in the "Red Eagles" on that September day, 13 had been graduates of the USAF Aggressor program or were former US Navy Fighter Weapons School IPs. Until recently, ten had been flying with the 64th or 65th ASs at Nellis.

One of the requirements to qualify for consideration for an assignment to the 4477th was to be a graduate of the USAF Aggressor program, the FWS, or TOPGUN. Several "Red Eagles" were graduates of both the Aggressor and FWS courses. A few who had attended both were Majs Dave Bland (F-4 FWS), "Paco" Geisler (F-15 FWS) and John Skidmore (F-16 FWS).

Opportunities for anyone to fly against the 4477th's MiG assets were limited, and this also held for the Aggressors at Nellis. Consequently, the bulk of the available *Constant Peg* sorties allocated to the USAF Aggressors were to support their own training syllabus. With rare exceptions, only those pilots going through the five-month-long Aggressor course would get an opportunity to fly against the top secret MiGs operating at TTR.

This meant that approximately every 16 weeks, a class of eight to ten pilots new to the F-5E would be scheduled for their opportunity to pit their skills against the MiGs of the "Red Eagles". When these students were at the *Constant Peg* exposure phase of the program, they had been flying the F-5E for about two to three months. That was not a lot of time to get comfortable in any new aircraft, and incredibly few when given the task of going up against a highly skilled and experienced "Red Eagles" pilot in a MiG-21. While some had had exposure to the MiGs during earlier assignments in either F-15s, F-4s, or F-16s, this was a whole new ballgame when flying an F-5E.

For obvious reasons, the best match-up and most challenging opponent for them was the MiG-21. I'll be the first to say this wasn't usually a fair fight, as these guys were still pretty new to the F-5E, having only logged maybe 20–25 hours in the fighter by the time they were scheduled to lock horns with us. Predictably, if they decided to slow down with the MiG-21, it usually ended up with them on the receiving end of a "gun's tracking" call. Having flown both aircraft extensively, here's my assessment of the advantages/disadvantages of each, and why the MiG-21 in a visual turning fight was the better of the two. I'll also explain why it gave fits to most fighter pilots who flew against it.

At first glance, the attributes of each fighter appeared similar. Each was roughly the same size, speed, and had similar weapon loads. But that's where the similarities stopped. In reality, the MiG-21F-13, better known as the "Fishbed-C," was a much faster aircraft, could fly slower at high AOA, and was an absolute pleasure to slow down in and get into the "phone booth" with – particularly against an F-5E.

It's important to note that this sharply contrasts with the Soviets' experience gained from exploiting a former Republic of Vietnam Air Force F-5E flown by two highly experienced test pilots from Akhtubinsk AB in 1976–77. Notable was their finding that the F-5E bested the MiG-21bis ("Fishbed-L") in every setup they attempted. Initially skeptical of their report, I found the following explanation the best possible reason for such an outcome.

While we in the "Red Eagles" flew the MiG-21F-13 "Fishbed-C," the Soviet Union exploited the F-5E against its then-most modern variant, the MiG-21bis "Fishbed-L/N". While the -bis had a much more powerful Tumansky R-25-300 engine producing approximately 15,500lb of thrust in full afterburner, it was also a much heavier aircraft, being fully 2,000lb heavier (empty weight) than our simple and, by 1977 standards, basic MiG-21F-13s. The "Red Eagles'" MiG-21s were better slow-speed fighters than the later models.

A study of the performance statistics of the F-5E and the "Red Eagles'" MiG-21s showed that they were very comparable. The most significant difference was the almost 2,600lb more thrust our MiG had over the F-5E. Combined with no radar in the nose and thousands of pounds less fuel, this made for a highly agile fighter, and one that the F-5E couldn't stay with.

While the F-5E had an excellent initial pitch rate and nose authority, the MiG-21F-13 was even more impressive. At high AOA and slowed to around 90–100KIAS, where the F-5E would struggle to maintain level flight, the MiG-21 could perform a rudder roll around it and proceed to "camp" at the fighter's "six o'clock." Such was the agility of the MiG that, with its large rudder and light stick forces, a "flat" or "rolling scissors" with almost any adversary was a comfortable position to be in. The two exceptions were when engaging the F-16 and F/A-18.

This wasn't to say the F-5E couldn't beat the MiG-21. On the contrary, on two occasions I was sufficiently humbled by a couple of sharp Aggressor students who, despite being new to the F-5E, managed to counter my initial hard defensive turn and not allow themselves to get drawn into a slow-speed fight. The common denominator in both fights was my losing sight of an aircraft that could prove lethal if not given the respect it was due, especially in the hands of a skilled pilot.

They learned something from those engagements, as did the somewhat cocky MiG driver who was on the receiving end of both "guns kill" calls! Something that made me feel a bit better about those humbling experiences was that one of those pilots, years later, would go on to notch up two Iraqi Mirage F1 kills on the first day of *Desert Storm*.

Despite my fondness for the MiG-21F-13's performance, the F-5E was, by far, a better fighter overall. In almost every conceivable scenario, I would have chosen it over the MiG-21. The operative word here is "almost." In a tight visual engagement, I'd have taken the MiG-21F-13 over the F-5E every time. In a "flat" or "rolling scissors," it simply excelled. Assuming pilots of equal skills in this regime, the MiG-21 would consistently outperform its rival. But that's a damn small regime, and one that is almost non-existent in modern-day air combat. That leaves the other 99 percent of the combat environment. In that arena, I would have taken the F-5E every time, as the aircraft had numerous advantages over any model of the MiG-21.

The bottom line is that the USAF, US Navy, and US Marine Corps made a wise choice in equipping their Aggressor and Adversary squadrons with the F-5E. What the aircraft did in emulating the MiG-21 threat was superb, and it has provided two generations of fighter pilots with invaluable DACT.

19

The Crapper

> "Do you realize that several Marines were killed by the Japanese at Pearl Harbor while taking craps? A fighting man must be vigilant to surprise attack, no matter where he is. The survival of our nation depends on the readiness of Marines all over the world."
>
> LT COL BULL MEECHUM (ROBERT DUVALL),
> THE GREAT SANTINI

If you question any "Red Eagles" pilot about life up at TTR, particularly the squadron Operations area, one topic sure to come up is the shenanigans centered around the single, unisex bathroom halfway down the hallway. For most, this may seem ridiculous, perhaps even juvenile, but it was part of the routine and culture everyone became accustomed to. When you had the mix of jokers and pranksters we had in the 4477th, there was bound to be raucous laughter almost daily, usually at the expense of someone new and unsuspecting as to what embarrassment awaited them. Follow along.

October 1985
"Red Eagles" Operations
Tonopah Test Range

The place just exploded! Out of the second toilet stall, away from the entry door and the all-important light switch next to it, flew a 50-gallon plastic trash can over the top of the stall's wall, bumping up against the ceiling and banging around as it then bounced on the tiled floor. This clamor, of course, was accompanied by a line of vulgarity that only a sailor could appreciate, and no doubt heard by everyone throughout the entire squadron Operations area.

"God damn it! What the fuck is going on? Son of a bitch," yelled the big Marine who, a moment before, had been quietly, peacefully, "sitting on the throne," minding his own business while simply trying to take a crap. "You assholes!"

Maj Marty "Fog" Macy, US Marine Corps, the newest pilot to join the ranks of the "Red Eagles," had just been welcomed to the 4477th in the most humbling way. Marty was our token Marine and had replaced Lt Col George "Cajun" Tullos, who had left the previous month to assume command of VMFA-232 at Kaneohe Bay, Hawaii. Macy had joined the "Red Eagles" following a tour with MAWTS-1 at Yuma, Arizona, where he had been an IP flying the F-4S. Macy's first exposure to *Constant Peg* had come five years earlier as a student at TOPGUN, where his experience flying against the MiG-17 and MiG-21 sparked a desire to become a "Red Eagle" someday himself, if possible. Ironically, this "exposure" wasn't what he had envisioned, especially on his first day "up North."

Macy had just been initiated into one of the many quirks that existed at TTR. That being, if you were going to take a dump, never do so from the second stall from the door. For inevitably, whether you were a general officer or an airman basic, someone would turn the lights off on you and leave you to finish your business in the dark and make you fumble your way out of there on your own. A humiliating experience, to say the least. Here's what led up to Macy's "initiation."

A few minutes earlier, as was routine before a flight, I had entered the bathroom to relieve myself, unzipped my flight suit by the urinal, and was generally minding my own business when in walked Maj Paul "Stook" Stucky to do the same. As Stucky saddled up to use the single remaining urinal to my right, he leaned back, looked behind me in the direction of the stalls to our left, and noticed a pair of black flight boots and a flight suit bunched down around the ankles of someone, his identity unknown to us, camped out in the second stall.

Ohh, ohh. This can't be good for whoever is in that stall.

Now finished, as I zipped up my flight suit, Stucky looked at me quietly and cocked his head toward the second stall. Following a quick glance of my own, I nodded silently in acknowledgment. Stucky was up to something, and I was game to play along.

As a bit of background, Stucky had joined the squadron within weeks of my arrival, and we quickly became good friends, spending a lot of time together as we qualified in the MiG-21. Stucky had begun his career as a young F-4 pilot, serving at both Clark AB and, later, Holloman AFB, where he transitioned to the F-15. Soon after, he was selected to attend F-15 FWS, where he had most recently served as an instructor. Oh, one other thing. Next to "Paco" Geisler, Stucky was perhaps the biggest practical joker in the squadron. If "Stook" was around, no one was safe from any number of pranks and jokes, which brings me to where I was currently standing, next to Stucky in the bathroom at Tonopah.

"Stook's" a crazy, practical joker. What's he planning?

Our "duties" at the urinal complete, Stucky and I made our way over to the basins on the opposite wall and washed and dried our hands. All routine, right? We traded small talk about who we were about to fight, the takeoff, intercept tactics, and so on. But it was all a ruse to throw off the unsuspecting victim behind the door in stall No. 2. Next, he looked at me and put his right index finger to his lips, signifying to me to keep quiet. He motioned with his left hand to stay where I was. I had no clue what the squadron's giant prankster had in mind, but I was pretty sure it would be epic.

With that, he took two steps to his right, reached for the door handle, opened the bathroom door wide, and then allowed it to swing closed, all the while remaining inside. And then, predictably, just as the door was about to close fully, he turned off the light switch. Predictably, a sigh of exasperation emanated from the still unidentified victim sitting on the commode behind "lucky door No. 2."

Of course, unbeknownst to the as-yet-unidentified pilot in that stall, Stucky and I were still inside. I stood motionless, having not moved from the basin. It was as black as two in the morning, as there were no windows, and barely a sliver of light entered from the hallway beneath the door. I couldn't see a thing, but I sensed some movement of sorts. It was Stucky, tiptoeing silently back towards the basin.

A giant predator is lurking in the darkness, and whoever's sitting behind that door is about to get a most humbling surprise.

Now, I had no idea what Stucky was planning, but I was now committed to seeing this charade through, as I was stuck there. What happened next surprised me, as I couldn't see a thing. So, my first indication that something had happened was the sound that accompanied the 50-gallon plastic trash can being dumped and launched over the stall wall onto the unsuspecting crapper by Stucky!

As the place exploded, and I heard the torrent of profanity coming from the stall, I had one of those hilarious panic attacks and decided I'd better make for the door. Once we heard the shouting, it was now apparent the victim was our new Marine pilot, "Fog" Macy, who was just sitting there in the dark trying to take a simple crap. Most unfortunate for him.

Fuck, I'm out of here!

I wanted to get out, but Stucky was laughing his ass off and blocking the main entry as I bumped into him, trying to escape. But getting past Stucky, built like an NFL lineman, proved impossible.

THE CRAPPER

I can't see shit. I'm stuck. Fuck me!

Thinking quickly, and perhaps fearing for my life at the hands of an enraged Marine, I decided the only other option was to exit through the seldom-used rear door. I bolted for the door and, moments later, made it out of the crapper and into the safety of the VIP hangar.

Whew! Made it.

As I was leaving, all I could hear was Stucky's deep voice, belly laughing. Moments later, having exited the VIP hangar, I ducked around back through the squadron lounge adjacent to the hangar and re-entered the main hallway just outside the bathroom door in time to see Stucky exiting the crapper, the light inside still off, and him still howling in laughter as only he could.

With that, the two of us, still laughing, walked down to the Operations counter at the far end of the hall, signed out for our upcoming flight, and waited to see who would exit the crapper. As we had a few minutes to spare before heading to our jets for our flights, we decided to wait and see our "new guy" exit the crapper. A good practical joke is even better when you can witness the outcome and share in the fun. We most definitely wanted to give the recipient of our joke a proper welcome to the squadron.

Less than two minutes later, we saw the new guy, Marty Macy, step out into the hallway, red-faced and, for an instant, looking more than a little upset. But, being new to the squadron, he wasn't quite sure who to be pissed at, as he was the "FNG" and still getting accustomed to this strange place he was just now getting a grip on.

Stucky and I broke out into another round of laughter when Macy came out of the crapper, and he looked like he was going to go on a tear. But when he saw us laughing it up at his expense, he quickly warmed up to us and, with a shit-eating grin on his face, yelled down the hall, "You fuckers! Thanks a lot. This is a god-damn dangerous place to take a shit."

"Welcome to the squadron, 'Fog,'" "Stook," still howling, managed to reply.

"You assholes! A guy can't even take a dump in peace around here," Marty continued, red-faced. Fortunately, he immediately sensed this was going to be an excellent assignment. With that, "Stook" and I filled Macy in on some of the little idiosyncrasies of the squadron and the rules of engagement, so to speak, of using the crapper.

These kinds of harmless shenanigans went on all the time. For instance, if you somehow discovered your security badge was missing, there was a better than even chance that someone had lifted it, and you would find it taped to the inside of one of the urinals. If you went to the bathroom, needed to use one of the urinals, you would always pick the one with the security badge taped to it and take good aim to avoid missing the target!

Hours later, if you hadn't noticed your badge was missing, someone would announce over the public address system, which was heard throughout the entire complex, that it had been located and where it could be retrieved. It didn't matter your rank; everyone was fair game.

Fast forward a few months, and the stage was set for what turned out to be a pretty comical and unforgettable experience for one unsuspecting visitor.

Being a prankster at heart, Maj "Paco" Geisler was known to play practical jokes on just about everyone, rank notwithstanding. If he didn't like you, he didn't, and you got the picture pretty quickly. One of his favorite targets was the handful of enlisted personnel assigned to the squadron's administrative section. When I say targets, it was all in good fun, and they knew it. While Geisler might have played jokes on them, he was still an officer, and they didn't lose sight of that fact. Yet, they knew he was always up to something, and they could always be counted on to play along. By now, you guessed it, several of these practical jokes involved that single bathroom midway down the hall.

On numerous occasions, Geisler would see one of our enlisted personnel about to enter the bathroom as he was coming out. He'd stop them, holding his arm across the entry, blocking the doorway, and say to them, with deadpan seriousness, "Hey, sorry, but the shitter is for officers only. You guys need to go outside." For a second, he had them going, thinking he was serious. Inevitably, they would chuckle, knowing Geisler was, again, screwing around with them, and reply good-naturedly, "Ah, come on, Maj Geisler, I really gotta go."

"Okay, just this once. But next time, it's outside for you and the rest. I'm tired of making exceptions for you guys," Geisler would add without breaking a smile. Seconds later, of course, he'd break out in a big smile, and they'd laugh about it and go on as if this were normal, because it was. Geisler wasn't afraid to test his humor on anyone, regardless of rank, and was one of those individuals who always got away with it.

Additionally, our enlisted men who worked in the squadron office were easy targets, as they conspicuously stood out in their dark blue polyester pants, light blue shirts, and highly polished black shoes, which were part of their everyday uniform. Everyone else in "Red Eagles" Operations was a pilot, all of whom were readily distinguishable by their flight suits and black boots.

On this particular day, as was routine before heading out to fly, Geisler entered the bathroom and headed for the urinal. As he was standing there, he looked over and saw a pair of dark blue polyester pants and shiny black shoes beneath the second stall. Upon finishing, he zipped up his flight suit and headed to the basin, washing and then drying his hands. As he was about to leave, he said in a loud, serious voice, "Hey, I thought I told you guys, if you need to take a shit, you gotta go outside."

With that, he walked out of the bathroom and, true to form, reached back and turned the light switch off before the door fully closed. Chuckling to himself, he headed back down the hallway to the Operations counter to sign out for his upcoming sortie. Once there, he decided to delay a bit to see who he'd turned off the lights on. Once again, like any practical joke, it was always more fun if you could see who the brunt of the joke was to get a laugh out of it yourself.

A couple of minutes went by – nothing. Geisler, sensing something was amiss, asked TSgt Jerry Howell, who was staffing the duty desk, "Any idea of who's in the shitter?" If anyone would know, Jerry would. He was the sort that always had his finger on the pulse of seemingly everything going on anywhere up at TTR.

"I have no idea," he said, "but I do know that there was an unscheduled VIP visit earlier. Some officers from the Pentagon were here along with some Congressional staffers, but other than that, I don't know who it might be."

Oh, shit!

Right about then, Geisler heard the bathroom door open and quickly looked down at the flight sign-out sheet, doing everything he could to make himself look busy, but not so much that he didn't sneak a glance down the hall to see who was stepping out of the bathroom.

Just then, out from the bathroom doorway, stepped a "full bird" (O-6) colonel, apparently one of the escort officers from the Pentagon, dressed in, you guessed it, blue polyester pants, blue uniform shirt, and shiny black shoes. He stopped just outside the doorway, looking up and down the hall. He must've been thinking to himself, "Who are these guys? I'm a full colonel, and I can't take a crap in peace!"

With that, Geisler looked at Howell and said, "Well, time for me to go flying," and headed for the door just a few steps away. But before stepping outside, Geisler looked back at Jerry and said, "Good luck. I hope that O-6 doesn't chew your ass. If he does, blame it on Stucky. I'm out of here."

Seconds later, Geisler waltzed out the door to make his way down to fly his awaiting MiG-21. Jerry Howell never heard a word about it, nor did our squadron commander. I'm sure that colonel, whoever he was, was no doubt too shocked and embarrassed to tell anyone. Another fine welcome to the 4477th. Luckily, it was Geisler that day instead of Stucky, or the colonel might've wound up wearing a trash can.

20

"You're Grounded!"

"No matter how bad you screwed up to get grounded, it's only a matter of time before someone else screws up worse than you, and you'll be back on the flying schedule in no time."

ROB "Z-MAN" ZETTEL

Rules – everyone's got them. And if you fly fighters, you're no exception. Ask any fighter pilot over a beer what one of their biggest gripes is, and high up on the list will be a passionate diatribe of the latest hair-brained rule or restriction that they're convinced will somehow keep them from being the best fighter jock in the world. We in the "Red Eagles" had ours. In the big scheme of things, not too many. However, we did have one that stood out from all the rest, and it was this – there was to be no air-to-air fighting in-house involving MiG assets.

You learned this rule early upon arrival in the 4477th TES, and assumed it was chiseled on a tablet of stone somewhere, handed down from Wing HQ. So, you could never expect to fight against one of your fellow MiG-21 or MiG-23 buddies 1-v-1. The rationale was simple. The limited number of assets we had shouldn't be wasted on training in-house, for which we could use another aircraft (e.g., T-38s and F-5Fs). The risk of losing one or more was deemed too significant in the event of a mid-air collision while conducting such training. Or so the logic went.

When upgrading a squadron pilot to fly either the MiG-21 or MiG-23, we would use a T-38 as a suitable adversary, thereby preserving the use of the MiGs solely for flying against USAF, US Navy, and US Marine Corps fighters. This rationale made sense to me, and most of us didn't question it. Plus, after flying an assigned air-to-air training sortie against an American fighter, you usually didn't have the fuel to dogfight with another MiG anyway. However, like many rules, it seemed there ought to be exceptions. This was one of them. Or perhaps it was more a case of thinking that exceptions should exist.

"YOU'RE GROUNDED!"

Okay, here's a little background to set the scene because you can sense what's coming. When a "Red Eagles" pilot had finished his flight in the area with his scheduled opponent, either because one of us had reached "bingo" fuel or the scheduled time for our range space had ended, we'd simply return to the pattern at TTR and land. This usually took a few minutes, and depending on which range you were flying back from and the traffic pattern configuration at TTR, it would also pretty much define your ground track back to the airfield.

Additionally, during the return, you also had to be aware of your squadron mates who possibly had ongoing engagements in adjoining areas, thus ensuring you didn't conflict with them. Hence, while recovering, we'd use our GCI controllers to help us avoid this traffic.

Naturally, there were plenty of times when you would be on your way back to the pattern at about the same time as one of your squadron mates. We rarely joined up, but we were often visual with each other as we approached the pattern. When you entered Initial, you'd be at traffic pattern altitude (1,000ft) and would typically be at 300KIAS. You planned your pattern arrival to be rolling wings level one to two miles from the approach end of the runway, and when "over the numbers," you would begin a hard turn with the throttle near idle and 60°–90° of bank, all the while slowing down to below 250KIAS and rolling out on the "Downwind" leg of the traffic pattern.

From there, you began to lower your landing gear and flaps as you approached the "Perch," from which you'd be at your final turn airspeed, and you started your descending turn to roll out aligned with the runway and land. It was a straightforward flight profile, one that fighter pilots have followed since their earliest days of flight training.

Now, as I previously mentioned, we often recovered at about the same time as one or two of our buddies at the TTR. Fighter pilots, being who we were, would eventually want to roll in on one of our squadron pals and discreetly call "Atoll" over the shared radio frequency to "pull their chain" a bit and let them know we were camped at their "six o'clock" and in a perfect position to "smoke 'em" with a simulated heat-seeking missile. Naturally, the other guy wasn't going to take kindly to this either. Having been the brunt of the joke, you could bet he would be on the prowl the whole way back to the pattern the following day to try to do the same should the opportunity present itself. You can see where this is headed.

In the early spring of 1985, these occurrences started simply enough with a couple of "dust-offs" by "Paco" Geisler on a few of the other "Red Eagles" pilots during returns to the pattern. Slowly, the word got out amongst the guys, "Hey, 'Paco' tapped me over Cactus Peak on the way back to Initial for RWY 14, so heads up. Don't let him bounce you like he did me. Better keep your speed up and head on a swivel." Of course, no one informed the squadron commander or the operations officer.

Over the next few weeks, a group of us, including Geisler, Lt Guy Brubaker, US Navy, Maj Paul Stucky, and Capts Denny Phelan, Steve Brown, and John Saxman, would not only be "checking our six" when returning to the pattern but also actively looking for others who might be on their way back too. After all, wasn't that what we trained all good fighter pilots to do – be on guard and never assume you were alone?

Due to this new "heightened awareness," many of us were also increasing our "bingo" fuel minimum by a small amount, perhaps by 100–200 liters. This additional margin allowed us to both recover at a higher airspeed and have an extra margin in case we had to execute a subtle, hard defensive turn on the way back home. I can distinctly remember tapping Phelan and Brubaker at least once on their way back to the pattern during this time, and I'm sure I was bounced once or twice as well. After a while, it was damn hard to surprise anyone as everybody had their eyes out and airspeed up.

By the end of April, pilots were entering Initial at 400KIAS, occasionally higher. I distinctly remember John Saxman entering the pattern one day, supersonic in his MiG-23! That was the extreme, but damn impressive when experienced from the ground.

If you happened to be in the tower as the SOF when this was happening, you'd see guys coming up Initial just hauling ass. A few seconds later, you'd know why, as you'd see another MiG-21 scorching up Initial and doing the same, and you knew they had been chasing each other.

It was even more impressive if you happened to be out on the ramp and could hear the distinct roar of the jets' Tumansky engines as they screamed up Initial at such airspeeds. Then suddenly, it'd all go quiet as the guys hit the break, snapped their throttles to idle, and broke hard to dissipate the 200–250KIAS they needed to lose in order to be able to safely lower the gear and flaps for landing. All good fun, and when you'd get on the ground, you'd go and chuckle about it with your buddy who'd been chasing you back. This went on for several weeks, but there was no mention of upping the ante and getting into a full-scale "furball." That all changed late one Friday afternoon during the last sorties of the day.

"YOU'RE GROUNDED!"

Friday, May 3, 1985
1450hrs Pacific Standard Time
Nellis range complex
MiG-21F-13

I was out in Area 71 and had just finished a series of engagements with an F-4 from George AFB that had reached its "bingo" fuel minutes earlier and had already received its ATC clearance to depart the area and return home. With no additional adversaries to engage and left with several hundred liters of fuel above my "bingo" limit, I was about to return to TTR when, out of curiosity, I asked my GCI controller, Capt Billy Bayer, where Capt Steve "Brownie" Brown, in "Bandit 32," was, and his status.

"Brownie" and I had taken off together 20 minutes earlier, each of us flying a MiG-21F-13. Following our 2-v-2 tactical intercept with the pair of Phantom IIs from George AFB, we split up to work with each F-4 separately in our respective areas. I knew "Brownie" was flying a similar sortie about 20 miles south of me in Area 76, and his adversary was probably at, or close to, "bingo" fuel as well, and would also be heading for home shortly. Knowing that Brown would then head back to TTR, flying in my direction, I told Bayer that I'd like a snap vector to him.

Our GCI controllers had begun to get in on the fun themselves and, for the previous few weeks, had been exceedingly helpful in telling us where our buddies were when we were on recovery so we wouldn't get tapped unawares – God bless 'em! Bayer told me Brown was just finishing up with his fighter, and he gave me a snap vector – "'Bandit Three-One', 'Bandit Three-Two' is One-Eight-Zero for 20." I immediately turned my fighter to a 180° heading and pushed the throttle up to the MIL power position. If I was going to dust off "Brownie," I wanted to do it at 400KIAS.

While heading his way, Bayer provided me with his best "bogey dope" on Brown's altitude. He also told me that Brown was RTB and was possibly aware that I was heading in his direction. I figure "Brownie's" controller had a bet going with Bayer as to who could find the other first, and pretty soon, you had two controllers doing their best to get their pilot's eyeballs on the other guy. I'm sure at the time, our controllers had no way of knowing this intercept was about to turn into the "furball" that it did. My intention was merely to dust off "Brownie" and then make a high-speed recovery back to the airfield, put the jets on the ground, and laugh about it later at the O'Club over beers. What happened next was unexpected, but after entirely predictable.

I was heading toward Brown's MiG-21 at 400KIAS and level at 17,000ft AGL. While I wasn't sure what altitude he was at, I had a good idea he was a bit higher based on the radar return Bayer was seeing at his control station back on the ground at Nellis. With our two MiGs closing fast, we each tried to gain a visual advantage before the other. If this had been actual combat, sighting him first would have been crucial for my survival. And when bragging rights and inflated egos are concerned, it may as well have been the real thing.

"One-Seven-Zero for three miles, slightly high," came the last call from Bayer.

Three miles! Damn, we're almost upon each other.

Luckily, the sun was farther to the southwest and not a factor as my eyes scanned an area just inches above my canopy, slightly to my left and higher. Today, I was flying one of our Soviet-built MiG-21s, and there was no canopy bow to obstruct my view, unlike in our Chinese F-7s. In another second, I spotted his desert-camouflaged MiG, slightly high at my "11 o'clock," now just a mile away. Wasting no time, I immediately started a left-climbing turn to close the lateral and vertical distance between us, attempting to give Brown nothing more than a dot to acquire visually. On his frequency, Brown was getting excellent "bogey dope" from his controller, Capt Jim "Smack" MacDonald, and he knew exactly where to look for me.

At about the same time I initiated my climb, I noticed "Brownie's" MiG roll sharply left, beginning a hard descending turn toward me. Our fighter pilot minds were in sync – he knew exactly what I was doing and instinctively what he needed to do with his aircraft. It would be a left-to-left pass, with Brown in a slight descending left turn, and me in a climbing left turn up and into him. We were about to merge 180° out from each other, separated by a scant 100 to 200ft.

As quickly as I saw him, and began to maneuver, we merged. As we passed, I noted he was continuing his left descending turn. Not wishing to allow Brown to escape so easily, I quickly reversed the direction of my turn, blending in full aft stick and pressing down hard on the right rudder pedal, compelling my fighter to reverse direction in as tight a turn as possible.

Immediately, I rolled my MiG onto its back and slammed the throttle fully forward, commanding full afterburner as I snapped my head around and spotted Brown's MiG-21 low and to my right at "four o'clock," and beginning to climb into me. His aircraft's subtle forward movement on my canopy told me he had a bit more speed, and I was quickly forcing him to react to my nose as I began to position myself to his "high six o'clock." As my fighter began to bleed airspeed swiftly in my hard 6G turn, I reached down and selected maneuvering flaps to help with what I knew would most assuredly be a slow-speed engagement.

In no time, we were a classic "right-rolling scissors," each trying to fly to the other's vulnerable "six o'clock" position. Brown was no slouch. An F-15 FWS graduate with years of experience in the Eagle before coming to the 4477th, he countered my moves with deft control of his aircraft. Our airspeeds were now well below 200KIAS. Locked together in a tight swirling spiral, our airspeeds were further slowing as we went through several revolutions of our "scissors," alternating positions on our backs, and then quickly rolling the airplane upright to stop our forward momentum. Three complete turns later, and our airspeeds hovered at 110KIAS, our two MiGs just 200–300ft apart, virtually canopy to canopy. I could see Brown in his cockpit as he countered each of my moves, his flight controls responding to his commands. It was simply an incredible visual spectacle.

After about 30 seconds of this stalemate, during which time neither our controllers nor ourselves had uttered a word, the radio came alive – "Knock it off!"

Oh shit! Who called "Knock It Off"? I thought we were trying to be discreet here.

Conditioned as we were to hearing a KIO call, we each acknowledged it on our separate frequencies. As quickly as the fight started, it was over, and we rolled apart and headed back to the airfield. We recovered separately to keep up the appearance of having just finished our sorties in our respective areas, the pitchout and landing being uneventful. What awaited us once we both got on the ground was anything but routine, and something neither of us had counted on.

Back on the ramp, as soon as we had both unstrapped and gotten out of our aircraft, we were met by the duty officer, Maj Tim "Stretch" Kinney, and he quickly told us we were to report to Maj Dave Bland's office as soon as we got our helmets and G-suits put away. "Oh, and by the way," Kinney added, "Blazo" [Bland] was in the tower as the SOF, and he saw you two knuckleheads knotted up in a fight on the Bright-Scope. Get ready for incoming, he's pissed!"

Oh shit – this isn't good!

Kinney was my flight commander, and without saying so, I'm sure he was a bit upset, as my stunt has probably put him in an uncomfortable position as well. Whatever the case, he never mentioned it to me – perhaps that was the reason I never became the Chief of Staff of the Air Force!

Maj Dave "Blazo" Bland was the 4477th TES's operations officer, having taken over the position upon Maj Monroe Watley's departure roughly a year earlier. As such, he was directly responsible for all squadron flight operations. I'd known Bland for years since I'd gone through the Aggressor course in the 65th AS as a student, where he had been an IP. Before becoming an Aggressor, Bland had completed several tours in the Phantom II, as well as being a graduate of the F-4 FWS. For him to have been in the tower was almost unheard of, as it was a duty usually relegated to more junior officers in the squadron. Whatever the case, he had seen Brown and me in a close-in engagement, and in a few minutes, we were about to find out what fate awaited us.

The Bright-Scope was a display unit in the tower that showed the position of airborne traffic in direction and range relative to the airfield. It was now apparent that Bland had been able to see our two separate radar returns merge and then stay that way for the brief duration of our "furball." He'd made a quick call to our controllers, verifying as much, and he was the one who had called the KIO.

Our goose was cooked. Some sage advice I'd heard years before as a young lieutenant immediately sprang into my head – "Fuck up and Fess up." As we walked together to Operations, it felt a lot like going to see the principal when I was back in grade school, following some prank for which I was about to get handed some punishment. "Brownie" wasn't too happy and was visibly worried. I was joking with him and trying to tell him not to worry.

"How bad can it be?" I said to him as we walked back to Operations. "We'll probably get grounded for a bit and have to pull SOF a day or two, and that'll be it. No sweat."

Minutes later, we were standing in Bland's office, at attention, and kept that way even after having reported as ordered and saluting sharply. Despite the dressing down we were about to absorb, here's where it gets interesting. Bland shared his office with "Paco" Geisler, who, as the assistant operations officer, was conveniently sitting at his desk to our right, purposely pretending to look busy and uninterested as Bland proceeded to rip each of us a new one. That's right, the verbal tongue-lashing he was handing out was loud enough that there was no mistaking down the hallway that "Z-Man" and "Brownie" were up shit creek with no paddle in sight.

As I stood there, I admittedly had a slight smirk on my face as I thought about the irony of being in the same room as Geisler, who had somewhat instigated all this months ago, and I knew was silently laughing his ass off. After all, for him, this was better than being the proverbial fly on the wall. He had a ringside seat to a first-class ass-chewing of epic proportions!

And, of course, being proper "Officers and Gentlemen," we never gave a moment's thought to ratting out Geisler for his part in it all. No, we took our medicine in our stride. Thank goodness Bland never asked if others in the squadron had been engaging in similar frolics – phew!

"YOU'RE GROUNDED!"

After five minutes of getting our shit handed to us, Bland dished out our punishment. While Bland was on vacation the following week, Brown and I would be grounded until he returned. Furthermore, we would be the only two guys in the squadron scheduled to pull SOF duty while we were grounded. Then, to top it off, Bland said he'd decide once he was back the following week whether he would put us back on the flight schedule.

Ouch! This is going to hurt.

The most painful part for me wouldn't be the mere grounding. No, it was losing out flying four to six MiG sorties to my buddies while exiled to the tower undertaking SOF duty. That absolutely sucked! But I deserved it. So, I just stood there, hoping the following week would pass quickly. I also expected Bland would ease up by the time he returned, and things would return to normal. After all, I knew Dave Bland to be a good guy, but there was no way he could overlook something as flagrant as what "Brownie" and I had done.

Time to pay the piper, "Z-Man"!

Upon finishing, he told "Brownie," who by now was looking like a kid who had just lost his puppy, to quit looking so put out. Next, glaring at me, he told me to wipe the smirk off my face and to start taking this seriously. The smirk was gone pretty damn quickly.

Our butt-chewing over and punishment meted out, he asked us if we had anything to say. Of course, we didn't. Rule No. 1 – never whine and whimper when you're as guilty as sin. With nothing more to say, Bland dismissed us. We both saluted and turned to leave the room. As I trailed Brown out the office door, Geisler caught my attention, giving me one of his famous cross-eyed "man with dementia" looks that told me he thought this was funnier than all hell, and not to worry – also, by the way, thanks for not ratting me out. I almost laughed right there and then, and was glad Bland couldn't see my face as I left the room.

The flight back to Nellis that Friday afternoon was a quiet one. The rest of the guys on the MU-2 understood what had happened, and I'm sure they were glad it hadn't been them who got caught. Naturally, there was the usual ribbing from them and plenty of laughs, all at "Brownie" and my expense. But I can't say it was a fun flight back south. Once at Nellis AFB, and following our debriefs, a good number of us made our way to the O'Club and the usual Friday night crowd that entailed. A few beers later, it was all behind me. Or at least that's what I told myself.

I've got a saying that goes like this. "No matter how bad you screwed up to get grounded, it's only a matter of time before someone else screws up worse than you, and you'll be back on the flying schedule in no time." Little did I know that was exactly what would happen, but the biggest surprise was the who and how. I wouldn't have to wait long. Squadron wives – you gotta love 'em!

The following evening, the squadron hosted a "going away" dinner party at a local Las Vegas restaurant for one of our GCI controllers who was leaving for another assignment. As was customary, following dinner, before the squadron commander made a few remarks about the departing officer, the commander's wife had her turn to say goodbye to the officer's spouse. Typically, this would include thanking the departing officer's wife for her involvement in the Officers' Wives Club, offering a few other pleasantries, sharing a few humorous anecdotes, and then presenting her with a bouquet of roses. Mild applause, photos, and so on always followed this. It was usually pretty standard and sedate, but not this night.

Apparently, this man's wife had little to no interaction with the rest of the squadron wives and harbored a total disdain for anything and everything related to the Officers' Wives Club. Right or wrong, such loathing for this group was not exactly helpful to your husband's career. Additionally, and unbeknownst to me, the departing officer was not exactly in Lt Col Phil White's good graces either – he had been the 4477th TES's commander for much of the past year following George Gennin's departure the previous July. As a bachelor, and unaware of the potential for internal catfights among the wives, I was clueless about the reasons for what happened next.

When Phil's wife began to talk, what started as a mild and polite thank-you and wishes for good luck on the next assignment suddenly and unexpectedly turned into a back-handed send-off. Now, in her defense, I doubt this was what she intended, but more likely, it was a case of someone's mouth not being engaged with their brain. I'm giving her the benefit of the doubt, and also assume several "adult beverages" might've been involved. Regardless, after she finished, the noticeably shocked wife, to her credit, accepted the bouquet and, without saying anything, sat back down. There was a palpable uneasiness in the room.

Damn! That sucked. What the fuck was that?

Next, Phil White stood up and went through his remarks, presenting the officer with a squadron plaque, thanking him for his contributions to the mission, and wishing him luck in his next assignment. I'm sure there was more, but after his wife's performance, I don't think many in attendance paid much attention to what Phil had to say. All were still trying to comprehend what they'd just witnessed minutes earlier.

"YOU'RE GROUNDED!"

Shortly after, the send-off concluded, and most of us retired to the bar, had a few drinks, and called it a night. However, amongst the wives, trouble was just about to start brewing. Again, being a bachelor, I was spared all the drama that was soon to take place, oblivious to the shitstorm that irate wives can generate. All that was on my mind was that I would be carrying out SOF duty the following week, and along with "Brownie," would most certainly miss out on at least four to six flights in the MiG-21 while Geisler and my other pals happily picked up the slack. Lucky bastards!

Tuesday, May 9, 1985
"Red Eagles" Operations
Tonopah Test Range

TSgt Jerry Howell popped his head into Geisler's office with the news that the commander was on the phone for him. "Maj Geisler, Col White is on line two for you," Howell said. "He sounds stressed." Jerry, from his position staffing the Operations desk in the squadron, was one of the best at screening calls – a gifted NCO, the squadron was lucky to have him. In short, Jerry had his finger on the pulse of everything in the squadron and was your go-to guy if you needed the inside skinny on what was happening behind the scenes. Today was no different, with his "heads-up" to Geisler being spot on.

"Thanks, Jerry," replied Geisler. "Does he sound pissed or just worried?"

"Not pissed, just not the usual laid-back tone I normally get from him," Jerry replied.

Geisler nodded, reached for the phone on his desk, and hit the blinking light connecting him to Phil White, who had remained at Nellis today, attending to other "pressing business." The previous afternoon, he'd told Geisler, now the acting operations officer while Bland was away on leave, to go to TTR with the rest of the pilots without him in the morning, but he'd planned on coming up on Wednesday.

"So, 'Paco,' how's everything going today?" White asked. "Things running smoothly?"

Geisler filled him in on the unit in town for their week of *Constant Peg* exposures, and thus far, the morning schedule had come off without a hitch. He then quickly added another tidbit that he knew would send White through the ceiling.

"Yeah, other than 'Z-Man' and 'Brownie' pulling SOF duty all week, things are going great," he added, knowing the grenade was about to detonate in White's head. There was dead silence on the other end of the line for a moment. Geisler knew his last comment had surprised White, for he was sure Bland had never told him about the shenanigans "Brownie" and I had been up to the previous Friday afternoon.

"What the fuck are they doing pulling SOF duty?" White asked. "All week?"

Geiser filled him in on the "furball" in our MiGs, the dressing-down Bland gave us, and as punishment, exiling us to the tower for the entire week until he returned from vacation the following Monday. White exploded. "Fuck that, 'Paco'," he yelled. "Get 'Z-Man' and 'Brownie' back on the schedule ASAP! I've got a shitstorm going on down here with colonels calling me, wives calling me, as this going-away party debacle has turned into a fucking mess. And keep this under wraps as well. The last thing I need is for fucking Ashy to ask why two of my pilots are grounded."

White was correct about the last part. Had Brig Gen Joe Ashy, the 57th FWW commander, found out we had been grounded for wrapping it up as we had, there's no telling what he would've done. Undoubtedly, "Smoking Joe" would've come unhinged, as Ashy was apt to do over almost anything. Had he found out, my days as a "Red Eagle" would most likely have been over, and this book would never have been written.

"Yes, Sir. I'll make sure they're on tomorrow's schedule," Geisler replied, "not a problem." After exchanging a few other remarks, White hung up.

Geisler quietly chuckled as, ironically, he knew the scheduler for tomorrow's flying was none other than me. He called me in the tower minutes later, where I was working off my penance as SOF, and gave me the news. My theory held. Given enough time, someone else would fuck up enough to overshadow anything you might've done to get yourself grounded, and you would be back on the schedule in no time. I made sure "Brownie" and I "double-banged" (sortied) the next day. After all, they were the commander's orders!

Thursday, May 11, 1985
"Red Eagles" Operations
Tonopah Test Range

Just finishing his lunch at the duty desk within "Red Eagles" Operations, Jerry Howell picked up the phone and pushed the illuminated button, answering the incoming call. "4477th Operations, TSgt Howell speaking."

On the other end of the phone was Dave Bland, who asked if Geisler was around.

"Yes, sir, he's standing right here," replied Howell. "Just a moment." With that, Jerry hit the hold button and looked at Geisler, standing at the Operations counter. "Sir, it's Maj Bland. He'd like to speak with you."

"Thanks, Jerry. I'll go pick it up in my office," Geisler replied, before turning and heading across the hall, entering his office, and shutting the door behind him. He knew what was about to happen and wanted to set up Bland for maximum effect. Seconds later, he hit the blinking light on his phone.

"What's going on, 'Blazo'? You missing us so much that you can't enjoy your vacation without calling?" came Geisler's smartass answer.

"Hardly," was Dave Bland's quick reply. After discussing how things were going at TTR and the units arriving over the weekend for next week's flying schedule, Bland cut to the question Geisler knew was coming.

"So, how are 'Brownie' and 'Z-Man' doing?" Bland asked. "Enjoying their SOF tours?"

Geisler, fully anticipating Bland's smug question, was ready, knowing full well his answer would send him through the ceiling. "Yeah, they're doing great," he said. "They 'double-banged' yesterday, and I think they're out flying right now as we speak." Geisler pauses a moment for effect and then continues, "Yeah, everything is going well. They're happy campers." Geisler knew precisely how to push Bland's buttons, and his deadpan delivery was pitch perfect.

Just seconds later, the phone exploded. "What the fuck are they doing flying? I grounded those two until I say otherwise!" shouted Bland.

Geisler laughed into the phone and simply replied, "Yeah, but you're not the squadron commander, and White told me Tuesday to put them on the schedule as he had more important things to deal with, namely, irate wives. So, I did what he ordered me to do."

Turning a bit more serious, Geisler then offered this, "And by the way, here's just a bit of advice. If I were you, I'd let this one go, as White is pissed that you grounded them without telling him. He is worried that 'Ash-nuts' might find out. That's the last thing we need. Fucking Ashy jumping in our shit. So, I'd drop it."

Geisler's answer was met with a few moments of silence on the other end of the line. It was apparent that Bland hadn't expected "Brownie" and me to be back flying so soon, and by the direction of the squadron commander, no less. "Okay, he's the boss. But I'm not happy about it." His curt reply told "Paco" that Bland was seething on the other end of the phone line. Sensing an opportunity to put the issue behind them, Geisler quickly replied, "Hey,

I think they and the rest of the guys got the message. I wouldn't worry about it any further. 'Brownie' and 'Z-Man' are great guys. No need to pile on any further, 'Blazo.'"

With that, the issue was behind us, and with Bland's return the following week, things were back to normal as expected. Nothing more was said or mentioned about it by anyone. The days of getting dusted off by your buddies returning from the ranges were over, and it was time to move on to more significant issues.

In five weeks, several others and I would fly a handful of MiGs to Area 51, where we'd be operating for nine weeks at a reduced schedule while the runway at TTR was being lengthened (see Chapter 16 for details). In the meantime, "Brownie" and I were flying full schedules, the beneficiaries of a handful of irate wives whose internal catfight had unwittingly saved our bacon. Oddly enough, I never got a chance to thank them!

21

TOPGUN

"The difference between men and boys is the price of their toys."
ANONYMOUS

September 24, 1985
"Red Eagles" Operations
Tonopah Test Range

"Hey, Capt 'Z,' there's a call for you on extension nine-eight," called TSgt Jerry Howell from his seat at the squadron Operations desk, immediately adjacent to the flight room I was working in. "Someone from TOPGUN, a lieutenant commander. I missed the last name. Wants to know about the schedule later this week," Howell added. I pushed back from the working copy of tomorrow's schedule I was busily trying to finish up, picked up the phone, and punched the flashing button labeled "98," answering the call, "Capt Zettel here. May I help you, sir?"

"Hey, 'Z-Man,' 'Hollywood' here at Miramar. How's it going today?" he asked. "Are my guys kicking ass and taking names?" "Hollywood's" opening line was jokingly referring to this week's flying schedule, heavily laden with MiG sorties dedicated to the current class of TOPGUN F-14 and F/A-18 students going through the US Navy's premier air-to-air combat training program at the Fighter Weapons School at Naval Air Station (NAS) Miramar, in San Diego, California.

"I haven't heard any reports of total buffoonery on the part of the Navy and Marines so far, but it's early in the week, so they've still got plenty of time to fuck it up!" I chuckled.

Lt Cdr Greg "Hollywood" Dishart, US Navy, was a great guy and someone I'd gotten to know professionally over the past couple of years while he was an IP at TOPGUN. Oh, and by the way, the callsign was perfect. Although the movie *TOP GUN* wouldn't be released until the following year, the director missed the mark when he cast Tom Cruise in the lead role. This "Hollywood" was authentic. Not only was he an actual fighter pilot (and taller!), his natural good looks were sure to turn every female head in any O'Club or bar he entered. Plus, he was, as fighter pilots are apt to say, "a great shit!"

"I hear ya," "Hollywood" laughed. "Hey, 'Z-Man,' I've got a request for this Thursday's schedule," he added, then paused as if hesitant to proceed. "Would it be possible for me to bag a sortie against a MiG-21 Thursday afternoon?" he continued. "Normally, I wouldn't ask, but this is the last opportunity I'll have before I head back to the fleet in the Tomcat, and I was hoping to knock heads with a MiG-21 as sort of a farewell send-off."

While assigned at NAS Miramar, one of "Hollywood's" additional duties was as TOPGUN's liaison to the 4477th TES whenever one of its classes was scheduled to fly against our MiGs as part of the curriculum. This occurred roughly once every eight to ten weeks. So, as the squadron scheduler, I'd had the opportunity to interact with "Hollywood" quite regularly. But this was the first time he'd ever asked for a sortie for himself – moreover, a dedicated MiG-21 sortie at that.

"No problem at all, 'Hollywood.' What time would you like?" I countered.

"How about the last sortie of the afternoon? After that, when I land back here at Miramar, I'll be ready to pound a few beers," he added quickly. "Oh, and one more thing," he said.

"Yeah, sure. What is it, 'Hollywood'?"

"Well . . . I want to fight you!"

Me? Not one of our Navy guys? Like "Rookie," "Bad Bob," or "Brudog"?

I was a bit taken aback. In the fighter world, it was a particularly flattering gesture to be asked by name to fly against anyone. This request was even more of an honor as it came from an esteemed and capable member of the US Navy's highly regarded Fighter Weapons School. While unorthodox, "Hollywood's" request was one I couldn't pass up. Being the squadron scheduler had its perks, and one of them was penciling yourself into the schedule to fight against a TOPGUN IP, not a student. If there was yet another way to measure my true air combat skill set, going 1-v-1 with "Hollywood" would undoubtedly be it. Then again, perhaps "Hollywood" was thinking the very same.

To provide proper context to his request, it was nearly impossible to simply ask to fly with the pilot of your choice from another squadron. Additionally, this wasn't just any squadron "Hollywood" was asking to snag a sortie with, but the very top-secret MiG squadron few even knew about. Moreover, to be paired against the fighter of your choice, and arguably one of their best pilots, was simply unheard of. No amount of money anywhere could buy you this. This was the epitome of "big boys and their toys."

"You're on, 'Hollywood,'" I quickly replied. I proceeded to pencil my name in the line adjacent to a box dedicated to a TOPGUN/MiG-21 sortie on Thursday afternoon, presumably for a TOPGUN student. But this wasn't to be a student but a formidable opponent, one who taught the very best of the US Navy's fighter jocks how to be even better. Depending on the outcome, this would be one air combat training engagement to remember, or perhaps one to quickly forget.

"Better bring your A-game, 'Hollywood'," I added. "The loser buys the beers at the next Tailhook convention. See you airborne Thursday afternoon. Oh, and 'Hollywood,' thanks. I know you could've asked for anyone. I look forward to it."

"See you then, 'Z-Man.' Remember to 'check six!'" And with that, he hung up.

Who said chivalry was dead? This was a request to fight me because "Hollywood" knew I'd give him the best-flown MiG-21 possible. If he could beat me, that would be a high note to leave TOPGUN on. If he couldn't, he'd know which MiG-21 pilot not to get into a fight with!

Two days later, I met up with "Hollywood" in Area 76 of the Nellis range complex. I don't remember doing a tactical intercept with another "Red Eagles" pilot beforehand, or whether I had just launched as a single bandit. Whatever the case, it doesn't matter.

What did matter was the type of fighter I was about to face. TOPGUN IPs flew both F-5s and A-4 Skyhawks in the adversary role. For some reason, I'd just assumed "Hollywood" would be flying an F-5E, the same as those I'd flown previously while an Aggressor – an aircraft I was all too familiar with. What surprised me, however, as I neared my opponent that afternoon, was the tiny silhouette of an A-4E turning into me, level for five miles. It was a mere speck of an airplane. As a fighter pilot, it's never good to be surprised by anything when you're about to enter a fight. Today, I was surprised.

This engagement would be something new to me, as I hadn't previously flown a dedicated sortie against an A-4E. It was a formidable adversary and, in the hands of a top-notch fighter jock like "Hollywood," simply lethal. TOPGUN IPs had briefed their students that the MiG-21 was similar to an F-5E above 300KIAS and more like an A-4E below that speed. Since we'd be engaging in a visual setup, we'd be unlikely to exceed 300KIAS, except for the initial start of the fight. That being the case, "Hollywood" would be pretty comfortable fighting me in the "phone booth."

Today, I expected to be on the low side of the 300KIAS figure and, more likely, closer to 100KIAS. That's where I preferred to be when dealing with just one bandit in the visual arena, working the fight to the advantage of my airplane. My thinking was to keep the opponent close and out-fly him until he made a critical mistake. In "Hollywood's" cockpit, he must have been thinking the same – wrap up the MiG-21 in a tight turning engagement where the A-4E could negate its speed advantage. Hopefully, it wouldn't be a mistake on my part that defined the outcome.

The "Mongoose," as the modified Skyhawk was affectionately known in TOPGUN circles, was an excellent aircraft with a reliable track record, making it a favorite among many IPs. The A-4s flown at TOPGUN were generally E- and F-models powered by the Pratt & Whitney J52-P-6A engine developing 8,500lb of thrust. Additionally, stripped of unnecessary equipment and weapons, the aircraft were as lightweight as possible, making them all the more maneuverable in the slow-speed regime.

It wasn't long before we were both on the same frequency and had visuals on each other. Moments later, I started an easy left-hand turn and directed "Hollywood" to join up on my left wing. As he came alongside, I was amazed at the small size of his mottled-gray camouflaged A-4E. It was one thing to see it sitting on the ramp. There, it didn't look so small. But when it was just a couple of hundred feet away off my left wing, with nothing but empty sky or barren desert behind it, well, that was yet another surprise. All I could see of "Hollywood" was his helmet and some of his shoulders!

How does he fit into that thing?

Part of the "briefed" visual scenarios were both offensive and defensive setups, whereby we'd typically give the adversary we were flying against the option to choose either or both, fuel permitting. There were to be no "neutral" setups – an intentional directive from higher headquarters, supposedly in the interest of safety. But today's engagement called for something a bit different. After all, "Hollywood" wasn't some nugget on his first flight up-range. Also, it would have been a bit of an insult to ask him to take the offensive setup option or, worse, be defensive. I intended to make this a neutral setup on his last flight against a "Red Eagles'" MiG-21. It would be a fitting test of two top-notch fighter pilots at the top of their game.

I asked "Hollywood" to maintain his heading while I gently turned away from him, slowly increasing the distance between us until we were roughly 1,000ft apart, with me slightly ahead of his wing line at "two o'clock." With the lateral distance set, I did a slight roll back to my left, matching his heading, and called for us to accelerate to 400KIAS.

Right now, "Hollywood" was sucked back to my "seven" to "eight o'clock," and if I wanted to make this a neutral setup, I needed to do it subtly, lest anyone be monitoring our frequency and hear the word "neutral" be uttered. The solution was simple.

"TOPGUN, check 40 left." I directed over the radio.

At my call, I immediately saw "Hollywood's" A-4E roll into a level 30° left-banking turn and hold it until he again rolled wings level seconds later, now established on a new heading. Watching him, I did precisely the same, the quick maneuver now placing our two fighters 1,000ft apart and line abreast, level at 20,000ft, and steady at 400KIAS. With our jets established on a south-southeast heading, the late afternoon sun was high at "two o'clock" and not a factor – visibility was unlimited. It was a perfect day for a "knife fight" – fighter pilot lingo for close-in air combat maneuvering (ACM) at distances too close to allow for the employment of missiles, which meant the gun was your primary weapon. This was about as manly as it got!

"'Bandit Four-One' is ready. Call when you're all set, 'TOPGUN,'" I informed "Hollywood" over the radio, indicating that the MiG-21 1,000ft away at his right "three o'clock" was "ready to rock."

Hard turn into him. Single-circle fight. Work to his "high six." Force him to pass below. Drive the fight!

As I'd mentioned, while I knew what my capabilities were, I was a bit unsure of my opponent. Other than the A-4E having an excellent reputation for being an incredibly agile, slow-speed adversary, I was aware that "Hollywood" had set me up in his comfort zone, where he should excel. I would find out if this was indeed the case in the next few minutes.

"'TOPGUN' is ready," was his quick response. A double click of my mic button told "Hollywood" that I'd understood. He was all set to go, and expecting my next radio call to start this aerial gladiatorial match.

Game on, "Hollywood," time to rock!

"'TOPGUN,' fight's on, fight's on," came my call to commence full-on, unrestricted maneuvering. I hadn't even released the mic button when I saw "Hollywood's" A-4E roll hard right and immediately begin a high-G turn into me. Even at just 1,000ft, the planform view of the "Mongoose's" 27ft wingspan simply looked tiny. Then again, with an even narrower wingspan of 23ft, my MiG-21 must have seemed farther away to "Hollywood" than, in reality, it was.

The MiG-21's size was deceptive. No matter how often you told yourself it was small, and tried to mentally prepare for its diminutive dimensions before engaging the fighter in DACT, you never fully appreciated the challenge the "Fishbed's" size presented until you experienced it in a close-aboard dogfight.

Without hesitation, I simultaneously mirrored his initial move, while also shoving my single throttle fully forward and commanding full afterburner. While both initial turns would deny the possibility of either fighter attaining nose position inside each other's turning circle, there was no doubt our two fighters would cross paths dangerously close within seconds. With my lift vector placed imperceptibly above his fuselage, I aimed to gain a subtle positional advantage above him as I prepared to lead-turn the fast-approaching A-4E and force the engagement into a "knife fight."

God, that thing can turn. Pass him on the high side. Get ready to reverse.

Such a fight generally favored the tighter-turning fighter. Once our airplanes crossed, "Hollywood" would either reverse back left and into me, committing to a classic slow-speed engagement, or continue his hard right-hand turn away and try to escape. I was betting on the former, as "Hollywood" knew all too well that his A-4E couldn't escape my much faster MiG-21. At this close range, he was committed, as was I.

My initial turn had placed me slightly inside and higher than the A-4E, and as we closed inside of 300ft, I began a hard reversal back to the right, blending in full right rudder and positioning the stick nearly full aft and right. Despite my engine at full afterburner, both of us were dissipating airspeed at a tremendous rate. Not that I needed to, but a glance inside at the airspeed indicator showed the needle dropping below 275KIAS, with no sign of stopping. It was a regime in which I felt comfortable, and my airplane performed exceptionally well.

Flaps down, full aft stick, better pitch rate than the A-4 – continue what you've got.

Without delay, I selected flaps down, enabling my fighter to continue slowing even further without any degradation in handling. Without the flaps extended, the MiG-21 was incapable of fighting effectively at slow airspeeds, which would give "Hollywood" all he needed to saddle up and eventually gun me. But not today.

Our fighters crossed within 150ft of each other, my MiG-21 slightly higher and just aft of "Hollywood," who had also led his left reversal back into me by this time. He was now slightly lower and at my "two o'clock" as we prepared to cross flight paths for a second time, now in a classic "flat scissors," each of us vying to flush the other out in front. From my vantage point, I could clearly see that the leading-edge slats of his fighter were fully extended, providing every ounce of additional lift they could muster, enabling the agile A-4E to stay with me. It was an incredible sight to see someone handling a fighter so smoothly and with such skill.

Damn, he's good. Keep inching it a bit higher. I've got better high AOA capability than the "Mongoose"!

I was slowly gaining a bit of altitude separation from "Hollywood," as my MiG-21's pitch authority at these slow speeds was ever so slightly better than that of the A-4E. As our two jets crossed paths yet again, I was about 200ft above and slightly aft of him, at his right "three" to "four o'clock," but still in no position to bring my nose to bear and gun him. I just didn't have the necessary turning room yet. I'd have to flush him farther out front and force him into committing an error.

Roll off to the left at the cross. Force a "rolling scissors." The "Mongoose" can't stay with me!

In the scant 30 seconds since we had locked horns, it had subtly become apparent the A-4E didn't have the slow-speed, high AOA capability of my MiG-21. I'd assessed all this in just two quick passes, the ever-so-slight forward movement of "Hollywood's" fighter on my canopy and my slight increase of altitude separation being the telling signs. We were at less than 175KIAS and slowing further, yet I still had plenty of pitch and roll authority. Now was the time to exploit that advantage. The next move would determine the outcome. It was three-dimensional chess, and I was about to move my Queen to a position he couldn't escape from. His subsequent moves would only work to my advantage, as each turn and roll further depleted his energy, allowing me to slowly squeeze his A-4 out in front of me.

I had just about got the control stick fully aft, and could sense, at this high AOA, that the ailerons were beginning to lose their effectiveness – the outer portions of my wings were nearing the stall. Luckily, the trump card in this fight was the MiG-21's large rudder and its incredible effectiveness. With the stick now centered and just about in my lap, I was asking for every bit of lift available, the rudder being my only means of effective directional control. Adding slight pressure on the left rudder pedal, my MiG banked gently in that direction, moving me toward "Hollywood's" "high six o'clock." From where he sat, all he could see was my MiG-21 crossing high and behind him. What I had in store wasn't just another "flat scissors" crossing, but something more aggressive that would force his hand.

Bury the stick, full rudder – NOW!

Judging that I had sufficient separation, I immediately pushed down hard on the left rudder pedal and pulled the stick fully aft. An aggressive but smoothly flown maneuver put the MiG-21 into a fully loaded roll to the left. Without relaxing an ounce of stick pressure, the rolling jet continued through a fully inverted position before becoming upright again and then ending up below and slightly aft of my adversary. I was showing 110KIAS on the airspeed indicator, and there was no hint of a stall or hesitation as the MiG carved a smooth arc around the A-4E.

As soon as I rolled off, "Hollywood," being no slouch, immediately reacted to my maneuver and initiated his own loaded roll to the left, desperately trying to counter my move. As I rounded out at the bottom of the loaded roll, I noted the A-4E attempting to follow me. I'd anticipated this, as I would have done the same.

Good move, "Hollywood." Now let's see how tight and slow your "Mongoose" can fly!

Seeing this, I didn't stop my loaded roll but continued with the stick buried and the left rudder pedal still fully depressed against its stop. For the uninitiated, our two fighters were locked in a classic "rolling scissors," where the pilot who could fly slower and still maintain control would slowly flush the other out in front. We were canopy to canopy in a swirling aerial vortex, separated by less than 200ft, and losing 400–500ft of altitude with each full 360° roll.

We continued through four complete revolutions of this maneuver, with me gaining incremental vertical and nose/tail separation with each pass. Simply stated, my MiG-21 could fly slower and at a higher AOA than "Hollywood" in his A-4E, which was slowly squeezing him out in front of me.

Gaining separation. Passing 15,000ft. Another cycle, and you'll have what you need!

Coming over the top and inverted on the fifth cycle of this "rolling scissors," I had enough nose/tail separation to make my move, and one I was adept at. The trick was to stop the "rolling scissors" and simultaneously roll inside your adversary, bringing your nose to bear on him. However, it could only be done with sufficient room and AOA authority to pull it off.

Okay, "Z-Man," unload and roll!

Instantly, I eased the stick forward and pushed it fully left. With the airplane now unloaded to near-zero Gs and the ailerons again effective, the MiG's roll response was immediate and stunning. Eyeing "Hollywood" just a few hundred feet away, I adjusted my roll rate to place him in the lower right-front quarter of my canopy and then came back with full aft stick, centering the rudder and anchoring me inside his turn. The MiG-21 did the rest, making me look like a magician.

In seconds, I'd stopped my loaded rolling maneuver and gone from "Hollywood's" "high 12 o'clock" in a "rolling scissors" to a position inside his turn, with fuselages nearly aligned. With me now at his "low seven o'clock" and just 500ft away, his options were few as his aircraft couldn't outmaneuver me and survive. "Hollywood's" two additional attempts to shake me proved futile as my more powerful and agile MiG was on him like a dog with a bone. Furthermore, he was hard-pressed to see my attacking MiG-21 except for a few fleeting glances between jinking maneuvers, making a credible defensive game plan impossible.

Checkmate!

With the A-4E unable to evade further and filling my gunsight, there was no need to call a gun kill. Instead, I rendered "Hollywood" the professional courtesy he was due and made a simple call. "'Bandit Four-One,' knock it off!"

"'TOPGUN,' knock it off!" came his acknowledgment that the fight was over.

It was an incredible fight against a very credible and skilled pilot. We had a second engagement that ended in much the same fashion, proving yet again that the MiG-21F-13, in that setup, was the superior aircraft. I'd like to think that if the roles had been reversed and I had been in the A-4E, "Hollywood" would've lined me up in the MiG-21's gunsight as well.

Following the second engagement, and reaching his "bingo" fuel to return to NAS Miramar, "Hollywood" wasted no time picking up his clearance from Los Angeles Center for his 240-mile flight back home. On the other hand, I had only 30 miles to get back to TTR, yet I was close to my minimum fuel limit just to do that. The takeaway was that, despite narrowly beating the A-4E in a close-in visual fight, the severe range and endurance limitations of the MiG-21 were readily apparent to both of us. In actual combat, such a limitation would limit how and where the "Fishbed" could effectively be employed – a lesson borne out years later during *Desert Storm*, where Iraqi MiG-21s were in large part notably absent in the ensuing air battle.

Lest you think that all my experiences flying against TOPGUN instructors or students were favorable for me in the MiG-21, I can assure you that was hardly the case. Moreover, just as with USAF F-15s and F-16s, it was generally a mixed assortment of success and failure for my adversaries. And in those engagements, whether they were successful or not, came many lessons learned, often by me. One notable drubbing I was on the receiving end of was by an F/A-18A TOPGUN student. To this day, it remains perhaps the best display of aircraft handling in a slow-speed dogfight I have ever seen.

On this occasion, I witnessed the incredible slow-speed, high AOA capabilities of the Hornet during a close-in, "flat-scissors" engagement. Just when I thought I was about to "tree" my adversary high above me, with neither of us having the turning room nor power to bring guns to bear, I learned a valuable lesson – don't get slow with a Hornet because he could sting you badly! In this particular case, I watched, fascinated, as the pilot worked his way from a position at my "high 12 o'clock" to one where he, in short order, gunned me like a stationary strafe panel. All this, as I was hanging like a kite at high AOA and at no more than 110KIAS. It was an impressive feat, and a testament to TOPGUN's skilled IPs and comprehensive training program. Well done TOPGUN, well done!

22

Coincidence or a Prelude to History?

"Coincidence is God's way of remaining anonymous."
                                                        ALBERT EINSTEIN

September 17, 1985
1410hrs Pacific Daylight Time
Nellis Military Operating Area 23 nautical miles north-northwest of Groom Lake
MiG-21F-13 "Bandit 14"

"'Control,' 'bogey dope.'" With his radio call, Maj "Paco" Geisler queried our GCI controller, who today was Capt Jim "Smack" MacDonald, as to whether he was showing any contacts to the north of our established Combat Air Patrol (CAP) orbits.

"Negative 'Bandit One-One,' the scope is clean," came MacDonald's quick response. The AN/FPS-27A radar antenna that he was reliant upon, perched atop Angel Peak at more than 8,800ft MSL, 25 miles to the west of Nellis AFB, simply couldn't detect any low-altitude targets much below 10,000ft MSL. The mountainous ridgelines, prevalent throughout the Nellis range space in south-central Nevada, with several rising to more than 9,000ft MSL, simply precluded any low-altitude coverage. It was the perfect setting for a high-speed, low-altitude ingress.

For today's mission, the attacking aircraft we sought to intercept, USAF Europe-based F-111s, were fully expected to be hugging the surrounding desert floor, ingressing at a minimum speed of 480KIAS and accelerating to 540KIAS during their Initial Point to target runs. On egress, it wasn't uncommon to hear of F-111s at airspeeds of more than 600KIAS. Whatever the case, we, in our MiGs, would be hard-pressed to threaten them down low in the environment they were so accustomed to, but which was so foreign to us.

Meanwhile, MacDonald, working from his scope nestled within the range group building 103 miles away at Nellis AFB, was doing his best to pick out any possible radar contacts from the interference of the

COINCIDENCE OR A PRELUDE TO HISTORY?

surrounding mountainous terrain. It was a frustrating task knowing that attacking fighter-bombers, somewhere, were approaching the target area, but he was unable to detect and vector our MiGs to intercept them.

Geisler had planned for our four MiGs to split into two elements, in two separate orbits, oriented roughly north–south, approximately 15 to 20 miles apart from each other. In the western most element, Geisler and his wingman, Capt Gary "Goldie" Craig ("Bandit 13"), both flying MiG-21s, were established in a left-hand orbit anchored by Quartzite Mountain in the south and the southern tip of the Kawich Mountains ridgeline ten miles to the north. Geisler's CAP area was just 30 miles southeast of our airfield at TTR. Their position was optimal to cover the west and central valley ingress corridors that lay directly north of Area 51.

To the east-northeast of Geisler's CAP point, Maj Dave Bland, in "Bandit 13" (a MiG-23MS), and I, "Bandit 14" (in a MiG-21), were established in a similar north–south orbit just northwest of Bald Mountain, the peak that defined the northern edge of the highly classified Area 51. We'd been loitering for the past 15 minutes at 300KIAS, conserving our fuel to ensure we covered the vulnerability window from 1400 to 1430hrs. I was flying a loose formation, two to three aircraft-lengths back, off his right wing and to the outside of our left-turning orbit. While still reasonably close to my element leader, the loose formation allowed me to scan the desert below for fast-moving intruders. Our position would cover the easternmost valley corridor, which lay just to the west of Rachel.

Nothing! It's almost too quiet. This mission could all be a colossal waste of time – unless!

All of these valleys served as a perfect conduit for attacking fighters, acting almost like a funnel, with their termination point in Emigrant Valley, located just to the west and at the base of Bald Mountain. The broad valley led directly to Groom Lake and the target range to its south. There was an excellent chance that if the attacking F-111s were near, we'd see them and pounce.

The mission today was unique in every respect from our normal flight operations in the 4477th. Just a week earlier, the squadron had received an Air Tasking Order (ATO) from none other than HQ USAF at the Pentagon via HQ TAC to support a "special mission." For starters, an ATO is a rarity, especially one coming from HQ USAF. For a top secret unit such as the "Red Eagles," it was unheard of.

Soon after the squadron received the ATO, Dave Bland, as operations officer, handed over all coordination, planning, and leadership of the mission to Geisler. After conferring with an action officer at TAC HQ, Geisler soon discovered that this operation was very different from the norm, and would indeed require greater scrutiny and planning beyond our everyday *Constant Peg* sorties. This mission was way outside the realm of that. Quietly, he wondered what was driving such an order.

To begin with, as Geisler soon discovered, the request was for a minimum of four MiGs of unspecified type. For today's mission, Geisler, in addition to himself and Bland, who insisted he was to be a part of it, had chosen Craig and me to be their wingmen. Like "Paco," we were both MiG-21 IPs.

The objective of the F-111s, as told to Geisler, was to see if they could penetrate undetected into and out of the target area without either our GCI seeing them on radar or being picked up visually by our MiGs. And, to add even more mystery to this mission, their targets would be located inside Area 51!

Okay, let's stop right here. To put this into perspective, anytime the mere mention of Area 51 was part of any plan, and someone had clearance to fly into it, that went way beyond eyebrow-raising stuff. Access to Area 51 just didn't happen unless the stars, moon, and planets all aligned. Geisler couldn't get over these authorizations. They were unprecedented.

Oh, and one other thing. The F-111s wouldn't be entering from the usual starting point for all large-scale Nellis-based exercises – a break in a ridgeline 40 miles east of Area 51 commonly known as Student Gap. Instead, they would be inbound from north of the Nellis range space – something that had never previously been done. Finally, as the F-111s would be dropping inert 2,000lb GBU-10 Paveway II bombs, our MiGs, despite having routine clearance for access into Area 51, would not be allowed to pursue any engaged strikers past the area boundary due to safety concerns. That was a legitimate issue we have never encountered before.

What Geisler was finding out raised more questions than answers. When he enquired about how the F-111 crews would be in-briefed on *Constant Peg*, and the security concerns that went with it, not to mention what the ROE was for such a mission, he was simply told it would all be taken care of, and we in the 4477th needn't concern ourselves. It was becoming increasingly evident to him that whoever was driving this mission had given the green light to do whatever it took to accomplish the task. Geisler wasn't about to argue with that approach. Whoever it was, no doubt, wore four stars!

To make the training as realistic as possible, we weren't told of their ingress route, nor did we want to be. All we knew was that we had a vulnerability window to cover with our MiGs and a sector, approximately 50 nautical miles wide, somewhere through which the F-111s would be ingressing. What was even more unique was that the entire Nellis range space would be closed to anyone except our MiGs and the attacking F-111s.

COINCIDENCE OR A PRELUDE TO HISTORY?

Geisler's plan called for each of our fighter pairs to CAP between 13,000 and 15,000ft MSL, which, over the desert floor below, put us at roughly 8,000ft AGL, with the surrounding mountain ranges jutting up to around 8,500ft MSL. It was high desert, and the one thing we could be sure of was that the F-111s wouldn't be over the high terrain, exposing themselves.

Another ten minutes passed in our CAP orbits, and there had still been no sign of any intruders. As mentioned, Jim MacDonald wasn't seeing anything on his scope except the radar contacts of our two CAPs boring holes in the desert sky. In each cockpit, pilots individually wondered whether this mission would be a waste of time and fuel. Just when it was beginning to look like the latter, the calm was broken.

"'Bandit One-One,' tally four bandits, on the deck, northbound, ten south of the 'Dogbone.'" Having sighted four F-111s, Geisler was quick to relay their altitude, heading, and location. As its nickname implies, the "Dogbone" is an easily identifiable combination of two dry lake beds connected by a thin desolate patch of desert that stretches for ten miles, lying on the western edge of the Cactus Flat area, due east of our airfield, TTR. If there was one landmark every "Red Eagles" pilot was intimately familiar with more than any other, it was the "Dogbone."

Even though I was still on Bland's wing and roughly 15 miles east-northeast of Geisler's position, I instinctively turned my head in that direction, impossibly hoping to at least get a visual on the two-ship of MiG-21s that undoubtedly were now in hot pursuit of the egressing F-111s.

Ten miles south of the "Dogbone," heading north as expected, on the deck.

At that instant, I saw Bland's MiG-23 surge ahead, beginning a left-hand descending turn in the direction of the "Dogbone." Almost simultaneously, I saw and heard his afterburner light as his MiG-23 began noticeably walking away from me, the variable-sweep wings starting to inch their way back to their high-speed, 72° setting. From the position I was flying at his "four o'clock" and roughly 100ft aft of his accelerating "Flogger," the noise, while not deafening, was considerable. Fully lit, the afterburner plume looked like a gigantic acetylene torch extending 30–40ft behind Bland as he brought his MiG-23 around before rolling out on a westerly heading.

Okay, this shit's about to get real! Stay with him.

As Bland was bending his "Flogger" around in a hard left turn, I cut to the inside of him, seeking every bit of advantage to stay with his fast-accelerating MiG-23. Pushing over from 15,000ft, our two MiGs were soon racing through 500KIAS. While I'd heard for years about the "Flogger's" impressive acceleration, this was the first time I'd been able to witness it. There was no other way to describe it other than jaw-dropping.

"'Control,' 'Bandit One-Three,' 'bogey dope,'" Bland asked MacDonald.

"'Bandit One-Three,' snap Two-Six-Zero, for 18. 'Control' is only painting 'Bandit One-One's' position," replied MacDonald. It was readily apparent that the F-111s were just too low for his radar to pick them up.

In full afterburner, I managed to stay with the MiG-23 out ahead of me until approaching Mach 1.2, at which point Bland's "Flogger" almost disappeared. I was soon hitting a performance wall that the "Fishbed" just wouldn't push through, and all I could see of Bland and his MiG-23 was the bright dot of his afterburner slowly disappearing into the desert background ahead of me.

Holy shit. He's fucking gone!

With no chance of staying with Bland, I pulled the throttle out of afterburner, thinking it was a waste of fuel even to try. Now, back at MIL power and having lost my visual on Bland's MiG-23, I simply picked up an intercept heading, aiming for the middle of the "Dogbone," somehow hoping to cut off the fleeing F-111s. While I was doing so, I continued to scour the desert floor below, not convinced there weren't more F-111s than those currently the center of attention. If experience had taught me anything, when you weren't the engaged fighter, you kept your head on a swivel, looking for trailers.

Geisler's verbal narrative, which described his position relative to the egressing F-111s heading up the west side of the Kawich ridgeline, told us exactly where they were currently and where they were headed. From his descriptive commentary, they were in a four-ship offset box formation, with the wingmen spread 5,000–6,000ft and slightly staggered aft of each leader. The second element was two to three miles in trail. With that as guidance, it was now up to Bland to intercept the fleeing strikers. I'd lost sight of his MiG-23, so he was on his own.

In the meantime, Geisler and Craig, accelerating in their descent, were trying to catch the trailing two-ship of F-111s. Despite having already converted all their altitude for 600KIAS of airspeed, Geisler simply couldn't close the gap to within range for a simulated "Atoll" missile shot. Realistically, even if he had been able to, at this low altitude, any chance of an infrared homing-missile to guide would be wishful thinking, the surrounding heat coming off the desert floor being just too much for an older-generation missile, whether it be an "Atoll" or a US-made AIM-9 Sidewinder, to overcome.

Since the initial tally and ongoing exchanges between Geisler, Bland, and MacDonald regarding positions and intentions, minutes had slipped past. By now, the egressing F-111s were midway up the "Dogbone," still heading northbound and hugging the western base of the Kawich Mountain range. It appeared they were going to egress just to the northeast of the Sandia

COINCIDENCE OR A PRELUDE TO HISTORY?

Laboratory target area, located at the northern end of the "Dogbone." Bland asked Geisler, one last time, for an update on the F-111s' position.

"'Bandit One-One' is two miles in trail, just approaching the southern end of the north 'Dogbone,'" replied Geisler, relaying his current position relative to the fleeing F-111s. What I heard next surprised everyone.

"Ah, hell, I'm already past the north end of the 'Dogbone.' No joy on any strikers. 'Bandit One-Three' is climbing and coming back west," replied Bland, sounding more than a bit puzzled that somehow he had flown past and missed the fleeing four-ship of F-111s.

It was only then that he looked down and noticed the airspeed. His airspeed indicator was showing 860KIAS as he pulled back on the stick, climbing up from 200ft above the desert floor. To put what had just happened into perspective, when Geisler had first gotten his tally on the fleeing strikers abeam Quartzite Mountain, the distance to the northern end of the "Dogbone" was roughly 35 miles. At an egress airspeed of 540KIAS, what had taken the fleeing F-111s approximately four minutes to cover, Bland, covering more than 14 nautical miles per minute, has traveled the same distance in less than three minutes and somehow missed the entire gaggle to boot!

I never did manage to intercept the fleeing F-111s, nor were any of our MiGs ever in a position to threaten them. With the outcome no longer in doubt, we abandoned our pursuit of the strikers and returned to TTR, our airfield conveniently located just a few miles west of the "Dogbone."

The following day, Geisler would debrief the mission with his contact at HQ TAC, effectively stating, from his perspective, the mission was a waste of time, especially since it was doubtful that F-111s would ever be so foolish as to attack during the daytime. Furthermore, should they attack at night, it was inconceivable that they would ever face any MiG threats. Little did "Paco" know at the time just how prophetic and accurate his words would be.

Seven months later, at 1713hrs, on April 14, 1986, 24 F-111F fighter-bombers from the 48th TFW took off from RAF Lakenheath, 80 miles northeast of London, marking the start of Operation *El Dorado Canyon*. Hours later, at 0200hrs in Tripoli, Libya, they made their presence known, and the sky lit up with SAM launches and AAA fire while bombs rained down on the forces of Libyan leader Muammar al-Gaddafi. Of the F-111s that went across the beaches early that morning, all but one returned to RAF Lakenheath some 13 hours later. They had just completed the longest mission in the history of any fighter squadron.

What part did the 4477th play, if any, in the success of that mission? It's hard to say. Our task months earlier was for a small contingent of MiGs during a daylight ingress by F-111s to see if we could detect the approaching fighter-bombers. Even during optimal daylight conditions and despite being informed in advance of the expected vulnerability period, we still failed to detect the strike package before it reached its targets.

Operating at night with the element of surprise against actual MiGs with little more capability than ours in the 4477th had, there was little doubt the F-111 crews would make it, likely undetected, to the beach. How they fared with the rest of the Libyan air defense system was another matter entirely. Perhaps our purpose was more a case of "leaving no stone unturned" in preparation than anything else. Or, quite possibly, it was all a total coincidence.

However, when you add up all the exceptions to normal operations, the answer is less clear and points more to it being a prelude to the much larger *El Dorado Canyon* mission. The following cannot be ignored. Why was the 4477th given an ATO by HQ USAF? This was a first. The route of ingress was, for the first time, from due north of the Nellis Military Operations Areas (MOAs), whereas all other training missions (e.g. *Red Flag*, FWS mission employment phase, etc.) entered the range space from the eastern part of the Nellis MOAs.

Furthermore, the entire Nellis training area was closed to all other traffic. And perhaps most puzzling of all, the strikers were given authorization to not only enter Area 51, but drop their ordnance on targets within it. This simply never happened without permission from the very top of the Air Force chain of command. Finally, when you put all that together, and then add the use of top-secret MiGs as defensive CAP, you're likely onto something that was just a bit more than coincidence. Nevertheless, whatever small way the "Red Eagles" helped make the mission a success will never be known. Regardless of that fact, I am proud to have been a part of it and feel fortunate to have done so with such a select group of "Red Eagles."

23

MiG-21 vs F-15

"Son, your ego is writing checks your body can't cash!"
                    CAPT TOM "STINGER" JORDAN, TOP GUN

October 1985
1330hrs Pacific Daylight Time
Nellis AFB, Range 71
MiG-21F-13

The setup was simple. The F-15 FWS student, having been given the option, had elected to start from a defensive perch for this, his likely singular outing against a "Red Eagles'" MiG-21. Minutes earlier, the pilot and his leader, an F-15 FWS IP, had completed a textbook-perfect tactical intercept against my wingman and me in our MiG-21s. Textbook – they had sorted through our Soviet-style high-low pincer attack and targeted my wingman and me well before the merge, employing simulated AIM-7M missiles. When the intercept portion of the mission was completed, the leader and wingman split up as previously briefed and vectored to Ranges 76 and 71, respectively, to meet up with their MiG-21 adversaries for the real challenge.

While the tactical intercept portion of the mission was nothing to take for granted, the demanding 1-v-1 setup for this phase of the FWS syllabus was what tested a fighter pilot's real mettle. In other words, how well could you employ your fighter against another in the visual arena? A pilot's grueling physical and mental requirements, as well as his ability to master his aircraft in close-in aerial combat, were the ultimate challenges for any fighter pilot. The visual setup of an attacking MiG-21 at relatively close range, and one's ability to counter and ideally destroy the adversary, was the metric against which all self-respecting F-15 FWS pilots measured themselves.

On paper, assuming pilots had equal air combat capabilities in their respective aircraft, the F-15 would win the vast majority, if not all, engagements with a MiG-21, be they offensive or, in this case, defensive.

The Eagle held all the advantages – more power, better initial and sustained turn capability, speed, range, radar, and weapons, among others. You get the picture. As in most engagements, the pilots would be the single variable in this clash.

From the moment of the impending "Fight's On" call, this was an unrestrained aerial fistfight. Only the absence of live weapons and explicit ROE separated this from the real thing. These ROE – well-established and standardized sets of "rules to play by" – were the norm for air combat training across the air arms of the US sister services and NATO allies alike, and an integral part of every mission briefing. As long as everyone adhered to these guidelines, all fighters, regardless of their similarity or dissimilarity, could conduct high-intensity air combat training with reasonable assurance of safety. "Reasonable," of course, is a relative term.

Following the split-up of the Eagles, the F-15 FWS student soon joined up with me in a loose formation off my right wing. The rejoin complete, I rolled out on a southerly heading and climbed our aircraft to 20,000ft at 350KIAS. My focus was on planning the setup to minimize wasted time and get both fighters into position to start the engagement. As mentioned previously, my MiG-21 had "short legs," and I intended to provide all the training I could to this aspiring F-15 FWS student with what precious fuel remained.

Once leveled off, and respective fuel and aircraft checks were out of the way, I directed him to maintain his heading and keep a visual on me as I banked 45° away to generate some space between my MiG-21 and his fighter. After ten seconds on diverging headings, I was roughly two nautical miles (12,000ft) to his left, "seven o'clock." Eyeballing my spacing as sufficient, I smartly rolled into a 90° right-banked turn and smoothly pulled back on the stick to match the 180° heading he'd been holding.

Time to crank this thing up!

"'Raven One-Two,' push it up. 'Bandit One-One' is level at your 'seven o'clock.' Confirm visual and call when ready," I radioed the F-15 FWS student.

Following my call, we both selected full MIL power settings. The student's engagement against the best-flown MiG-21 he was ever likely to encounter was just seconds away. Accelerating to 400KIAS wouldn't take long. Within a few seconds, I received his reply,

"'Raven One-Two,' visual. Ready."

"Start your turn," I replied.

The F-15 at my right, "two o'clock" for 12,000ft (I was at his "seven o'clock"), smoothly rolled into a level, 45° left-banked turn into me. Its pilot's eyeballs were glued to my sleek MiG, now nose-on to him, the distance decreasing rapidly. While the forward visibility from the cockpit of the Soviet variant of the MiG-21 I was flying today could have been better, there was no missing the unmistakable planform of an F-15 turning in my direction. It looked like a flying tennis court!

As the range closed, I was about to see what this student would give me. Had he listened to my briefing to his FWS class weeks earlier about how to fight this airplane? Or would he, like so many others, dump that expert advice, put on a "Genghis Khan" jacket, and try to prove he knew better? At an estimated range of 9,000ft and now coming through an easterly heading, I keyed the mic and told my opponent, "'Bandit One-One,' fight's on, fight's on!"

I'd barely released the mic switch on the throttle when the clean F-15C on my nose at a distance of 1.5 miles broke into a 9G hard left-hand turn – the planform shape of the entire top of the light gray Eagle was bright, almost glaring, in the high afternoon sun. His hard turn quickly presented me with a face full of heading crossing angles, none of which I could solve if I didn't want to overshoot and expect to do anything but take a high-deflection gunshot and disengage. But that would only challenge the student a little, and I intended to maneuver to see if it was possible to get this Eagle driver to make a mistake – one that he wouldn't soon forget.

I kept my nose on him in "pure pursuit" until I estimated he'd turned about 90–100° and I'd closed to approximately 3,500ft. With the fight geometry just too tight to stand without jeopardizing my offensive advantage, it was time to counter his defensive move. Instantly, I selected full afterburner and smoothly rolled my fighter 90° to the right, pulling the stick back toward my lap.

The airplane's response was immediate, welcome, and one I had grown to trust and rely upon in such pitched ACM. In doing so, I'd aggressively maneuvered to the Eagle's "high six," preserving valuable turning room and forcing his next move. As soon as I rolled and pulled my MiG into the vertical, I noticed the F-15's nose dip abruptly, its pilot aggressively unloading his airplane and trying to regain some of the 120KIAS he'd just lost in that break turn to defend against my attack.

Good move, keep it up, get your energy back, and then take the fight to me!

With him committed to an unloaded maneuver, I had no time to waste keeping the pressure on him. Allowing him to accelerate back to his cornering velocity would give him an advantage, and I couldn't afford to give my adversary that chance, especially in an F-15.

Just seconds after I broke nose-high off the attack to save my turning room, I reapplied the pressure instantly. By blending in nearly full left rudder and aileron, I quickly rolled back hard left, now in a slicing turn, nose low.

Simultaneously, selecting the flaps during the maneuver had helped me place my aircraft's lift vector well out in front and below my adversary, now 2,500ft below me and still in an unloaded acceleration maneuver.

In this high-stakes duel, there was no time to think through the mechanics of what your hands and feet were doing on the controls. You and your airplane were inextricably joined. You were the brain, and the aircraft was your muscle. Either you were part of the jet or along for the ride, such was the nature of gut-wrenching, hi-G, visual air combat, whether actual or simulated. And all of this was done against an adversary you hoped hadn't mastered DACT yet. One critical mistake, and you were dead.

If the FWS student had been sharp and had assessed the fight correctly, he would have smartly used his regained energy to reposition his lift vector on me and, again, force my nose off. Doing so would defeat my subsequent attack and prevent me from regaining expended energy myself. In essence, he'd be reinitializing the fight in the same relative position we'd begun at, albeit now closer, slower, and at the cost of several thousand feet of altitude – but he didn't!

Instead, I saw his aircraft reverse direction in a loaded right climbing turn while pulling about 60° nose high. This move, no doubt, was to see if he could flush me out in front of him to his right. It was a huge mistake, as he had misjudged my energy state, which was fatal in air combat. I was in a controlling offensive position, and the Eagle out in front of me had neither the energy nor the room to flush me to even a neutral position, much less out in front of him.

Well, if that's your idea of how to defeat me, you guessed wrong today.

He'd gone from what had been a promising position of regaining the energy advantage to one where he had squandered any potential to capitalize on the performance benefits the F-15 had in such a fight over my MiG-21. In doing so, he'd failed to negate my positional and energy advantage, all in the hope of forcing my MiG-21 to overshoot his flight path. There was no chance of that happening – I had been there and seen that too many times.

While he was pulling up, I'd deftly rolled left and pirouetted to the outside and high of his right-climbing turn, maintaining both my energy and turning room, the latter now being a commanding 2,500ft behind him. I was holding all the cards at this distance and had more than 300KIAS on my airplane. I estimated he had less than 250KIAS, which was decreasing rapidly, and his F-15 couldn't regain the advantage. Nor could he thwart what was sure to be a gun-tracking kill shot from my MiG-21 in less than 30 seconds unless a miracle occurred. Looking down through the forward right quarter of the canopy, I could see him low and below me at "one" to "two o'clock," rapidly running out of energy and, more importantly, ideas. If he was praying for that miracle, it needed to happen soon.

What happened next was both surprising and painful to watch. The F-15 FWS student was at my low "two o'clock" for 2,000ft AGL, at what I'd estimated was now no more than 200KIAS. I was lagging his position from above, preserving my turning room and enjoying a comfortable 50–80KIAS advantage. I was in the driver's seat, and he was helpless against what he surely knew was an impending gun attack. But that didn't mean he'd quit.

I suddenly saw my adversary's flight control surfaces moving – and not in a good way. Trying to bring the Eagle back into a left climbing turn, the horizontal stabilizers had gone full opposite deflection in the blink of an eye. Correspondingly, the ailerons were fully deflected, commanding full left roll, as were both rudders. All of this happened in less than a second, and I could almost sense what the ride must have been like in my adversary's cockpit. It had to have been violent.

While air combat is an aggressive and demanding endeavor, the pilots who excel at it are those who first master their aircraft and energy management. Key to this is learning to fly it smoothly while optimizing its performance. Flying your airplane too hard and abruptly is detrimental to conserving energy and outmaneuvering your opponent. Precious energy (read, airspeed, and altitude) is pissed away when any airplane is operated in such a haphazard manner. The aircraft I was attacking wasn't just being flown improperly; it was being abused. And it was painful to watch.

With the high afternoon sun illuminating the Eagle, I next saw something I'd never witnessed before or since – an F-15 instantly going out of control. The jet, attempting to do a loaded climbing turn to the left, abruptly snapped into a rolling departure to the right; exactly opposite of what the pilot had intended. Just a moment earlier, I had been looking down at the planform of the entire top of the F-15, but now I was seeing only its belly. Afterburners aglow, with the nose dropped precipitously below the horizon, the fighter was now inverted and beginning a second departure roll to the right.

Whoa! What the fuck!

"Knock it off, knock it off. 'Bandit One-One,' knock it off," I radioed over our shared UHF frequency.

When you had experienced as many air-to-air engagements as I had against a multitude of fighters flown by pilots with varying levels of skill, you began to think you'd seen pretty much everything that could happen. Mistakes that pilots (myself included) tended to make were similar and predictable for each airplane. But now and then, something so unexpected occurred that it snapped you back to the reality that this was a dangerous and often unforgiving profession.

And perhaps that's part of the allure of what I do. Whether perceived as hazardous or not, that part of this endeavor gives all who have undertaken it over the decades an adrenaline rush that makes them the most willing of prisoners. Hopefully, this new and unexpected rush doesn't cause you or someone else to lose an airplane or, worse, its pilot. Luckily, today's mission wasn't one of those.

"Negative. Continue," came the immediate reply from the F-15 FWS student. Wishing to salvage this debacle, he wanted to press ahead, convinced he could fight his way out of his predicament. While he'd immediately neutralized his controls, unloaded his aircraft, and regained control, little did he know there was no way he would ever survive had this been actual combat.

You've got to be fucking shitting me!

"Negative! Knock it off, knock it off! 'Bandit One-One,' knock it off!" I adamantly radioed.

"Copy, 'Raven One-Two,' knock it off," he replied tersely. His exasperation at the outcome of his first fight against the MiG-21 was readily apparent in his tone.

With the engagement over, I radioed the F-15 pilot to recover to a wing's level attitude and climb the aircraft as soon as possible. During the fight, he'd lost a lot of altitude, and his aircraft's departure had increased that loss even more. His eventual recovery had occurred just above the 10,000ft AGL maneuvering hard deck. I wanted him and the nose of his Eagle safely pointed skyward – now!

With the FWS student now safely climbing back to 15,000ft and accelerating to 300KIAS, I radioed that I'd be rejoining his right wing and closing to look his airplane over for any telltale signs of flight control issues. Having been in gun range and with closure before the KIO, it wasn't long before I had rejoined to a loose position while directing him to start an easy turn southbound. Whatever the cause of the departure, my immediate concern was that there could be something amiss with his aircraft, and if so, a full recovery to Nellis AFB would be in order.

Once he'd steadied out on a southerly heading and was aware of my intentions, I slipped my MiG below his fighter and slowly crossed under to his left wing, all the while looking for any obvious flight control issues. Seeing no external problems that would have caused such a departure, and the aircraft appearing to be flying normally, I advised him to return to Nellis and debrief the occurrence with maintenance. We'd debrief at the 4477th TES building after my landing at Nellis AFB later that afternoon.

With everything seemingly in order, and he in concurrence, I directed Bandit Control to affect his handoff to Nellis Approach for his recovery.

That complete, I gave him a quick salute and was gone in a climbing afterburner turn back to the north and began my return to Tonopah.

Hours later, we would have an in-depth debrief at Nellis with his F-15 FWS instructor in attendance. I could sense his discomfort at having to sit through my explanation of what had occurred and where he'd made his initial and then follow-on mistakes. When pressed, he couldn't explain what had happened or how he'd somehow departed an otherwise perfectly flying F-15. His instructor sat in silence, tight-lipped but occasionally nodding in agreement with my recreation of the engagement on the whiteboard before him and the lessons learned from it. No doubt there'd be another debrief once they returned to the FWS. Regardless, the takeaway was that the student had learned a great deal about the maneuvering capabilities of the MiG-21, and perhaps more about his limitations in handling his Eagle.

Later, the three of us chuckled about it at the O'Club over several beers, none of which I remember buying. While we gave the student a good-natured ribbing, what was left unsaid was that the MiG-21 he had engaged that afternoon was undoubtedly the best-flown example he'd likely ever encounter. While there may have been some small measure of solace in that, the fact that he hadn't been able to measure up to F-15 FWS expectations no doubt left him troubled and disappointed. How about pissed? Remember those fragile fighter pilot egos?

While the reasons for the outcome of the previous engagement were unique, the loss by many an F-15 pilot to a well-flown "Red Eagles" MiG-21 in a visual attack certainly wasn't. Let me explain why.

The visual arena was where the MiG-21 excelled, and I loved flying it in that role. Designed as a point defense interceptor, the early models, without radar and all-aspect missiles, weren't much of an offensive threat except as a deterrent to an opposing adversary. Just ask any Vietnam-era USAF or US Navy fighter pilot. While knowing they were airborne and on the prowl was, without doubt, nerve-racking, the pucker factor was at its highest when VPAF MiG-21s got within visual range, and American pilots had to react to the threat they presented. It was simply a superb fighter in the visual arena. Did I mention they were damn small?

Conversely, this was the area in which most fighter pilots, whether USAF F-15 or F-16 jocks or US Navy F-14 or F/A-18 drivers, tended to be less proficient. That wasn't to say their aircraft or pilots weren't capable – quite the contrary. The explanation lay in pilots' experience or recency of exposure to dissimilar aircraft in this arena.

Most training for frontline fighter pilots focuses on their aircraft's primary and secondary combat missions and roles. In the case of F-15 pilots, it also involves honing the skill sets necessary to achieve and maintain air superiority. While proficiency in BFM is essential, it's simply lower in the hierarchy of the many skills required to sweep the sky of enemy fighters. Hence, you spend much more time on radar search, targeting techniques, and four-ship tactics than you do in 1-v-1 dogfights with your squadron mates. If you can't work your radar and target your adversary well before the merge, being the best in the squadron in aerial "knife fights" is only marginally helpful when it comes to overall mission objectives.

This visual arena, however, was the daily bread and butter of every "Red Eagles" MiG-21 pilot. Moreover, we had years of air combat training experience behind us before joining the 4477th. Pair us with the MiG-21, which, as mentioned previously, was hard to see and still more challenging to defeat if one got slow with it, and you can begin to see why it was a tall order to ask of anyone to defeat a TTR-based "Fishbed" unless they regularly trained at that level.

As previously alluded to, the ability to showcase and demonstrate the MiGs' best capabilities to our frontline fighter pilots was at the core of the "Red Eagles'" mission. With in excess of 10,000 MiG-21s and 2,400+ Chinese J-7s built and exported to more than 30 countries, the odds were good that our airmen would encounter any number of them if US forces got into hostilities in almost any theater worldwide.

Our objective, therefore, dictated that we fly the MiG-21 to its absolute limits and demonstrate the "worst case" scenario – a sudden encounter with a MiG-21, either offensively or defensively (most unfortunate!), in a close-in visual arena – for those we were training. The challenge we, the "Red Eagles," presented was simple. Either defeat the attacking MiG-21 and destroy it from an initial defensive position, or eliminate this highly maneuverable adversary in minimal time from an advantageous offensive position. Sounds easy enough. Trust me, regardless of pilot experience level or aircraft capabilities, it wasn't.

During more than two years serving as a MiG-21 pilot and instructor, I fought the F-15 more than any other type. A few memorable sorties stand out in stark contrast to the rest, often due to a lesson learned.

But it would be disingenuous of me to leave the reader with the impression that my other squadron mates and I never found ourselves in the gunsights of a well-flown USAF or US Navy fighter, jinking for our lives. We certainly did, although rarely on a student's first exposure to a MiG. During a week's deployment, it wasn't uncommon for a participating pilot to get two to three sorties and perhaps as many as four to six visual setups against our Soviet aircraft (MiG-21 and MiG-23).

And there lay the genius of the *Constant Peg* program. Visiting aircrew were exposed to multiple MiGs flown to their absolute limit in DACT sorties. Students quickly learned from their mistakes throughout the week, receiving in-the-air coaching from the very "Red Eagles" "Bandits" they were then fighting, followed by in-depth debriefs upon our return to Nellis. This usually meant that the learning curve for these fighter jocks was often as steep as it was invaluable. With that being the case, by week's end, we "Red Eagle" MiG-21 pilots usually had our hands full dealing with aggressive and confident adversaries who would then summarily thrash us using their aircraft's full potential and, often, a newfound personal skill set. For many, this would prove invaluable years later in the skies over Iraq.

Two months later, I had the opportunity to engage in a head-to-head DACT clash with another F-15 pilot, a young, talented graduate of the FWS, in the same Range 71. Throughout two neutral engagements, neither one of us ever got so much as a snapshot on the other; the tight maneuvering of our "rolling scissors" simply prevented us from bringing our noses to bear on the other. With me hitting my "bingo" fuel despite being a mere ten miles from my airfield, I gave my worthy opponent a salute and made for TTR, landing just minutes later.

Once back in the squadron, "Paco" Geisler approached me and asked what I thought about the weapons officer from the 9th TFS at Holloman AFB. I gave him my assessment that this guy really knew how to handle an Eagle. Geisler then shared with me that he was being considered for an assignment with us early the following year. My reply was a simple thumbs up and the words, "That's a no-brainer. He's great. Give him a 'Red Eagles' patch now."

Just a few months later, the 4477th welcomed aboard Capt Herbert "Hawk" Carlisle as "Bandit 54." He would prove to be an invaluable addition to the squadron and subsequently further distinguished himself throughout an enviable Air Force career, eventually rising to the rank of general and leading Air Combat Command, the successor to our then-TAC. Simply a top-notch guy and superb Eagle driver!

24

"Sir, Can He Do That?"

"There are pilots, and there are pilots. With the good ones, it is inborn. You can't teach it. If you are a fighter pilot, you have to be willing to take risks."
                                                                BRIG GEN ROBIN OLDS

November 15, 1985
1535hrs
Control Tower Cab
Tonopah Test Range

It is often said that fighter pilots live on the edge. In some ways, I suppose that's true. After all, that's what the public is fed by Hollywood and the stereotypical behavior accompanying that image – hard-flying, hard-drinking, skirt-chasing antics. And if you've watched the movie *TOP GUN*, you know it's got to be true. Without a doubt, there is an element of truth to that image. At one time or another, many of the pilots that I've known could have come right out of central casting for such a movie.

But along with the image, whether right or wrong, is the knowledge that because of this association, you're less disciplined and less professional than others. Indicative of behavior from a bygone era. Indeed, it is out of place in a peacetime military, where it is assumed that you must compartmentalize your ego and aggressiveness until called upon on the eve of conflict to bring it forth. Yeah, right!

Show me one fighter pilot who never broke a regulation, speed, or altitude restriction, and I'll show you one guy I wouldn't want to have on my wing in combat for anything. It's part of who we are and what we do. Fighter pilots don't wake up intent on breaking rules and regulations or defying the command structure. Moreover, if it is done at all, it's to push the envelope and, by extension, ourselves. Both physically and mentally. Let's face it, if you never push your limits, you'll never know what they are.

"SIR, CAN HE DO THAT?"

Anyone trained in an athletic discipline inherently knows they have to push themselves to the point of pain and beyond for ultimate success. In many ways, it's no different from preparing for air combat. As a fighter pilot, I always felt it was better to find that out before the bullets and missiles started flying than when the shit hit the proverbial fan once in combat. Furthermore, if you relied solely on what the Air Force regulations "allowed" you to do to prepare yourself for combat, you were probably already a step behind your opponent.

Here's an example. Let's say you're a new lieutenant assigned to my flight in your new squadron, and you're about to go flying with me, each in our respective F-15s. Damn, "good luck," you tell yourself, as that's what you'd been looking forward to doing for years. Not to fly with me(!), but to fly the hottest fighter anywhere. Okay, so we set out on a training flight, and it's just the two of us. We will conduct a sortie known as BFM, where you and I will each attempt to outperform the other in our F-15 during a series of one-on-one engagements.

Okay, the stage is set. We go out to our jets, start them up, taxi out for takeoff, and so on. As we're awaiting takeoff, a problem develops with my aircraft. Hydraulic, engine, radar, it doesn't matter. The bottom line is that it's serious enough that I have to return to the ramp and have maintenance look at it. In the meantime, you've been briefed that if I abort, your backup plan is to proceed to the planned working airspace and execute the briefed backup mission, which for you would be "Advanced Handling." It's code for, "Go out and max perform the aircraft," and then bring it home in one piece before running out of fuel.

The unspoken rule is to avoid doing something stupid, like hitting the ground or anything attached to it. Pretty simple. So, you take off and go to the working area, and for the first time, you're all alone with the hottest fighter on the planet. And for the first time in your young career, you're faced with a real dilemma. Fly to the limits of the regulations and be safe, or push the boundaries and begin to know your fighter and, by extension, yourself.

Remember the movie *Ferris Bueller's Day Off*, and specifically the 1961 Ferrari 250 GT California Spyder that Matthew Broderick couldn't keep his hands off? Today, this F-15 is the equivalent of that Ferrari, and you've just been given the keys to it. Let me ask you this. If given this opportunity, do you think you'll tamely fly it around at 250–300KIAS, straight and level, pulling perhaps 2Gs only, treating it like some civilian with his Cessna who has never been inverted in his life and has no concept of performance? Exactly – no way!

So, what you do is what every red-blooded American boy has done for generations before when given a similar opportunity. You open that baby up! And for the first time, you fly that F-15 like you've never flown it before. You take it as low as you care to go and as fast as you can, and then rocket skyward to see how high you can take it and how fast you can push the Mach indicator. Will it be Mach 2 or something higher?

This is what you do as a developing fighter pilot. In the process, at some point, you probably scare yourself shitless or at least do something to give yourself pause and tell yourself not to try that again until you get a bit more experience. To do anything less is bullshit, and if you do, you might as well resign your fighter slot and apply to be an airline pilot. But we all know that's not what happens. Okay, you're reading this and thinking, "Cool, 'Z-Man,' I get it. So, how does this all tie in with stuff at Tonopah?"

My answer is simple. That young lieutenant who takes that fantastic fighter, whether it be an F-15, F-16, or whatever, for his first "wild ride" never entirely grows up or leaves us. We all grow older and more experienced as we accumulate more time in the air. However, the thrill remains to excite the senses, push our limits, and share what we've learned from those experiences with others. What could be better than to do it all in one stellar flight? That's what happened this Friday afternoon in mid-November 1985. And I had a first class seat from which to view it.

On the schedule this particular day was the final flight for our operations officer, Maj Dave "Blazo" Bland, as his assignment with the "Red Eagles" drew to a close. Air Force tradition, being what it is, called for anyone's final flight in the squadron to be celebrated upon his landing by available squadron pilots, friends, wives, girlfriends (hopefully not both!), children, etc., out on the ramp next to the jet. And, as was the case with Bland, it was usually accompanied by a bottle of champagne, followed by the pilot being hosed down by squadron mates armed with fire extinguishers or, on this occasion, the ample hoses of the airfield's crash recovery fire trucks.

Of course, with TTR being a restricted area, Dave's wife and friends couldn't be present, so today, instead, numerous squadron pilots who had completed their flying duties for the day had gathered together with a fair number of maintenance and support personnel. In total, they numbered around 20 to 25 people.

Bland had taken off 30 minutes earlier in a MiG-23MS "Flogger-E" and flown a 1-v-1 sortie with another fighter deployed to Nellis AFB for his exposure to our MiGs. Also, airborne this afternoon was Maj Jim "Thug" Matheny, who had taken off with Bland in a T-38. Together, they had done a 2-v-1 intercept with the "friendly" fighter out of Nellis before Bland broke off on his own. The plan that had been briefed early that morning was simple enough. Bland would fly his sortie, which was scheduled to be the last that day, and upon completion, well-wishers would meet him as he stepped off the aircraft ladder to celebrate his successful tour as a "Red Eagle."

This afternoon, I was the SOF for the flight schedule. As such, I was already positioned in the control tower and working alongside two enlisted air traffic controllers on duty. While they were responsible for all aircraft entering and exiting the airfield, my responsibility was solely to support the safe operation of the "Red Eagles" aircraft.

Shortly after Bland's engagement had ended, I got a call from Jim MacDonald at Bandit Control telling me "Blazo" was returning to the field. This was my cue to call down to the squadron and alert the troops to make ready for his arrival, get the champagne out of the refrigerator in the squadron bar, and get everyone's butts out to the ramp where he would taxi his "Flogger" to and shut down, thus signaling the start of the festivities. All good.

Currently, the only two individuals airborne were Bland and Matheny. There was no other traffic inbound or moving on the airfield. Things were slow in the tower. Sometime during Bland's recovery to the field Matheny rejoined him, and they were returning together in formation. Okay, with the "table set," here's where it got interesting.

Part of my job as the SOF was to keep an eye on operations and stay informed about what was happening with your squadron's aircraft, both on the ground and in the air. To help you do this, there were many available radios in front of you, along with phone lines that could put you in touch with anyone from the squadron to the airfield fire department within seconds.

Another piece of equipment that came in handy for keeping track of aircraft approaching the field or in the traffic pattern was a Bright-Scope. A televsion-like monitor positioned in the upper left corner of the tower cab, it allowed everyone to see the radar "big picture" of the airfield and any traffic in the pattern or approaching it out to approximately ten miles in any direction. On the scope, the airfield was at its center, with two concentric rings scaled at five-mile increments. It was an excellent piece of equipment for maintaining high SA when traffic was outside of visual range.

Shortly after I received the call from MacDonald that Bland and Matheny were on their way back, I turned my attention to the scope to gauge their distance. Immediately, I saw a small radar return positioned just outside the ten-mile circle on the scope south of the airfield and tracking toward the extended centerline of RWY 32 for the approach and landing to the north. Minutes earlier, MacDonald had told me that Matheny had joined Bland, so the radar image on the scope made sense for a pair of fighters returning to the field and setting up to land. Again, everything seemed straightforward, as this happened 99 percent of the time when we were flying.

While in the tower, I monitored its working frequency, unless there was an emergency or something unusual happening that required me to monitor another frequency, as was the case today. However, as the radar return approached ten miles, I saw two targets, versus the single contact I'd been looking at just moments before. One return was aligned with the runway and proceeding to Initial. At the same time, the other appeared to be moving east, obviously in a turn, as evidenced by the diverging blips on the scope. As the aircraft were still too distant to acquire visually, I reached for high-powered binoculars and looked for the single aircraft approaching the break for RWY 32.

As the contact neared five miles on the scope, I lifted the binoculars to look for the now obviously single jet without knowing which aircraft it was. Within a few seconds, I acquired what looked like a dot, fast approaching Initial for the runway. Shortly thereafter, I hear Matheny in his T-38 check in on the tower frequency, reporting his position. Adjusting the focus on the binoculars soon brought the sleek lines of the T-38 into sharp view, obviously now proceeding to the break for landing by himself. Bland and his MiG-23 were nowhere in sight.

Hmmmm? What the fuck are you guys up to?

I lowered the glasses, and glancing outside, I now saw the assembled group of 25–30 people standing near where they expected Bland to park and shut down, and where the champagne would likely soon be flowing. Their heads were cocked skyward, hands shielding their eyes from the afternoon sun as they scanned the sky for the guest of honor. By now, I could see Matheny's T-38 without the aid of the glasses as he approached the break at 300KIAS. Still, there was no sign of Bland, even though I knew from GCI's earlier call that he was returning. Another look at the scope, and the picture I saw made what was about to happen plainly evident.

On the radar monitor, I noted a single return heading eastward and flying at a relatively high rate, as indicated by its movement on the screen. I lifted the glasses once more, this time looking south of where one typically picked out arriving traffic, and focused farther out, about seven miles. Still nothing. Another sneak peek at the scope had the radar return, which was Bland, farther east, and now just touching the inner five-mile concentric ring on the radar monitor. About this time, I heard Matheny's T-38 in the break, the sleek supersonic trainer shattering the afternoon silence in a hard turn to downwind in preparation for landing.

Within seconds, I had the binoculars back to my eyes, looking due south of my position to the skies beyond the airfield boundary to approximately where I was guessing, from the indication of the radar

"SIR, CAN HE DO THAT?"

monitor, Bland's "Flogger" should have been. I eventually acquired him with a couple more scans of the horizon to my south – a tiny side profile view of a MiG-23 in a gradual descent, its faint trail of engine smoke indicative of a non-afterburner throttle setting. Having estimated that he was at about 500ft AGL, I quickly detected a change in attitude as I was now looking at the planform of a MiG-23 with its wings swept back and moving fast as he began a hard left turn toward the airfield. Whatever Bland had planned, it wasn't your standard arrival to the pattern, and given that it was his last flight with the unit, I had a feeling it would be one to remember!

While all this was happening, the assembled crowd of well-wishers had no clue what was about to occur. Furthermore, they simply weren't expecting him from the direction he was approaching. What mere seconds before had been visible in the binoculars as a descending and fast-moving silhouette of a MiG-23 was now beginning to blur into the background of the desert scrub, for he was nose-on to me and moving – fast! Any signs of a smoke trail were now gone, indicating that the aircraft was in full afterburner.

From my vantage point in the tower cab, roughly 75ft above the airfield and adjacent to the "Red Eagles" ramp, Bland appeared to be just feet above the ground, his approach aligned with the flightline where the troops had gathered. Even the tower controllers were clueless as to what was about to happen. If they had known, I wonder if they would have said anything. And as this was going to be epic, I was not about to let them in on it.

Through my headset, I heard Matheny call his final turn with the landing gear down and get clearance from the tower controller to land. With binoculars still raised, I glanced up and noted his T-38 fully configured in the final turn.

Everything's good – no need to worry about "Thug."

It was time to look back for Bland and one fast-moving "Flogger" about to do a fly-by that everyone would remember. With another glance at the ramp where the group of well-wishers had gathered, I could see everyone intently focused on Matheny's T-38 and seemingly asking each other where Bland's "Flogger" had gone, as it was now apparent he was not returning as a flight of two. Another noteworthy item that was not part of the norm was the presence of the squadron commander's Jeep on the ramp, with what appeared to be a couple of people riding along to witness the event.

Uh-oh! VIPs! Shit!

That afternoon, Lt Col Phil "Hound Dog" White, current commander of the 4477th, was showing his boss, Col Bob LaTourette, around TTR. Accompanying them, and stuffed into the back seat of the Jeep, was

Lt Col Jack "Mad Jack" Manclark, who had recently been named as White's replacement and who would take over the command in a few short weeks. Both had come up to Tonopah for the day to get the tour from White and most likely discuss how we operated here at Tonopah. None of us had been told that they would be around for Bland's finale. They were about to get a close and personal view of something a little non-standard.

Oh, crap. Nothing good is going to come out of this act.

In the meantime, Bland's MiG-23 was quickly approaching the airfield boundary, just feet off the deck and moving like a scalded-ass ape. As I noted Matheny's T-38 touchdown, another glance south revealed a MiG-23 just feet off the deck, its shadow appearing as one from the angle of the high afternoon sun and the jet's proximity to the ground below.

You've got to understand something. The runway, which one normally lined up with on approach to the airfield, was about a quarter-mile west of where Bland was lining up. He was aligned directly with the aircraft parking ramp, which was flanked to the east by several large hangars. The control tower from which I was watching events unfold was farther north of the assembled troops by about a quarter-mile. The distance from me to the beginning of the parking ramp that Bland was fast approaching was less than a half-mile. He and his MiG were lined up to pass between me and the hangars, directly over the ramp. Add to this the low altitude and high speed of the "Flogger," and you begin to get the picture with respect to what was about to happen.

In a flash, the "Flogger," seemingly a mile or more away, was upon us. Roaring over the ramp mere feet above the group, it covered the half-mile distance from the south edge of the ramp area to me in seconds. Flying at close to 500KIAS, Bland's MiG-23 was moving at more than 800ft per second. To put that speed into perspective, if you're driving at 80mph down the freeway, you're doing about 120ft per second – a big difference with respect to the distance covered. Plus, you're not working in the third dimension – the vertical. I don't think anyone on the ramp saw Bland until he had passed them. They could probably smell the jet fuel exhaust before they heard the fighter or saw it pass them.

Just as he was about to pass behind the tower, I quickly turned around to see what will always be one of the most impressive sights I've ever witnessed in aviation – the top of a MiG-23MS, its wings swept back at 72°, going past me at close to 500KIAS, its trailing afterburner plume and accompanying shock cones lit up like a Saturn V rocket! He might've been going even faster. Whatever the case, when he flew past, I estimated him to be at about 50ft AGL – I was sitting in the control cab of a 75ft tower looking down at him.

"SIR, CAN HE DO THAT?"

Bland continued past me for a few more seconds at low altitude, overflying the deserted ramp outside the F-117 hangars before starting a hard left-climbing turn to downwind. In the process, he began to burn off the epic amount of airspeed he had come past us with, slowing to get his wings forward, landing gear down, and flaps set, all in preparation for landing. Back on the ramp, the guys who had just gotten "dusted off" were laughing and hooting it up. Some were just now getting up off the tarmac and brushing themselves down. A few hats went flying on the ramp. The crowd was utterly taken aback, yet ecstatic by having just been bounced by "Blazo" on his final flight.

With Bland on downwind and the "show" apparently over, the two enlisted air traffic controllers turned and looked at me, unsure of what to say and seemingly overwhelmed by what they'd just witnessed, but wanting to say something.

"Sir, can, ahh, can he do that?" the senior controller managed to blurt out.

"Well, he just did," was my reply, not knowing what else to say about something NOT covered in the training these two gentlemen had received regarding the control of aircraft in the traffic pattern.

Minutes later, Bland completed his landing and soon exited the runway, dropped his drag chute he'd deployed upon roll out, and was quickly approaching the parking spot around which the crowd, now even larger following the fly-by, was gathered. My duties in the tower over for the day, I hurried down the stairs for the Jeep we kept for the SOF's use and quickly made my way to the spot where Bland had shut down. He was now out of the cockpit and had already popped the champagne in celebration of the end of not only a remarkable assignment but an even more remarkable final flight.

Remember, a few paragraphs back, I'd mentioned that the squadron commander had been on the ramp, too, toting around his boss and his replacement? Well, when there was that much brass around and someone had just done something that clearly wouldn't be tolerated, no matter what squadron you were in, all pilots were understandably guarded. The enlisted guys couldn't care less. It wasn't their ass in the sling. They figured that as long as the pilots did it and it wasn't their responsibility, what the heck? They were laughing and whooping it up, backslapping the whole time and telling Bland what an incredible display of flying that had been. And you know what? They were right.

However, this celebration was somewhat muted, as the brass was present for the final flight, which our previous commander had cleverly avoided until the pilot had landed. Yeah, handshakes were exchanged, and swigs of champagne were poured, but what was missing was the unabashed celebratory enthusiasm that naturally occurred when there were no colonels present. I felt both happy and a bit sad for Bland following his flight.

Without a doubt, he was a great fighter pilot. He'd been a fine operations officer and was a guy I respected, even if he had grounded me months earlier for that 1-v-1 with Steve Brown in our MiG-21s. Still, it was his final flight, and it was an impressive one. I'm sure he hadn't counted on the commander and the others being there to witness his fly-by. Or perhaps he had, and it was his final "middle finger" to the lot of them.

Bravo, "Blazo," Bravo!

25

"Flogger!"

"Every time I went to fly the MiG-23, I reminded myself it would try and kill me today if I let it."

MAJ TED "GABBY" DRAKE
(294 SORTIES IN THE MiG-23)

February 20, 1986
0900hrs Pacific Standard Time
Tonopah Test Range
MiG-23MS "Flogger-E"

While I stabilized the MiG-23's throttle at MIL power (the Soviet flight manual referred to this setting as "Maximum"), I made a quick cross-check of the engine instruments and warning lights for any telltale signs that something was amiss with my machine. With everything appearing normal, I released the brakes and, as the airplane began to roll, squeezed back on the throttle-lock lever with the index finger of my left hand, allowing me to smoothly move the "Flogger's" sliding throttle to its forward position, commanding full afterburner.

With the throttle now at the full-forward setting, I immediately felt and heard the afterburner ignite, accompanied by the illumination of the "Reheat" light, located on the upper-right portion of the instrument panel just outboard of the tachometer.

Wow! No delay in the light-off like the MiG-21. Damn, this thing is loud.

A glance at the exhaust gas temperature (EGT) needle, stabilized near the 620° Celsius mark, along with an unmistakable kick in the ass, told me nothing was holding this beast back. The "Flogger" leaped forward down the runway on this, my first flight in the Soviet swing-wing fighter. If the MiG-21's afterburner light-off set you back in the seat, the "Flogger's" Tumansky R-29-300 twin-spool turbojet engine with 27,500lb of thrust – more than twice that in the "Fishbed" – was at another level entirely. Even on this bright morning, the 35ft-long afterburner plume was easily visible to the occupants of the control tower more than a half-mile away. On the hangar aprons across the airfield, the deafening roar of a "Flogger" at full takeoff power was unmistakable.

Despite a gross weight of 34,000lb, more than twice that of the MiG-21, the MiG-23 accelerated quickly. On this wintry morning, with light winds coming off the high desert from the northeast, there was little need for directional braking to keep the airplane tracking down the centerline of RWY 32.

As the airspeed needle passed 135KIAS, I slowly inched the stick back and felt the nose lighten. Seconds later, accelerating through 153KIAS, I felt the nose wheel lift off the runway and the thundering jet break loose of the runway surface at 163KIAS. Now airborne, I gradually increased aft pressure on the stick and established a 15° nose-high pitch attitude for the climb.

Holy shit! This thing is moving. Not as light as the MiG-21. Heavier, much like a Phantom II.

No longer bound to the earth, the airplane was accelerating rapidly. At 190KIAS, I raised the gear handle and both felt and heard the hydraulics surge through the airframe. The nose gear quickly retracted with a distinct "thump" into its gear well directly below the cockpit, the vibration felt by my feet resting lightly on the rudder pedals just two feet above.

Gear indicator lights are out. The ventral fin light is out. So far, so good!

With the landing gear fully stowed, I moved the gear handle to the neutral position, releasing all hydraulic pressure from the system and reducing the load on the main pump. Without delay, I dropped my hand to the flap control quadrant, just aft of the throttle, and depressed the forwardmost of three flap control buttons, commanding the flaps to the "Up" position. The "Flogger" was now racing past 235KIAS, and I hadn't yet passed the departure end of the runway.

Established in the climb and passing 300ft AGL, I glimpsed a fast-descending T-38 behind me in the periscope atop the cockpit canopy, crossing left-to-right to carry out the usual "clean and dry" check. While I'd been focused on the initial portion of the takeoff, Major Ted "Gabby" Drake, flying the T-38 chase airplane, had swooped in from downwind RWY 32 to rejoin my fast-accelerating MiG. Ted closed up on me to inspect the gear and doors, ensuring that no fluids were visible trailing from the jet.

An additional item Ted would look for was the MiG-23's folding ventral fin – a unique feature of the "Flogger." If functioning correctly, it would extend with the retraction of the landing gear. Without the ventral fin extended, the aircraft was susceptible to directional stability issues, which limited its top speed to just under 380KIAS. Any sign to the contrary would have meant an aborted mission, a quick recovery, and a landing, which was not exactly what one wanted in any new airplane, much less your first hop in a MiG-23.

"'Bandit Four-Two,' clean and dry. Button Four, Go!" Drake's radio call told me he had passed below my sky-bound fighter and hadn't seen anything out of order on my aircraft – today, the fighter interceptor variant of the MiG-23, NATO code-named "Flogger-E." My simple reply of "Two" over the radio told him I understood everything was a "Go" with my MiG, and I'd meet him on the frequency for Range 71 preset in our radios. Seconds later, we were up on our working frequency and checked in with our GCI controller at Bandit Control. This morning, Capt Jim "Smack" MacDonald was on the scope 120 miles away at Nellis AFB, and he would be keeping a watchful eye on us throughout the sortie.

As my IP for the checkout, Ted had spent several days preparing me for today's flight. In the week since my last flight in the MiG-21, he had painstakingly guided me through the academic aspects of the MiG-23's systems, emergency procedures, performance, and flight characteristics. It was exhaustive but necessary.

Unlike any other fighter squadron in the USAF, the 4477th TES did not have simulators or two-seat trainers to help pilots become acquainted with its MiGs. You could listen to all the tales and experiences of the other MiG-23 pilots in the unit and read everything available in the flight manuals many of them had helped write, but until you were airborne, it was all just a concept in your head. The bottom line was that if you were going to check out in the MiG-23, Ted Drake was the guy to have as your IP – he would end up flying more "Flogger" sorties than any other "Red Eagles" pilot. I could not have asked for a better instructor anywhere. Once again, good fortune had landed on my shoulders.

A graduate of Johns Hopkins University with a degree in engineering sciences, Ted received his USAF commission through Officer Training School and had earned his Air Force wings at Moody AFB, Georgia. Finishing second in his UPT class, Drake had selected the F-4 for his first assignment. Since then, he had amassed an enviable amount of fighter experience. The top graduate of his F-4 FWIC class, Ted had completed three tours in the venerable Phantom II before transitioning to the F-16 as part of the initial cadre to fly the aircraft with the 474th TFW at Nellis. During almost two years in the 4477th, Ted had spent 18 months flying the MiG-21 before checking out in the MiG-23. Such a distinguished flying record meant that Drake had plenty to offer me as my IP.

I stabilized the "Flogger" in a 320KIAS, 20° nose-high, left-climbing turn to the west. It was a clear morning, and from my vantage point, streaking skyward, I could easily see down the entire length of the Cactus Peak ridgeline, five miles west of the airfield, extending south toward Range 76. At this airspeed and with the MiG's wings in the full-forward position, my rate of climb was more than 7,000ft per minute. It was an exhilarating feeling.

While gradually becoming accustomed to the airplane and refining my priorities in a radically different cockpit to what I was used to, I was subconsciously taking in the subtleties of this jet. As with every fighter I flew, the MiG-23 talked to you through subtle feedback in the control stick, various vibrations associated with flight control movements, and sounds that were unique to it. While it may have been an inanimate object, the aircraft demanded respect like that given to a highly charged thoroughbred, and it would either reward or discipline its pilot, sometimes harshly, if not handled with a firm yet gentle touch.

It was not until you were climbing out in full afterburner that these nuances, and their impact on your flying, became known, and I'd only been airborne in this airplane for less than a couple of minutes. That is what this initial sortie was all about. Take off, explore its operating envelope, get comfortable, and slowly adapt to the jet's cockpit. Mastering the MiG-23 and its capabilities would be the focus for my final ten months as a "Red Eagle." It all begins right here, right now.

Following his visual inspection, Drake cut to the inside of my left-arcing climb and comfortably took up a loose chase position off my left wingtip. Or that's where I believed he was, because I couldn't see him from where I was sitting in the "Flogger," despite his assurances that he was off my left wing at my low "eight o'clock" position. Moreover, I couldn't see much of anything aft of a line drawn from "three" to "nine o'clock" passing through my cockpit. The ejection seat headrest and high fuselage bulkhead immediately aft of the cockpit made rear and side visibility difficult, except when looking through the periscope mounted on top of the canopy.

Climbing through 12,000ft MSL (roughly 7,000ft AGL), I smoothly retarded the throttle aft from the maximum available power position to the MIL power setting, keeping a close eye on the engine instruments for any signs of an engine anomaly. As with the MiG-21, it was squadron procedure to leave the engine in full afterburner until climbing through this altitude, should an issue or failure require an immediate return to the field.

If that were to occur, the pilot would have little time to waste turning back to land. While we were all seasoned pilots, this would be a handful even for us, and even more so for someone on their first hop in the MiG-23. You really had your hands full trying to lower the gear in time to make the runway, all without flaps. So, just as on my first flight in the MiG-21, I was in no rush to pull the throttle out of afterburner, and stayed at the minimum afterburner position until well through 17,000ft MSL.

Once comfortably out of afterburner, I throttled back still further, smoothly setting the power at 90 percent RPM. Having done so, Ted, who had been at full afterburner in his T-38 this whole time, finally closed up. Rolling out on a southwest heading into Range 71, I saw him pull up alongside me, level at my "nine o'clock." I continued the climb to 20,000ft MSL, lowered the nose, accelerated to 350KIAS, and set up for the sequence of maneuvers Drake had outlined in our pre-mission briefing.

As with any checkout in a new fighter, much of the first flight was about getting a feel for your new mount. While pretty straightforward with conventional fighters, with the variable-geometry wing design of the MiG-23, much more time was spent exploring the performance envelope of not just one wing-sweep setting but three, all with their unique airspeed, G, and AOA limits.

Today's flight's profile focused on getting used to the aircraft at 16° wing-sweep, in both clean and landing configurations, a go-around demo, a configuration change to 45° wing-sweep, high AOA handling, and an acceleration demo followed immediately by a loop. After the latter, I would perform a zoom climb while transitioning back to 16° wing-sweep, then return to the airfield and set up for an SFO pattern. Finally, once there, with some luck and good planning, I was hoping to have enough fuel for two to three landing patterns. It was an ambitious flight profile, especially for one's first hop.

Whenever discussing our wing-sweep configuration openly, for communications security purposes, we (both pilots and maintenance) referred to the various wing positions of the MiG-23 as either "Alpha" (16° wing-sweep), "Bravo" (45° wing-sweep), or "Charlie" (72° wing-sweep). Similarly, we referred to the MiG-23 as an "F-4," whether on the radio, over the phone, or even at the O'Club over beers. I always found these attempts at secrecy a bit laughable since anyone with an inkling of knowledge of US fighters would surely have been able to figure out we weren't flying a Phantom II while doing more than 700KIAS in a configuration called "Charlie." However, to the casual listener, they wouldn't have had a clue.

"'Bandit Four-One,' Ops check. Lead is Three point Two," radioed Drake. Following our level-off, Ted wanted to get the status of our remaining fuel. His call told me he has 3,200lb aboard his T-38.

A glance down at my fuel gauge, located on the lower right side of the instrument panel, showed the pointer squarely at 4,500 liters. As a "Red Eagles" pilot, once you became accustomed to the metrics used by the Russians to indicate anything aboard their fighters, whether it be fuel quantity, hydraulic pressure, pneumatics, etc., it was all relative. In this instance, I had approximately 8,000lb of fuel remaining. Mentally, in practice, I didn't even try to convert liters to pounds. Still, I quickly learned to convert any fuel quantity into what I could accomplish with the airplane in terms of time, whether it was an engagement at full afterburner or completing circuits in the traffic pattern. Another way of looking at it was how much time did I have to get the most out of this fighter, regardless of the mission?

"'Bandit Four-Two,' Four point Five," I quickly answered.

Following the airplane's refueling an hour earlier, the assigned crew chief had set the fuel gauge needle at 5,300 liters, or 9,500lb, of JP-4 when conducting his pre-flight preparations for this sortie. A pilot could also tell a fully fueled aircraft just by looking at it as he approached the jet on the ramp. When fully loaded, the MiG-23 "sat on its haunches," its nose easily a foot higher than when returning from a mission and low on fuel.

Since starting the engine, taxiing, takeoff, and climbing out using full afterburner, I'd used 800 liters of my starting fuel load. Unlike our Western-designed fighters, the fuel gauge, similar to that fitted to the MiG-21, didn't rely on capacitive sensors to measure fuel quantity. Instead, the indicator simply reflected the amount of fuel remaining, based on a simple measurement of the JP-4 that had passed through a sensor in the fuel manifold before reaching the engine fuel pump. While inexpensive and straightforward, the major shortcoming of such a design was that this system could not detect trapped fuel or, worse, a leak. Such a scenario was something Drake had addressed during a review of the fuel system. Today, the odds were good that I wouldn't be experiencing either issue. My fingers were crossed!

Following the "Ops check," Drake took up a high chase position in trail of my aircraft, allowing me to put the airplane through a series of ever-increasingly steep turns with various G-loads in each direction. Having gotten a good sense of how the big Soviet fighter handled in the "clean" configuration, it was time to gauge its handling qualities and engine response when "dirtied up" with landing gear and flaps extended and slowed to final approach airspeed.

Reducing my speed to below 300KIAS and constantly trimming the aircraft to maintain level flight, the "Flogger" slowed relatively quickly once both gear and full flaps were extended. Once fully configured, I stabilized at 180KIAS in level flight. During this configuration exercise, the only unusual handling characteristics were a slight but noticeable yaw and rolling moment that quickly dampened out following the extension of the landing gear and flaps. The initial yawing moment associated with gear extension was believed to be caused by the MiG-23's ventral fin folding to the right as the pilot lowered the gear. When the flaps were extended, I experienced much the same. Both characteristics were subtle and easily overcome by slight corrective movements of the control stick and rudder.

These minor flight control characteristics were present in every MiG-23 we operated, leading us to conclude that they were inherent to the design of the "Flogger" rather than due to the aircraft having been mis-rigged.

Following roughly a minute in this configuration, during which time I made several gentle turns in both directions to get a feel for the aircraft, the radio suddenly came alive.

"'Bandit Four-Two,' go around!"

At Drake's directive, I smoothly advanced the throttle to maximum power and eased the control stick back, establishing a 10° pitch attitude. The engine response was immediate, accompanied by a corresponding surge in power and thrust. This was a welcome change compared to the MiG-21's R-11F-300 engine, which could take 11 to 14 seconds to reach maximum power from idle.

Noting a positive rate of climb, I immediately raised the gear handle, followed quickly by the flaps. As I'd experienced during takeoff, with both retracted, the "Flogger" promptly accelerated. I lowered the nose to almost level flight and let the big fighter stretch its legs. In no time, the airspeed needle had passed 300KIAS and was racing toward 350KIAS. "'Bandit Four-Two,' selecting 'Bravo' (45° wing-sweep setting)," I radioed to Drake. My call with my configuration change was perhaps more for my benefit than his – a verbal placeholder of where I was in this sortie's planned profile. Should there be any doubt, the apparent movement of my wings aft and quick aircraft acceleration showed that I was proceeding as planned.

Accelerating through 350KIAS, I dropped my left hand from the throttle to the wing-sweep control. The handle smoothly moved to the middle detent with a gentle pull aft, commanding the wings to the "Bravo" position. A glance at the wing position indicator to the right of the gunsight confirmed that they were moving steadily aft from their 16° position. As the wings began to move slowly, the corresponding decrease in aircraft drag allowed the airspeed needle to rapidly exceed 400KIAS. This profile demonstrated the jet's engine response and commensurate acceleration and stability, with the wings now at their 45° setting.

At 450KIAS, I reduced power and stabilized the fighter, once again leveling off at 15,000ft MSL. As I had previously done with the wings swept at 16°, I performed a series of increasingly complex turns in both directions. Meanwhile, Drake stayed in a comfortable chase position high and behind me. As he did this, I occasionally got a glimpse of him through the periscope – I quickly became a fan of the goofy-looking appendage atop my canopy. While having a "rear-view mirror" may have seemed archaic, given the visibility limitations of the "Flogger," I was glad it was there. As I soon discovered, the MiG-23 was a fighter design with numerous compromises – visibility from the cockpit was just one of them.

Only years later, with designs such as the MiG-29 and Su-27, did the Soviets finally field fighters with cockpits that began approaching the near-unrestricted visibility of Western aircraft like the F-15, F-16, and F/A-18.

To set up the acceleration exercise, I brought the throttle to idle and trimmed the aircraft for level flight. As it slowed, I closely watched the AOA gauge, prominently mounted just to the left of the gunsight. Its various hatched areas in yellow, red, and black indicated the limitations of controlled flight and where the "knuckle-rapper" commenced, adding its tactile warning that a continued increase in AOA would result in a departure from controlled flight and, if allowed to progress too far, would most probably lead to a spin.

It was important to note that, unlike the MiG-21 I had flown just a week earlier, the MiG-23 was a very different fighter. Perhaps the label "fighter" is where the similarities ended. Both were called fighters, but the MiG-23 was more a pure interceptor. While I could take the MiG-21 into the pure vertical and run it out of airspeed without any adverse handling characteristics, I didn't dare attempt that in the "Flogger." Hence, I paid close attention to the AOA indicator in all configurations during my initial checkout in the airplane. Aside from significant limitations to its AOA, the MiG-23's turning potential was also extremely poor. I quickly discovered that the "Flogger" wasn't the agile fighter the Mikoyan-Gurevich design bureau had initially hoped it would be.

As if on cue, as the AOA needle passed the 20-unit mark, the "knuckle-rapper" lightly began tapping my right hand, which was loosely gripping the control stick, while I trimmed off the stick pressure to stabilize at this setting. Slowing to 240KIAS, I added power to maintain level flight while keeping the AOA indicator between 20 and 24 units. Pulsing the stick ever so slightly fore and aft, the AOA needle hovered in this range, accompanied by a corresponding rhythmic rapping of my knuckles. Had I abruptly yanked the stick fully back, the aircraft would have stalled, with a departure followed by a spin being highly likely. Not wanting to tempt the demon within the "Flogger" on my first hop, I gently eased the stick forward. Now for some fun.

"'Bandit Four-One,' Ops Check, Lead is Two point Three. The visual is at your 'eight o'clock high.' Ready when you are." Drake's call indicated that he was well-positioned to chase me through the next part of the profile, and was currently at 2,300lb of fuel. "'Bandit Four-Two,' Three point Four on the fuel." My reply informed Ted that I had about 1,000 liters of fuel

"FLOGGER!"

to work with before we needed to head back to TTR to complete the approach and landing portion of the flight. But now, I was focused on readying myself to take the "Flogger" into the vertical.

As scripted, I was to stabilize at MIL power, unload in a slight descent, select full afterburner, accelerate the big fighter to 550KIAS, and take the Flogger into the vertical for a loop. While I'd performed many loops during initial checkouts with all the previous fighters I'd flown, this aircraft was entirely different. The airspeed, power settings, and AOA limits were far more restrictive than anything I'd previously experienced.

Drake's guidance in the briefing about performing the loop was succinct and straightforward, and all I needed to know. "Don't fucking ham-fist it, 'Z-Man,'" he had warned, "and pull beyond about 24 units AOA. If you do, ensure the rudder is centered. Any yaw at high AOA will get you in trouble. If the nose starts to wander, immediately unload to less than 18 units AOA, but keep the nose coming down below the horizon."

Ted spoke from experience. Just months earlier, he had departed and spun a "Flogger," both inverted and upright. Luckily, he was able to recover from the spin. He had given me valuable information that wasn't to be found in any of the manuals obtained from various US intelligence sources.

Message received and understood. Okay, don't fuck this up!

"'Bandit Four-Two,' ready. On my count. Three, Two, One, afterburner now."

The engine was stabilized at the MIL power setting to prepare for selecting the afterburner. On my call, I wasted no time lifting the throttle lock and pushing the throttle fully forward to the maximum afterburner setting. With the afterburner lit, I unloaded the aircraft until I could feel that "light in the seat" sensation as the airplane did what it did best – accelerate, unlike any other fighter I've ever flown, before or since!

Smooth light-off, REHEAT light illuminated, engine low and high-pressure rotors are stabilized. Damn!

In seemingly no time, the airspeed needle rapidly passed through 450KIAS, leaving Drake's T-38 well behind. A quick peek in the periscope at where he had been just moments before showed little more than a dot fading back at my "seven o'clock," the Talon struggling to stay with me despite both of its engines being at full afterburner.

This thing is a rocket!

As planned, upon reaching 550KIAS, I smoothly pulled back on the stick and initiated a 5G climb. The MiG-23 responded immediately and blasted into the vertical. While it was a fantastic ride, I was also bleeding off airspeed at an alarming rate. In what seemed like just seconds later, approaching the top of the loop, I eased off the back pressure to 2Gs, the AOA gauge hovering at roughly 18–20 units, and the airspeed indicator showing 245KIAS, having gained approximately 11,000ft on the front half of the maneuver – all in less than 15 seconds.

Coming over the top of the loop inverted at 26,000ft MSL, I tilted my head back as far as I could, looked through the top of the canopy toward the desert floor more than three miles below, and continued the pull, smoothly bringing the nose below the horizon. Now established on the backside of the loop and beginning to accelerate, I was careful to smoothly retard the throttle to the minimum afterburner setting, being wary of picking up too much airspeed during the descent. With its nose buried below the horizon, the MiG-23 wanted to accelerate quickly. If left at full afterburner, the airspeed would easily exceed 600KIAS, requiring more than 15,000ft of altitude and heavy Gs for recovery.

Coming through pure vertical, I brought the throttle out of the afterburner position. I let it stabilize at MIL power before further retarding it to idle as it pushed through 450KIAS while beginning a 20–22 unit AOA pull-out of the ensuing dive. A light rap on the knuckles reminded me that I was performing at my maximum turn rate in my current configuration. As the airspeed increased, so did the G loads, now showing 5Gs on the cockpit accelerometer.

No more aft stick, ease off a bit. First flight. Give yourself some margin.

Should I have inadvertently increased the AOA beyond 28 units, which would have required moving the stick an inch farther aft, the airplane's departure was almost guaranteed. Worse yet, it would do so without warning, and the altitude needed for recovery from any ensuing spin would likely exceed 10,000ft. While pointed almost straight down, even slight pulses of the stick made the needle on the AOA gauge float between 22 and 26 units. With the desert floor below at roughly 5,500ft MSL, losing control here and initiating a recovery below 15,000ft MSL would be incredibly risky, even if it were flawless. The completion of the loop was uneventful, but the maneuver didn't stop there.

"Okay, now bring the nose up and start an easy turn back toward the field," Drake reminded me, as I started the recovery toward the runway. Having plenty of excess energy, I smoothly pulled up into a 30° climb as per Drake's briefing and began an easy turn to the northeast, back towards TTR. Following the loop, the plan was to "zoom" the airplane while at idle, trading nearly 300KIAS of excess airspeed for altitude.

Established in the climb and making an easy left turn towards TTR, as the airspeed decreased through 450KIAS, I moved the wing-sweep handle forward to the 16° position and continued the climb, setting up for an SFO recovery.

"'Bandit Four-One,' Ops check. Lead is Two point One."

"'Bandit Four-Two,' Two point Three," came my prompt reply. We had planned for the MiG to still have 2,500 liters of fuel when it was time to

RTB, which meant I had enough to conduct an SFO and perhaps two, maybe three landings before reaching the squadron's 800-liter "wheels on the ground" minimum fuel limit for the "Flogger."

"'Control,' say distance to the field for 'Bandit Four-One' flight," Ted queried our controller. Back at the Range Control Center, our GCI controller, Jim MacDonald, who had been silently monitoring the flight's progress for the past 20 minutes, was on it immediately.

"'Bandit Four-One,' 'Control' shows the field at Zero-Five-Zero for 20 miles. The active runway is Three-Two. Do you need assistance?"

"Negative 'Control.' We're RTB. Thanks for the snap. 'Bandit Four-One,' Button Three, Go." With a double-click of the microphone switch on the throttle, I acknowledged Drake's directive and immediately switched to Channel 2 on the radio control head, awaiting his check-in.

"'Bandit Four-One,' check." My simple reply of "Two" let Ted know we were both on the tower frequency and ready for the SFO portion of the flight.

With the airfield now squarely on my nose, I climbed to almost 23,000ft MSL just as the airspeed needle approached 250KIAS. At this airspeed, with the engine at idle and the wings fully forward at 16°, the MiG-23 was a worse glider than the MiG-21, even with the gear and flaps retracted. I next assessed whether I'd have made the field from this position had I experienced an actual engine-out emergency. As with the MiG-21, with the runway on the nose, speed brakes extended, and holding 250KIAS, the relative movement of the airfield, either below my nose or above it, dictated my next course of action.

With plenty of altitude at less than 20 miles from the field, the approach end of the runway was slowly moving below my nose, indicating that I would not only make it but had a bit of excess energy (altitude) that I needed to dissipate to make the landing manageable. Having completed dozens of similar SFOs in the MiG-21, I was well-prepared for this profile, which, for all practical purposes, was virtually identical in its mechanics with respect to airspeeds and altitudes, save for the apparent differences in aircraft.

Nonetheless, with this being my first attempt at such a feat in the MiG-23, I'd start from a controlled position over the threshold of RWY 32, stabilized at 20,000ft MSL and 250KIAS. Having checked in and received clearance from the tower for the maneuver, once "over the numbers," I smoothly retarded the throttle to idle, extended the speed brakes, and began a reasonably steep left-descending 45–50° turn in the SFO pattern.

Same ground track as in the MiG-21. The airspeed's the same, just way more sluggish.

In his T-38, flying a loose chase position outside my turn, Drake kept an ever-present eye on my progress. Anyone watching from outside the "Red Eagles" hangars below would be hard-pressed to see us in our descent. Having started at 15,000ft AGL, we were little more than a silent pair of dots in what appeared to be a graceful spiral more than two miles above the southwest corner of the airfield.

As with any flame-out approach, whether actual or simulated, the real test came when the pilot extended the landing gear. This was the decisive moment. Underestimate the increased drag associated with the landing gear extended, and you would likely not make the runway. If you were too cautious and extended the landing gear too late, there was a good chance you'd not get the stricken jet onto the runway with enough distance to stop. You would end up "four-wheeling" across the desert beyond the overrun. In either case, there was a better-than-even chance you'd lose the aircraft and, with it, yourself, as the envelope for ejection while strapped into the MiG-23's KM-1M seat, with its associated sink rates in either scenario, was zero.

But today, despite flying an appreciably different aircraft, I benefited from having made dozens of similar approaches in the MiG-21. As such, coming around the base turn, I lowered the gear at 3,000ft AGL while still 1.5 miles from the runway threshold. With the gear down, the corresponding increase in drag on the airplane was significant, requiring further lowering of the nose to maintain my airspeed. Fortunately, I'd chosen the proper time to commit to the gear, and even with the increased descent rate, the likely point of touchdown was approximately 2,000ft down the runway.

At a half-mile on final approach and 1,000ft AGL, I began the transition from a 250KIAS gliding "brick" to what hopefully would be an acceptable touchdown at 160KIAS. The required pitch rotation from approximately -15° nose-down to one where you were touching down in a slightly nose-high attitude of +2/−3° was substantial, and needed to be accomplished in seconds, requiring it to be initiated while still 300ft AGL. Committed to landing with no engine and decreasing airspeed, the point at which you began the flare was the only variable you could control without an operable powerplant.

"'Bandit Four-Two,' go around." At 200ft AGL, Drake's call to "go around" approaching the touchdown point was both expected and prudent. While the SFO was a valuable exercise for anyone checking out in the MiG-23, carrying it out to completion with a full touchdown was also fraught with risk, especially on a pilot's first flight. At Ted's call, I smoothly moved the throttle to the MIL power setting, and the response was immediate and impressive. With the added thrust, the MiG-23 quickly climbed following the simple aft movement of the stick. Accelerating through 200KIAS,

I reached for the gear handle and raised it. Flap retraction followed at 230KIAS, and with the MiG-23 now cleaned up, it was just seconds before the airspeed needle was well past 250KIAS.

If asked to name one thing I liked better about the MiG-23 than the MiG-21, it was engine response. Initiating a similar go-around from idle in the MiG-21, equipped with its R-11F-300 engine, would have resulted in the aircraft touching down well before it had time to spool up. The response of this engine reminded me of the GE J79s fitted in the F-4, but with significantly more thrust – it was excellent!

"'Bandit Four-Two,' request closed."

"'Bandit Four-Two,' left-closed approved. The pattern's yours."

Having clearance from the tower, with the throttle at MIL power and the "Flogger" now approaching 300KIAS at the departure end of the runway, I began a smooth but conservative left-climbing turn to downwind, rolling out on a slightly wider downwind leg than I had in the MiG-21. While I was comfortable with how the jet was handling, one's first trip in the traffic pattern with a "Flogger" wasn't the time to be overly aggressive. I rolled out with plenty of room between myself and the runway.

Once level at pattern altitude and steadied out on a comfortable heading parallel to the runway, I smoothly throttled back and began slowing the "Flogger." The airplane quickly decelerated, so there was no need to worry about over-speeding the landing gear or flaps. Fully configured, I slowed to 215KIAS while trimming off the stick pressure to hold altitude.

"'Bandit Four-Two,' gear down, Runway Three-Two, touch and go."

"'BANDIT Four-Two,' winds are Zero-Two-Zero at seven knots, cleared touch and go, Runway Three-Two."

Slight right crosswind. Gear, flaps, all green. Don't fuck it up!

Having been in the tower many times as the SOF for pilots on their first flight in the "Flogger," I knew firsthand that the occasion attracted additional attention from every controller on duty. Without it being said, even they knew it was a different beast from the MiG-21, and there was a heightened sense of excitement in the air whenever a MiG-23 was in the pattern for its pilot's first landing. As I started the base turn, I imagined no less than three sets of binoculars trained on our two airplanes, giving them an added bit of scrutiny.

I slowed to 185KIAS in the left-descending turn to final, looking to roll out at least a mile from the runway with wings level at 300–400ft AGL. The visual pattern was something I'd done more than 1,000 times in other fighters over the past eight years. While the mechanics were the same, it was still another "first time" in this airplane that I was slowly becoming acquainted with. The roll out on final was uneventful. The flight control response was somewhat sluggish, as only wing spoilers, rather than conventional ailerons, provided the primary means of roll control.

Nothing close to the MiG-21 – even the Phantom II was much crisper in roll response.

With my aimpoint for the touchdown established, a slight power reduction was all that was needed to nail an approach speed of 165–170KIAS. Just moments from landing, what caught my attention next was a stark reminder of the risks and dangers of flying these aircraft, particularly the MiG-23. To my left, only a quarter-mile from the runway threshold, lay a plowed-out section of ground devoid of the usual desert scrub brush. This barren area, measuring approximately 20 x 50 yards, was a silent reminder of where we had lost one of our own just three-and-a-half years earlier in a MiG-23 similar to the one I was flying today. But this was no time for sightseeing.

Focus! Aimpoint, airspeed, sink rate.

As I approached the runway threshold at 50ft AGL, I had already begun preparing for the landing, having reduced my speed to 150–155KIAS on short final. In the next few moments, I shifted my focus through the windscreen towards the far end of the runway, allowing my peripheral vision to sense the approaching runway and gauge when to begin my final flare for landing and throttle reduction. Done correctly, I'd touch down with a minimal sink rate between 135 and 145KIAS.

Don't chop the power, ease the stick back, and don't bounce!

A second later, I felt the main wheels contact the runway, and I held the stick where I had it, preventing the nose wheel from slamming down. With the "Flogger" tracking straight, I slowly lowered the nose wheel to the runway. I then used a touch of left rudder, along with a slight right stick, to minimally raise the right-wing spoilers, keeping the airplane from drifting left in the prevailing right crosswind conditions.

Damn good, no surprises. Okay, power up and do it again!

As planned, I flew another closed pattern for one final landing. With 1,300 liters of fuel remaining, I had enough for only one more. Seconds later, with the "Flogger" quickly accelerating down the runway in MIL power, I was airborne again for one last trip around the pattern. There would be many more over the remaining nine months of my assignment in the 4477th, along with experiences that would later prove invaluable.

In the ensuing days, I would log three additional training sorties before taking a qualification check ride on the fifth hop in the big Soviet fighter, all in less than two weeks after unstrapping from the MiG-21 for the

"FLOGGER!"

last time. The day after the qualification flight, I was introduced to the ground attack model of the "Flogger," the MiG-23BN. Although it had some unique flight characteristics, in most respects, throughout much of the flight regime, the ground attack variant wasn't too different from the fighter interceptor MiG-23MS. Nonetheless, we didn't waste more than a single sortie getting a new "Flogger" pilot used to it, and one week later, I was flying a full schedule against visiting fighter units.

As the saying goes, "There's no slack in a one-link chain!" The ops tempo as a "Red Eagles" "Flogger" pilot was limited only by how well the aircraft held up under a reasonably high sortie generation rate for such a complex fighter. This proved quite a challenge for our maintenance troops, as, despite their seemingly limitless talents in doing the impossible with what they had, we undoubtedly flew the airplanes much harder than their designers had ever intended.

As much as our maintenance troops were learning about the MiG-23, so were we, the pilots who flew it. The exploitation of the aircraft years before, while valuable, merely provided a baseline of performance expectations, but little more. My fellow "Red Eagles" pilots and I would only discover the actual capabilities and limitations of the "Flogger" through experience, as we max-performed the aircraft daily during hard DACT. I soon realized that our wider understanding of the jet wasn't gained without significant risk to us, and we lived to share our experiences only through skill and often a healthy measure of good luck.

26

"Knock It Off!"

"The ordinary air fighter is an extraordinary man, and the extraordinary air fighter stands as one in a million among his fellows."

PRESIDENT THEODORE ROOSEVELT

April 1, 1986
Tonopah Test Range
MiG-23MS "Flogger-E"

Not everything always goes quite as planned, and when flying our MiGs, it was neither unexpected nor a surprise when something untoward occurred. While flying a 2-v-2 mission on this early spring day, the unexpected happened, making for an exciting recovery and, eventually, the saving of a most valuable asset. To say the pucker factor was not present would be total bullshit. During such moments, when we were surprised by events or circumstances that no one else had experienced up until then, all you could do was rely on your piloting skills to recover the airplane and, by extension, yourself. Without it being said, no one wanted to be the pilot who had to eject from a MiG unless it was the only remaining choice available.

This particular incident began with two of our MiGs racing south at 400KIAS to engage a pair of F-15s that were committed toward us at 28 miles, which our GCI controller reported to be at 26,000ft. We were slightly lower at 22,000ft and deployed in a loose formation. Today, I was the tactical lead in a MiG-23, with my wingman, Capt Gary Craig (in a MiG-21), in a 200–300ft right-echelon formation, stacked slightly higher and to the west of me.

With our two MiGs close together, we appeared as a single target to the F-15 pilots, despite the power of their sophisticated AN/APG-63 pulse-Doppler radars. Remaining in close formation allowed us to better mask our intentions, fooling the opposing F-15 pilots into thinking that they were intercepting a single radar contact. We could be a single bandit or

"KNOCK IT OFF!"

many – there was no way for the Eagle pilots to tell, as their radars could not break out multiple fighters within a tight formation at such a range. When we got the call from our controller that the F-15s were at 22 miles, we made our move.

"'Bandit Three-One,' execute!" At my radio call, Craig and I split our formation. I delayed my maneuver for a brief second and, with a slight glance to the right, noted Craig's MiG-21 beginning a climbing turn to the southwest, its afterburner plume now visible in the late-afternoon sky as the nimble fighter quickly headed for its pre-briefed altitude of 31,000ft. A split-second later, I began a hard rolling left turn to the southeast. In an instant, our two MiGs were headed in opposite directions, both now in full afterburner and quickly changing the dynamics of the attack. In my hard-slicing turn, the force of the 4G maneuver snugly wedged my body farther back into the ejection seat, the sensation being both intimately familiar and welcome.

As I began my roll-out on a southeasterly heading, I momentarily dropped my left hand off the throttle and reached for the wing-sweep control lever on the left console just inches below. Within seconds, I had quickly selected the full-aft detent position, commanding the variable-sweep wings of the MiG-23MS "Flogger-E" I was flying that afternoon to the fully-aft, or 72° "high-speed," position from their current 45° "cruise" setting. Coupled with my steep descent, reduced aerodynamic drag, and 27,000lb of thrust from the big Tumansky engine, the airplane quickly accelerated through 550KIAS. All this happened within seconds of the "execute" command. I was now "hauling ass," still accelerating and trying to out-flank the F-15s to my south.

Already five miles to my west, Craig had leveled off and was himself accelerating his "Fishbed" to 1.2 Mach, putting added distance between our two fighters as we completed the initial move of our high/low "pincer" attack on the F-15s, now approaching from our south at a distance of 15 miles.

"'Bandit Three-One,' targets 15 miles, breaking out two contacts, line abreast formation," came the call from our GCI controller, Jim MacDonald. Quickly looking back inside, I noted the airspeed indicator needle hovering near the 630KIAS mark as I eased the stick back to begin my level-off at 13,000ft. It was time for both of us to start our hard turns back toward the F-15s and finish the attack. If all had gone as planned, Craig and I would easily have out-bracketed the Eagles, and with a bit more luck, one or both of us would have been able to engage the targets undetected and unseen – me, attacking from low and to the east, Craig, high and from the west.

I had just started the turn, with my head twisted far to my right and looking toward the targets through the upper right side of the "Flogger's" canopy, when the sudden appearance of a bright light grabbed my attention. The red "Master Warning" light flashed brightly below the canopy bow, just to the left of the gunsight's combining glass. While still in the hard turn, my eyes darted over the instrument panel, looking for a telltale sign of the warning light's offending source. I found it on the lower right corner of the instrument panel, just above my right knee, in a group of indicator lights that were usually blank. Shining bright yellow, it highlighted the words "Main Hydraulic."

"'Bandit Three-One,' knock it off, knock it off!" I quickly transmitted on the discreet UHF, letting Craig and MacDonald know that something was amiss with me, or more probably, my airplane. In disciplined order, they promptly acknowledged the call, and the "Knock It Off" was quickly passed to the F-15s' GCI controller sitting beside MacDonald at their radar at Nellis. Within seconds, everyone knew that the engagement was off, and what had been looking like a promising intercept for us was now over. The F-15s were instructed to loiter until the nature of the KIO could be determined. With all parties alerted and the calls acknowledged, Jim MacDonald was the first to speak.

"'Bandit Three-One,' state the reason for the Knock it Off."

"'Bandit Three-One' is declaring an emergency and RTB," I replied. "'Three-Two,' I'm going to need you to join up on me." My simultaneous reply and directive signal to Craig and MacDonald that something serious was happening with my airplane, and I needed "Bandit 32" to join up with me as soon as possible.

"'Bandit Three-Two,' snap left, Zero-Seven-Zero, ten miles for 'Bandit Three-One.'" MacDonald was on my request in a flash, giving Craig my bearing and range from him to help facilitate the rendezvous with me.

While all this was happening, I had shifted from attack mode to one focused on getting the stricken fighter back on the ground. Very quickly, my mind took in everything that was happening with my airplane and assessed the situation, hands and feet subconsciously moving the control stick, rudder pedals, throttle, and wing-sweep control. My eyes darted from the instrument panel to outside the cockpit and then back to the instruments once again, my brain crunching through the criticality of the situation regarding altitude, airspeed, attitude, system status, and, ultimately, survivability!

A pilot's senses are attuned to the slightest differences in the aircraft's feel and sound compared to what they're accustomed to. At this instant, at this airspeed, I'd no clue as to the nature of this hydraulic issue other than that it was serious, with the emergency action procedure calling for the pilot to move the wing-sweep control fully forward immediately. By this particular "April Fool's Day," I had been flying the MiG-23 for all of five weeks. In that time, I had logged 16 flights in the "Flogger-E" and nine in the "Flogger-H." With this being only my 26th hop in the MiG-23, it was safe to say I was not yet totally aware of all the subtleties of the jet's performance at varying airspeeds, configurations, and G loads.

In the seconds since I had first seen the warning light, I had reversed direction and begun a steep left-climbing turn, converting 630KIAS of airspeed into precious altitude and, hopefully, time. Although my steed may have been "wounded," the jet didn't know it yet. Responding to my command, the control stick acting as my "reins," the MiG rocketed skyward at more than 10,000ft per minute.

Before I proceed, let me explain why any type of hydraulic problem was such a significant issue in the MiG-23. Like the MiG-21, the "Flogger" featured two independent hydraulic systems, namely the main system and the boost system. As the name implies, the main system handled all the essential high-demand components of the airplane, the most critical being the variable-geometry wing-sweep motors. Other systems, such as the leading and trailing edge wing flaps, landing gear, speed brakes, nose wheel steering, etc., I could work around, but without the wings coming forward, there was no recovery – just an ejection, or the "nylon let-down," as we jokingly called it. With my takeoffs and landings being equal up to this point in my career as a pilot, I was in no mood to alter the balance and go one down in the landing column.

I needed the wings to be at the 16° setting or the fully-forward detent on the wing-sweep control mechanism, which was necessary for landing. Otherwise, I'd eventually have to eject from the airplane. Even the MiG's designers advised against attempting to land in my current configuration with the wings full aft. My immediate priority was to move the wings forward quickly, making the best possible use of whatever residual hydraulic fluid remained in the system.

Next, my eyes were drawn to the periscope atop the canopy as I established my climb and reduced my airspeed to where the wings would begin to inch forward. What I saw next was both eye-opening and telling. Whatever the cause, the left-wing root of the airplane, where the movable wing was hinged in the fuselage, had erupted into an angry, grayish-looking cloud of hydraulic fluid, quickly vaporizing as it escaped into the 500KIAS slipstream.

Whatever amount of hydraulic fluid remained had better get the wings forward, or you could say goodbye to this MiG.

With the engine-driven hydraulic pump normally pressurizing the system at between 180–210kg/cm² (2,560–3,000psi) and venting as it did, I didn't have any margin for error. By now, I had steadied out heading northbound as I quickly approached 20,000ft AGL. During the climb, I traded 330KIAS of airspeed for 7,000ft of altitude, all the while keeping the throttle pulled back to idle.

Decelerating to 300KIAS, the wings had been slowly easing their way forward during the climb and were inching toward the 45° mark. With the loss of the main hydraulic system, the wing movement was painfully slow – only half the standard rate of 3.1 degrees per second. There was hope that enough fluid remained in the hydraulic reservoir to power them for the last few degrees of travel. At this point, the safe recovery of the airplane rested solely on the boost system, shouldering the burden of moving the wings and supplying partial power to the stabilators and spoilers. Should the boost system fail, the "Flogger" would become uncontrollable.

Another glance at the periscope atop the canopy visibly confirmed that the fluid was almost depleted, for the grayish-looking cloud was now barely visible in the wing root area. A sneak peek at the main system pressure gauge on the lower pedestal, located in front of the control stick, showed a reading well below 130kg/cm² and slowly decreasing. The boost system needle hovered at 200kg/cm² on the same hydraulic gauge. So, whatever the cause of the main system's loss of pressure, the boost was holding on.

Additionally, the location of the hydraulic leak was troubling. The wing carry-through area of the MiG-23 was one of the two most vulnerable locations on the "Flogger," where the hydraulic lines for both systems, fuel lines, and flight controls ran from the fuselage to the wings. Damage in this area could quickly lead to the loss of more systems. For the moment, I dismissed any "what if" thoughts for the emergency at hand.

"'BANDIT Three-One,' say the nature of your emergency?" asked MacDonald.

"Main hydraulics. I'm losing it fast."

"'Three-One,' say altitude," asked Craig. Having knocked off his part of the intercept while level at 31,000ft AGL, he had been in a full afterburner tail-chase for the last minute and was approaching me at 600KIAS. He needed to know my position to affect the rendezvous without wasting any time.

"'BANDIT Three-One,' level at 20,000ft, steady, headed Three-Four-Zero," I was quick to respond.

"'BANDIT Three-Two,' lead is Zero-Three-Zero, for five miles," MacDonald added. His snap vector, along with my altitude call, allowed Craig to get a visual on me at his low "one o'clock." He instinctively

"KNOCK IT OFF!"

snapped his throttle to idle to help dissipate the 350KIAS of overtake he had on my now much slower fighter.

"'Two's' visual. Your 'seven o'clock for three.'"

I sneaked a slightly longer glance into the periscope and saw a dot, high in my left rear quarter and slowly growing larger. Eventually, I made out Craig's mottled-gray camouflaged MiG-21, closing rapidly in a descent exactly where he described and conveniently in line with the ever-diminishing hydraulic cloud atop my fighter's left-wing root.

"'Lead' is visual. 'Three-Two' cleared to join on my left wing. I'm slowing to 250[KIAS], starting a slight descent. 'Bandit Three-One' flight, switch tower. Button Two – Go!"

"Two!"

Seconds later, following a switch in radio frequencies, I checked in with the SOF, Maj Marty "Fog" Macy, who was operating the tower, and explained the situation. We were still ten miles south of the airfield, heading north. As we did so, and without my prompting, I saw Craig's fighter disappear from my view through the periscope off my left wing to commence what I assumed would be a visual inspection of my airplane. Initially, he would fly low and below me to eyeball any irregularities that may be obvious to him on my fighter's belly, before heading under my right wing to do the same thing once again, and then returning to take up formation just off my left wing. All the while, he would be closely looking at the MiG-23 to spot any tell-tale sign of something more ominous that would prevent a safe landing.

"'Three-One,' the top of your left wing and fuselage is covered in hydraulic fluid. I don't see any fluid still leaking, though," Craig informed me.

"'Three-One' copies," I replied.

By this time, my wings had reached to the fully forward position, visually confirmed through the periscope and the wing-sweep position indicator on the upper right side of the instrument panel. Any immediate thought of having to bail out at some point was at least, for now, farther down the list of essential items on my mind. Over the next few minutes, in coordination with Macy in the tower, I reviewed the checklist covering the procedures for such a failure, our options, the order in which Craig and I would land, the positions of emergency response vehicles on the airfield, and other relevant details.

Of immediate concern was the amount of fuel I had remaining. That alone would dictate how long we had to troubleshoot my predicament. Another issue was how the airplane would handle in the landing configuration without deployment of the leading and trailing edge wing flaps. I would have to significantly increase my approach speed to compensate for the lack of these important lift devices, while striving to maintain controllability so that I could still land safely. Main hydraulic failure in the MiG-23 and the resulting compromised landing configuration were problems that had never previously been encountered by the 4477th TES.

Typically, pilots everywhere practice specific emergency procedures. Those of us flying MiGs did as well, but such drills were usually associated with engine problems or failures, mainly because you only had one. So, any "cough" or "sneeze" of your "one-and-only" motor quickly got your attention. Hence, the procedures for landing an airplane with degraded engine performance were the primary focus during any "Red Eagles" discussion of probable emergency recoveries.

However, no squadron pilot has ever had a hydraulic emergency of this nature before in a MiG-23. So, all we had to go on was what the Soviets had published in their flight manual. The latter, of course, had been translated from Russian into English and then rewritten and transcribed in a format and style most of us US fighter jocks were accustomed to.

Isn't this going to be fun? I hope they got the translation right!

As I mentioned earlier, this was no ordinary hydraulic failure. Every significant component that relied on hydraulics now depended on the boost system. Thankfully, with the wings fully forward, at least I'd be able to attempt the approach. However, without the availability of the leading and trailing edge flaps, the procedure required an approach airspeed of 210KIAS and a touchdown of the main gear at 190KIAS. To put those numbers into perspective, our typical approach speed in the MiG-23 was around 150KIAS, with touchdown at approximately 140KIAS. For comparison, a typical airliner would land at around 120–130 KIAS. At the very least, I'd be 60KIAS faster than your average airliner approach. But hey, I was a fighter pilot. What could possibly go wrong that I couldn't handle?

While this emergency was nothing to take lightly, it wasn't necessarily alarming, nor was it something I had not had some exposure to, although I had obviously never experienced it in a MiG-23. Six years earlier, as a young lieutenant piloting an F-4D while flying out of Kunsan AB, I experienced a similar compound hydraulic emergency. In that instance, I had lost two of my three hydraulic systems in the Phantom II. If the sole remaining system had failed, pitch control of the jet would have been lost, and my WSO and I would've had to eject.

In that instance, the safe recovery of the F-4 required jettisoning the six live Mk 82 500lb bombs on my centerline station, dumping fuel, emergency extension of the landing gear, a no-flap landing, and an approach end barrier engagement with the tailhook. If that were not enough, should the tailhook have somehow skipped the BAK-12 aircraft arresting cable, then I'd have

"KNOCK IT OFF!"

to execute a go-around and try again as my Phantom II didn't have any functioning brakes. But back to my current predicament in the "Flogger."

Before I could attempt a landing, I needed to lower and lock the landing gear. No problem. I could "blow down" the landing gear using the emergency pneumatic system. Luckily, after activating the latter, all three green lights on the gear control panel illuminated, indicating the gear was down and locked. Great!

Next, I did a "controllability check." With the landing gear down, I slowed to the planned approach speed of 210KIAS from my present speed of 250KIAS. Again, all was fine and dandy. There was no airframe buffet at 210KIAS, which would have indicated a potential problem with the configuration or possibly an improper airspeed. With the proper airspeed confirmed and the checklist completed, the only thing left to do was to land the airplane, bring it to a stop, and hand it back to Maintenance. Simple.

After conferring with Macy in the tower and Maintenance, we decided to have "Bandit 32" land first in case I botched my landing and closed the runway. The rationale was that it was better to have Craig on the ground rather than risk him being airborne with nowhere to land except for the narrow taxiway.

So, not needing his assistance any further for chase duties, I cleared him off and he landed, while still allowing me plenty of time to set up for my approach, which today was to the south-southeast on the airfield's Runway 14. When planning my approach to land, I ensured that I had enough fuel to execute a "go-around" should the first attempt be questionable. With everything in position on the airfield, I was cleared to land, commencing my turn to final before setting up on a four-to five-mile straight-in approach.

Now, one more piece of the story was unique, at least at TTR, compared to any other USAF installation. Throughout the 4477th complex, a public address (PA) system was installed that allowed anyone to transmit messages or information deemed necessary to everyone within earshot of the PA speakers. It was an excellent system if you suddenly needed to get the word out on an un-briefed Soviet satellite over-flight of the airfield, the arrival of a high-ranking official, or an emergency. Today, it was being used for the latter.

So, as I was setting up for the final approach, word went out by some unseen voice, "'Bandit Three-One,' F-4, hydraulic emergency. Estimate five minutes to landing." I imagine it sounded like an announcement of some impending doom. Hey, it was not every day that someone experienced an emergency like this. And let's face it, without it being said, everyone knew there was a good chance that this airplane and its pilot could end up in a giant fireball at the departure end of the runway if things didn't go quite to plan. So, with the PA announcement made, no less than two dozen maintenance troops dropped what they were doing and quickly ran out to the west side of the hangar complex to witness what could have been "Z-Man's" last hurrah. How touching. Now, I like to think no one had their fingers crossed, hoping to witness a fireball.

Landing the MiG-23 under normal conditions wasn't necessarily a "no-brainer." Today, I would be landing one with a ton of extra airspeed. For the unfamiliar, these additional "knots" would require some deft stick and rudder work once on the ground, as the airplane still wanted to fly at my planned landing speed. It wanted to fly, I wanted to land. It would be a bit of a dilemma if not handled well when all your wheels were on the ground.

As I have previously mentioned, the MiG-23 was squirrelly even on a good day. The high wings, narrow landing gear, and lack of ailerons made for some "interesting" approaches and landings even when everything was normal. Today, I had all that to contend with, plus diminished flight controls due to the lack of main system hydraulics.

The last couple of miles took but a minute. On short final to the runway, I could see the emergency vehicles' flashing lights set up and positioned at the mid and far end of the runway, should I need help (read, flaming fireball). But right now, I focused on the point of the runway, 1,000ft from the approach end, where I wanted to make my touchdown. The alignment had to be near perfect, the airspeed spot on, and the blending of throttle reduction and pitch control orchestrated precisely to keep the fast-moving jet from touching down too hard and bouncing.

In its stricken state, there simply was not the controllability to arrest a possible botched landing and a handful of "Flogger" at this airspeed. If the aircraft became uncontrollable and headed off the runway, there was no "punching out." At this altitude, the ejection seat was worthless, except to keep me strapped in. Attempting to eject should I lose control was a death sentence commutable only by the grace of God. It was all up to me.

In the last few seconds before touching down, I gently eased the control stick back and slowly reduced the throttle, bleeding off my airspeed to synchronize my touchdown with as little descent rate as possible at 190KIAS. At that speed, I sensed the end of the runway going past in a flash out of my periphery, the surrounding desert a blur. I was focused on my touchdown point, and, in a moment, I was there. The main gear touched down, and I held the nose off for a few seconds while I pulled the throttle to the idle stop.

The airplane was tracking perfectly – no yaw to compound the problem. I'd almost made it. With the throttle now at idle, I quickly reach to deploy the drag chute, its control button just above and outboard of the throttle quadrant. A few seconds later, I felt the familiar tug of the drag chute as it deployed from its housing at the base of the rudder. A quick peek through the periscope confirmed a full chute, rapidly helping to slow the airplane. It worked so well that I made an early exit off the runway rather than having to taxi the whole length of it.

Exiting the runway, I was surrounded by five emergency and maintenance vehicles. TSgt Jerry Fields, who was on Crash Recovery alert duty that afternoon, was out of his truck before I stopped, signaling me to hold my position while his crew chocked and secured the airplane.

With the chocks in place, Jerry gave me the signal to shut down the engine, and I quickly did just that, then popped open the canopy. With my oxygen mask dropped, the rush of fresh air across my sweat-covered face was brisk and welcome. I could relax for the first time since the warning light had illuminated 20 minutes earlier. I did not move for a few seconds. In short order, Jerry had the boarding ladder in place and was quickly up the side of the airplane to congratulate me on bringing the bird back, reaching out to shake my hand. I took it firmly in mine and, looking at him, gave him a wink, saying, "Other than the hydraulics, good airplane, Jerry!"

Back at Nellis AFB later that evening, several other "Red Eagles" and I made off to the O'Club, where I don't remember paying for a single round. I tried to, but I was told my money wasn't good that night. The celebration was on, and it lasted a while. Naturally, we could not discuss what had happened amongst the other patrons, but we all knew how close we'd come to losing an airplane and perhaps a fellow pilot that afternoon, especially those of us who knew and flew the MiG-23. With the night over, we all went our separate ways, knowing we'd return to the squadron the following day to do it all again. We were "Red Eagles." It's what we did.

At this point, I'm sure you're wondering what caused the hydraulic leak that started all this fuss. The following day, deputy maintenance officer Capt Fred "Jose" Garcia walked into the squadron, entered the flight room where I was seated, and approached me, carrying a peculiar-looking piece of hardware. Next, he tossed me about a foot-long section of what appeared to be four high-pressure aluminum hydraulic lines affixed together, each about the diameter of your index finger. A closer look reveals a rather large crimp at their center point, with two lines ruptured, showing gaping holes of jagged metal.

This section, Garcia explained, was what his maintenance troops had discovered upon removing the access panels at the top of the left-wing root, where I had seen the hydraulic fluid venting. Next, he produced another piece of hardware that appeared a bit more familiar. This resembled a giant electrical plug, approximately the size of your fist. It, he explained, was part of the wiring harness that typically extended into the wing pylons and supplied the circuitry for missiles, ejection racks, and other components.

Never having been used by us in the "Red Eagles," the large plug-like connector had, years before, been "tucked away" within the recesses of the wing and forgotten. Whenever the wings had been moved over that period, the plug and its associated cable had somehow gotten caught in the wing-sweep mechanism. Little by little, it worked its way up to the hydraulic lines, where yesterday the plug and cable had conveniently caused the damage that had led to the failure. My selection of the wings to the 72° position was the final act, causing the plug to be forcibly pulled through the main hydraulic lines, resulting in the failure.

It has often been said that timing is everything. This is especially true when flying fighters – even more so when you were flying MiGs in the 4477th. Had the failure happened right after I had landed and brought the wings to their full aft post-flight position, it would have been a non-event. On the other hand, had the two remaining hydraulic lines in the wing root, just inches from the others, been compromised, the aircraft would have been uncontrollable. I would've had no option but to eject from the airplane, had that even been possible, which would have ruined my takeoff-to-landing ratio. As I said, timing is everything. Luck isn't a bad thing, either!

27

"We Lost One"

"Our flag does not fly because the wind moves it. It flies with the last breath of each soldier who died protecting it."

UNKNOWN

July 11, 1986
0150hrs Pacific Daylight Time
21,000ft above the Central Valley of California
F-117A "Ariel 32" (85-0814)

Capt Greg "Curly" Nicholl had been airborne for roughly 50 minutes. He and his F-117 were level at flight level 210 with the autopilot engaged as they headed southward down the Central Valley of California on this, his second sortie of the evening. While notably busy with the usual duties of flying the single-seat stealth fighter, everything about the flight was reasonably routine as he prepared to acquire his last "target" located amongst the maze of buildings and structures of downtown Bakersfield, California. Unknown to its sleeping citizens below, nearly four miles overhead, the USAF's latest and most secret weapon system was routinely using their city as part of its targeting practice.

In "Ariel 32," Nicholl was roughly 40 miles in trail of "Ariel 31," another F-117 Nighthawk assigned to the 4450th Tactical Squadron (TS) of the 4450th TG. While officially based at Nellis AFB, the 4450th's operating location, like that of the 4477th, was also at TTR. As evidenced by the growing number of hangars dedicated to each F-117, the scope of the unit's operation had grown considerably over the past few years. Where it once numbered a mere dozen hangars when I first set foot on the TTR airfield nearly three years earlier, its sprawling ramp now sported more than 50.

Nicholl's training mission this evening was simple, one he and other F-117 pilots with the top secret stealth fighter squadron had done repeatedly over the past 14 months – fly the route beginning near Sacramento, California, and along their flight path, practice the switchology, acquisition, and tracking of the Designated Mean Point of Impact (DMPI) targets for that mission. Handling all of these tasks while employing the Nighthawk's Infra-Red Acquisition and Designation System was crucial for honing the skills necessary to place an actual LGB on an enemy target should they ever be tasked to do so by the National Command Authority.

Flying America's super-secret stealth fighter and exercising everything associated with employing its capabilities in a realistic environment was crucial for maintaining the 4450th's combat capability. No longer limited to operating within the confines of the Nellis AFB ranges, F-117s had been venturing out all over the western US almost on a nightly basis for the past 14 months since they'd successfully passed their first Operational Readiness Inspection.

The conditions at TTR when both jets had taken off were near perfect for the two pilots. For starters, it was an absolutely clear night, with light winds out of the north-northwest and a moon illumination forecast of only 14 percent. The darker the night, the better, as such cover was then still necessary to keep America's best-kept secret safe from even a chance discovery. Painted jet-black, the F-117 was virtually invisible to the naked eye in the night sky.

Nicholl had departed from RWY 32 at TTR roughly eight minutes after "Ariel 31" took off. While flying the same training profile, they were not a formation flight but operated distinctly as separate fighters. The primary objective for both pilots this evening was a successful bomb run on a target located on the Superior Valley Range within the Edwards AFB, California, range complex. There, they were to each drop a single 25lb BDU-33 practice bomb, which would be scored and graded for accuracy and timing by the Range Control Officer (RCO).

As he neared Bakersfield, over the assigned UHF radio frequency, Nicholl could hear chatter between "Ariel 31" and the air traffic controller at the Los Angeles (LA) Air Route Traffic Control Center (ARTCC) as the F-117 ahead of him coordinated his descent and changed radio frequencies to the RCO at Superior Valley. The communication was so routine that it was much like background noise. Nicholl mostly tuned it out as he concentrated on nailing his last DMPI target in Bakersfield. Intent on doing just that, he was oblivious to repeated calls by the LA ARTCC controller to "Ariel 31." Finally, the controller reached out to "Ariel 32."

"'Ariel Three-Two,' Center."

Reflexively, hearing his callsign, Nicholl replied instantly, "Center, 'Ariel Three-Two.' Go ahead."

"Yeah, we've lost radar and radio contact with 'Ariel Three-One.' Perhaps he's already switched over to Superior Valley. Are you in contact with him?"

"WE LOST ONE"

"Negative Center. But let me check with the RCO. I'll be back on frequency in a minute and will let you know."

For the next two minutes, Nicholl made several attempts to raise "Ariel 31" on their current LA ARTCC frequency and then switched over to that of RCO to raise his squadron mate, all to no avail. The RCO told him "Ariel 31" hadn't checked in with him yet. Nicholl assumed that he must have had an aircraft issue and headed back to TTR. However, he thought that it was odd that his squadron mate hadn't told anyone.

Returning to his frequency with LA ARTCC, Nicholl told them that he had had no luck raising "Ariel 31." At about this time, Nicholl was approaching the turning point over Bakersfield, and he coordinated with LA ARTCC for his descent, canceling his IFR clearance and switching to the Superior Valley Range frequency. With so many things happening, he was preoccupied with them and didn't suspect anything amiss regarding "Aeriel 31's" status.

Over his turn point, Nicholl executed a smooth but aggressive 70° roll to the left and began a moderate descending turn toward the Superior Valley Range on the eastern slopes of the Sierra Nevada mountain range. With the Nighthawk banked up and coming through an easterly heading, his view of the mountains below and before him was unhindered by the front canopy area, which had earlier masked much of what was below him. His attention was immediately drawn to a massive fire at "ten o'clock" and approximately ten miles ahead along the Kern River Valley.

Traveling at nearly 400KIAS, his Nighthawk quickly closed the distance to the blaze. Offsetting slightly to the south, as he sped past the inferno below, Nicholl steeply banked his aircraft to the left to get a better view of the raging fire out of the left side of his canopy. He could see a ring of flames rapidly expanding outwards, climbing the surrounding canyon walls. A hot mass of what appeared to be the burning, charred remains of something was readily apparent at the center of the blaze. It looked like a cauldron of angry flames.

Nicholl had the presence of mind to switch quickly to the UHF emergency frequency of 243.0 MHz to check for signs of an emergency beacon, but his efforts to raise his squadron mate were only met with cold silence. If this was indeed the accident site of "Ariel 31," he hoped that its pilot had been able to eject safely and, although not responding to Nicholl's radio calls, would eventually turn up okay. Nonetheless, while he couldn't be sure, Nicholl had a haunting feeling that "Ariel 31" wouldn't be on the ground when he landed at TTR later that evening. The grim reality suddenly hit him. The USAF had lost its first operational F-117.

Seconds later, Nicholl checked in with the RCO at Superior Valley and told him of the fire that he had just observed 15 nautical miles east of Bakersfield. Additionally, given that he couldn't raise "Ariel 31," he wouldn't continue with his planned bomb run that evening. Something gnawed deep within him. Nothing more needed to be said. Even the RCO could connect the dots, and the picture they formed was not a good one. Instead, Nicholl picked up a clearance back to TTR and climbed to altitude for the 30-minute flight home. It would be the longest 30 minutes of flying in his Air Force career.

Following his landing back at TTR, Nicholl taxied to his assigned hangar. As he approached, he noted that the front and back doors were open, and his crew chief was waiting with lighted guidance wands to marshal him in. When he shut down his engines, the signal was immediately given to close both doors. With security concerns paramount, hangar doors throughout the complex were rarely ever opened, save for the immediate launch and recovery of each Nighthawk.

Before he had time to unstrap and exit the aircraft, there was already a small cluster of senior officers from the 4450th at the base of the ladder to meet him. Their mere presence told him his suspicions were correct – his friend aboard "Ariel 32," F-117A 81-0792, hadn't returned. The ensuing debrief back at the command post lasted well over an hour. Through it all, there wasn't much Nicholl had to add to the fact that LA ARTCC had suddenly lost radar and voice communications with "Ariel 31" just as he approached the Superior Valley Range. All attempts made by LA ARTCC, the RCO, and himself to contact "Ariel 31" were to no avail.

It was now well past 0400hrs, and Nicholl was physically and emotionally drained. Despite his exhaustion, there was some comfort in being in the company of his fellow squadron mates. Hours later, unable to even think about sleeping, he and several others headed to the dining hall seven miles away. As welcome as the thought of a warm breakfast was, it was a small comfort.

July 11, 1986
0600hrs Pacific Daylight Time
Tonopah Test Range

As was his usual routine most mornings after spending the night in the main camp at Tonopah, "Paco" Geisler had gotten up about a half-hour earlier, at around 0530hrs. This gave him plenty of time to get ready, head

"WE LOST ONE"

out the door, and stop at the dining hall for a bacon, egg, and cheese breakfast sandwich on the way to "Red Eagles" Operations seven miles away at the airfield. It was a beautiful morning in the high desert country of Nevada, almost perfect. Clear skies, cool early morning temperatures that would later give way to a high of 93° Fahrenheit, barely a trace of humidity, and light winds out of the north-northwest. It promised to be an ideal day for flying.

The short six-block drive to the main camp's dining hall in the squadron's rickety SOF Jeep was routine, and one he'd driven dozens of times over the past few years. Two minutes later, he pulled into the dining hall parking lot and noticed an unusual number of vehicles. Typically empty at this time of the day, almost two dozen USAF vehicles were clustered near the entrance. When he walked into the dining hall, he was taken aback by the number of people there from the 4450th, who, at that hour, were usually fast asleep following a full schedule of F-117 night operations.

Something was different. Geisler could feel it. Sense it. Typically, the dining hall was empty save for a handful of "Red Eagles" maintenance troops, who were up early to ready our MiGs for that morning's flying schedule. Today, however, there were dozens of 4450th personnel at the tables. Missing was the usual buzz amid the din of ongoing conversations. Today, it was noticeably subdued. Even the body language of those picking at their breakfast was different. They had slumped postures, eyes fixed straight at their meals, with little to no eye contact between them.

He was sure something was amiss when he noticed one table with no less than six 4450th pilots clustered together, a bit away from the others. Following a typical night's flying schedule, these guys were usually asleep in their assigned officers' quarters by 0430–0500hrs. Today, they were here with all the others. None of it made sense.

After getting his sandwich, Geisler walked over, looked at the group of pilots, and asked what was happening this morning. As was his usual jocular style, he laughingly asked if they'd been on a bender at the "TOCACL" (TTR's O'Club, jokingly nicknamed the "Tonopah Officers Club and Chinese Laundry") and were now trying to sober up. His attempt at humor was met with an awkward silence. A few heads shake to the negative. Still fewer look at him.

Just then, one of the pilots, whom Geisler knew well from previous assignments, stood up and tilted his head to the right, motioning for "Paco" to follow him. He walked a few steps away and, making sure he was out of earshot of the others, whispered, "We lost one last night, 'Paco'." Geisler could hardly believe what he had just heard.

"God damn!" he whispered, trying to contain his surprise. While he was about ready for anything he may have been told, losing a top secret stealth fighter wasn't even remotely on his radar. "Did he get out?" he asked. This was almost the universal question all fighter pilots first asked when they heard about an accident. His friend's facial expression, filled with emotion, gave him his answer.

"We don't know for certain now, but it doesn't look like it. It's not good, 'Paco'." Both were well aware of the security concerns surrounding the F-117 program and how this would undoubtedly affect the 4450th and, indirectly, the "Red Eagles" program as well. That said, Geisler was curious about another aspect of the accident – where was the crash site?

"Is it here on our ranges or somewhere else you were operating?"

"I can't get into that just now," his friend answered, "as you can appreciate the sensitivity, but it's off-range."

"Hey man, I'm sorry. Let me know if there's anything we can do to help." Even though "Paco" knew there was little that could be done to assist when such a tragedy occurred, he nevertheless expressed his understanding, as was customary whenever a sister squadron lost a pilot.

"Thanks, 'Paco.' Catch you later, perhaps."

Looking his friend in the eye, "Paco" gave him a heartfelt nod, a gentle pat on his shoulder, and headed for the door. He knew that a shitstorm was about to descend upon the F-117 program and, due to our physical proximity to them at TTR, it would indirectly affect us as well, at least in the short term. It was time to get to "Red Eagles" Operations and ensure Lt Col Jack "Mad Jack" Manclark was fully briefed. With his sandwich in hand, he was quickly on his way to meet the other squadron pilots, me included, aboard two Beechcraft C-12 aircraft inbound from Nellis and due to land within minutes, all onboard clueless about what had happened over the Sierra Nevada mountains just east of Bakersfield barely four hours earlier.

After the two C-12s that ferried us to TTR each morning had landed, we quickly exited the aircraft and piled into the squadron van for the short drive from the transient ramp to "Red Eagles" Operations. As soon as I stepped through the door of the building, I saw TSgt Jerry Howell standing in front of the daily scheduling board, busily erasing it.

What the fuck? This isn't good.

"Jerry, what's going on?" I ask indignantly.

"You'll have to ask Maj Geisler, 'Captain Z,'" Jerry replied. "I was only told that today's schedule has been canceled."

I know this is selfish, but I was anxious to get airborne again after being off the previous week due to the Fourth of July holiday. During this period, we typically skipped flying to give our maintenance troops some well-deserved

"WE LOST ONE"

time off at home. As I'd only flown a single MiG-23 flight earlier this week, I was disappointed that I wouldn't be able to head out and provide DACT for a visiting F-15 squadron that had been flying with us all week.

Within a few minutes of entering the squadron, the news quickly spread to everyone in Operations and throughout the Maintenance complex that flying for the day had been canceled. Instead, we were instructed to be in the squadron's main briefing room at 0730hrs, where our commander, Lt Col Manclark, would address us and explain what was happening. In the meantime, Manclark and Geisler were in the commander's office behind closed doors for the next 20 minutes on the STU II secure phone line with TAC HQ. Whatever it was, it was serious, but no one outside those two knew about it.

Armed with our early morning coffee and donuts, we all filed into the main briefing room moments before 0730hrs and waited for the news. Shortly thereafter, Manclark entered, went to the podium, and prepared to brief us on the current situation. Whatever the subject was, you knew it had to be serious when he got behind the podium to address the officers – he never did that. Manclark didn't waste any time and got straight to the point.

Firstly, the 4450th TS had lost an F-117 early that morning. Although they were still unsure, it was believed that the pilot had not survived the crash. Secondly, the location of the accident was sensitive. Worse yet, it was not on the Nellis range complex. Thirdly, with security concerns of paramount importance, both for the 4450th program and our own, all "Red Eagles" operations were canceled for the next few days as a team of accident investigators was expected to descend upon TTR. While those investigators would be briefed on the F-117 program, most had no knowledge of *Constant Peg* and our MiGs, and there we had no intention of providing them with such information.

Our MiGs would remain hidden within their hangars and out of sight. Therefore, to minimize security breaches, we would stand down operations today. As the investigation would certainly be ongoing for some time, we weren't expecting to recommence operations until at least the middle of the following week. That directive came straight from TAC HQ.

While we all had plenty of questions, we knew that little information would be released until much later, and only then on a strictly need-to-know basis. We also sensed we would never honestly know what had led to the first loss of an operational F-117 and its pilot.

Two hours later, we boarded our C-12s and flew back to Nellis AFB. While there was plenty of speculation about what might have occurred, none of us knew. With both programs tightly shrouded in secrecy, only a select few back at Nellis had been made aware of the incident. The rest of the base wouldn't be told about the accident until much later in the day, and only then after the local television stations broke the story mid-afternoon. Even when news of the accident went public, no mention would ever be made of the existence of the F-117. To the outside world, the aircraft didn't exist. If it didn't exist, it couldn't be lost. And therein lay the answer and the ever-present cover story. The 4450th openly operated A-7 Corsair IIs, and the official USAF press release acknowledged that one had crashed in the Sierra Nevada mountain range in the early morning hours of Friday, July 11, 1986.

July 11, 1986
1000hrs Pacific Daylight Time
682 North Straight Street
Las Vegas, Nevada

Marcie Nicholl had just returned home after dropping off her youngest daughter at preschool. With the two older children already in classes for the day at the local elementary school and the house now "empty," she looked forward to a brief respite from the myriad duties and responsibilities she dealt with all week while Greg was away. Kicking back with a good cup of coffee for even 30 minutes was a luxury. Things wouldn't get hectic until later in the afternoon, once everyone got home.

She had just sat down at the breakfast bar and was astonished to hear the garage door opening. Other than herself, only Greg had another remote to operate the door. A quick look out the front window showed his truck pulling into the driveway. "Oh great!" she thought to herself. "There goes any hope of a relaxing morning! Wait a moment. What's he doing at home so early? He's never been home this early on a Friday for over two years."

Greg entered the kitchen a minute later, looking exhausted and emotionally drained. Marcie knew something terrible had happened. But in that instant, whatever it was, her husband was home, and he was safe. In their ensuing embrace and the flood of emotions afterward, she learned of the accident and the identity of the squadron mate, but little else. Such was the case whenever the squadron lost a pilot.

Over their four years in the 4450th, Greg and Marcie would attend four funerals for pilots lost in aircraft accidents. Oddly, the weight of not knowing whether your husband would return home suddenly hit home

"WE LOST ONE"

some months later while Marcie was browsing the latest women's fashions on the sale rack at Neiman-Marcus at the nearby mall. She came across a lovely black dress and, holding it up to the mirror, a disturbing thought crossed her mind. "This is beautiful. It would be perfect for a dinner party – or a funeral." The last thought shocked her, and she quickly returned the dress to the rack and promptly exited the store. In that instant, she knew it was time for them to leave Nellis.

In its top secret accident report, the USAF Accident Board listed spatial disorientation as the likely cause of the crash. While pilot fatigue was known to be an issue among the squadron's aviators, it was not listed as a contributing factor. Ironically, there were rumors of a fatigue study and final report on the 4450th commander's desk at the time of the accident. The story holds that it vanished without any members of the accident board ever seeing it.

What is known is that the aircraft hit the ground while traveling at more than Mach 1. The airspeed limitation for the Nighthawk was said to be approximately 0.95 Mach. Moreover, the flight control software only gave the pilot a 49 percent "vote" on what he was allowed to do in the fly-by-wire design that enabled the jet to fly. The rest was reportedly left to the three flight control computers to decide. Whatever the case, whether the pilot knew he was in peril or not, there was no evidence that he made any attempt to eject.

At my home in Las Vegas, directly across from Greg and Marcie Nicholl (both close friends that I saw regularly), in the ensuing days and weeks following the accident it was never acknowledged, much less discussed. Moreover, my roommate, Dick Hoey, who had been an F-117 pilot for more than two-and-a-half years and was in the squadron at the time of the accident, never mentioned it, even in passing. And I never asked. We were aware of the security sensitivities of the program, and we avoided discussing any aspect of our respective missions outside of TTR.

In the 4477th, we recommenced flying the following Wednesday, July 15, 1986, when I undertook a single MiG-23MS sortie. While we were back to "normal operations," it would be some time before the 4450th TS followed suit. The importance of the secrecy of our program and others, to which we were privy, was something we lived with and took for granted. Indeed, it was as natural as breathing. If it didn't concern the person you might be talking to, no mention of such events was ever uttered. Such was life behind the "black curtain."

28

Pushing the Envelope

"It's a fine line between bravery and foolishness."
                                                              ANONYMOUS

August 1986
Late afternoon
Range 76
23 nautical miles south-southwest of Tonopah Test Range
MiG-23MS "Flogger-E"

It was day three of a week-long *Constant Peg* deployment for the F-15 pilots of the 8th TFS visiting from Holloman AFB. As line Eagle squadrons went, the "Black Sheep" had progressed on par with their counterparts across TAC. Typically, almost all fighter units started a bit shaky on days one and two of any deployment. Still, by Thursday, those pilots who'd had an opportunity to see and fight a MiG-21 at least twice were doing well, making life difficult for my fellow "Red Eagle" squadron mates, knocking heads with them in the MiG-21. Additionally, a few had been exposed to the MiG-23, and this afternoon's sortie would provide yet another F-15 pilot with the opportunity to fly against the "Flogger" during a Performance Profile (PP) and perhaps a couple of 1-v-1 engagements.

It was my second sortie of the day, having flown an earlier one with another member of the "Black Sheep" in a MiG-23BN model hours earlier. While the ground-attack variant didn't have the high-speed capability of the fighter interceptor MiG-23MS I was flying on this sortie, for all practical purposes, there wasn't an appreciable difference in performance, especially in the visual arena in which visiting crews were exposed to our MiGs. It would have been an entirely different story in a beyond visual range scenario against a later model "Flogger-K" fitted with RP-23 Sapfir (NATO reporting name "High Lark") radar and armed with AA-7 "Apex" (Vympel R-24R) radar-guided missiles.

Today, however, following a demonstration of the "Flogger's" acceleration, turn, and zoom capabilities, it was to be a pure 1-v-1 visual setup, with me attacking the F-15 pilot from his aft quadrant, outside of 9,000ft, and closing. Even if starting defensively, I always told visiting fighter units that if they could see an attacking "Flogger," they could defeat it. My theorem was about to be put to the test.

With the PP portion of the mission complete, I wasted little time setting up the visual 1-v-1 with my F-15 adversary. As a bit of background, the Eagle pilot I was paired with this afternoon coincidentally happened to be a former Nellis-based Aggressor pilot and someone I had known since attending the 65th AS conversion course at Nellis AFB four years earlier. Seeing that he had now been in the Eagle for a few years, odds were good that my opponent would quickly turn the tables on me, and at the very least, I'd be absorbing simulated missile shots somewhere during the engagement. How's that for confidence?

We were steady on a northbound heading, level at 20,000ft MSL, with the F-15 in a loose visual formation off my right wing, holding at 350KIAS. After instructing him to maintain our current heading, I rolled left, making a wide S-turn to put some distance between us, and took up an offensive position on his left at "seven o'clock" and approximately 1.5 miles away.

"'Ram One-One,' push it up and start an easy left-hand turn. 'Bandit Two-One' is at seven o'clock and level. Call when you are visual and ready," I radioed. As briefed, my directive was for the F-15 pilot to throttle up to 400KIAS, establish a visual on me, and call when ready to commence maneuvering. The information provided in this brief transmission was something fighter pilots did with regularity whenever they were about to engage in 1-v-1 combat training. The message acted as a prelude to unrestricted maneuvering once the fight was on. Two audible clicks over the radio indicated that "Ram 11" understood my instructions and was throttling up.

As I pushed the throttle to the MIL power position, I felt the "Flogger" surge forward and begin accelerating. The "feel" of the aircraft responding to the throttle movement told me everything was normal, and the big Soviet fighter was ready for whatever I had in store for it. Still, my eyes darted over the engine gauges and warning lights, habitually checking to ensure everything was okay.

EGT stable, wings at 45°, fuel 3,200 liters – enough for at least two fights. Middle of Range 76. Steady northbound. Game time!

"'Ram One-One' is ready," he quickly replied a few seconds later. In a moment, at the "fight's on" call, I expected the pilot of "Ram 11" to roll his Eagle into a 90° left banked break-turn into me, generating close to

24° per second of instantaneous turn rate and making any attempt to get inside his turn-circle impossible for a MiG-23. Needless to say, my options were limited.

"'Bandit Two-One,' fight's on, fight's on!" With my radio call, I shoved the throttle to the full afterburner setting and felt it immediately light, noticeably pushing my torso back into the ejection seat ever so slightly. As anticipated, within seconds, the entire planform shape of the F-15 was visible, its light gray paint scheme almost reflective in the high afternoon sun, its pilot cranking the big fighter around in an 8G turn, his lift vector squarely on my attacking MiG.

Damn. This never gets old!

As my MiG's afterburner was lighting, I wasted no time bringing the tight-turning Eagle onto my nose and, pulling lead on him, placed the big fighter at the base of my windscreen, well below the gunsight in an 80° left banked turn of my own. While there was no way I'd ever be able to turn with him, the MiG-23, equipped with its internal GSh-23L 23mm twin-barrel autocannon, was enough of a threat that it required him to honor my nose position and continue his hard turn, bleeding precious airspeed the whole time.

Very quickly, my "Flogger" had accelerated well past 450KIAS while my adversary's airspeed depleted with every second he was in his hard turn. With my estimated range to him now less than 4,000ft, I was guessing he'd pissed away close to 100KIAS and was at just above 300KIAS. While he may have been depleting his energy, he was generating enough angles for my attack that I faced a decision point – and quickly.

Blow through him, sweep the wings to 72° and "bug-out," or go vertical and fight?

With my wings at 45°, if I were going to stay and fight, this was the configuration I wanted to be in. While the odds of success in a turning fight weren't in my favor, he wasn't expecting any MiG-23 pilot to be foolish enough to try it. With my airplane approaching 500KIAS and crossing angles building rapidly, I made my move. Approaching a separation distance of 2,500ft, I rolled out of my hard turn and slightly unloaded the aircraft. As expected, with my nose now off of him and no longer posing an immediate gun threat, I saw my adversary react. But instead of unloading his Eagle and regaining his lost airspeed, as would have been prudent, he reversed his turn direction with a quick 180° roll to his right.

Foolish move. Should've unloaded and gone for energy, and better options!

Probably anticipating a "hit-and-run" tactic, he was "betting the farm" that my high-speed "Flogger" would grossly overshoot his turn, and his reversal would leave him on the attack. What happened next was both telling and surprising.

While I had thought about turning away, sweeping the wings to 72° and extending out of the fight and radar missile range, his unexpected reversal presented an opportunity that rarely happened when flying the MiG-23 – one that few "Flogger" pilots would contemplate, much less attempt. With him now momentarily blind to me while in his turn reversal, I immediately pulled back on the stick and launched the "Flogger" into a nearly pure vertical climb. As I rocketed skyward, a slight left pirouette in the vertical axis enabled me to keep a visual on my opponent, who had by now completely reversed his turn and come back hard right, frantically searching for the MiG-23 that he was sure would be "bugging out" back at his right "four o'clock" and low.

In my climb, I maneuvered to his high "six o'clock" and to a height he couldn't have imagined. I was now nearly 7,000ft above his energy-depleted Eagle, watching as he finally gained sight of me while I began to arc over the top of my oblique loop and commenced my descent in pursuit. With the MiG-23 now driving the fight, the tables had been turned, but most unexpectedly.

Having spent much of the previous 20 seconds in two energy-depleting turns, the F-15 pilot lacked the airspeed to take his fighter into the vertical in pursuit. I estimated that at this point his airspeed was less than 250KIAS, which became evident as I momentarily saw him attempt to bring his nose up to meet my attack. Without the energy to do so, I watched as his nose abruptly fell off after he had only been able to raise it roughly 60° to counter my position of advantage. The F-15's airspeed was now well below 200KIAS. With the Eagle almost out of airspeed, he dropped off into a steep dive in a desperate attempt to escape.

Coming over the top inverted at just 220KIAS, I had the stick back as far as I was comfortable with. The "knuckle-rapper" was letting me know the MiG-23 had nothing more to give, it's rhythmic tapping on my right hand increasing to a rate I'd never previously experienced. A glance at the AOA indicator showed the needle hovering at the 27-unit mark. As much as I'd like to have "stomped" full left rudder and got the nose slicing down to pursue the attack as I would've done in the MiG-21, I had to keep the rudder pedals centered, lest any hint of yaw at this AOA put the "Flogger" out of control.

Just take what it gives you – you're on the edge of departing this beast. Don't fuck it up. Gentle, you've got him!

Seconds later, I was 70° nose low, still at full afterburner, and quickly accelerating. The F-15 was now less than 3,000ft in front of me, but I was gaining. As previously mentioned, almost nothing accelerated like the "Flogger," especially downhill. I was closing on him – fast!

Out of afterburner. Preserve your distance. Center him in the gunsight.

My adversary attempted everything to escape, his engine's afterburners glowing bright and distinct against the desert floor far below us. Careful not to overshoot him, I quickly slid the throttle back out of afterburner to idle and extended the speed brakes, looking to conserve my distance as I brought the flailing Eagle into my gunsight. At under 250KIAS, the F-15 out in front of me was wallowing, and its pilot was out of energy and ideas. While the MiG-23 was not an agile fighter, I was seconds away from squeezing the trigger for a simulated guns-tracking kill on the F-15 from a commanding position and with an energy advantage.

"Knock it off, knock it off. 'RAM One-One,' knock it off – 'bingo fuel,'" the cornered F-15 pilot transmitted over the radio.

What? You've got to be fucking shitting me!

"'Bandit Two-One,' knock it off. Copy the 'bingo,'" I replied, with a tone of both surprise and disbelief undoubtedly present in my retort.

Call me skeptical, but F-15s didn't typically "bingo" out on a routine *Constant Peg* sortie, especially one where we had barely had a full engagement. While it may have been a legitimate KIO for fuel, if it were, it'd been the only time I "bingo'd" out an F-15 in all my years as a "Red Eagle." More likely, and I'll never be able to prove this, the F-15 pilot, not wanting to suffer the humiliation of being gunned by a MiG-23, conveniently played the "fuel card" to save his bacon. But that was largely irrelevant.

Whatever the case, the fight was over, and what had looked like a sure guns-tracking kill of an F-15 by a MiG-23 never happened. It probably would've been a squadron first. And, for what it's worth, somewhere out there is a former F-15 pilot who knows what it's like to look over his shoulder and see a MiG-23 bearing down on him for a gun attack and being unable to defend against it. Had he, instead, unloaded his Eagle and gotten his energy back when my nose first came off of him, the clash would've ended appreciably differently. But we'll never know.

The lesson learned from this engagement was the same as had been discovered by aviators contesting the first aerial duels of World War I. "In air combat, greed will get you nowhere, and underestimating your opponent will get you killed!" Once again, the value of the concept of *Constant Peg*, flying against actual threat aircraft, was unmistakably proven.

That was the closest I ever came to scoring a gun kill on any fighter I flew against while in a MiG-23. As I previously mentioned, if you could see a "Flogger" behind you closing for a gun attack, you could defeat it. Well, as had just been proven, that was probably true 99 percent of the time.

And that, to a fighter pilot, says it all when the topic arises regarding the merits of the MiG-23 as a fighter.

To properly understand MiG-23 operations within the 4477th TES, it is helpful to recap the unit's experience with the aircraft. By the time I began my checkout on the jet, the USAF had been secretly operating the "Flogger" for less than eight years, starting with Project *Have Pad* – a top secret tactical exploitation of the MiG-23MS by AFSC, which commenced in March 1978 from Area 51. A further two years passed before the 4477th made its first flight with the MiG-23 on November 1, 1980. Five years later, I became the 23rd "Red Eagle" to fly the "Flogger."

While much had been learned about how to effectively employ the MiG-23 during its early years of operation with the 4477th, these lessons were often only passed along verbally. Moreover, while the *Have Pad* exploitation had done a superb job of outlining how each system and component in the aircraft worked, what was lacking was the availability of any in-depth manual on aircraft handling and performance that would be of value for "Red Eagles" pilots transitioning to the "Flogger" in the future. Understandably, this was outside the scope of the evaluation. While a *Have Pad* Section III Operational Evaluation report on the MiG-23 was said to exist, neither I nor any other "Red Eagles" "Flogger" pilot interviewed during the research for this book had ever seen a copy of it.

This essentially meant that there was scant information beyond the collection of individual notes kept by 4477th pilots early on, with nothing being formalized outside of crude checklists and operating guidelines.

Once Lt Col George Gennin took command of the squadron in August 1982, all that changed. Under his leadership, by the time I began the transition to the MiG-23, we had flight manuals for both the MiG-21 and MiG-23. They were an "in-house" effort, converting volumes of intelligence data on our aircraft into something any USAF or US Navy pilot would recognize. The manuals' outline, style, font, and other features resembled all other USAF "Dash-1" manuals. This was invaluable in providing pilots with a single repository of what we had learned, both good and bad, about operating these aircraft without the filters of various intelligence agencies or the need to sift through poorly translated foreign-sourced manuals.

Additionally, their creation addressed a recurring challenge faced by the 4477th – the departure of our most experienced MiG-23 pilots following their assignment as "Red Eagles," taking with them a vast reservoir of knowledge about the aircraft. For example, in the months leading up to my transition to the MiG-23, we saw Capt Larry "Shy" Shervanick and Majs Dave "Blazo" Bland and Jim "Thug" Matheny depart with Permanent Change of Station orders for F-16 assignments. Together, they accounted for 415 sorties in the "Flogger." This was significant, considering that in the entire history of the "Red Eagles," only half of all squadron MiG-23 pilots managed to attain even 100 sorties, with seven pilots never exceeding 30.

The respective training syllabuses and checklists for each aircraft were revised in conjunction with the new flight manuals. This 18-month overhaul of our in-house training program aligned the squadron with most other fighter units in TAC. In short, I benefited from the tremendous work of people like Cdr John "Black" Nathman, US Navy, and "Thug" Matheny, both of whom spent months exhaustively crafting the MiG-23 manual together.

As alluded to earlier, the MiG-23's poor turning performance was the biggest disappointment for pilots who flew it in the 4477th. As every "Red Eagles" pilot came to the MiG-23 after having just flown the agile and forgiving MiG-21, the "Flogger" was almost the complete opposite in so many ways. Moreover, the aircraft's susceptibility to departing controlled flight suddenly and without warning at high AOA was particularly startling, and to some, frightening. Whereas the MiG-21 was forgiving and docile if stalled, to achieve maximum performance from the MiG-23, the pilot needed to closely monitor the AOA indicator and heed warning signs from the "knuckle-rapper." In short, it required a pilot's full awareness of his energy state and strict limitations associated with every wing position.

That said, the primary goal of the *Constant Peg* program was to highlight the aircraft's full potential in a controlled visual air combat setting. Those of us who flew the "Flogger" pushed its capabilities far beyond what Soviet pilots would ever consider. A prime example was our use of the MiG-23BN ground attack model in intense visual engagements, a mission for which it was never intended. Quite often, it was not unusual to see the "Flogger-H" model occupying the flying schedule because all of our "Flogger-Es" were in the hangar for maintenance.

As previously mentioned, "Red Eagles" pilots wrote the definitive guide to flying the MiG-23, primarily based on the squadron's firsthand experiences with the aircraft during the five years the 4477th operated it before my checkout. However, most pilots had in-flight "experiences" beyond what was mentioned in the squadron's flight manual, especially when the jet was flown in the high AOA regime. This was where our expertise proved invaluable, allowing us to safely return damaged airplanes to TTR and recover from departures at high AOA. The latter scenario was never far from a "Flogger" pilot's mind when flying the jet.

Without the advantage of simulators or two-seat trainers, high-performance experience – often gained across multiple aircraft types – before joining the "Red Eagles" proved invaluable. Notably, at the time of my checkout in the MiG-23, all 4477th pilots flying the MiG-23, bar Capt Steve Brown (F-15), had flown the F-4 Phantom II at some point during earlier assignments before joining the unit. While this wasn't particularly surprising, given that the F-4 had been the backbone of the USAF, US Navy, and US Marine Corps fighter forces for years before the introduction of the F-15, F-14, and F/A-18, it emphasizes the Phantom II's significance.

Despite the apparent differences between the basic aircraft, both exhibited similar handling characteristics, which undoubtedly made my transition to the MiG-23 easier. With the "Flogger's" wings swept back at 45° and speeds ranging from 400 to 550KIAS, the feel and turn rate closely resembled those of a "hard-wing" F-4 (i.e., without maneuvering slats). Moreover, the "hard wing" Phantom II was prone to violent departures at high AOA if the pilot attempted to roll using only the ailerons. The adverse yaw caused by the downward-deflecting aileron (i.e., left roll, right aileron) would abruptly, without warning, cause a snap roll in the opposite direction. If you didn't make an immediate correction by unloading the aircraft, this uncontrollable departure could likely lead to a spin. It's often said in Phantom II pilot circles that if you had flown a hard-wing F-4 and never experienced a departure, you had never really "flown" the Phantom II. Ask me how I know.

While the F-4 and the "Flogger" had similar aircraft departure recovery procedures, they differed in one crucial aspect – the Phantom II's included deploying the drag chute if the aircraft did not recover after stick and rudder inputs. A significant difference in the MiG-23's procedure was the step to shut down the engine once it was determined that the aircraft had entered a fully developed spin. Although this was aimed at preventing engine damage from the anticipated bending moments caused by such a maneuver, none of the 4477th pilots who experienced spins in the MiG-23 ever seriously considered shutting down their sole engine.

That's where the similarities between the F-4 and the MiG-23 ended. In the Phantom II, regardless of whether it was a hard-wing F-4C/D/E model or the F-4E equipped with leading-edge slats, you quickly learned to always use the rudder to lead any turns while maneuvering, especially at high AOA during air combat training. This technique would later influence how I flew the F-5E and the MiG-21, as maximum performance in either was highly dependent on proper use of the rudder as aileron effectiveness diminished.

In contrast, avoiding the use of the rudder in the MiG-23 at high AOA was a must, as any introduction of yaw could quickly lead to a loss of controlled flight and potentially result in a spin. Generally, I would only actively use the rudder in the "Flogger" during crosswind landings or, heaven forbid, during spin recovery. Ironically, the first step in spin recovery required applying full rudder in the opposite direction of the spin. Fortunately, I never found myself out of control in the MiG-23, despite often flying it right to its AOA limits. Several of my squadron mates weren't so lucky.

The most incredible spin recovery of a MiG-23 by any "Red Eagle" took place during Maj Ted Drake's flight against a pair of F-16s. He was the only pilot to experience upright and inverted spins in the "Flogger." Unbelievably, he achieved this remarkable feat on the same flight!

The first of these events began at the merge with a pair of F-16s following a tactical intercept ten minutes into the flight. Drake was in a level, hard right-hand turn, with the "Vipers" (F-16 is officially called the Fighting Falcon, but it is universally known as the "Viper" by those that fly and maintain it) off his right wing line, but with high angles off his tail, about one mile back at "five o'clock." With it being obvious the F-16s were going to overshoot his tail, Drake initiated a moderate left turn to kick them across his "six o'clock," fully expecting to reacquire them seconds later at "seven o'clock" at a distance of about two miles. However, as he rolled left, the MiG-23 unexpectedly began a slow roll to the right, which he initially thought was simply adverse yaw. Drake eased off the Gs slightly, anticipating that the roll would stop. It didn't.

Instead, the MiG-23 persisted in its lazy roll to the right, completing two full rolls, with the second being more pronounced than the first, before pausing and momentarily hanging in space at approximately a +40° nose-high pitch attitude. The "Flogger" then briefly yawed to the right, followed by violent yawing in the opposite direction, slamming Ted against the right side of the canopy as the MiG-23 entered a left-hand stabilized upright spin.

Without hesitation, Ted applied full right rudder to counter the spin and unloaded the "Flogger," keeping the stick well forward of neutral and aligning it with the prominent white stripe running vertically down the center of the instrument panel – a feature so characteristic of later model MiG-21s and all MiG-23s. In less than one additional turn, the MiG-23 exited the spin with its nose positioned at -70° below the horizon.

Convinced he had safely recovered from the spin, Drake gently pulled back on the stick to raise the buried nose. With minimal Gs on the aircraft and no "knuckle-rapper" alerting him of anything amiss during his pullout, everything seemed like a normal recovery. As he neared a nose-low attitude of -40° to -45°, the nose suddenly popped up to the horizon. As before, the MiG-23 yawed again, this time slamming Ted against the left side of the canopy, flipping inverted, and entering a right-hand inverted spin.

For a brief second, Drake, now hanging inverted and in a spin for the second time in less than a minute, seriously considered ejecting. However, in a moment of calm, knowing he had just recovered from the previous spin, he decided to try again, immediately applying the recovery procedures. After two additional turns, the MiG-23 recovered from its spin, nose low at -70° but still inverted. When the spinning stopped, he gently rolled the "Flogger" upright and smoothly began recovering from the ensuing dive, reminding himself that he didn't have the altitude to recover a third time should it depart again. Now upright and gaining airspeed, Drake allowed himself a bit more altitude than was necessary to ensure there was no chance of departing a third time. Feeling confident the "Flogger" was safely flying, he bottomed out of his recovery at less than 2,000ft AGL above the desert floor.

Luckily, there was no apparent damage to the engine, as it responded to his slow and deliberate throttle movement. He then smoothly increased power, beginning a climb back to altitude. After recovering from two spins, and less than 15 minutes into the flight, Drake, not wanting to tempt fate further, turned and put TTR on the nose and headed home. Minutes later, he was rolling out on RWY 32 following an uneventful straight-in approach. Only then, with the MiG-23 safely on the ground and the adrenaline apparently now wearing off, did the enormity of what Drake had just experienced hit him. After exiting the runway, he pulled into the de-arming area, shut the airplane down, and sat motionless for two minutes, contemplating what had just occurred minutes earlier.

Maintenance arrived within five minutes of his landing, and soon after, with the aircraft ladder in place, he slowly exited the cockpit, holding his helmet in his hand. Ted then began the one-mile walk back to the squadron. He hadn't gotten more than 100 yards when "Paco" Geisler arrived in the squadron Jeep and drove Drake back to Operations. During the short ride, he told his squadron mate about what he'd just experienced.

In keeping with the high operational tempo of the 4477th, Drake experienced no downtime. He was back on the schedule the following day, again in a MiG-23 and flying another sortie against a visiting adversary. Two days later, Drake flew the incident "Flogger" to Area 51 to let the "Red Hats" and their maintenance folks give it an exhaustive inspection. The jet returned the following week with no discrepancies noted. As per usual with the "Red Eagles," we pressed ahead with MiG-23 operations!

Another "Flogger" handling experience, while not developing into a spin, was no less surprising to its pilot, Lt Cdr Dan "Bad Bob" McCort, US Navy, who had a wealth of experience before ever strapping into the "Flogger." "Badly," as Dan was known to his squadron mates, had completed multiple tours in the F-4 before becoming a Fighter Weapons School IP at NAS Miramar. When his stint instructing on the TOPGUN course was over, McCort transitioned to the F-14 and was assigned to Fleet Replacement Squadron VF-101 as an IP. After three years in the Tomcat, Dan was selected to join the "Red Eagles," an assignment he'd had his eye on since his days as an IP teaching students at Miramar.

Following a year of flying the MiG-21, McCort checked out in the MiG-23 in the fall of 1985 – an airplane he had been anxious to fly since he first arrived at TTR in June 1984. Despite all the talk and tales about the jet's strange peculiarities from fellow "Red Eagles" pilots, he had anxiously awaited his opportunity to get qualified in the Soviet swing-wing fighter. Additionally, having extensive experience in both the Phantom II and the Tomcat (aircraft that shared some base similarities with the "Flogger"), he was eager to explore the flight envelope to achieve better turning performance from the MiG-23.

With this in mind, soon after checking out in the aircraft, he began experimenting with different wing-sweep settings, hoping to find the "sweet spot" where, while not expecting stellar performance, he at least had a better option than the 45° setting typically used for air combat engagements and resulting high AOA maneuvering.

The opportunity presented itself one afternoon when the adversaries he'd been fighting against "bingo'd" out and headed back to Nellis. With the range to himself and ample fuel remaining, McCort decided that now was the time to put his theory to the test. Already comfortable with the aircraft's performance with the wings set at 45°, he tried various settings, ranging from 20° to 40°, settling on a configuration between 25° and 30°, which showed the most promise.

It's important to point out that the MiG-23 had the least amount of AOA stall margin with the wings full forward at the 16° wing-sweep setting – the configuration used for all takeoffs and landings, and the only setting where flaps were available. As the wings were moved aft to 45°, while flaps were unavailable for maneuvering, the airplane was capable of much higher airspeeds and G loads. So, in essence, anything between 16° and 45° was a compromise and, in my opinion, of little value, as the incremental improvement in available turn rate was offset by the higher susceptibility to departures should you stall the "Flogger." But that was just my approach to flying it. You can begin to see where this was going.

With the wings set near 30°, McCort had established the aircraft in a steep climb and high AOA when the "Flogger" suddenly, and without warning, departed violently to the right. As McCort still had a decent amount of forward airspeed, the airplane's nose pitched down, and the MiG-23MS tumbled forward, similar to a Lomcovak maneuver, the tail pitching up and over. Adding to the surprise of the departure was the loud banging caused by successive engine compressor stalls, accompanied by orange flames shooting out of both intakes just aft of the cockpit, shaking the big fighter to its core. While tumbling forward, McCort couldn't help but look into the periscope and see flames repeatedly shooting out of the tail in sync with each loud compressor bang. It was one wild and disorienting ride.

Despite the violent nature of the departure, following McCort's quick application of full-left rudder and forward stick, the aircraft recovered almost immediately. With the "Flogger" flying once more, Dan's primary concern was the engine. Having experienced similar compressor stalls with the finicky Pratt & Whitney TF30 engines that powered the F-14, he gingerly moved the throttle aft, allowing the R-29-300 to recover, hopefully without causing further damage. After returning to idle, a slow and deliberate advance of the throttle up to MIL power showed no signs of damage.

Happy to have recovered the aircraft and relieved that he still had a functioning engine, McCort was in no mood to push his luck further. Minutes later, he safely returned to TTR and handed the MiG-23MS back to Maintenance. It was a long debrief covering what had occurred. As with Ted Drake's MiG-23BN, no discrepancies could be found following an extensive airframe and engine inspection. Days later, it was back on the flying schedule.

While the turning performance of the MiG-23 left much to be desired from a fighter pilot's perspective, the jet excelled in one area – its ability to generate and maintain high airspeeds regardless of altitude. Within the squadron, it was said that the "MS" suffix of the fighter interceptor variant stood for "Max Speed." Those of us who flew the "Flogger" knew that was an accurate descriptor. Without doubt, it is simply the fastest fighter aircraft I have ever flown.

My first real exposure to the MiG-23's raw power and speed came just a few months after my qualification. In mid-May 1986, Ted Drake, now the assistant operations officer, asked if I'd like to check out as a Functional Check Flight (FCF) pilot in the "Flogger." With the departure of several highly experienced MiG-23 pilots in the previous months, Drake had been left as the sole qualified "Flogger" FCF pilot, and he needed help to share test-flight responsibilities. Without hesitation, I jumped at the opportunity.

Being an FCF pilot allowed me to frequently test-fly the airplane after visits to the maintenance hangar whenever significant issues (e.g., engine and flight control problems) arose. As one of only two pilots qualified to do so, I had the legitimate opportunity to explore the full performance envelope of the MiG-23. During my last six months in the 4477th, I flew no less than seven test flights on both "Flogger" variants. This was substantial, considering that Ted Drake and I were splitting FCF duties for the squadron's nine MiG-23s.

Typically, the final item of any FCF test-flight profile was a high-speed run performed at high altitudes, which allowed us to check the operation of the aircraft's variable intake ramps and speed coast-down interlock feature. As each could only be adequately checked when flying at more than 1.5 Mach, it wasn't much of a stretch from there to push on to the top-end placard limit of 2.35 Mach. On two occasions, while flying the MiG-23MS model, I reached a speed of 2.35 Mach at a 1G level at 40,000ft MSL. Even then, the airspeed needle continued to increase and showed no sign of slowing down. I'm sure the MiG-23MS would've gone well past the placard limit if I'd let it and had available range space ahead of me. Remind me again of that saying about a fine line between bravery and foolishness!

The "Flogger's" high-speed performance was equally impressive at the other extreme – low altitude. With fuel available on one notable FCF while returning to TTR, I took the opportunity to let the airplane stretch its legs at a "comfortable" 200ft AGL over the high desert of the Nellis ranges on a cool fall morning. Selecting full afterburner with the wings back at 72°, the "Flogger" wasted no time pushing through the placarded limit of 755KIAS. When I approached my "bingo" fuel limit, the MiG-23MS was streaking across the desert floor at 830KIAS and showed no signs of being thrust-limited. I'm sure it would've gone up close to or exceeded 900KIAS if I had let it.

And through it all, the "Flogger" was rock steady and stable, as if it were on rails. What would've happened had I hit a bird at that speed is anyone's guess, but most assuredly, I wouldn't be around sharing this story – that bravery versus foolishness thing again, with perhaps a healthy dose of common sense mixed in as well. One thing was sure. I wasn't afraid to fly this airplane to its limits, and often beyond what its designers had ever intended. A good number of my fellow "Red Eagles" pilots felt the same way.

My experiences in the high-speed regime were by no means the exception among pilots in the 4477th who flew the MiG-23. Ted Drake, who would go on to log 294 sorties as the most experienced MiG-23 pilot in the program's storied history, saw 910KIAS one afternoon – unintentionally. It occurred not during an FCF but a tactical intercept. In this instance, Drake found himself merging without a tactical advantage. Choosing not to turn with the adversaries, he elected to exit the fight and re-attack if conditions allowed. "Bugging out" from the merge in full afterburner with the wings back at 72°, he got distracted trying to keep a tally on his adversaries behind him through the periscope.

Seconds later, he looked back inside the cockpit to check his airspeed, expecting to see approximately 700KIAS. Instead, the airspeed indicator was already well past 800KIAS. By the time he had leveled off and throttled back, he had hit 910KIAS! This was 1,685km/h, and well beyond the placard limit of 1,400km/h (1,047mph). Putting it into perspective, he crossed the ground at a rate of one nautical mile every four seconds! And yet, the "Flogger" showed no signs of being thrust-limited.

The extent of the stress placed on the MiG-23's engines and airframes remains uncertain. However, it can be argued that the stress from high G-forces in the twisting and turning environment of air combat training far exceeded what our intelligence indicated the Soviets or other "Flogger" operators around the globe were experiencing. This was especially true for the MiG-23BN variant, which we operated like the fighter interceptor model – a role for which it was never intended. Once again, that was part of our mission: to demonstrate to our fighter pilots what the aircraft was capable of, not just what we observed others doing. I doubt many MiG-23 pilots anywhere could fly the "Flogger" as well as we did – certainly none in the third world.

Additionally, maintenance made significant improvements and resolved issues such as cracked engine turbine blades and wing box cracks in the fuselage, greatly enhancing the MiG-23's operational reliability. It had previously been uncommon for squadron "Flogger" pilots to fly more than a few sorties each week. However, by mid-to-late 1986, it became routine to fly between four and six times during the four-day week we operated at Tonopah. In a notable period from October 14–17, I logged an unprecedented ten sorties, all in the MiG-23, none of which were FCFs.

Such a high sortie tempo was a testament to our maintenance troops who transformed the extraordinary into the ordinary. I have never respected a group of USAF professionals more than our enlisted maintenance and support personnel. Each time I prepared to fly, I relied on their ability to ensure the aircraft was ready and as safe as possible. I can honestly say that trust was never misplaced.

29

The Final Push

"The engine is the heart of the airplane, but the pilot is its soul."
SIR WALTER ALEXANDER RALEIGH

August 13, 1986
"Red Eagles" Operations
Tonopah Test Range

"Hey, numb-nuts, I've got 'Digger' on the line at TAC Assignments," said Lt Col "Paco" Geisler, who'd just stuck his head in the flight room. "Where do you want your F-15 assignment to, Langley or Eglin?"

On the phone back at Langley AFB was Maj "Digger" Baldwin, one of several staff officers at HQ TAC who routinely handled follow-on fighter assignments for those of us about to leave the 4477th TES. Geisler, who had just recently been promoted to lieutenant colonel, had a good relationship with Baldwin and usually got what he requested for "his guys." In retrospect, I could've had a posting to any of the three operational Eagle bases in the US or, for that matter, an F-16 unit anywhere.

I had made it known to Geisler months before that I was only interested in an Eagle for my next assignment. After all, I was, and had been, an air-to-air fighter jock for the past six years and had no intention of returning to hauling iron. Without Geisler even asking me, he'd ruled out Holloman AFB and simply narrowed my options to the two he'd mentioned. He knew the only place for me was in a fighter wing flying the latest models of the F-15C versus older A-model Eagles at Holloman, his rationale being that, if it came to it, only F-15Cs would be chosen to go to war – and kill MiGs!

I looked up from what I was doing, gave it a few seconds, and replied, "Tell him, Langley. It'll be one less move should I have to do a staff tour at TAC a few years down the road."

"Are you sure?" he asked, as if trying to convince me otherwise. "You'll be there with all those headquarters geeks." He chuckled and shook his head. "Okay, I'll tell 'Digger.' Expect your orders to Langley in a few weeks. But I still wish you'd come to Eglin with me." Geisler already had orders in hand that would send him to the 33rd TFW at Eglin AFB in a short two months. Ironically, it was there, 13 years earlier, that he'd started his fighter career as a brand-new lieutenant and an F-4 pilot in the 58th TFS.

Lt Col Frank Geisler, or simply "Paco" to us in the "Red Eagles," as well as to an entire generation of fighter pilots USAF-wide, was, in the truest sense of the phrase, "a fighter pilot's fighter pilot." Following initial tours in the F-4 at Eglin AFB and Korat AB, Thailand, Geisler volunteered to join the 64th AS at Nellis AFB as part of TAC's fledgling venture into providing dedicated adversary DACT for fighter crews, the unit initially flying T-38s. Months later, he was among the initial cadre of Aggressors that transitioned to the F-5E in the newly formed 65th AS in 1975. From there, with a follow-on assignment in the Eagle at Holloman AFB, a graduate of the brand new F-15 FWS, later, back to Nellis AFB as an F-15 FWS IP, and his selection to join the "Red Eagles" in early 1983, his reputation in the fighter world was fast becoming the stuff of legend.

Having served alongside "Paco" for the past three years and having become good friends along the way, I couldn't have had a better man running interference for me. Just a year earlier, Geisler had similarly poked his head into the flight room where I was working on the daily flying schedule with a proposal. Would I be interested in serving on the F-20 Tigershark Operational Test and Evaluation and Tactics Development and Evaluation teams? Recently, Geisler had been approached by the F-20 program manager at the Northrop Corporation and asked to lead the team and select the members who would be among the first to fly what promised to be the USAF's hottest new fighter. With "Paco" leading such a team, my answer was a quick and emphatic "YES"!

Again, always looking out for "his guys," Geisler had singled me out to join the initial cadre should the Northrop Corporation get the contract to proceed with full-scale production. However, in the months that followed, the USAF elected not to proceed with F-20 production, and with it went what could have been a stellar opportunity. Still today, I ask myself, "What if?"

Thanks to "Paco," with my next assignment already secured, I looked forward to finishing out the following few months and then moving on to the F-15.

Lest you think it was all work with the 4477th TES, you'd be wrong. Just days before my chat with "Paco" Geisler about my future posting,

THE FINAL PUSH

Lt Cdr Marty "Streak" Chanik, US Navy, had asked me and "Hawk" Carlisle if we were interested in a T-38 cross-country flight to NAS Miramar the following Friday. Oh, and by the way, according to his sources, there was a rumor of a toga party being held at the O'Club there that Saturday night! NAS Miramar was home to the Pacific Fleet's F-14 squadrons, as well as the Fighter Weapons School and its TOPGUN course. All I knew from Chanik was that this cross-country, which the Air Force legitimized as "instrument training," was one not to miss. I was all in.

"Streak," as Marty went by, was a 1973 graduate of the US Naval Academy and, following earning gold wings as a Naval Aviator, had multiple tours in the Tomcat, as well as serving as an IP with the Fighter Weapons School. More recently, just before his selection to join the 4477th, Chanik had been assigned to VX-4, the US Navy's Air Test and Evaluation Squadron, where he flew both the F-14 and F/A-18. Besides being an accomplished Naval Aviator, "Streak" was just one great guy and never one to forego a good party. What was to follow was right up there with the best.

By the Wednesday before the weekend in question, Chanik had turned in our request to Geisler, who by now had been the operations officer for the past nine months, to take two T-38s that Friday afternoon, agreeing to be back at TTR the following Tuesday morning in time for the start of "Red Eagles'" flight operations. With the report submitted and Geisler's quick approval, it wasn't long before TSgt J. B. Neal, the NCOIC of the squadron's five T-38s, sauntered into my flight room early Thursday morning to confirm our request to take two of "his" jets on the road that weekend. He also asked, almost in passing, if we wanted our names painted on the canopy rails?

Knowing Neal as I did (he was a former crew chief for the Thunderbirds), the airplanes were guaranteed to turn heads wherever we landed. As a side note, "J. B.'s" T-38s were hangared every night when at TTR and meticulously maintained. No one's Talons in the entire USAF were as pristine. With a promise to bring him and his guys back a case of beer of their choice, undoubtedly one they couldn't purchase locally, it was a deal. Sure enough, in keeping with the highest "Red Eagles" standards, when Chanik, Carlisle, and I stepped to our T-38s that Friday afternoon for the 50-minute flight to NAS Miramar, there our names were, neatly painted on the canopies of each of our glistening T-38s – nothing but a first class service from J. B. Neal and his troops.

The very next evening, Saturday, August 9, Chanik, Carlisle, and I made our way from our rooms at the Visiting Officer's Quarters (VOQ) on base at Miramar to the O'Club, clad in the only thing we could fashion togas from – our bed sheets! Somehow, none of us had thought about needing togas, whatever they were made from anyway. So, complete with the words, "Property of NAS Miramar Officers' Quarters Laundry," stamped at regular intervals along the edges of the sheets, while not impressive, at least we were properly attired. Although we didn't garner any points for style, we most definitely did for resourcefulness. With sunglasses in place, bedsheets for togas, and little else beneath, away we went.

To begin with, whoever was in charge of decorating the place did an outstanding job, as it resembled the frat house from the 1978 movie *National Lampoon's Animal House*, both inside and out. Not to be overlooked was every significant one-liner from the film emblazoned on impossible-to-miss three-foot-high posters that adorned every wall in the O'Club. The party, coming right on the heels of the blockbuster movie *TOP GUN*, much of which was filmed at NAS Miramar, was alive and buzzing with excitement.

Adding to the festive event were most of the officers and wives of the F-14 units assigned to NAS Miramar, all of whom turned out in togas representing their squadron colors. In addition to the Tomcat crews and their wives or girlfriends, dozens of attractive young ladies from the San Diego area, having heard of the party, were also in attendance, all dressed in togas. In total, several hundred people were at the party. Chanik had been correct – this event was going to be epic.

Several hours into the evening, with the first of two bands having finished its performance, it was time for the main event. Next to take the stage was none other than Otis Day and the Knights, the fictional rhythm and blues band from *National Lampoon's Animal House*, performing live. If the place hadn't been rocking by then, once Otis Day and the Knights launched into their hit, "Shout," made famous by the movie, it certainly was then.

Somewhere along the way, I lost track of both Chanik and Carlisle. "Streak" had wandered off with old friends from his days at Miramar, and "Hawk," who'd grown up in nearby El Cajon, California, headed off-base with newfound friends to continue the party elsewhere. Knowing that this would most likely be the case, we had agreed to rendezvous the following morning at 0700hrs in the Billeting Office to check out and then take off in our T-38s, with the ambitious goal of making it across the country to Warner-Robbins AFB, Georgia, that same day.

The following morning, as planned, I met up with Chanik in the office promptly at 0700hrs to check out. About 15 minutes later, in walked Carlisle, looking like he'd had a rough night. Knowing "Hawk" as we did, we also knew there had to be a good story to accompany his current appearance. What followed next had us howling.

THE FINAL PUSH

Apparently, after partying in downtown San Diego, Carlisle was dropped off at one of the gates at NAS Miramar, not far from the VOQ where we were staying. As "Hawk" told it, it was close to 0200hrs – not good! Approaching the US Marine Corps sentry posted at the gate, wearing just his toga, he realized he didn't have any identification on him, only, miraculously, his room key. When the corporal asked him for his identification, Carlisle told him of his predicament, but managed to produce his room key, with the line, "I'm staying in that building, right there," pointing to the VOQ just blocks from the gate.

The sentry, sizing up the toga-clad individual before him claiming to be a USAF captain, and realizing that Carlisle, in his current state, was harmless and no doubt would be a lot more trouble than his time was worth, snapped to attention, his right hand raised smartly rendering Carlisle a sharp salute with the words, "Have a good evening, Sir."

"Hawk," ever the professional and master of SA, his toga unravelling, sunglasses still on, did his best to return the salute smartly. With that, Carlisle was through the gate, where he slowly made his way back to his room. His wake-up call came just a few short hours later for what would prove to be a long day, especially for "Hawk" (whose story would be retold a dozen times over upon returning to the squadron days later).

An hour later, having filed a flight plan that would take us to Albuquerque for the first leg of our journey east, our two T-38s joined a long line of fighters that had descended on Miramar for the previous night's epic event and were now taxiing to takeoff for air bases scattered across the US. It was quite the scene. Over the next hour, no less than 25 to 30 US Navy and US Marine Corps fighters, along with our two T-38s, broke the serenity of a clear San Diego Sunday morning with our afterburner takeoffs, all headed to different destinations. Needless to say, Carlisle sat out the first leg of our trip in the back seat of the T-38 I was flying with Chanik on our wing. Was this a great job or what?

The final few months passed quickly, with the normal pace of MiG operations supporting various fighter deployments into Nellis AFB for *Constant Peg* exposures. Fortunately for both our pilots and those we flew against, our operational reliability was as high as it had ever been. Even for me in the MiG-23, during a typical four-day flying week, I would participate in between five and seven sorties against visiting fighter units.

At the same time, this routine was interspersed with final flights and farewell parties for squadron mates finishing up their assignments in the

4477th and heading back to frontline fighter units. In mid-October, "Paco" Geisler, following his 500th sortie in the MiG-21 (a record for the most in any single MiG aircraft by any "Red Eagle"), left for Eglin AFB amid much fanfare, laughter, and well wishes.

A month later, Lt Cdr Guy "Brudog" Brubaker, my closest friend in the "Red Eagles" and fellow bachelor, returned to NAS Oceana, Virginia, and the F-14. He had joined the "Red Eagles" two years earlier and quickly checked out in the MiG-21. Brubaker, like all other members of the 4477th, had come to the squadron with an impressive résumé and could fly with the best of us. With assignments in both F-4s and F-14s, an East Coast Fleet Adversary pilot and IP in VF-43, and a TOPGUN graduate, Brubaker brought with him a lot of credibility.

Another fun-loving guy, Brubaker and I quickly bonded, and could regularly be found at the Nellis O'Club on most Wednesday and Friday nights following a day's flying up at Tonopah. On weekends, it wasn't uncommon for us to take a pair of T-38s and head to destinations as far away as the East Coast and Florida. Wherever the destination, there was always a reason, usually involving good-looking girls. There's nothing quite like having the "keys" to individual T-38s and "Uncle Sam's" gas card, with almost no limits to where you could go. Why we never went to NAS Key West, Florida, still escapes me! It wasn't long before Ted Drake dubbed us "The Fun Brothers."

With me due to depart the squadron just weeks after Brubaker, our farewell party was a joint one held on Saturday, November 15, 1986. To be sure, it was quite the celebration with Brubaker and me showing up wearing tuxedos. Despite our over-the-top attire, our departing gift to the squadron was a serious one.

Brubaker and I designed and had made a large wall plaque adorned with engraved brass plates featuring the names and "Bandit" numbers of every "Red Eagles" pilot that had ever been a member of the 4477th TES. When presented, it contained the names of 61 "Red Eagles." Adorned with the squadron patch at the top-center, and flanked by large renderings of Air Force and Navy wings, it was a fitting way to say thanks to a unit and the people who were the absolute best of our fighter careers. Whatever became of the plaque and the eventual 69 names listed on it is unknown. A piece of history, it was last seen hanging on the wall of the lounge in the 64th AS.

With Geisler and Brubaker having departed, it was just three weeks before I, too, would say goodbye to the 4477th and take my last flight in a posting that had been the highlight of my career.

THE FINAL PUSH

December 5, 1986
1455hrs Pacific Standard Time
Tonopah Test Range
MiG-23MS

"Tower, 'Bandit Three-One,' Cactus Peak, for Initial, One-Four." My call to the control tower alerted them to my position and my intention to enter Initial and the overhead pattern for Runway 14. It didn't give them my airspeed.

As I headed back to the airfield on my final flight as a "Red Eagle," while I wouldn't put on an arrival show quite like Dave Bland had a year earlier, I could still hit Initial with a ton of airspeed and give everyone assembled on the ramp the chance to experience, both visually and audibly, the sight and sound of a clean MiG-23MS doing what it did best – go fast!

"Roger, 'Bandit Three-One,' the winds are one-eight-zero, at ten, altimeter is two-niner-niner-four. Report Initial, One-Four." Came tower's reply, confirming the runway in use and winds exactly as they had been for my takeoff 30 minutes earlier.

At least I won't have to deal with a nasty crosswind for my final landing.

No doubt, the two controllers in the tower, along with the SOF, were monitoring the fast-approaching radar blip on the Bright-Scope. Where they were accustomed to seeing our MiGs entering the pattern at 300KIAS, the rapid movement of my radar return on the monitors hanging in the corners of the control tower was indicative of a pilot coming in with a whole lot more "smash" on his jet than was usually the case. Indeed, with my wings back at 72 degrees, I was "smokin" at 450KIAS and about to select minimum afterburner to go just a bit faster. Thirty seconds later, after passing Cactus Peak, five miles to the west of the runway, I was rolling out on a two-mile Initial and taking in one last look at what had been my home for more than three years.

It's been awesome. One more trip around the pattern . . . don't fuck it up!

"Tower, 'Bandit Three-One,' Initial, One-Four." My check-in with TTR tower would be the last of my career as a "Red Eagle."

"Roger, 'Bandit Three-One,' cleared for the break. The pattern's yours." Tower's clearance informed me that our other MiGs, which had taken off earlier that afternoon, had already returned and were on the ground. I was, as expected, the last MiG airborne that Friday afternoon, and there were no conflicts in the pattern.

My MiG, my pattern, my airspeed – one last time!

At one mile out from the approach end of the runway, I smoothly selected full afterburner and watched, still amazed after all these months flying the MiG-23, as the airspeed needle jumped effortlessly to nearly 500KIAS. By mid-field, not wishing to overdo a good thing, I had pulled the throttle back to the MIL power setting. If I hadn't, there's no doubt I would've easily been at 600KIAS by the departure end of the runway.

That's enough for now . . . plus, you're gonna have to slow this beast down!

As I streaked the length of the runway, a glance out the left side of the canopy showed a crowd of approximately 15 to 20 people gathered where they had planned for me to shut down my MiG minutes later. Oh, and there was no mistaking the fire truck on hand with its lights already flashing to make sure that when I exited the cockpit, I wouldn't get away dry. It was all part of the tradition associated with a pilot's final MiG flight in the 4477th.

Once I reached the departure end of the airfield, I rolled the "Flogger" into a smooth 4G-level break, bringing the throttle smoothly to idle, and simultaneously moved the wing-sweep control lever to the fully forward detent, selecting the 16° wing-sweep position. With the wings inching their way forward throughout the hard turn to downwind, the light rhythmic tapping of the "knuckle-rapper" on my right hand told me I'd be wise to pay attention to the AOA gauge. The movement of the wings and the resulting shift in the center of gravity forward would affect the airplane's handling as I slowed for landing.

As the Gs on the aircraft began to dissipate with the reduction in airspeed throughout the turn, I nonetheless looked to keep the needle of the AOA gauge well below the stall region, which was significantly lower when the wings reached their fully forward position for landing. Rolling out wings-level on downwind, I'd managed to dissipate 250KIAS of airspeed in the 180° turn, which was a bit wider than usual due to the increased turn radius – the result of hitting the break at 500KIAS versus the more usual 300KIAS!

The remainder of the pattern was uneventful, and, as I had done hundreds of times before in our MiGs, I made one final call for clearance to land.

"'Bandit Three-One,' gear down, full-stop, One-Four."

"Roger, 'Three-One,' winds are one-seven-zero, at eight, cleared to land Runway One-Four. Congratulations, Sir. It's been a privilege serving with you," came a heartfelt clearance from the controller, one whom I'd had the good fortune of working with while a SOF throughout the years.

"Thanks, it's been my pleasure. I'm gonna miss it all, you guys included. You're the best." My short reply was non-standard phraseology for an air traffic control pattern, but then again, at this point, who cared?

THE FINAL PUSH

Rolling out on short-final for the runway, I made one last check before landing to ensure my flaps and landing gear were indeed down, the three green indicator lights confirming yet again what I had already checked on downwind before beginning the descending turn to final.

Gear and flaps – down. Not the time to screw that up!

Seconds later, I smoothly touched down for the final time at TTR. Within two minutes, following the landing rollout, runway exit, and dropping of the drag chute, I had taxied in through the south entry to the "Red Eagles" ramp. I noted a crowd of no less than 20 pilots and maintenance troops assembled near where the crew chief was marshaling me to shut down. As I approached, it was a bittersweet moment.

On the one hand, I'd just completed my final flight of my three years as a member of perhaps the most talented assembly of fighter pilots anywhere in the USA. For that, I was justifiably proud. Just ten years earlier, I hadn't even begun my Air Force career, wearing a hard hat and working on construction sites while still awaiting orders to report for pilot training following graduation from college. And here I was about to bring to a stop one of the USAF's most closely guarded secrets.

On the other hand, while the assembled crowd was there to celebrate the end of a successful tour as a member of the "Red Eagles," many members of the squadron who had contributed to making the assignment such a rewarding experience were missing, leaving behind memories that would last a lifetime. Don't get me wrong, those awaiting my arrival were the next generation of "Red Eagles" who would continue to fill the cockpits of America's top secret MiGs, providing the absolute best in air combat training to our frontline fighter pilots.

Of the 15 aviators who had been in the 4477th when I'd first arrived, I was the last one still there, and now I was about to leave. The squadron had undergone a complete turnover during the past three years, but that was true for just about any squadron, and not necessarily unique to the "Red Eagles." However, the complexion of the squadron had changed during that period. As I prepared to exit the MiG-23 that Friday afternoon, I knew it was time to leave. Next man up!

In retrospect, it'd be remiss of me not to provide some quantitative measure of how well the 4477th TES performed from an operational standpoint. But before I delve into the numbers, which by any measure are impressive, let me first say, at the risk of repetition, that none of this would have been possible without the simply amazing team of maintenance and support NCOs who kept our MiGs flying. Despite literally writing the books on the proper "care and feeding" of MiG-21s and MiG-23s, they continually made the extraordinary look ordinary. While they might have been maintenance technicians by profession, I can honestly say, they were more like magicians.

Thanks to their magic, I safely completed a total of 476 sorties in our Soviet-built MiGs – 338 in the MiG-21 and 138 in the MiG-23, which ranks me third on the list of "Red Eagles" with respect to the number of sorties flown with the 4477th TES. Perhaps the most gratifying reward for me personally was helping hundreds of pilots over the years through innumerable briefings, engagements, and debriefings.

During my tour with the 4477th, which lasted just over three years, my squadron mates and I flew nearly 6,670 MiG sorties, accounting for 43 percent of all MiG sorties in the program's ten-year history, while exposing 5,930 fighter pilots to the best-flown threat aircraft they'd likely ever encounter. Once again, this made up 41 percent of all exposures for the program's ten-year existence.

While I've alluded to it throughout this story, the level of talent among the pilots of the 4477th TES was simply unmatched anywhere in the military. Of the 32 aviators I served with who completed a military career, more than 56 percent of them went on to reach the rank of O-6 (colonel/captain) or higher, with 15 percent attaining general/flag rank. This compares to only three to four percent, historically, of all officers achieving the rank of O-6 or higher across all services. If one needed any further indication of the level of talent within the 4477th TES, it's borne out in those statistics.

To say I am humbled to be included within their ranks would be a complete and gross understatement. That's coming from a guy who, as a young boy, was told by his high school guidance counselor that perhaps I should think about pursuing a different career path, as achieving my goal of being a pilot looked unlikely. Thank you, Mr. Liljegren!

Three days later, Monday, December 8, I walked into the 426th TFTS at Luke AFB, Arizona, to begin my checkout in the F-15 Eagle, marking the beginning of the next chapter in my career as a fighter pilot. Little did I know at the time that just 14 months later, I'd return to the skies south of Tonopah to do battle yet again, this time in the F-15 and against my former "Red Eagles" squadron mates. The legacy of what I had learned and the value of the program known as *Constant Peg* would be on full display.

30

Going Back

"An excellent weapon and luck have been on my side. To be successful, the best fighter pilot needs both."

GENERALLEUTNANT ADOLF GALLAND

Nellis AFB Range Complex
Thursday, March 18, 1988
1012hrs Pacific Daylight Time
F-15C 82-0014

"'Droid Two-One,' snap Three-Two-Zero for 43. Bandit Control is showing one, possibly two contacts, southbound, fast movers," came the hurried directive from our assigned GCI controller. His quick narrative told us possible enemy fighters were airborne and heading our way.

Show time, "Z-Man." Time to make all of your experience pay off!

"'Droid Two-One' copies, possible bandits airborne," I replied after receiving the information. This was the "bogey dope" my wingman and I had been waiting for, telling us suspected bandit aircraft were airborne heading our way and had met our pre-briefed commit criteria. We were about to put our training to the test. Today's tactical scenario called for us to intercept, identify, and, if able to, engage and destroy "enemy" aircraft entering the area north of our position.

We were now southbound in a north–south-oriented racetrack orbit, ten miles long, awaiting our commitment. In tactical formation high off my right wing for a mile and a-half at 26,000ft, my wingman, Capt Jim "Boots" Bowman, was watching my aircraft for the cue to bring our F-15s around northbound for our commit. A quick dip of my left wing silently told Bowman to begin a hard turn in my direction. A glance high off my right wing a moment later revealed the planform silhouette of his F-15 against the blue morning sky, confirming he'd seen my signal and was cranking his big fighter around for the commit.

Satisfied that my wingman was in the turn, I moved the control stick hard to the left while smoothly blending in the left rudder to reel the jet over into a 100° bank, easing it back to establish a comfortable 4G, slightly descending turn. Simultaneously, I pushed the two throttles up to their MIL power stop, not wanting to deplete any of my airspeed in this hard turn back toward the threat. Our two fighters carved identical descending left-hand turns, rolling out on a new heading of 320° line abreast and indicating close to 400KIAS.

"'Droid,' push it up!"

At my call for more airspeed, we jammed our throttles fully forward to the stage five afterburner setting. The electronic engine controls responded to the throttle setting and immediately commanded the twin Pratt & Whitney F100-PW-220 turbofan engines of each F-15 to full afterburner. The desert valley below awakened to the roar of nearly 100,000lb of combined thrust from the two fighters. Our Eagles were inbound and on the hunt, with Bowman high off my left wing to the west of me in our offensive formation. Approaching 500KIAS, I smoothly throttled back out of afterburner to a bit less than full MIL power. We were "smokin" at a high tactical airspeed advantageous to us when we were about to enter the fight.

"'Droid' flight, Control's contact, Three-Three-Zero, for 35. Radar is now painting only one return." Our GCI controller radioed the latest radar update as we accelerated northbound.

Slightly right of my nose, 35 miles. A lone return. I bet there are two or more MiGs in there!

While in our turns, we'd each re-checked our pre-briefed radar settings to afford the F-15s' powerful AN/APG-63 pulse-Doppler radars the best chance of detecting the threat aircraft as soon as we rolled out of the turn. The fingers of both my hands deftly glided over the myriad of radar and weapons control switches positioned on both the stick and throttles. Within seconds, I selected a 40 nautical miles scope display. I positioned my radar's acquisition symbols at the 20 nautical miles range while adjusting the elevation control knob of the antenna to search an area from the ground up to 25,000ft MSL. Bowman had done much the same, although he had positioned his radar's antenna slightly higher to sanitize the airspace between 20,000ft MSL and 45,000ft MSL. We would find them quickly if there were hostile aircraft ahead of us.

As I rolled out of the turn, an instinctive glance at the Vertical Situation Display (VSD) at the upper left corner of the instrument panel showed the distinctive digital radar return symbology squarely centered in the display and just outside of the 30 nautical miles range scribe. In an instant, I centered the target designator cursor on the return and pressed the switch down with the index finger of my left hand. The powerful radar reached out and locked onto the target, filling the Heads Up Display (HUD) and VSD with the unknown aircraft's vitals – bearing, range, altitude, and aspect angle. This was a sample lock. To further sanitize the airspace before us, I depressed the auto-acquisition switch on the stick grip with my right thumb, quickly returning the radar to its four-bar sweep and continuing its search for additional targets.

If you're out there, we'll find you!

"'Droid Two-One's' contact, Three-Two-Zero, 24, head."

With the disciplined conveyance of the sample lock's information, both Bowman and our controller had a verbal image of what my Eagle's radar was "seeing" out ahead of me. My display concurred with what Bandit Control was telling us: a single contact, bearing 320° for 32 miles, at 24,000ft, head aspect – coming straight at us.

"'Droid Two-Two's' showing same, clean high," Bowman radioed, adding his piece to the three-dimensional puzzle before us as part of the practiced litany amongst Eagle pilots.

We were both showing a single contact at the same bearing and range, and soon had our radars back to their four-bar scan search mode, continuing to sanitize our areas of responsibility. While our radars were powerful, they couldn't discern individual fighters in close formation at these ranges. At some point, the enemy would show his hand and begin to maneuver, changing the dynamics of the intercept. This usually came via altitude splits, lateral maneuvers, and spacing feints – often, all three.

For the seasoned F-15 pilot, rewards came through measured discipline and patience in working the radar and interpreting what it began to tell you. If we did our job right, there would be no need to reach the merge and engage in a turning fight. If executed precisely, this radar-led tactical intercept would reduce the targets in front of us to shards of flaming, twisted metal well before we closed to within visual range of them.

And that's when it happened. As the targets approached the 25 nautical mile range, the VSD began to show two digital returns, where before there had been just one.

Now you're talking, and beginning your ruse just as I expected.

When I locked up the easternmost contact and began to decipher the target's data yet again, it was barely breaking out as two separate returns.

"'Droid Two-One's' contact, eastern bogey, Three-Three-Zero, 25, One-Eight-Zero descending, One-Three right!"

My brisk narrative told Bowman I'd broken out an easternmost target, slightly right of my nose at 25 miles, who was in a left descending turn at 18,000ft. With another quick press of the multi-function button, I dumped my lock and searched for possibly another bogey that had gone undetected. Bowman was quick to add "bogey-dope" as part of our effort and began to fill in the missing pieces of the radar picture.

"'Two-Two's' contact, western bogey, Three-One-Zero, 25, Two-Eight-Zero, climbing, One-Six left."

From Bowman's call, I'd ascertained we'd got at least a pair of bogeys 25 miles out in front of us and attempting to bracket us in a classic Soviet "pincer" style attack. My target was in a hard left descending turn toward the east, trying to get outside of us undetected, and was last seen in a descent at 18,000ft. The other bogey that Bowman was monitoring was bracketing high to the west, and at the last radar lock, it indicated an altitude of 28,000ft.

Our tactical briefing today called for us to target bogeys that meet our criteria at a distance of 20 miles. In the few precious seconds remaining before we reached that range, we sanitized our airspace assignments one last time to ensure no possible trailing targets had slipped past us undetected.

"Bandit Control is showing the same, negative additional contacts." The picture was now mostly complete. We were fast approaching our targeting range. When my contact reached 20 miles, I made the call.

"'Droid Two-One' flight, target side-side, cleared off. Visual's at 'three o'clock.'"

"'Two-Two' copies, targeting western bogey, visual lead."

At the targeting call, we both turned our radars on our respective targets. In an instant, I again established a lock on the eastern bogey, which was now at a lower altitude. The apparent split between him and the western bogey was almost ten miles.

Classic high-low, side-side pincer. No, fooling me. I've seen this act before and have been there. I know what you're doing and what you're capable of. I am you!

With my radar now locked onto the low bogey to the east, the HUD quickly told me precisely what my opponent was doing. His indicated airspeed was close to 650KIAS, and he had leveled out at 12,000ft.

Too fast for the typical MiG-21. I'll bet all the beers at the O'Club tonight you're a "Flogger," you sneaky bastard!

Moments later, the radar display's aspect readout told me he was making a hard turn toward me as we approached 16 miles. Twice, I thumbed the multi-function control switch on the stick forward, directing the radar's computer to search its database and inform me of the type of aircraft with an engine exhibiting the unique Doppler frequencies it was detecting. In a nanosecond, my question was answered in the form of a readout at the bottom of the HUD and VSD – MiG-23MS.

He's no longer a bogey – he's a bandit! Time to kill.

"Bandit, bandit . . . 'Droid Two-One,' Fox-1," came my response to the information filling my HUD. Simultaneously with my "bandit" call, I depressed the weapons launch button atop the control stick. Two seconds later, I depressed it again, and the bottom right corner of the HUD was filled with the countdown timer of the last launched missile's predicted Time Of Flight (TOF). In an instant, I heard Bowman call the same, telling our GCI controller and me that "Droid" flight had simulated AIM-7M missiles in the air, and that the likely outcome of two splashed MiGs was less than 30 seconds away.

"'Droid Two-One's' cranking west. Lead's visual, 'four o'clock low.'"

I rolled my Eagle into a hard left descending turn, all the while making sure to keep my radar lock on the bandit, now electronically identified as a MiG-23MS "Flogger-E," that was still 12 miles away and nearly at the edge of my radar scope. While my turn had helped keep me closer to my wingman for mutual support, it had also decreased the chance of absorbing possible missile shots from my target, should he also have weapons in the air. A glance at my "11 o'clock" showed Bowman 4,000ft above my altitude at a distance of three miles.

Air combat is the ultimate chess game, and those who cannot think and operate in all three dimensions while employing their fighter will soon be toast. Ten miles from the bandit, I wheeled the F-15 back into a 6G turn, bringing him to the nose while snapping my throttles to idle to thwart any chance of his infrared-homing missile attack and to get a visual on my target. My turn brought the Target Display Unit back into view of the HUD. With the distance now eight miles, I could begin to make out the dark, narrow silhouette of a MiG-23 with its wings swept back, its nose onto me, slightly low, and indicating 630KIAS.

My left thumb commanded the weapon selector switch to the middle position, or short-range missile, and I immediately heard the growl of the left inboard AIM-9M heat-seeking missile filling my ears, telling me it had acquired the target. If my radar-guided missiles happened to miss or were countered, I was ready to dispatch the MiG with any of the four AIM-9Ms the Eagle typically carried. I was awaiting the shoot cue to launch one of the "heaters" when the AIM-7M's TOF counter elapsed, signifying missile impact.

"'Droid Two-One,' Fox-1 kill on the F-4 [for security purposes over the radio, any reference to "Red Eagles'" MiGs by Blue Air always used the term "F-4" for MiG-23s and "F-5" for MiG-21s] low to the east at 12,000[ft]. Lead's coming hard left, visual at two's 'four o'clock.' Press!"

My call let Bowman know the bandit to the east had been destroyed. I had my wingman in sight at his "four o'clock" position, providing mutual support and allowing him to continue his attack and kill his target.

"Bandit Control copies kill on the F-4 low to the east."

Back at the Range Control Center, our controller passed the kill call to his counterpart, who was working the MiGs. On the other frequency, the "Red Eagles" pilots were quickly getting the word that the MiG-23 low and to the east had been targeted and killed by an AIM-7M from the opposing F-15s.

I didn't wait to pass the "Flogger," but banked my Eagle toward Bowman and his bandit to maintain support and help him kill his target if necessary. It wasn't.

"'Droid Two-Two,' Fox-1 kill on the F-5 at 27,000ft to the west."

"Roger Two, check 45 right, lead's visual at your 'four o'clock' for five miles."

"Two's visual," Bowman replied to me seconds later.

And just like that, this portion of the fight was over. Moments later, Bandit Control passed us a "knock it off" call, informing everyone that the engagement was over, which we acknowledged individually. Bandit Control directed us to split up, with me heading north to Range 71 and Bowman south to Range 76 to join our respective bandits.

Over the radio, on our flight's discreet frequency, I cleared Bowman off to his assigned area and told him we'd rejoin upon completing our engagements for the flight back to Nellis. I heard two mic clicks as an acknowledgment, and then I watched as he banked his clean F-15 away from me in a hard left turn, heading south.

Bandit Control next instructed me to switch frequencies and establish contact with my adversary, who had been pre-briefed to be a MiG-21 for visual engagements. Bowman and I had just splashed a pair of MiGs as part of our intercept. Now it was time to see how I do in the close-in visual arena with a very dangerous and formidable adversary – one I was intimately familiar with and knew all too well.

Without it being said, I knew that my former squadron mates were out to show me that I hadn't yet mastered the F-15, and any of them would have loved to have boasted about gunning me in the visual arena. In my mind, I envisioned a drawing at this morning's briefing to see who would get to fight me. Whatever the circumstances, today's pilot, who will remain nameless, had drawn my straw and would do his best to humble me. I intend to be up to the challenge, knowing fully well that if I ended up being gunned down by him in his MiG-21, I'd surely never hear the end of it. Did anyone mention fighter pilot egos?

Following a switch of frequencies, I checked in with our GCI controller, who quickly provided me with a snap vector to "Bandit 11," five miles north of me at 20,000ft, awaiting my rejoin. I got a quick radar lock on a lone MiG-21 at that location, and acquired a tally on him seconds later at my "two o'clock" some three miles away. The show was now his, and having established both radio and visual contact, he asked me what sort of setup I'd like today, offensive or defensive. I told him defensive, which I'm sure was no surprise to him. Let's get real. No self-respecting former "Red Eagle" would ever ask to be on the offensive, especially this one!

This setup would put me 9,000ft ahead of an attacking MiG-21. The objective was to defeat the attack and, if possible, turn the tables and kill the MiG – easier said than done for many an experienced fighter pilot, even in an F-15. But I'd flown the MiG and had been the attacker in hundreds of engagements against some of the best. I knew exactly what he could and couldn't do. Now I was about to put all that experience to the test against an adversary that would give me nothing but the best the MiG-21 was capable of. It was time to show him a thing or two and demonstrate what an expertly flown F-15 was capable of.

With this, he directed me to make an easy left turn at 20,000ft at 350KIAS. He commented that he'd cross behind me during the turn and slide inside and aft of my left wing line. I watched as his MiG-21 crossed my tail roughly 12,000ft back and moved smartly to my "seven" to "eight o'clock" position. Once there, he told me to steady out of my turn, heading southwest, and accelerate to 400KIAS. Then, I should call when ready. As he was now just a mere dot aft of my left wing, I'd be working hard to keep sight of this formidable opponent.

With the throttles up at MIL power, I was quickly at 400KIAS and passed the word to him that I was ready to begin the engagement. At my ready call, he told me to start an easy turn towards him and that he'd call the fight on as he closed to 9,000ft. Established in a 45° banked turn and eyeballing the bandit, I didn't have long to wait as the MiG-21 was now nose-on and closing fast.

This is the moment of truth, "Z-Man". Kick his ass!

"Fight's on, fight's on," came the call from the MiG pilot.

We were now both cleared to maneuver unrestricted, and I immediately jammed both throttles fully forward to their max afterburner stops and rolled the Eagle hard left, stopping only when I'd placed the attacking MiG-21 high at the top of my canopy. The nearly instantaneous onset of close to 9Gs as I pulled the stick back almost to my lap was making it increasingly difficult to keep sight of the sleek fighter – my head was now cocked back as far as it would go, tight against the ejection seat headrest.

Looking up through the very top of my visor as I grunted and strained to constrict my abdominal muscles, I was fighting against gravity to keep the blood in my head from draining too fast and robbing me of my eyesight.

As had happened countless times throughout my career, the sweat beneath my helmet ran down my forehead and through my eyes, only momentarily impeded by my oxygen mask on its way down my neck as I strained further to keep sight of the tiny fighter. The battle was on!

Damn, you're a tricky bastard to see. Keep the turn going until you force him to maneuver nose-off of you!

In the first few seconds of my gut-wrenching turn into the MiG-21, I'd been generating close to 22° of turn per second, but at the cost of significant airspeed bleed-off despite the power of the twin turbofan engines now roaring at full afterburner. I'd started the turn at about 400KIAS, and a quick peek at the HUD showed my airspeed fast decaying through 330KIAS, as evidenced by a lightening of the stick forces in my right hand.

At this point in the engagement, I was desperately trying to compound the attacking MiG's geometry problem and give him a corner he couldn't possibly solve if he wanted to saddle up and gun me. The continual hard turn forced the issue as I saw his speck of an airplane almost imperceptibly inching forward along the top of my canopy. The angles I was generating were becoming impossible for my opponent to handle. Even with the excellent turning capability of the MiG-21, it was just too much. If he didn't reposition soon, he'd grossly overshoot me and risk becoming defensive himself. But there was no way this guy was going to make that mistake.

I'd now turned through roughly 110° of heading change when I noticed the bandit abruptly roll right out of his hard left turn and pull up into the vertical, attempting to reposition on me, the angular problem just too harsh to solve. Not only was my jet generating a ton of turn rate, but with my airspeed bleeding off, the radius of my turn itself had shrunk dramatically, further compounding his problems.

His nose is off. Unload and get some airspeed back, and don't lose sight of him, dammit!

As soon as I saw the MiG reposition, I immediately dumped the nose, pushing the stick slightly forward of neutral while keeping my eyes trained on the MiG, which was now moving high to my fighter's "seven o'clock" position and well back of me. With my Eagle unloaded and the nose about 20° below the horizon, the "light-in-the-seat" feeling told me my fighter would accelerate as fast as possible, but there was no time to take my eyes off my opponent for fear of losing him.

Within seconds, the feeling of the jet through the control stick told me I'd gained a lot of my lost airspeed back – precious knots I'd need to defeat this attack and turn the fight to my advantage. I further sensed the aircraft picking up speed as the subtle sounds of the airstream over the canopy told me I could soon pull back hard into the MiG-21.

All this happened in just a very few seconds. I sneaked a peek at the desert floor below and sensed that I'd descended a couple of thousand feet during my unload. I reacquired my adversary, who by now had rolled onto his back and was about to pull down into me a few thousand feet below him. Since the fight began, I'd tracked through approximately 200° of heading change and was now roughly pointed north and about to pull back up and into my adversary.

Okay, he's repositioned, putting his lift vector on me, and about to come back down. It's time to take this fight to him and into the vertical!

With no time to waste, I again pulled back hard on the stick and rolled the aircraft to place the MiG high above me atop my canopy. This was a game of energy and angles, and I would force him into the first mistake. The Eagle responded to the airspeed I'd regained and smoothly carved a tight turn into the vertical as I fought to keep my opponent in sight. The next second, I was squinting hard as I watched the MiG disappear into the high, bright morning sun.

You have got to be shitting me! Damn it. Of all the times to lose your tally!

This was the worst possible scenario. A tiny bandit was still high and aft of my wing line, aggressively maneuvering to gun me, and I'd just lost him in the blinding sun. This very scenario was something I'd briefed countless times before to visiting pilots when I was in the MiG-21's cockpit. Now it had happened to me, and if I didn't reacquire him soon, I could easily be the one jinking for my survival.

I know where you're at, you little son of a bitch!

As I brought the Eagle into the vertical, I knew where the MiG had to be. I'd been there, and I knew his capabilities. He had to be high and to my left – directly in the sun and on his back coming down into me, slightly in lag.

While still in my hard climbing turn, I instinctively thumbed forward twice on the multi-function button on the control stick. At the same time, my left index finger jabbed the target designator control button on the left throttle, commanding the radar into its Vertical-Scan mode. As I pirouetted the Eagle in the vertical, I placed the lift vector where I expected the MiG to be – the radar did the rest of the work. In an instant, the AN/APG-63 stopped its typical side-to-side four-bar level search aligned with the horizon to instead scan a narrow sliver of airspace only 6° wide from my aircraft's nose to 60° high aligned with the longitudinal axis of the fighter. Anything in that tiny slice of sky within 20 miles would be acquired and locked automatically.

My hunch was correct, and a second later, the "LOCK" lights illuminated on the canopy bow and the HUD once again filled with information indicating the bandit's location. Having pulled up into the pure vertical, I then rolled the Eagle and put the target designator box at the top of the HUD. I quickly saw that the MiG-21 was in a 60° nose-low dive and slightly above my altitude. Having reacquired a tally on the "Bandit," I began a lead turn of it, converting my energy in one smooth pull to roll out slightly above and behind the MiG. My adversary was at a disadvantage in terms of energy and couldn't counter my move.

I rolled out high and 1,500ft behind the MiG-21, with both of us nose low in a 60° dive, and my opponent now desperately trying to elude me. Out in front of me, he began a series of jinking maneuvers known to fighter pilots as the "funky chicken," trying to shake me. But I was squarely on his "six o'clock" and about to saddle up for a gun attack. Even with my engines throttled back to idle, slowing my rate of closure, the F-15 quickly reduced the gap between our fighters. He was hurting and vulnerable, and he knew it. Worse still, he knew I knew it.

He probably couldn't see me, and he certainly couldn't shake me. It was a terrible feeling knowing there was little you could do before you were about to be gunned. If this had been actual combat, the MiG pilot would have had just a few precious seconds left to live before 20mm armor-piercing incendiary cannon shells ripped him and his aircraft apart with devastating effectiveness. At least it'd be quick. But thankfully for him, today wasn't actual combat.

I closed the range to just outside 1,000ft, thumbed the Weapons Select Switch on the right throttle aft to the GUNS position, and smoothly eased the weapon's pipper to position it atop his canopy. Following another half-roll to the left, then right, of the MiG-21, I stabilized the pipper just aft of his canopy and squeezed down on the trigger. The shoot cue in the HUD illuminated, and following a solid second of tracking the MiG-21, I released the trigger and rolled off to the right, my adversary now out of fight, airspeed, and ideas. For a fighter pilot, there was no worse feeling than knowing someone just gunned your brains out, especially after starting from an offensive position of advantage.

"'Droid Two-One,' gun tracking kill. Knock it off!"

"'Bandit One-One' copies, knock it off."

Immediately after acknowledging the call and ending the engagement, I watched the MiG cease maneuvering and begin a slow pull-up out of its dive, low to my "ten o'clock." A quick fuel check had the MiG-21 pilot just about at his "bingo" level, and moments later, he called for his recovery back to TTR and cleared me off.

From my vantage point, loosely off his right wing, I could see him twist his head around to visually acquire me. As he started a right-hand turn back toward the airfield, I joined up a bit more, now almost in close formation.

I could see his helmeted head turn again, accompanied by an ever-so-slight salute followed by a head nod. This acknowledgment was a silent tribute to a worthy opponent who, in textbook fashion, just gunned him after having started defensively less than 90 seconds earlier. I said nothing, but instead returned the head nod and gave him a thumbs up, before peeling off in an afterburner climb to the right as I began my flight south to rejoin Bowman and return to Nellis.

Later that afternoon, when I returned to the "Red Eagles'" squadron building at Nellis, where we F-15 pilots of the 94th TFS were being hosted, I was summoned by the 4477th's operations officer, whom I knew well. We had been squadron mates together before I'd left the unit 14 months earlier. I casually entered his office and asked what was up. He seemed a bit hesitant, but then proceeded to speak.

"Hey 'Z-Man,' some of the "Red Eagles" pilots are saying you and your guys are being a little too aggressive, like passing too close aboard. You in particular."

The look of disbelief I gave him must've irked him because he went on. "So, talk to your guys, have them back off a bit, and finish the week safely." These words didn't sound like the guy I knew before. Delivered a little half-heartedly, I don't think he genuinely believed he was uttering them.

"Okay, so what I'm hearing you telling me is you expect my guys to keep from gunning your guys' brains out because they're not used to it," I snapped back, all semblance of professional courtesy and respect for rank thrown aside. "Sorry, I guess it's not much fun being on the receiving end. Did I hear you right?" I added. My voice was a bit louder than proper decorum dictated, with an edge to it.

"No, that's not it. Just have everyone watch it," he responded rather feebly, my retort having caught him off guard.

My pushback was probably a little more forceful than it needed to be, but that was mainly because I couldn't believe what he had said to me. My guys, young lieutenants and captains, were doing exactly what they had been trained to do. They were flying their F-15s exactly like I had briefed them to – and they were kicking ass! And in epic fashion, at that, more so than most F-15 FWS students. Any mention of violating training ROE was pure bullshit, and this guy knew it. Remember those fighter pilot egos? Be careful now, they're fragile at times!

That was it. Nothing more was said. I turned and left his office. In short order, the F-15 jocks of the 94th TFS headed to the fighter bar at the Nellis O'Club, and like the evenings before, those who had bested their paired MiG drivers that day were all too happy and downright eager to buy the beer. And as they had done exceedingly well, there was plenty of it.

In two days, it was over for us, and our deployment to Nellis AFB was complete. Just two weeks later, on March 4, 1988, the "Red Eagles" of the 4477th TES would fly their last sorties, the storied program canceled and the MiG hangars shuttered forever – all a decision based upon DoD and impending Cold War budget cutbacks. With its closure, one of the most successful air-to-air programs ever conceived for training the world's finest fighter pilots would be gone forever.

In retrospect, by then I'd come full circle in my career. Less than nine years earlier, as a "puppy" lieutenant without much air-to-air experience and flying an F-4D, I'd been gunned by an attacking Aggressor in his F-5E on an almost identical setup to the one that had seen me so rapidly defeat the MiG-21. Now, having gained invaluable experience along the way in the F-4E at Osan AB, as an Aggressor, a "Red Eagles" MiG pilot, and, finally as an F-15 IP and mission commander, I'd taken a career's worth of lessons learned and not only turned the tables on my "foes" but, more importantly, passed on that experience to a new generation of fighter pilots.

It was this experience and the sharing of it that is the legacy of the value of the 4477th TES and the *Constant Peg* program. Along the way, I can count myself lucky to have been the beneficiary of hundreds, perhaps thousands, of air-to-air engagements and the sage advice and wisdom of countless squadron mates, flight leads, and IPs during that period.

The time I spent as a "Red Eagle" was undoubtedly the highlight of my service in the USAF, and the experiences and stories chronicled here are among the most cherished of my lifetime. During the three years I was assigned to a program that arguably was one of the best-kept secrets of the Cold War period, I helped prepare our fighter pilots to be the absolute best. Less than three years later, the value of the MiG pilots of the 4477th TES, and what they taught, would be validated over the skies of Iraq.

Epilogue: Desert Thunder

"The duty of the fighter pilot is to patrol his area of the sky and shoot down any enemy fighters in that area. Anything else is rubbish."

RITTMEISTER MANFRED VON RICHTHOFEN

1240hrs, January 17, 1991
"Bunker" air refueling track
North central Saudi Arabia

"'Zerex Seven-Three,' offload complete, disconnect now," the metallic voice of the KC-10 Extender tanker's boom operator came over the assigned air refueling frequency.

A quick glance at the fuel gauge verified that the F-15's tanks were topped off. Fully fueled, Capt Rhory "Hoser" Draeger simultaneously clicked the throttle mic switch twice to acknowledge the call and depressed the air refueling disconnect button on the control stick. As the tanker's refueling boom released from the air refueling receptacle in the aircraft's left-wing root, the few gallons of JP-4 that inevitably escaped quickly vaporized into the frigid wind stream generated at 27,000ft and 300KIAS.

Refueling complete, Draeger smoothly moved from low and behind the massive tanker to a position just outboard of his wingman, Capt Tony "Kimo" Schiavi, who was flying alongside the right wing of the KC-10, anxiously awaiting his turn in the refueling sequence. With the refueling behind him, Draeger turned his attention again to finding some way to get his aircraft's AN/APG-63 radar to return to life. After all, this was the most important mission yet in his Air Force career, and he didn't want a malfunctioning radar to keep him on the sidelines watching.

Today was the first day of Operation *Desert Storm*, the war against the forces of President Saddam Hussein following Iraq's invasion of Kuwait more than five months earlier. Draeger, serving with the 58th TFS, was No. 3 in the lead four-ship of F-15Cs providing air cover for a 50-airplane strike package tasked with the first daylight attack on Al-Taqaddum and Al-Asad ABs, 46 and 100 miles west of Baghdad, respectively.

After taking off from King Faisal AB in Tabuk, Saudi Arabia, he'd only covered 50 miles when his radar stopped sweeping, the antenna frozen at 40° left. For the past hour, while en route to the tanker, he had tried at least a dozen cycles of the On/Off switch and flown several maneuvers whereby he'd loaded the aircraft up from -1G to +2Gs in the hope of reviving the radar, all to no avail.

"'Zerex Seven-One,' MiGs airborne, 50 southwest of 'Bullseye,'" came the call from the radar controller aboard the Airborne Warning and Control System (AWACS) E-3A Sentry aircraft. The AWACS was orbiting northwest of their tanker track at 32,000ft MSL and 240 miles southwest of Baghdad. Today, the Iraqi capital itself was being used as "Bullseye" – the reference point from which AWACS broadcasted the position, range, and direction of enemy aircraft to all Coalition fighters.

"'Zerex Seven-One' copies," replied Capt Chuck "Sly" Magill, US Marine Corps, the token "Jarhead" in the 58th TFS serving a three-year exchange tour with his "brothers in blue." Today, "Sly" was both "Zerex" flight lead and mission commander for the eight F-15Cs comprising the 33rd TFW's contingent within the air support package.

"Shit, MiGs are airborne just south of the target area, and my radar is fucked to hell," Draeger thought to himself, still trying to exorcise the demon within his radar while mentally plotting the location and possible MiG types now airborne, apparently out of the strike package's target of Al-Taqaddum.

"'Zerex Seven-Two,' how 'ya doing?" Magill enquired of his wingman, Capt Mark "Nips" Arriola, who, following Draeger, had now been taking on JP-4 from the tanker for the past several minutes.

"'Zerex Seven-Two,' disconnect now," Arriola radioed the tanker, as if in answer to his leader's inquiry. Once again, the boom lifted out of the way, and Arriola smoothly rejoined "Zerex 71's" left wing and was quickly replaced in the refueling slot by Schiavi in "Zerex 74."

"'Pennzoil Five-One,' status?" "Sly" queried the flight lead of the second F-15 four-ship, also undertaking refueling operations on the trailing KC-10 two miles behind them and stacked 500ft higher in the tanker track.

"No. 2's on now – should be another eight to ten," replied Capt Rick "Kluso" Tollini as he watched the tanker's boom nestle silently into his wingman's fuel receptacle and securely lock.

"'Zerex Seven-One,' MiGs capping 100 miles southwest of 'Bullseye,'" said the senior controller aboard the AWACS, updating the previous information.

"'Zerex Seven-One,' copy" "Sly" replied, busily checking his map to mentally plot the MiG's location relative to their planned ingress route.

EPILOGUE

Draeger looked at his watch – 1250 hrs, 25 more minutes until the scheduled "push" time, when the eight F-15s would leave their pre-assigned orbit point and press into Iraqi territory. That was when the "pucker factor" was bound to be at its highest. And still, his radar wasn't showing any signs of life.

For a brief instant, Draeger's thoughts wandered to the uncertainty that lay before him and the grim reality it held. Someone, possibly on both sides, would, in all probability, die today in the skies ahead. Someone as devoted to his cause as his enemy was to his own in the other cockpit. Someone who would be savagely torn into unrecognizable fragments by the devastating effectiveness of a high-explosive warhead fitted within the radar-guided missile that would tear into his fighter at twice the speed of sound as he closed with his opponent.

"'Seven-Three,' how's your tube?" "Sly's" tentative manner seemed to indicate that he was aware of the impending answer to his question about the state of Draeger's radar.

"No change, still sick," replied Draeger, his thoughts returning to the idle antenna position indicator on the radar scope. His mind now squarely back on the task before him, he focused on the quintessential challenge faced by every great fighter pilot throughout history – accomplish the mission, take care of your wingman, and survive!

1305hrs
Iraqi Air Force MiG-29 flight
80 miles southwest of Al-Taqaddum AB, Iraq

The sky was clear, the air crisp, and the visibility superb. Yes, the day was beautiful. If only they'd had time to enjoy it. The two IrAF MiG-29 "Fulcrum" pilots from No. 6 Sqn who were manning their CAP area southwest of Baghdad that afternoon marveled at their luck in having clear skies to patrol. To the south, over Saudi Arabia, from where their threat would come, they saw solid cloud formations extending up to what appeared to be 20,000ft.

Their country was now at war with the Coalition forces ranged against them, which, hours earlier, in the dark of night, had launched an attack on their country and its people to liberate Kuwait. And even though the IrAF had suffered a handful of losses in those early hours of *Desert Storm*, the MiG-29 pilots were confident of success. At some point, however, they each recalled silently to themselves how their Arab brethren in their Soviet-supplied MiGs had been sorely defeated at the hands of Israeli-piloted Mirage IIIs in 1967, Phantom IIs in 1973, and, most recently, F-15s and

F-16s over the Beqaa Valley, in Lebanon, in 1982, when 82 Syrian MiGs were lost, and not a single Israeli fighter was downed in return. They, alone, would now take on the Coalition forces and face American pilots in the skies above their homeland.

Against that backdrop, they swore to each other that this was their moment, their opportunity to reclaim their ancestors' glory in the days of Nebuchadnezzar II. Their intelligence officers claimed to have learned the tactics of American fighter pilots from their Jordanian counterparts, who had flown outdated and outmatched French-built Mirage F1s and American-supplied F-5Es against visiting USAF F-15 and F-16 squadrons in joint training exercises in recent years.

The MiG-29 pilots were confident of success, with Iraqi intelligence providing more assurance by outlining why the poorly trained Syrians couldn't defeat their Israeli opponents nine years earlier, despite possessing numerical superiority. Furthermore, the IrAF was one of the most modern air forces in the region, equipped with the latest Soviet hardware, including 33 of the very MiG-29 "Fulcrums" they were flying, 68 MiG-23 "Floggers," and no fewer than 174 venerable MiG-21s and F-7s. It also had 88 Mirage F1s and 160 Sukhoi fighter-bombers and attack aircraft. Yes, the "Fulcrum" pilots were indeed very confident.

They had taken off from Al-Taqaddum AB 30 minutes earlier, piercing the midday calm with the thunder of their twin Klimov/Sarkisov RD-33 turbofan engines at full afterburner. Sitting atop 36,000lb of thrust, both pilots had reached 350KIAS by the time they left the airfield boundary and streaked skyward in a 20° climb. In less than two minutes, they had leveled off at 15,000ft southwest of Baghdad, activated their N-019 "Slot Back" pulse-Doppler radars, and reported to their assigned GCI controller for target information and intercept orders.

While the early-morning Coalition air attacks had targeted, among other sites, the four main IrAF integrated air defense system (IADS) control centers at Baghdad, Kirkuk, Nasiriyah, and Ar-Rutbah, much of the country's impressive early warning and GCI capability was still operative, albeit at somewhat reduced capacity. It was IADS controllers, manning their Soviet-supplied P-35 "Bar Lock" surveillance radars, that the "Fulcrum" pilots now contacted for further information concerning the very enemy fighters they anxiously awaited to engage and destroy. They would not have to wait long.

EPILOGUE

1315hrs
"Zerex 71" Flight

Draeger noted the 010° heading as the formation rolled out, piloting his jet in the direction of the inertial navigation reference point eight miles on the nose. He glanced at his wingman, Schiavi, in "Zerex 74," some 9,000ft off to his left, line abreast and stacked slightly higher in perfect tactical formation. To his right, Magill, in "Zerex 71," was somewhat lower than Draeger and a similar distance away. Magill's wingman, Arriola, in "Zerex 72," was slightly lower, yet in a similar tactical spread farther to the east.

Offset to their formation's "four o'clock," at four to five miles, were the four members of "Pennzoil 51" flight in a similar "Wall of Eagles" formation. The eight F-15Cs of the 58th TFS, making up the Coalition's "tip of the spear," were departing their planned push point 120 miles south of the IrAF's Mudaysis AB. Their timing and position were perfect.

"'Zerex' arm hot," came the call from Magill in the lead position. If they hadn't done so already, this was the final reminder to all eight pilots before crossing the Iraqi border to flip the master arm switch to "Arm," select "Combat" on the selective jettison switch, and arm the chaff and flares dispenser unit.

By this time, Draeger had already decided to press ahead despite his inoperative radar, 33rd TFW directives notwithstanding. His logic was simple. No one airborne in either flight had more experience in the F-15 than he. His three consecutive operational assignments in the Eagle and completion of the grueling FWIC at the FWS at Nellis AFB just four years earlier had enabled Draeger to hone his combat skills to a level seldom matched by any pilot anywhere. The value of his presence to the rest of the flight in terms of overall SA certainly outweighed his current lack of radar capability. Moreover, this was war, what he had trained for his whole career, and he wasn't about to miss it.

Ahead, the skies over Iraq were clearing, and MiGs were airborne south of the target area. As he glanced once again over to his left at Schiavi, it happened. His radar's antenna, as if by magic, began to sweep!

1320hrs
Iraqi Air Force MiG-29 Flight

The "Fulcrum" pilots settled into their CAP formation and communicated freely with their assigned GCI controller. Surviving Iraqi early warning radar units had picked up the Coalition strike aircraft, marshaling 180 miles south of Mudaysis AB at high altitude while on their tankers. Nonetheless, it took time for information on numbers and positions to filter through to the two MiG-29 pilots on their CAP station southwest of Al-Taqaddum AB. The intelligence that filtered down was sketchy and fragmented due to the system being saturated with requests and having only a handful of operable radars available to provide any answers.

The two fighters were armed with the best weapons the IrAF had been allowed to purchase from its Soviet suppliers in recent years. While the Iraqis had been prevented from receiving R-27 (NATO reporting name AA-10 "Alamo") semi-active radar-guided missiles, each "Fulcrum" carried four R-60 (NATO reporting name AA-8 "Aphid") infrared-homing missiles, with a maximum effective range of five miles, providing them with limited all-aspect capability. The "Aphid" was reportedly a formidable weapon in a tight-turning fight at close quarters. Add to this, the "Fulcrum's" GSh-30-1 30mm internal autocannon and phenomenal maneuverability so aptly demonstrated by Soviet pilots at recent Paris and Farnborough airshows, and one had a genuine contender in the air-to-air arena.

Their CAP orbit consisted of a patrol pattern, oriented roughly north–south, flown in ten-mile legs before reversing direction in right-hand turns. The racetrack pattern at 15,000ft AGL was designed to allow the fighters to remain on station at maximum endurance airspeeds and, using both onboard radar and GCI, seek out, intercept, and destroy any attacking aircraft within their assigned airspace. But today, the GCI part of the equation was sorely lacking. That being the case, the "Fulcrum" pilots were directed to concentrate their radar search at low altitudes where the threat was expected to appear, and GCI coverage was at its worst. Opportunity was about to come knocking.

1327hrs
"Zerex 71" Flight
30 miles into Iraq

"'Zerex' flight, SAMs, 12 o'clock!" Magill's charged call to flight members confirmed what was immediately apparent to everyone. Low and to the right of his HUD on the instrument panel, Draeger immediately noted the SA-8 tracking symbol squarely at "12 o'clock" on his Tactical Electronic Warfare System (TEWS) unit that displayed programmed threat radar locations.

"Three notching left – tanks!" Draeger radioed a millisecond later as he reeled the big fighter into a left descending 40° dive. While in his 4–5G pull to a heading 90° offset from the threat, he deployed chaff and

EPILOGUE

flares and pressed the jettison button to clear his Eagle of its external fuel tanks.

Within seconds of his call, eight 600-gallon external fuel tanks carried on the F-15s' outboard wing pylons had been sent free-falling to the desert below. With the added weight and aerodynamic drag of the drop tanks now gone, each Eagle was fast approaching its maximum maneuvering potential – precisely what a fighter pilot wanted while dodging SAMs. If the adrenaline hadn't been pumping before, it certainly was now. The temperature was in the low 40s on the ground below, but Draeger was already saturated with sweat, and he was barely into Iraq with a lot more to do before he'd be on his way out.

Then, as suddenly as it had started, it was over. The TEWS displays all went blank, and there wasn't the expected AAA barrage they'd been told would likely accompany an active SAM battery. One threat apparently behind them, all four pilots quickly rejoined five to seven miles north of the SAM position in the same line-abreast formation and accelerated, now in a climb.

"'Zerex Seven-One,' MiG aircraft now confirmed as 'Fulcrums,' number unknown, 100 southwest 'Bullseye,' indicating 13,000ft," the AWACS controller told them as the flight climbed through 21,000ft MSL.

"'Zerex' copies. 'Seven-One,' clean," replied Magill. He worked quickly, mentally converting the AWACS calls into the MiG's position relative to his own, now approaching 63 miles to the IrAF fighters. His eyes focused on the radar scope, located low and to the left of the HUD on the instrument panel, as the fingers of his left hand glided over the radar controls on the two throttle grips. In an instant, he'd commanded an 80-mile search from the radar, adjusted the antenna tilt, and reset the range position of the radar cursor, all with the flick of a couple of fingers. While the radar cycled through its four-bar scan pattern, he anxiously waited, confidently expecting the MiGs to appear as tiny digital radar returns near the 60-mile reference line on the scope. However, his efforts initially resulted in nothing but a blank radar display. Then suddenly, the radio came alive.

"'Zerex Seven-Three,' 50 right, 60 miles, 17,000[ft], head!" Draeger's now resurrected radar had picked up the MiG formation on the far right side of his scope, heading straight at them.

"Contact's target 'Zerex'," AWACS quickly confirmed.

"'Zerex,' check 60 right," directed Magill in the tactical lead position. Within seconds, the four F-15s had steadied out on a northeasterly heading. They began closing in on the enemy fighters, now directly on their nose, slightly low, as they accelerated their formation of Eagles to 440KIAS while descending through 19,000ft MSL. The sun was shining brightly at their high "six o'clock."

1335hrs
Iraqi Air Force MiG-29 Flight

The "Fulcrum" pilots had just begun a right-hand turn to the north when their SPO-2 Sirena-3M radar warning receivers (RWRs) suddenly came alive, their steadily glowing forward quadrant lights and aural warning tone attesting to the presence of enemy fighter radars somewhere out ahead of IrAF jets. Yet their radar scopes were blank. They'd been searching the low-altitude regime for nearly an hour now, with not so much as a single contact. Undoubtedly, the Coalition had more than a single nighttime attack in mind, and if their RWRs were any indication, they would show themselves soon.

They had received spurious reports of enemy air activity from their GCI controller, but nothing was nearby. The latest report was of intermittent long-range radar contacts of a large enemy formation more than 120 miles south of them. A glance at their fuel gauges told both pilots that they'd have less than 20 more minutes to spend in the CAP before having to return to Al-Taqaddum and refuel. Rolling out northbound and starting a slight descent, they maintained their loiter airspeed of 250KIAS, their RWRs having now gone blank.

"Zerex 71" Flight
50 miles south of Iraqi Air Force MiG-29s

"'Zerex Seven-Three,' contact nose, 50 miles, 13,000[ft], cold, showing single only," came Draeger's call, simultaneously dumping his sample lock of the MiGs and returning the radar to its search mode.

"'Seven-One' copies. Still clean," replied Magill, sounding slightly annoyed at not having contact with the MiGs, which were now heading away from them, the F-15s in a tail chase separated by 50 miles.

"'Seven-Two's' clean high," reported Arriola. His contribution completed the radar picture, confirming that there were no MiGs above 20,000ft MSL.

With both "Zerex 71" and "Zerex 72" having yet to detect the presence of MiG-29s, Draeger concentrated his efforts on the northbound contact.

EPILOGUE

The F-15s indicated close to 490KIAS as they passed through 16,000ft MSL in their descent, closing on the relatively slow MiGs at more than four miles per minute, despite the tail chase. The closure rate was apparent on the scope. Draeger placed the radar cursor over the single radar blip on his scope and depressed the target designator control button. The sample lock immediately filled both his HUD and radar scope with information, providing the target's heading, altitude, airspeed, and aspect angle, as well as his own aircraft's overtake, minimum, and maximum range cues for the AIM-7M radar-guided missile he had currently selected.

"'Zerex Seven-Three,' two contacts, nose, 45 miles, 13,000[ft], hot!" exclaimed Draeger. The MiGs were now seemingly alerted to their presence, for they were coming right at the Eagles, despite being unaware of "Zerex" flight's exact location, as evidenced by the F-15s' blank TEWS displays.

"'Seven-One,' clean," Magill called, surprised to still be without a contact, and his radar showing no apparent signs of degradation.

On their current headings, the two fighter formations were closing at a rate approaching 13 miles per minute. If this intercept geometry continued, the sky would be filled with AIM-7Ms missiles headed for the IrAF fighters in just over two minutes. Then, the geometry broke.

"'Seven-Three,' two contacts, nose, 40 miles, 12,000[ft], turning cold!" The disappointment in Draeger's voice acknowledged the obvious missed opportunity to engage what his radar had confirmed as two Iraqi fighters in close formation, slightly below the Eagles' altitude. Both MiG-29s had made a right-hand turn back north.

"They're running north and heading for home. We'll never catch them before we hit that SAM ring around Al-Taqaddum," Draeger thought to himself, anticipating their chances of catching the MiGs, "unless they turn to engage!"

1350hrs
Iraqi Air Force MiG-29 Flight
40 miles north of "Zerex 71" Flight

Since their last turn northbound at the southern end of their CAP, some 50 miles behind them, the two "Fulcrum" pilots had been in a constant descent from 12,000ft MSL and 250 KIAS. Just as they prepared to level off at 2,000ft above the desert floor, the lead pilot's RWR illuminated yet again for what had to be the tenth time in as many minutes. If enemy fighters were nearby, GCI certainly had been of no help in alerting them, nor did it appear they'd have fuel enough to engage anyway. It was time to recover at Al-Taqaddum and return later.

They were just northwest of Razazza Lake, immediately west of Karbala. Ahead, the fertile farmlands on both sides of the Euphrates River were visible, and it was a mere 35 miles to the airfield. Suddenly, their radios were alive with a frantic call from their GCI controller of enemy aircraft, closing rapidly at "six o'clock" and 23 miles. Although this information had taken them by surprise, both pilots reacted instinctively and without hesitation. They immediately selected afterburner and began swinging their nimble fighters around in a hard turn to the south, their radar antennas now slewed up in search of an enemy – approaching from above!

"Zerex 71" Flight
23 miles south of Iraqi Air Force MiG-29s

The four F-15s had been bearing down on the Iraqi "Fulcrums" for the past 14 minutes, descending from 20,000ft MSL to their present altitude in the "mid-teens." Draeger and Schiavi were still slightly high and to the west of Magill in "Zerex 71" and his wingman Arriola, who were presently descending through 13,000ft MSL. All four aircraft were now approaching the transonic region at about 0.98 Mach.

"'Seven-Three,' breaking out two contacts," said Draeger, his radar remaining in search, it being apparent the MiGs were continuing north.

"'Seven-Two's' same," chimed in Arriola, sneaking a peek from his assigned high-altitude search to check out the low bandits on their nose running northbound.

"'Pennzoil Five-One,' cleared off to your CAP point," directed Magill to Capt Rick Tollini in the other F-15 formation, which was still offset to "Zerex" flight some five to seven miles southeast at 21,000ft MSL. "'Pennzoil Five-One' copies," acknowledged Tollini, his formation now checking 40° left and preparing to pass high and behind "Zerex" flight en route to their CAP location 50 miles east of Al-Asad AB.

It was then that it happened. The movement was so subtle that it would have gone unnoticed by a less experienced pilot. The two contacts, at the center of the radar scope a moment ago, suddenly jumped to the right while the range closed abruptly from 20 to 18 miles. It was the digital radar signature of high-performance fighters carrying out a hard turn into the chasing Eagles.

EPILOGUE

"'Zerex Seven-Three,' bandit's coming hot!" exclaimed Draeger, quickly locking the westernmost contact. In an instant, Draeger's radar grabbed the tight-turning Iraqi fighter. As the range to the MiG began to register on the HUD, his right thumb pressed the missile launch button atop the control stick once, energizing the launch circuitry for the left forward AIM-7 radar-guided missile at 15 miles.

"'Zerex Seven-Three' – Fox-1!" he called moments later from behind his oxygen mask as the 500lb missile was forcibly pushed down and away from the aircraft, its motor igniting within seconds, and the weapon then accelerating to nearly three times the speed of sound as it raced towards its target.

Without waiting to see the missile rocket out in front of his Eagle, Draeger rolled the twin-tailed fighter into a 135° descending hard right-slicing turn, purposely offsetting the target to near the left edge of his radar scope. As he rolled wings level from this 7G maneuver, his head was instinctively turned to the left, his eyes looking for the threat aircraft. Instead of spotting the MiG-29, Draeger saw the single AIM-7 streaking northward, its motor trailing an angry tongue of flame ten feet long.

"'Seven-Three,' cranking east," he called, now in a 45° dive passing through 9,000ft MSL, the enemy fighters at 13 miles heading straight at them.

"'Zerex Seven-One,' Fox-1!" answered Magill five seconds later, his radar having picked out the Iraqi fighters only minutes earlier.

Draeger's F-15 was screaming toward the parched and barren desert floor at 550KIAS when he passed 1,000ft below his lead's Eagle in time to see two AIM-7s leave Magill's jet, their exhaust trails forming ribbons across the sky, pointing toward their target.

Iraqi Air Force MiG-29 Flight
11 miles north of "Zerex 71" Flight

The leading-edge maneuvering wing flaps on both "Fulcrums" had programmed out with the sudden change of each aircraft's AOA and the rapid onset of G forces as the jets made a slightly descending hard turn to the south. The lead MiG-29's RWR had lit up in the middle of the turn. All quadrant lights now illuminated, its shrill aural tone irritated the pilot's ears. Only the power of another fighter's air-to-air radar locked onto its target at close range could generate that type of response from the SPO-2 Sirena-3M. His wingman, spread 1,500ft in a right echelon formation, experienced much the same aural warning seconds later.

Midway through the turn, the trailing MiG-29 crossed low and aft of the lead aircraft as its pilot moved into a left echelon position. Just before rolling out, the wingman's N-019 "Slot Back" radar momentarily displayed, then lost, a target high and at least 15 miles to their southwest. Sensing the threat farther to their right, he continued his turn, rolling out on a heading of 210° at his leader's "four o'clock" position. Some 2,000ft to the wingman's east, at 700ft above the desert, his leader's attention was diverted by a bright flash due south of him. Looking high, his eyes squinting into the early afternoon sun at his high "one o'clock," the flash appeared not too unlike a sun glint reflecting off an aircraft's canopy. Seconds later, it vanished.

"Zerex 71" Flight
Seven miles south of Iraqi Air Force MiG-29s

When ten miles from the lead MiG-29, Draeger pulled the Eagle into another gut-wrenching left turn, bringing the targeted Iraqi fighter to his nose. Focusing beyond the greenly lit symbology of the HUD, he could distinctly make out the twin tails of the easternmost "Fulcrum," the box-shaped radar target designator now centered squarely on it. Draeger leveled off just 200ft above the ground, the desert now being little more than a blur, his F-15C now indicating 550KIAS.

While the TEWS scope was blank, he snapped both engines to idle, reducing his forward infrared heat signature to defeat a possible "Aphid" missile launch from one of the "Fulcrums." Fast approaching the merge, it was time for Draeger to visually acquire the rest of "Zerex" flight. A quick swivel of his head to the left allowed him to pick up Magill and Arriola, rapidly descending through 2,000ft MSL, three miles to his left. Schiavi was now slightly sucked back to his "seven o'clock" for 10,000ft and slightly high.

Above and ahead of him stretched the greyish-white smoke trails of three AIM-7s, reaching out like narrow fingers for three, perhaps four miles, then abruptly stopping, their solid propellant exhausted. Then came the rarest sight of all. Beyond the exhaust trails, yet still short of the MiGs, Draeger watched as all three missiles silently arced downward, guiding sweetly toward their intended targets.

Iraqi Air Force MiG-29 Flight
Five miles north of "Zerex 71" Flight

EPILOGUE

The Iraqi GCI controllers were no longer "painting" the enemy fighters with their radars, having lost them in the ground clutter at low altitude. They were useless to the "Fulcrum" pilots.

In the few seconds since the MiG-29s had steadied out south, the wingman had radioed about an intermittent radar contact high to the southwest. Still, he had not reported any solid locks to allow either jet to prosecute an attack on the intruders.

By this point, the "Fulcrum" leader had throttled back to conserve his precious fuel, the needle on his airspeed now indicating just under 400KIAS. His wingman, head down and perhaps preoccupied with his radar, had left his throttles up, his mottled gray jet piercing the early afternoon air at 540KIAS.

What occurred within the cockpit of the lead MiG-29 in the last few seconds of its pilot's life will forever remain a mystery. Perhaps he was preoccupied with his radar and didn't see it. Or, more likely, his eyes were fixated on a spot near the horizon where, just seconds earlier, he'd sighted the planform shape of Draeger's F-15, descending rapidly in a hard turn toward him and just as suddenly disappearing.

Although what happened next was too fast for the human eye to see and the mind to comprehend, it was recorded by the MiG-29's gun camera, looking forward through the HUD and the aircraft's windscreen beyond. Visible on the last few frames of film to survive the ensuing explosion was the blurred, ghostly gray image of Draeger's AIM-7 missile impacting the base of the windscreen – at Mach 2!

"Zerex 71" Flight
Five miles south of an Iraqi Air Force MiG-29

"Nothing came out of the front," Draeger thought to himself upon seeing the missile impact the Iraqi fighter, pieces of it now hitting the desert floor five miles north of him. "No huge fireball – must've been just about out of fuel."

The remaining "Fulcrum," however, was still apparently unscathed, and now the immediate threat. His mind absorbed the destruction ahead in the blink of an eye. It was simply astonishing. The MiG-29 that had been coming at him just seconds before at 400KIAS had, in an instant, been reduced to shards of burning and twisted metal, the most significant piece no bigger than a few feet in diameter, now suddenly strewn across the desert before him.

Draeger, having just selected his left inboard AIM-9M infrared-guided missile, banked left to place the remaining Iraqi fighter on the nose to get a front aspect shot off when it too suddenly turned into a flaming wreck as Magill's first AIM-7 found its mark. A few seconds later, "Zerex 71's" second missile flew through the remaining debris and detonated.

"Splash two, splash two!" Draeger yelled, his adrenaline now maxed out.

"AWACS copies splash two. Green south," replied the senior director aboard the E-3A on station 200 miles southwest of them. His color reference indicated to "Zerex" flight that the airspace south of them was clear for a safe egress home.

"'Zerex Seven-One' flight, in-place one-eighty left. Let's bug out," Magill radioed to the rest of the flight.

The two Iraqi MiGs that had challenged them for control of the skies were now part of the desert. AWACS was not identifying any airborne IrAF fighters, and the Eagles were running low on fuel. It was time to egress, plug into the tanker again, and then head home. Some would have called that mission a good day's work, but the pilots of 'Zerex' flight knew better – their second mission was just hours away.

1448hrs
"Zerex 71" Flight
250 miles east of King Faisal AB, Saudi Arabia

They'd left the tanker track ten minutes ago. King Faisal AB was still 35 minutes away. Cruising westbound at 32,000ft MSL, the four F-15s were in a loose, comfortable formation. The cruise portion of the flight home afforded them a brief respite from the seemingly constant "on edge" feeling associated with combat. It allowed Draeger to finally reflect on what had just happened in the skies above Iraq.

Elation? Not necessarily. Pride? Definitely. They had trained hard for just this eventuality. Not just the past few months but for years, an entire career's worth for some. And it had all paid off in those few minutes of their encounter with their enemy counterparts flying MiG-29s.

Draeger's mind raced with images of literally dozens of fellow squadron mates, past and present, whom he'd flown both with and against during his previous three assignments in the F-15, and consciously acknowledged their contribution to his MiG kill. A part of this victory belonged to all of them. And silently, as his mind continued to retrace the events, the training, and the people that had helped him in whatever small way down that MiG, he focused on yet one other event, one program, and its unrivalled contribution to his kill.

EPILOGUE

Of the thousands of sorties he'd flown over the past eight years, a mere half-dozen stood alone, unique as no others, preparing him for this truest of tests in the sky. On those sorties, Draeger had taken off in his F-15 from Nellis AFB and flown 120 miles northwest into the air combat training ranges just south of Tonopah, for it was there that he'd had his first real encounters with the enemy.

Within the ranges commonly referred to as 71, 76, EC West, and EC South by scores of American fighter pilots over the years, Draeger, along with many others like him, had indeed met the enemy. In those Nevada skies over the barren desert below, he had both won and lost, and yet lived to return home later with another set of tricks up his sleeve as an accomplished fighter pilot.

During those sorties, Capt Rhory "Hoser" Draeger had pitted his skills against those of a select few of the very best fighter pilots in the USAF, US Navy, and US Marine Corps, whose mission it was to challenge him in their MiGs. They were, of course, assigned to the top secret 4477th TES, based at a remote, inaccessible airfield in the Nevada desert. The program's unclassified codename was *Constant Peg*. The squadron's pilots were known simply as "RED EAGLES!"

Appendices

Appendix 1

"Red Eagles" Pilot Chart

The pilots listed below all had overlap with the author during his three-year assignment to the 4477th TES. Included are their "Bandit" numbers, as well as the type of MiGs flown and the total sorties in those aircraft.

Last Name	First Name	Rank	Bandit Number	Service	Callsign	MiG Sorties		
						MiG-21	MiG-23	Total
Bland	Dave	Maj/Lt Col	32	USAF	"Blazo"	241	124	365
Boma	Tom	Capt	59	USAF	"Boomer"	265	–	265
Brown	Steve	Capt	33	USAF	"Brownie"	344	51	395
Brubaker	Guy	Lt/Lt Cdr	48	USN	"Brudog"	278	–	278
Carlisle	Herb	Capt	54	USAF	"Hawk"	146	170	316
Chanik	Marty	Lt Cdr/Cdr	52	USN	"Streak"	166	190	356
Craig	Gary	Capt	43	USAF	"Goldie"	355	105	460
Drake	Ted	Maj	42	USAF	"Gabby"	147	294	441
Geisler	Frank	Maj/Lt Col	35	USAF	"Paco"	500	–	500
Gennin	George	Lt Col	31	USAF	"G²"	177	–	177
Green	Jim	Capt	26	USAF	"Wiley"	243	16	259
Kinney	Tim	Maj	45	USAF	"Stretch"	223	162	385
Larsen	Dudley	Maj	60	USAF	"Dud"	200	–	200
Macy	Marty	Maj	49	USMC	"Fog"	360	66	426

Last Name	First Name	Rank	Bandit Number	Service	Callsign	MiG Sorties		
						MiG-21	MiG-23	Total
Manclark	Jack	Lt Col	51	USAF	"Mad Jack"	301	–	301
Mann	John	Maj	56	USAF	"Flash"	271	61	332
Matheny	Jim	Capt	27	USAF	"Thug"	240	142	382
McCort	Dan	Lt Cdr/Cdr	44	USN	"Bad Bob"	119	160	279
McCoy	Brian	Capt	53	USAF	"Lazmo"	287	–	287
Nathman	John	Cdr	29	USN	"Black"	61	52	113
Phelan	Dennis	Maj	47	USAF	"Hog"	268	135	403
Prins	Orville	Lt Cdr	30	USN	"Orv"	168	90	258
Robb	Jim	Lt Cdr/Cdr	38	USN	"Rookie"	213	–	213
Rogers	Shelly	Capt	55	USAF	"Scotty"	237	–	237
Roy	Mike	Capt	36	USAF	"Mach"	230	–	230
Saxman	John	Capt	34	USAF	"Sax"	182	116	298
Shervanick	Larry	Maj	28	USAF	"Shy"	125	149	274
Silvers	Cary	Lt Cdr	61	USN	"Dollar"	160	22	182
Simmons	Michael	Capt	57	USAF	"Mick"	254	–	254
Skidmore	John	Maj	41	USAF	"Skid"	175	–	175
Stucky	Paul	Maj	40	USAF	"Stook"	230	96	326
Sundell	Charles	Maj	58	USAF	"Smoky"	234	–	234
Thompson	Fred	Capt	50	USAF	"T-Bear"	470	–	470
Tullos	George	Maj/Lt Col	37	USMC	"Cajun"	234	–	234
White	Phil	Lt Col	46	USAF	"Hound Dog"	131	–	131
Watley	Monroe	Maj	24	USAF	"Monroe"	200	78	278
Zettel	Rob	Capt	39	USAF	"Z-Man"	338	138	476

Appendix 2

Nellis Range Map

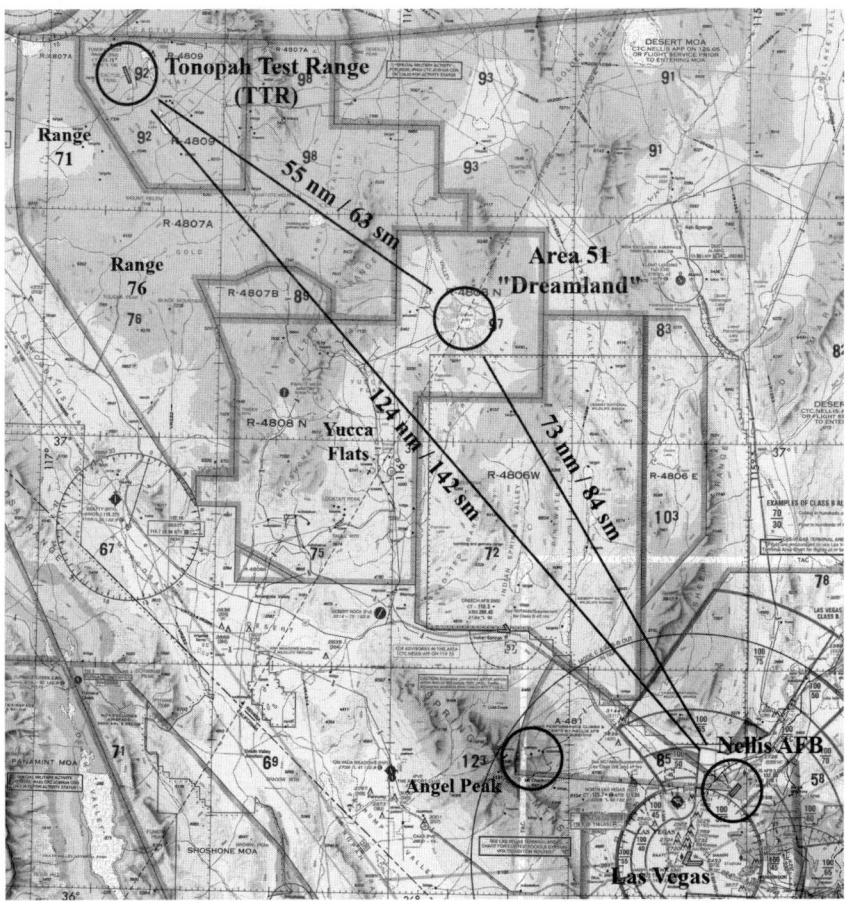

Note the location of the Tonopah Test Range in the upper left-hand corner of the range complex, with Area 51 ("Dreamland") near the center. Each morning the pilots of the 4477th TES would depart Nellis AFB in two turboprop aircraft for the nearly one-hour flight to TTR. They would fly back that same afternoon to debrief with the fighter crews they had flown with earlier in the day.

Appendix 3

MiG CAP Positions

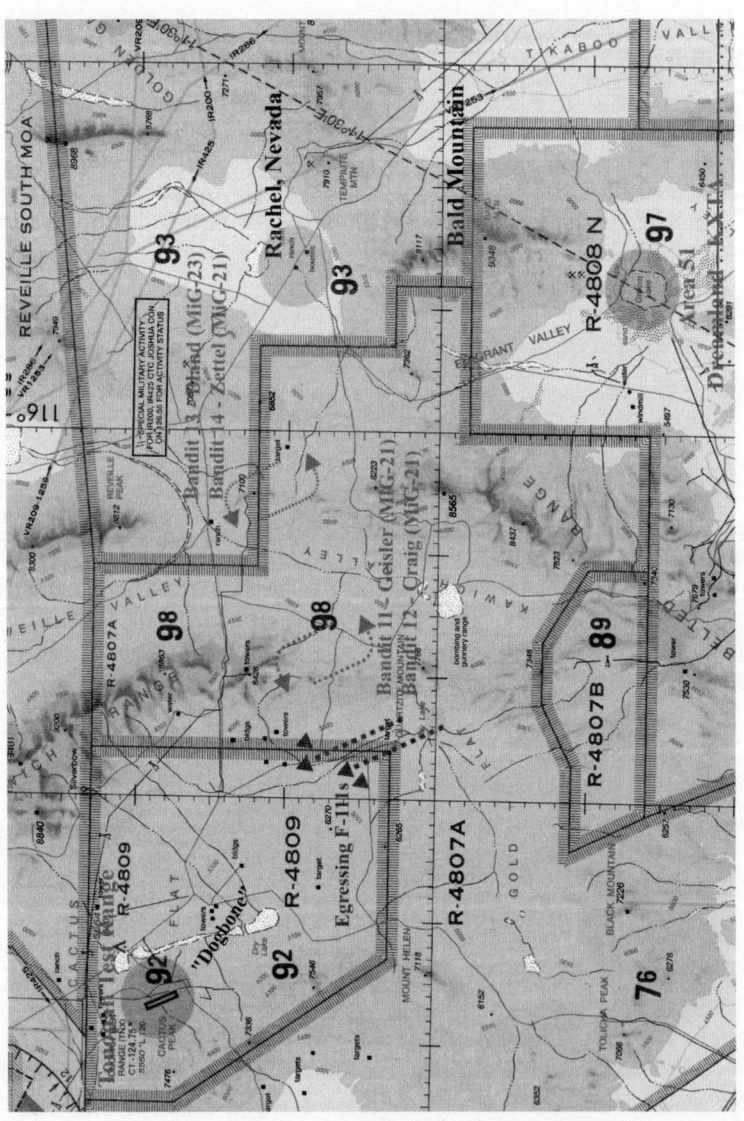

This view of the Nellis range complex shows the CAP positions of the four MiGs of the 4477th TES when tasked to intercept USAFE F-111s on September 17, 1985 (see Chapter 22).

Appendix 4

Fighter Comparison Chart

Fighter Specification Comparison Chart					
	F-5E Tiger II	MiG-21F-13 "Fishbed-C"	MiG-23MS "Flogger-E"	F-4E Phantom II	F-15C Eagle
Length	48ft 2in	44ft	54ft 0in	63ft 0in	63ft 9in
Wingspan	26ft 8in	23ft 5in	16° – 45ft 10in 72° – 25ft 6in	38ft 5in	42ft 10in
Height	13ft 4in	15ft 4in	15ft 10in	16ft 5in	18ft 6in
Aircraft Empty Weight	10,481lb	10,739lb	24,000lb	31,500lb	29,000lb
Aircraft Weight with Internal Fuel	15,050lb	14,977lb	33,860lb	44,012lb	42,455lb
Internal Fuel (lb)★	4,537lb	4,238lb	9,860lb	12,512lb	13,455lb
Liters	2,566	2,471	5,749	7,296	7,836
Gallons	698	652	1,517	1,925	2,070
Engine(s)	2 × General Electric J85-GE-21	1 × Tumansky R-11F-300	1 × Tumansky R-29-300	2 × General Electric J79-GE-21	2 × Pratt & Whitney F100-PW-220
Thrust (Afterburner)	9,300lb	12,676lb	27,500lb	35,800lb	47,540lb

★ JP-4 fuel at 6.5lb per gallon

Appendix 5

Initial Active Duty Orders

SPECIAL ORDER	DATE		DEPARTMENT OF THE AIR FORCE
AB-383	20 Jan 77	EXTENDED ACTIVE DUTY ORDER	HQ AIR RESERVE PERSONNEL CENTER 7300 EAST FIRST AVENUE DENVER, COLORADO 80280

BY DIRECTION OF THE PRESIDENT

1. GRADE, NAME, SSAN AND MAILING ADDRESS FROM WHICH INDIVIDUAL WILL DEPART FOR ACTIVE DUTY
   2d Lt Robert J. Zettel
   7009 Washington Ave
   Racine WI 53406

2. COMPONENT: [X] USAFR / [ ] ANGUS
3. ADN: 001

4. TEMPORARY ADDRESS: 102 S Broadway #25, De Pere WI 54115
5. HOME OF RECORD (Same as Item 1 unless otherwise indicated)
6. PQAFSC/CAFSC OR PRIMARY AND DIRECTED DY AFSC: 0006
7. DATE OF RESERVE APPOINTMENT: 22 May 76

8. AERO RATING AND FLYING STATUS
   [ ] RATED [X] NON RATED   AERO RATING   [X] NOT ON FLYING STATUS   [ ] ON FLYING STATUS

9. IS ORDERED TO EXTENDED ACTIVE DUTY [X] VOLUNTARY [ ] INVOLUNTARY IN ACCORDANCE WITH
   Sec 6d(1), Mil Selective Service Act of 1967   IN THE GRADE OF 2d Lt
   [ ] FOR AN INDEFINITE PERIOD   DATE OF SEPARATION: 16 Mar 81
   [X] FOR A PERIOD OF 48 MONTHS   DAYS UNLESS SOONER RELIEVED.
   [ ] APPOINTED TO THE TEMPORARY GRADE OF _____ USAF, ON EFFECTIVE DATE OF DUTY.

10. ON DAY PRIOR TO EFFECTIVE DATE OF ACTIVE DUTY IS RELIEVED FROM RESERVE ASSIGNMENT
    HQ ARPC (ORS-RC) (PAS: S7ØIFLX7)

11. ASSIGNED TO 71 Student Squadron, ATC, Vance AFB, Oklahoma 73701 (PAS: VHØJFCJ2) to attend Course P-V4A-A, Undergraduate Pilot Training Class 78-04. Duration of course is approximately 49 weeks, and approximately 9 days of processing and briefing enroute at Lackland Training Annex (Medina), Lackland AFB, San Antonio, Texas 78236 to attend Familiarization Training ROTC Delayed Accessions Course MORM0004, Class 77-14 ending 29 Mar 77.

12. EFFECTIVE DATE OF DUTY IS 17 Mar 77   ON OR AFTER EFFECTIVE DATE OF DUTY, INDIVIDUAL WILL PROCEED AND REPORT not earlier than 0800 hours and not later than 1200 hours 21 Mar 77 to Building 112, Lackland AFB, Texas 78236. Report not later than 7 Apr 77 to the Consolidated Base Personnel Office (In and Out Processing), 71 Air Base Group, Vance AFB, Oklahoma 73701.

13. [X] DD FORM 220 (PA) EFFECTED BY THE PRIVACY ACT OF 1974, WILL BE COMPLETED BY FIRST DUTY STATION AND/OR PROCESSING STATION AND FORWARDED TO AFMPC (DPMDRR) RANDOLPH AFB, TX 78148. IF FIRST DUTY IS TDY FOR 60 OR MORE DAYS, TDY STATION WILL SUBMIT PHOTO TO SERVICING CBPO. AFR 35-93 APPLIES.

14. [X] AUTHORITY HAFAN 0370NM2617   PCS CODE "A"

15. PERMANENT CHANGE OF STATION. TRAVEL AS DIRECTED IS NECESSARY IN THE MILITARY SERVICE.
16. PERMANENT CHANGE OF STATION CHARGEABLE TO
    5773500 327 P510 S503725 (Pay and Allowances)
    5773500 327 5741.0*(*Insert M,D,H,I,L,T,Y) 5748.0N S503725 (Tvl and Trnsp)

17. TDY CHARGEABLE TO (Except for overseas and active duty processing)

18. SPECIAL INSTRUCTIONS (See reverse)
    FOR THE COMMANDER
    AUTHENTICATION
    DANIEL L. GROGAN
    Directorate of Administration

    DISTRIBUTION: A-1 Plus
    1-AFROTC/SDAP
    2-AFRTOC Det 410, College of St Thomas, St Paul MN 55105
    5-OTS, USAF/MTR, Lackland AFB TX 78236
    7-3700 PRG/DPPRO, Lackland AFB TX 78236

AFPC FORM 75 MAR 76   REVISED   3db4

A copy of the author's initial orders sending him to USAF Undergraduate Pilot Training. (*Rob Zettel collection*)

APPENDICES

Appendix 6

UPT "Dream Sheet"

Air Force Form 439 that the author submitted showing his assignment preferences after earning his wings. Despite the F-15 being listed as his first choice, no Eagles were handed out to this UPT class. Fortunately, the F-4 turned up, with the author being the only second lieutenant to receive a posting to fly the aircraft from his class. (*Rob Zettel collection*)

Appendix 7

Behind the Scenes

DEPARTMENT OF THE AIR FORCE
HEADQUARTERS 3D TACTICAL FIGHTER WING (PACAF)
APO SAN FRANCISCO 96274

Colonel Michael C. Kerby
Commander 57th Fighter Weapons Wing
Nellis AFB, NV 89191

Dear Mike

I've got a top notch young Aggressor pilot who would be a strong addition to the 4477th TES. Capt Rob Zettel came to Clark as an Aggressor after consecutive F-4 tours at Kadena and Osan. While flying the F-4 air-to-air at Osan he caught my Aggressors' attention -- sharp officer, strong stick, good briefer and an excellent host for the Aggressors during several deployments to Osan.

Rob has more than lived up to our expectations since his checkout as an Aggressor. His 700 F-4 hours and 260 F-5 hours give him the fighter credentials to back his solid Aggressor skills. As an Aggressor academic instructor, his strong platform performance has prompted positive comments from critical audiences throughout PACAF. His enthusiastic style as an instructor is infectious. In addition, the PACAF Stan/Eval team just inspected my three fighter squadrons. Rob's Stan/Eval program was singled out for high praise.

With an October DEROS, Rob could be ready to fly with you this fall. If I can provide further info, please let me know. Hope you can find a slot for him - he's a good one.

Sincerely,

JOHN A. CORDER, Colonel, USAF
Commander

Little did the author know of the ongoing efforts by his wing commander and others to help secure his assignment to the 4477th TES. This letter was one of several the author discovered decades later during his research of files for this book. (*Rob Zettel collection*)

Appendix 8

MiG-21

CERTIFICATE OF AIRCREW QUALIFICATION					DATE COMPLETED 18 Nov 83	
I. EXAMINEE IDENTIFICATION						
NAME (Last, First, Middle Initial) ZETTEL, ROBERT J.				GRADE CAPTAIN	SSAN ▓▓▓▓▓	
ORGANIZATION AND LOCATION 4477 TES/Nellis AFB, NV				ACFT/CREW POSITION YF110/P (MiG-21)	ELIGIBILITY PERIOD N/A	
II. QUALIFICATION						
GROUND PHASE				FLIGHT PHASE		
EXAMINATION/CHECK	DATE		GRADE	MISSION/CHECK		DATE
Written	8 Nov 83		100% (S)	Initial Qualification		18 Nov 83
EP Eval	15 Nov 83		Q			
QUALIFICATION LEVEL			RESTRICTION (Explain in Comments) ☐ YES ☒ NO	ADDITIONAL TRAINING		
QUALIFIED 1		UNQUALIFIED 2 3		DUE DATES N/A		
EXPIRATION DATE OF QUALIFICATION Nov 84				DATE ADDITIONAL TRAINING COMPLETED N/A		
COMMENTS: Qualified - See Reverse.						
III. CERTIFICATION						
TYPE NAME AND GRADE	ORGANIZATION	CONCUR	DO NOT CONCUR	REMARKS	SIGNATURE	DATE
FLIGHT EXAMINER 1 JAMES D. MATHENY Captain	4477TES/DOV			X	*James D. Matheny*	1 Dec 83
REVIEWING OFFICER 2 JAMES M. WATLEY Major	4477TES/DO	X		X	*James M. Watley*	1 Dec 83
FINAL APPROVING OFFICER 3 GEORGE S. GENNIN Lt Colonel	4477TES/CC	X		X	*George S. Gennin*	9 Dec 83
I CERTIFY that I have been briefed and understand the action being taken this date						
DATE 9 Dec 83	TYPED NAME AND GRADE OF EXAMINEE ROBERT J. ZETTEL, Captain				SIGNATURE *Robert J. Zettel*	

AF FORM 8 (APR 79)   PREVIOUS EDITION WILL BE USED

November 18, 1983 – initial qualification in the MiG-21. Note the reviewing and approving officers, Maj James Watley and Lt Col George Gennin, respectively. (*Rob Zettel collection*)

Appendix 8 continued

IV. Examiner's Remarks:

1. Mission Description: This evaluation was accomplished for initial qualification in the aircraft. Elements included: takeoff, SFO approach immediately after takeoff, departure, selected aerobatics, windup turn and reversal, random SFO approach on recovery, no flap low approach, normal touch and go, normal full stop.

2. Discrepancies:

    a. EP Eval: None.

    b. Flight: None.

3. Recommended additional training/corrective action: N/A.

4. Additional comments: Capt Zettel flew an excellent mission. Patterns were very precise and both SFOs were excellent.

V. Reviewing Officer's Remarks: I was briefed on the results of this mission.

VI. Approving Officer's Remarks: I monitored the entire mission on UHF and observed all pattern work. Capt Zettel demonstrated outstanding radio discipline and performed superbly in the pattern.

On the reverse side of the certificate of aircrew qualification, the check pilot, Capt Jim Matheny, outlined exactly what was performed on this, my sixth flight in the MiG-21. (*Rob Zettel collection*)

Appendix 9

MiG-23 Qualification AF Form 8

CERTIFICATE OF AIRCREW QUALIFICATION			DATE COMPLETED 26 FEB 86		
I.	**EXAMINEE IDENTIFICATION**				
NAME (Last, First, Middle Initial) ZETTEL, ROBERT J.			GRADE CAPTAIN		SSAN ████
ORGANIZATION AND LOCATION 4477 TES/NELLIS AFB, NV			ACFT/CREW POSITION YF-113/P (MiG-23)		ELIGIBILITY PERIOD N/A
II.		**QUALIFICATION**			
GROUND PHASE			FLIGHT PHASE		
EXAMINATION/CHECK	DATE	GRADE	MISSION/CHECK		DATE
CLOSED BOOK	12 FEB 86	100 (S)	INITIAL QUALIFICATION		26 FEB 86
OPEN BOOK	12 FEB 86	100			
EP EVAL	12 FEB 86	Q			
QUALIFICATION LEVEL			RESTRICTION (Explain in Comments) ☐ YES ☒ NO	ADDITIONAL TRAINING	
QUALIFIED 1	2	UNQUALIFIED 3		DUE DATES N/A	
EXPIRATION DATE OF QUALIFICATION FEB 87				DATE ADDITIONAL TRAINING COMPLETED N/A	
COMMENTS (If more space is needed, continue on reverse) QUALIFIED					
III.		**CERTIFICATION**			
TYPE NAME AND GRADE	ORGANIZATION	CHECK CONCUR / DO NOT CONCUR / REMARKS		SIGNATURE	DATE
1 FLIGHT EXAMINER THOMAS E. DRAKE MAJOR	4477 TES/ADO		X	Thomas E. Drake	27 Feb 86
2 REVIEWING OFFICER FRANK K. GEISLER MAJOR	4477 TES/DO	X	X	[signature]	27 Feb 86
3 FINAL APPROVING OFFICER JOHN T. MANCLARK LT COLONEL	4477 TES/CC	X		John T. Manclark	27 Feb 86
I CERTIFY that I have been briefed and understand the action being taken this date					
DATE 27 Feb '86	TYPED NAME AND GRADE OF EXAMINEE ROBERT J. ZETTEL, CAPTAIN			SIGNATURE Robert J. Zettel	

AF FORM 8 APR 79   PREVIOUS EDITION WILL BE USED

February 26, 1986 – initial qualification in the MiG-23. Note the check pilot was Maj Ted Drake, with the qualification reviewed by Maj "Paco" Geisler, 4477th TES DO. (*Rob Zettel collection*)

Appendix 9 continued

IV. EXAMINER'S REMARKS:

    1. Mission Description: This evaluation was accomplished on a dedicated transition sortie at Tonopah Test Range. Examinee was responsible for planning, briefing, flight leadership, and debriefing. Elements included: Takeoff with simulated flameout immediately after first throttle reduction for heavyweight SFO low approach, departure to the working area for advanced handling (acceleration maneuver, sustained turns, instantaneous turns, and vertical reversals), approach to stalls (no-flap and full-flap), enemy tactical formations, random SFO from the working area to a low approach, precautionary approach to a visual straight-in touch-and-go, overhead no-flap low approach and closed normal full stop.

    2. Discrepancies: None

    3. Recommended Additional Training/Corrective Action: None

V. REVIEWING OFFICER'S REMARKS: I was briefed on the results of this evaluation.

VI. APPROVING OFFICER'S REMARKS: None

    4477 TES/DOV

        FLT CC

    57 FWW/DOV

    57 FWW/AT

    57 FWW/CV

Note the mission description on the reverse side of the certificate of aircrew qualification. From the time I took off until when I landed, there was very little time for relaxing. The qualification flight was my fifth sortie in the MiG-23. (*Rob Zettel collection*)

APPENDICES

Appendix 10

"Red Eagles" Helmet and Bag

The author's helmet and bag, which he used throughout his 476 MiG sorties while a member of the 4477th TES. The helmet bag was custom-made in Osan shortly after the author received orders to the "Red Eagles." (*Rob Zettel collection*)

Glossary

A

Adverse Yaw – The natural and undesirable tendency for an aircraft to yaw in the opposite direction of a roll. It is caused by the difference in lift and drag of each wing.

Afterburner – An additional combustion component used on some jet engines. Its purpose is to increase thrust, typically for supersonic flight, takeoff, and combat operations. The afterburning process injects additional fuel into a combustor section aft of the turbine section of the engine, significantly increasing the engine's available thrust.

Aggressor (USAF) – An adversary pilot in one of four USAF squadrons whose mission it was to provide DACT to USAF fighter units. They flew the Northrop F-5E, emulating Soviet formations and tactics.

AIM-7 – Air Intercept Missile. Designation given to the class of USAF/US Navy medium-range radar-guided air-to-air missiles (e.g., AIM-7M).

AIM-9 – Designation given to the class of USAF/US Navy short-range infrared-guided air-to-air missiles (e.g., AIM-9M).

Air Force Systems Command (AFSC) – Formerly a major USAF command whose mission was research and development of new weapons systems. The USAF Flight Test Center at Edwards AFB was a key focal point for AFSC activities. AFSC merged into the present Air Force Materiel Command in 1992.

Air Route Traffic Control Center (ARTCC) – Controls aircraft flying in a specified region of airspace. There are 22 ARTCCs in the CONUS (e.g., Los Angeles Center, Chicago Center).

Air Tasking Order (ATO) – A detailed document that synchronizes and directs air operations for a specific 24-hour period.

"Alamo" – NATO reporting name for the Soviet R-27 semi-active radar-guided missile. It is also designated the AA-10 missile by NATO.

"Alpha" – The reference used to describe the 16° wing-sweep configuration of the MiG-23.

Angle of Attack (AOA) – The angle formed by the chord line of the wing and the aircraft's flight path (relative wind), typically mentioned in fighter circles when discussing the maximum performance of an aircraft.
AN/APG-63 – A radar unit that equipped early models of the F-15 fighter.
"Aphid" – NATO reporting name for the Soviet R-60 all-aspect infrared-homing missile. It is also designated the AA-8 missile by NATO.
Area 51 – A highly restricted airfield located 70 nautical miles northwest of Nellis AFB, where many of America's most classified aircraft programs, including the U-2, SR-71, and F-117, were initially flown and tested. It is also known as "Dreamland" and "The Box." "Red Eagles" pilots had access to the airfield and operated out of "Dreamland" for nine weeks during the summer of 1985 while the runway at TTR was being lengthened.
"Atoll" – NATO reporting name for the short-range infrared-homing missile developed by the Soviet Union. It is similar in appearance and function to the American AIM-9B Sidewinder. It is also designated the AA-2 missile by NATO.
AUTOVON – Short for Automatic Voice Network, was a worldwide telephone system used by the US Department of Defense from the mid-1960s to the early 1990s.

B

Base – In an airfield traffic pattern, the base leg is a segment flown perpendicular to the runway's extended centerline, connecting the downwind and final approach legs.
Basic Fighter Maneuvers (BFM) – Classic maneuvers taught to fighter pilots everywhere to develop the aerial skills necessary to gain positional advantage over an opponent during visual 1-v-1 maneuvering. BFM, as the name implies, is fundamental to successful progression to advanced maneuvers and tactics where the fighter(s) may engage multiple adversaries.
"Big-Sky Theory" – An unofficial fighter pilot belief that, due to the relatively small size of a fighter compared to the vastness of the sky, the odds of hitting another airplane during air combat, whether in wartime or training, were minuscule.
"Bingo" – The term used to describe the minimum fuel quantity at which a pilot would begin a normal recovery to the airfield for landing (e.g., "Two's 'bingo.'"). "Bingo Fuel" is typically well above an emergency fuel state.
Blue Air – The term used to describe those aircraft in major exercises jointly operating in opposition to their Red Air counterparts.

GLOSSARY

Blue Angels – US Navy flight demonstration squadron.
"Bogey Dope" – Information GCI relays to fighters regarding the composition of enemy aircraft, including numbers, bearing, range, and altitude.
"Bravo" – The reference used to describe the 45° wing-sweep configuration of the MiG-23.
"Bug-out" – To leave an air combat engagement with no intention of re-engaging.
"Bullseye" – A pre-designated reference point from which radar contacts, both friendly and hostile positions, are called.

C

"Charlie" – The reference used to describe the 72° wing-sweep configuration of the MiG-23.
Chief Master Sergeant (CMSgt) – USAF enlisted paygrade E-9.
Clark AB – Located on the island of Luzon in the Philippines, Clark AB was a PACAF base and home of the 3rd TFW. The 26th AS (F-5E) and the 3rd and 90th TFSs (F-4E/G) were notable tenants.
Clueless – As the name implies, a person(s) without a clue. This expression is typically heard around the bar in the company of junior officers when describing any number of people whose exercise of judgment is regarded as a waste of their time, usually senior officers and anyone from headquarters.
Combat Air Patrol (CAP) – A type of mission for fighter aircraft, typically patrolling an assigned geographical area of a combat zone.
Combat Spread – A tactical formation where two friendly aircraft fly 6,000 to 9,000ft apart line abreast, with one stacked vertically higher (typically by 500 to 1,000ft) than the other.
Constant Peg – The unclassified code name for the top-secret USAF project that operated Soviet MiG-17, MiG-21, and MiG-23 fighter aircraft in air combat training against USAF, US Navy, and US Marine Corps fighter aircrew during the period 1978–88. The 4477th TES, while officially based at Nellis AFB as part of the 57th FWW, conducted all flight operations from TTR.
Cope Thunder – A PACAF two-week tactical air exercise involving fighter units operating as both "Red Air" and "Blue Air." Participating fighter and tanker crews operated out of Clark AB.
Crank/Cranking – A tactic whereby a fighter pilot turns his aircraft away from a targeted enemy fighter while maintaining radar contact, simultaneously reducing his closing speed on the target and increasing the distance an enemy missile has to travel to reach him.

D

"Dart" – TDU-10B towed target used in training aerial gunnery, simply referred to as the "Dart," was trailed behind the tow aircraft by a 1,500–2,000ft cable.

Designated Mean Point of Impact (DMPI) – A precise point on a target selected for the center of impact of precision weapons (e.g., laser-guided bombs).

Dissimilar Air Combat Maneuvers (DACM) – Air combat training involving dissimilar fighter aircraft (e.g., 2 × F 4 vs 1 × F-5) and typically a precursor to more advanced Dissimilar Air Combat Training (DACT) scenarios.

"Double-Bang" – Fighter squadron term meaning to fly two sorties in a day.

Downwind – A course flown parallel to the landing runway, but in a direction opposite to the intended landing direction, when in an airfield traffic pattern.

"Dreamland" – The term often used for Groom Lake/Area 51.

Dress Blues – The USAF service dress uniform, often referred to as the "Class A" uniform, is worn with the service dress coat.

E

Eagle – Official name given to the F-15 fighter.

E-3A Sentry – USAF Airborne Warning and Control System (AWACS) aircraft.

F

F-4 Phantom II – Twin-engined fighter built by McDonnell Douglas and flown by the USAF, US Navy, and US Marine Corps.

F-5E Tiger II – Lightweight twin-engined fighter built by the Northrop Corporation and flown by the USAF and US Navy as an adversary trainer for Dissimilar Air Combat Training (DACT).

F-7 – A Chinese copy (built by the Chengdu Aircraft Industry Group) of the Soviet MiG-21F-13 with minor changes. The 4477th flew at least eight of these aircraft alongside Soviet-built examples.

GLOSSARY

F-14 Tomcat – Twin-engined US Navy fleet fighter/interceptor built by Grumman.

F-15 Eagle – Twin-engined fighter built by McDonnell Douglas and flown by the USAF.

F-16 "Viper" – Single-engined fighter built by General Dynamics (and then Lockheed Martin) and flown by the USAF.

F/A-18 Hornet – Twin-engined fighter/attack aircraft built by McDonnell Douglas and flown by the US Navy and US Marine Corps.

F-20 Tigershark – A supersonic, single-engined lightweight fighter proposed by the Northrop Corporation. Despite building and testing several prototypes, the USAF elected not to buy the aircraft, and the program was canceled.

F-111 – A twin-engined, supersonic, medium-range fighter-bomber built by General Dynamics and operated by the USAF.

F-117 Nighthawk – A twin-engined stealth attack aircraft, built by Lockheed and operated by the USAF from TTR alongside the 4477th TES.

Final – The "final" leg in an airport traffic pattern is the last segment before landing, where the aircraft is aligned with the runway and descending for touchdown.

"Fishbed" – NATO reporting name for the MiG-21 line of fighter aircraft built by Mikoyan-Gurevich.

"Flogger" – NATO reporting name given to the MiG-23 line of fighter aircraft built by Mikoyan-Gurevich.

Fox-1 – Term used to describe the launch, simulated or actual, of a medium-range air-to-air missile (e.g., AIM-7).

Fox-2 – Term used to describe the launch, simulated or actual, of a short-range air-to-air missile (e.g., AIM-9).

Functional Check Flight (FCF) – A test flight during which a specially trained pilot checks out all primary functions of an aircraft to ensure proper operation. These flights typically occurred following major maintenance performed on the engine, flight controls, etc.

"Furball" – A tight-turning visual engagement between two or more aircraft.

G

GBU-10 Paveway II – A laser-guided 2,000lb bomb.

G-induced loss of consciousness – Blacking out due to the rapid onset of G forces while maneuvering a high-performance fighter.

Ground-Controlled Interception (GCI) – The use of ground-based radar equipment and controllers to affect the air-to-air intercept of aircraft. The term GCI was also used to refer to personnel who operated the equipment as their primary duty assignment.

Guided Bomb Unit (GBU) – General reference to those bombs equipped with a precision guidance system (e.g., laser guidance, GPS, or infrared).

H

Hard Deck – The term used in air combat training that designates the "floor" of the engagement area. It is usually set high enough to allow for a safe recovery margin above the underlying terrain (e.g., 10,000ft AGL).

Have Blue – The code name for Lockheed's proof of concept demonstrator for the F-117 stealth attack aircraft.

Have Doughnut – Project codename for the top secret exploitation by the Defense Intelligence Agency (DIA) of a single MiG-21F-13 obtained from Israel, the evaluation taking place from January to April 1968. Years later, this same aircraft was part of *Have Idea*, and it would eventually be one of a number of MiG-21s and F-7s flown by the 4477th TES during Project *Constant Peg*.

Have Drill – Project codename for the DIA's top secret exploitation of a MiG-17F that the US had acquired from Israel in 1968. This aircraft was one of two MiG-17s later operated by the 4477th TES during Project *Constant Peg*.

Have Idea – Project codename for the AFSC-led exploitation of MiG-17s and MiG-21s, with TAC and US Navy participation.

Have Pad – Project codename for the AFSC-led exploitation of the MiG-23MS in the spring/summer of 1978.

Heads-Up Display (HUD) – A transparent cockpit display that presents flight, radar, and weapons data without requiring the pilot to look down into the cockpit.

"High Lark" – NATO reporting name for the RP-23 Sapfir radar developed by Phazotron specifically for the MiG-23 fighter and used in conjunction with the Vympel R-24R (NATO reporting name "Apex") beyond visual range radar-guided missile.

"High Key" – The starting altitude of a Simulated Flame Out (SFO) pattern.

Hornet – Official name given to the US Navy/US Marine Corps F/A-18 fighter.

GLOSSARY

I

Infra-Red Acquisition and Designation System – Targeting system aboard the F-117 stealth attack aircraft.
Initial Point – A specific, identifiable location used as a starting point for a bombing run on a target.
Instructor Pilot (IP) – Aviator tasked with teaching UPTs how to fly, or improving the skills and mission effectiveness of frontline pilots.

J

Jink – A sudden, rapid, and unpredictable change in an aircraft's flight path, often involving sharp turns, rolls, and altitude changes, that is used to evade an enemy aircraft's gun attack.
JP-4 – Military aviation fuel, historically used by the USAF.

K

KC-10 – USAF tanker/transport aircraft based upon the McDonnell Douglas DC-10 airframe.
KC-135 Stratotanker – USAF tanker aircraft based on the Boeing 707 airframe.
Kilometers per hour (km/h) – The airspeed metric Soviet aircraft designers use to measure airspeed.
Kilogram per square centimeter (kg/cm^2) – Metrics used in Soviet fighter aircraft to measure and indicate hydraulic and pneumatic pressure versus pounds per square inch (PSI), as in US-designed fighters.
"Knife Fight" – Another term for a close-in visual fight between two fighter aircraft.
Knock it Off (KIO) – The term used by fighter pilots to terminate air combat training maneuvers (e.g., "'Bandit 11,' knock it off"). Once announced, each participant would reply with their respective callsign and repeat the term "knock it off," signifying acknowledgment that maneuvering had ceased.
Knots Indicated Airspeed (KIAS) – Often expressed as knots or abbreviated as kts. The standard metric by which most Western-designed fighters measure airspeed.

L

Lomcovak – A family of extreme maneuvers where the aircraft, with almost no forward speed, rotates on chosen axes due to gyroscopic precession and torque of the rotating propeller. Generally associated with high-performance aerobatics.

"Low Key" – The 180° position in a circular pattern used to position the aircraft for a final approach when simulating the loss of engine power.

M

Mach – Term expressed as a function of an aircraft's airspeed relative to the speed of sound (e.g., 0.95 Mach or 2.2 Mach).

Maple Flag – Royal Canadian Air Force air-to-air and air-to-ground exercise located at Canadian Forces Base Cold Lake, Alberta.

Master Sergeant (MSgt) – USAF enlisted paygrade E-7.

Mean Sea Level – The standard reference metric used in aviation for altitude reporting, it is often abbreviated as "MSL." This reference is different from Above Ground Level (AGL), which is a measurement above the local terrain over which an aircraft is flying.

MiG-21F-13 – The primary model of the MiG-21 flown by the 4477th. TES NATO reporting name "Fishbed-C."

MiG-23BN – The export ground attack variant of the MiG-23. NATO reporting name "Flogger-F."

MiG-23MS – The export fighter interceptor variant of the MiG-23. NATO reporting name "Flogger-E."

MiG-29 – Twin-engined fourth-generation fighter developed by the Soviet Union to counter the F-15 and F-16. NATO reporting name "Fulcrum."

Mikoyan-Gurevich – The Soviet design bureau that produced a long line of Soviet fighters, including the MiG-17, MiG-21, and MiG-23 fighters operated by the 4477th TES.

Military Power (MIL) – Full throttle setting with the aircraft's engine developing 100 percent power but not yet in afterburner. Commonly just referred to as "MIL power" or "full MIL."

"Mongoose" – US Navy pilots' nickname for the Douglas A-4E/F Skyhawk modified into a fighter for the Adversary role.

MU-2 – The MU-2 is a twin-engined turboprop aircraft built by Mitsubishi. The 4477th TES operated two MU-2s to shuttle pilots between Nellis AFB

GLOSSARY

and TTR each morning and afternoon. The aircraft were flown solely by squadron pilots.

Multi-National Operational Test and Evaluation – A collaborative effort between the US and multiple countries to test and improve the F-16 fighter.

N

Nautical mile – Measured as 6,000ft

Nellis AFB – Located in Las Vegas, Nevada. During the period covered by this book (1983–86), Nellis AFB was home to the USAF's TFWC and the FWS. The 64th and 65th ASs, 4477th TES, 4450th TG, 474th TFW, *Red Flag*, and the Thunderbirds were notable tenants.

Nellis Test and Training Range – A major military training area located at Nellis AFB. It is the largest contiguous air and ground space available for peacetime military operations in the free world, encompassing 2.9 million acres of land and 7,000 square miles of airspace.

Nighthawk – F-117 stealth attack aircraft, built by Lockheed.

Non-commissioned officer – Non-commissioned officer ranks in the USAF are enlisted personnel who have been promoted to positions of leadership and authority. NCO ranks are E-5 through E-9.

Notching – A defensive fighter maneuver executed by turning 90° to the suspected radar threat (SAMs and/or air-to-air missiles) and placing it on the beam, often accompanied by the dropping of chaff and flares.

O

O'Club – Officers' Club

Officer Efficiency Report – A formal document used to assess and document an officer's performance and potential with a military organization.

Officer Training School – A USAF officer commissioning program located at Maxwell AFB, Alabama.

Operation *Desert Storm* – The war against the forces of President Saddam Hussein following Iraq's invasion of Kuwait. It commenced on January 17, 1991.

Operation *Diamond* – Israeli Mossad operation to acquire a MiG-21F-13 from Iraq. This led to the successful defection of an IrAF pilot in his MiG-21 to Israel on August 16, 1966. That same aircraft was later flown for years by the pilots of the 4477th TES.

Operation *El Dorado Canyon* – A joint USAF, US Navy, and US Marine Corps air strike against targets in Libya on April 15, 1985.

Operational Readiness Inspection – A mission-oriented inspection given by a major command's Inspector General Team to evaluate a unit's ability to fulfill its mission.

P

Performance Profile (PP) – A flight profile flown by 4477th pilots when demonstrating to visiting aircrews the size and performance capabilities of their MiGs in comparison to visiting fighters.

Permanent Change of Station – Reference in USAF circles to formally published orders for reassignment and a change of duty locations.

Phantom II – Designation given to the McDonnell Douglas F-4 fighter aircraft.

"Phone booth" – A fighter pilot term for a close-in visual fight between two aircraft.

R

Range Control Officer (RCO) – Officer tasked with manning a bombing range, controlling access, active targets, and overseeing bomb scoring.

Red Air – The term used in major exercises to describe those aircraft simulating the enemy.

Red Flag – USAF air-to-air and air-to-ground exercise located at Nellis AFB.

Replacement Training Unit (RTU) – A squadron assigned the primary mission of training pilots in a specific fighter aircraft.

Rules of Engagement (ROE) – In air combat training, these are the specified rules that all fighter aircraft, whether engaged or not, will abide by to ensure safe operations (e.g., if meeting head-on, both fighters will alter their course to the right; when converging, the fighter with the higher nose position will continue to go nose-high; when not engaged, all fighters will maintain their assigned altitude blocks, etc.).

GLOSSARY

S

Senior Master Sergeant (SMSgt) – USAF enlisted pay grade E-8.
Senior Trend – The program name within TAC for the F-117 stealth attack aircraft.
Simulated Flame Out (SFO) – The recovery and landing of a single-engined fighter simulating the loss of power of its engine. Typically associated with an SFO pattern to be flown overhead of the landing airfield.
Sirena-3M – Soviet-built SPO-2 Sirena-3M RWR commonly fitted in the MiG-29 fighter.
Situational Awareness (SA) – The ability to understand and respond to what is happening around you.
"Slot Back" – NATO reporting name for the N-019 pulse-Doppler target acquisition radar fitted in the MiG-29.
"Space available" – Travel status given to DoD personnel traveling aboard USAF transport aircraft when not on official duty orders (i.e., if there's a seat available, it's yours).
Splash – The term used to convey the destruction of an enemy fighter by missiles or a gun.
Staff Sergeant (SSgt) – USAF enlisted pay grade E-5.
STU II – The second-generation Secure Telephone Unit developed by the National Security Agency for use by US and NATO forces.
Student Gap – The nickname given to a prominent geographical point used by many participants in *Red Flag* exercises as their starting point for low-level ingress.
Supervisor of Flying (SOF) – A duty position manned by an officer in the airfield control tower. Typically, an experienced pilot and current in the unit's primary assigned aircraft, he monitors and assists in the ongoing flight operations of the unit's assigned fighter aircraft.

T

Tactical Air Command (TAC) – Major USAF command, headquartered at Langley AFB, Virginia, that had operational control of all fighter squadrons in CONUS – predecessor of today's Air Combat Command.
Tactical Electronic Warfare System – The radar warning display in the F-15.
Target Display Unit – Symbol on the F-15 HUD in which a locked airborne target is displayed.

Technical Sergeant (TSgt) – USAF enlisted paygrade E-6. Most commonly referred to as simply "Tech Sergeant."
Threat Training Facility – An installation at Nellis AFB that housed auditoriums, classrooms, and static displays of Soviet MiGs and other Warsaw Pact equipment.
Thunderbirds – USAF Air Demonstration Squadron.
Tiger II – The official but rarely used name given to the F-5E fighter.
Tomcat – Official name given to the Grumman F-14 fighter aircraft.
"Tonopah Officers' Club and Chinese Laundry" – The nickname given to the Officers' Club at TTR.
TOPGUN – The US Navy Fighter Weapons School course taught to selected crews. Established on March 3, 1969, at NAS Miramar, the US Navy Fighter Weapons School (and its courses, including TOPGUN) merged into the Naval Strike and Air Warfare Center at NAS Fallon, Nevada, in 1996.
Top Secret/Sensitive Compartmented Information (TS/SCI) – A security clearance level usually only granted to personnel handling the most sensitive information, and well above the secret and top secret security classifications.
T-37 Tweet – The primary, Cessna-built twin-engined jet trainer for the USAF. The T-37 was the first aircraft USAF pilot trainees flew during UPT.
T-38 Talon – A twin-engined, supersonic trainer built by Northrop, the Talon served as the advanced jet trainer for USAF students during UPT. The 4477th TES operated as many as five T-38s primarily for chase duties with the squadron's MiGs.

U

Ultra-High Frequency (UHF) – Radio frequencies between 300 MHz and 3 GHz.
Undergraduate Pilot Training (UPT) – The 52-week training course that USAF pilots attend to earn their wings.

V

Vertical-Scan – A radar search mode in the F-15.
Vertical Situation Display (VSD) – The screen in the upper left corner of the F-15's instrument panel that displays radar data.

GLOSSARY

"Viper" – Unofficial name given to the F-16 fighter (which is officially called the Fighting Falcon).
Visiting Officer's Quarters (VOQ) – Lodging facilities at most military installations set aside for officers visiting the base temporarily.

W

Weapon Systems Officer (WSO) – In the USAF, flight officers involved in all aspects of a fighter aircraft's weapon systems and air operations. Most commonly associated with two-seat fighter aircraft (e.g., F-4, F-111, and F-15E).

Y

YF-110B – USAF flight records identifier for the MiG-21F-13.
YF-110C – USAF flight records identifier for the Chengdu F-7.
YF-113B – USAF flight records identifier for the MiG-23BN aircraft.
YF-113E – USAF flight records identifier for the MiG-23MS aircraft.

Z

"Z-Man" – The author's USAF callsign.

Abbreviations

A

AAA – Anti-Aircraft Artillery
AAF – Air Force Auxiliary Field
AB – Air Base
ACM – Air Combat Maneuvers
ADIZ – Air Defense Identification Zone
ADVON – Advance Party
AFB – Air Force Base
AFROTC – Air Force Reserve Officer Training Corps
AFSC – Air Force Systems Command
AGL – Above Ground Level
AIM – Air Intercept Missile (e.g., AIM-7M)
AOA – Angle of Attack
ARTCC – Air Route Traffic Control Center
ATO – Air Tasking Order
AWACS – Airborne Warning and Control System (e.g., E-3A Sentry)

B

BFM – Basic Fighter Maneuvers
Brig Gen – Brigadier General (USAF)

C

CAP – Combat Air Patrol
Capt – Captain (USAF, US Navy, and US Marine Corps)
Cdr – Commander (US Navy)

CMSgt – Chief Master Sergeant (E-9), most commonly referred to as simply "Chief"
Col – Colonel (USAF and US Marine Corps)

D

DACM – Dissimilar Air Combat Manaeuvers
DACT – Dissimilar Air Combat Training (e.g., F-5E vs F-15)
DMPI – Designated Mean Point of Impact
DoD – Department of Defense (United States)

E

EGT – Exhaust Gas Temperature

F

FAIP – First Assignment Instructor Pilot
FCF – Functional Check Flight
FTS – Flying Training Squadron
FTW – Flying Training Wing
FWS – (USAF) Fighter Weapons School
FWIC – Fighter Weapons Instructor Course
FWW – Fighter Weapons Wing (e.g., 57th FWW)

G

GBU – Guided Bomb Unit
GCI – Ground-Controlled Interception
Gen – General (USAF)

ABBREVIATIONS

H

HQ – Headquarters
HUD – Heads Up Display

I

IP – Instructor Pilot
IADS – IrAF Integrated Air Defense System

K

KIAS – Knots Indicated Airspeed
KIO – Knock it Off

L

Lt – Lieutenant (USAF, US Navy, and US Marine Corps)
Lt Cdr – Lieutenant Commander (US Navy)
Lt Col – Lieutenant Colonel (USAF and US Marine Corps)

M

Maj – Major (USAF and US Marine Corps)
Maj Gen – Major General (USAF)
MiG – Mikoyan-Gurevich
MIL – Military Power
MOA – Military Operations Area
MPC – Military Personnel Center (USAF)
MSgt – Master Sergeant (E-7)
MSL – Mean Sea Level

N

NAS – Naval Air Station
NATO – North Atlantic Treaty Organization
NCO – Non-Commissioned Officer
NCOIC – Non-Commissioned Officer In Charge

P

PACAF – Pacific Air Forces (USAF)
PLAAF – People's Liberation Army Air Force (i.e., Chinese Air Force)
PP – Performance Profile

R

RCO – Range Control Officer
ROE – Rules of Engagement
ROTC – Reserve Officer Training Corps
RTB – Return To Base
RTU – Replacement Training Unit
RWRs – Radar Warning Receivers
RWY – Runway

S

SA – Situational Awareness
SAM – Surface-to-Air Missile
SFO – Simulated Flame Out
SMSgt – Senior Master Sergeant (E-8)
SOF – Supervisor of Flying
SRM – Short Range Missile
SSgt – Staff Sergeant (E-5)

ABBREVIATIONS

T

TAC – Tactical Air Command (USAF)
TDU – Target Display Unit (F-15)
TDY – Temporary Duty
TES – Test and Evaluation Squadron
TEWS – Tactical Electronic Warfare System (F-15)
TFS – Tactical Fighter Squadron
TFTAS – Tactical Fighter Training Aggressor Squadron
TFTS – Tactical Fighter Training Squadron
TFW – Tactical Fighter Wing
TFWC – Tactical Fighter Weapons Center
TG – Tactical Group
TS – Test Squadron or Tactical Squadron
TSgt – Technical Sergeant (E-6)
TS/SCI – Top Secret/Sensitive Compartmented Information
TTR – Tonopah Test Range

U

UHF – Ultra-High Frequency
UPT – Undergraduate Pilot Training (e.g., USAF)
USAF – United States Air Force
USAFE – United States Air Forces in Europe
USMC – United States Marine Corps
USN – United States Navy

V

VOQ – Visiting Officers' Quarters
VPAF – Vietnam People's Air Force
VSD – Visual Situation Display (i.e., cockpit radar display in the F-15)

W

WSO – Weapon Systems Officer

Index

Note: All hardware is US unless otherwise stated.

accidents   110, 135, 149, 150, 170–173, 178, 179, 264–270
   and rate metrics   174–176, 177
ACM (Air Combat Maneuvering)   13, 21, 27–31, 72–75, 90–91, 95, 97–98, 101, 102, 137, 139–140, 141, 170, 171–172, 173, 194–195, 207–211, 220–223, 253–255, 273–275, 279–280, 297–298, 300–301, 303–306, 315, 319, 320
   Advanced Combat Maneuvers   71
   BFM (Basic Fighter Maneuvers)   71, 177–178, 226, 229
   departures   223, 224, 244, 246, 279, 281, 283
   "flat scissors"   22, 182, 183, 208, 209, 211
   "funky chicken"   306
   "knife fights"   207, 208, 226
   Lomcovak maneuver   283
   "rolling scissors"   22, 90, 182, 183, 195, 209, 210, 227
adverse yaw   100, 242, 245, 275, 279, 280, 281
Aggressor pilots and squadrons   71–74, 75, 78, 80, 81, 83, 85, 107, 110, 124, 149, 150, 151, 170–181, 273, 288
   and the Red Eagles   180–181
air configurations and formations   23, 41, 68–69, 95–96, 158, 213, 216, 220, 252–253, 297, 299, 313
air power evolution   12
air-to-air refueling   68–69, 309
aircraft   13, 25
   Beechcraft C-12   268, 269
   Boeing B-52 Stratofortress   43, 48, 55, 59, 60
   Boeing KC-135 Stratotanker   48, 59, 68, 111–112
   Cessna T-37 Tweet   54, 56, 60, 63, 64
   Convair F-106 Delta Dart   49
   Dassault Mirage F1 (Iraq)   312
   Dassault Mirage IIIO (Australia)   103
   Douglas A-4 Skyhawk   205, 206–211
   General Dynamics F-16 "Viper"   80, 84, 85, 90, 118, 142, 180, 181, 182, 211, 225, 244, 280, 312
   General Dynamics F-111   212, 213, 214, 215, 216–217, 218
   Grumman F-14 Tomcat   152, 203, 225, 279, 282, 289, 292
   Lockheed C-5A Galaxy   107, 128, 130, 132, 133, 134, 135
   Lockheed C-130   59, 81, 129
   Lockheed C-141   56, 59, 107, 111
   Lockheed F-117 Nighthawk   160, 162, 163–165, 166, 168, 169, 263–264, 265, 266, 269, 271
   LTV A-7 Corsair II   168, 270
   McDonnell Douglas F-15 Eagle   56, 57, 60, 69, 70, 78, 85, 89, 90, 92, 93, 124, 142, 167, 168, 175, 180, 181, 185, 195, 211, 219–224, 225, 226, 227, 229, 230, 244, 252–253, 254, 272, 273–276, 279, 283, 287, 288, 296, 307, 308, 309, 311, 312
      F-15C   287, 297–307, 309–310, 311, 313, 314–315, 316–317, 318–319, 321, 322, 323
   McDonnell Douglas F/A-18 Hornet   142, 182, 203, 211, 225, 244, 279, 289
   McDonnell Douglas KC-10 Extender   309, 310
   McDonnell Douglas Phantom II F-4   56, 59, 60, 61, 62, 63–68, 69, 71, 76, 77, 83, 84, 90, 93, 95, 110, 114, 115, 123, 124, 131, 149, 167, 180, 181, 185, 193, 239, 249, 250, 279, 282, 292, 311

F-4C/D 66, 72–75, 80, 258–259, 279, 308
F-4E 80, 81, 82, 86, 87, 92, 96, 97–99, 100, 279–280, 308
F-4S 185
RF-4 56
Mitsubishi MU-2 (Japan) 117, 124, 152, 153, 154, 197
North American F-100 Super Sabre 115
Northrop F-5E 23, 72, 73, 74, 75, 76, 89, 90, 91, 92, 93, 95, 98, 100–102, 128, 130, 141, 146, 149, 150, 170–172, 173–174, 175, 177, 180, 181, 182, 183, 205, 280, 288, 308, 312
Northrop F-20 Tigershark 288
Northrop F-89 Scorpion 32–33
Northrop T-38 Talon 54, 56, 59, 60, 61, 64, 119, 137, 139, 140, 141, 143, 146, 155, 245, 248, 289, 291
Piper PA-28-140 Cherokee 52, 67, 116
Republic F-105 Thunderchief 86
Sukhoi Su-27 (USSR) 244, 312
see also Mikoyan-Gurevich MiG aircraft (USSR)
airshows 30, 314
airspeeds (KIAS) 22, 23, 27, 28, 31, 65, 68, 73, 74, 75, 90, 95, 97, 100, 138, 139, 141, 143, 144, 145, 146, 158, 171, 172, 173, 182, 191, 192, 193, 194, 195, 205, 206, 208, 209, 211, 212, 213, 215, 216, 217, 220, 222, 223, 224, 234, 238–239, 241, 242, 243, 245–246, 247, 248–249, 250, 253, 254, 256, 258, 259, 260, 273, 275, 283–284, 285, 293, 294, 300, 304, 317, 321
al-Gaddafi, Muammar 217
altitudes 27, 137, 140, 143, 144, 145, 158, 191
AGL (Above Ground Level) 21, 22, 27, 28–29, 68, 73, 74, 90, 95, 98, 137, 140, 143, 144, 145, 158, 194, 215, 223, 224, 233, 234, 240, 248, 249, 256, 314
MSL (Mean Sea Level) 172, 215, 240, 246, 247, 273, 284, 298, 310, 317, 318, 320
AOAs (angles of attack) 22, 66, 141, 182, 208, 209, 210, 211, 241, 244, 245, 246, 275, 278, 279, 280, 282, 283, 294, 319

Area 51, Nevada 158, 159, 160, 202, 213, 214, 218
Arizona ANG (Air National Guard), the 168
Arriola, Capt Mark "Nips" 310, 313, 316, 318, 320
ARTCCs (Air Route Traffic Control Centers) 264–265, 266
Ashy, Brig Gen Joe 174, 180, 200, 201
ATO (Air Tasking Order) mission 213–217, 218
AUTOVON (Automatic Voice Network), the 79, 85
AWACS (Airborne Warning and Control System), the 310, 315, 322

BAK-9 arresting system, the 66, 67
Baker, TSgt Jerry 127–128, 130
Baldwin, Maj "Digger" 287, 288
Bayer, Capt Billy 140, 193, 194
Bell, TSgt Jim 131–134
Beverlin, SSgt Mike 129, 130
"Big-Sky Theory" 102–103, 175
"Black World" operations 125
Bland, Maj Dave "Blazo" 157, 181, 195–197, 200, 201–202, 213, 214, 215–217, 230–231, 232–233, 234–236, 278, 293
BLC (Boundary Layer Control) system, the 65, 66
Boldface (immediate action terms) 65
Bort numbers 119, 121, 131, 135
Bowman, Capt Jim "Boots" 297–298, 299, 300, 301, 302
Bright-Scope, the 195, 196, 231, 232, 293
Brown, Capt Steve "Brownie" 192, 193–195, 196, 197, 200, 201, 236, 279
Brubaker, Lt Cdr Guy "Brudog" 192, 292
Burzynski, SSgt Tom 129, 130

callsigns 109, 113, 119, 149, 150, 152, 203
see also names
camouflage paint schemes 23, 28, 120, 137, 194, 206, 257
CAP (Combat Air Patrol) missions 212, 213, 215, 218, 311, 313, 314, 316, 317, 318
Carlisle, Capt Herbert "Hawk" 227, 289, 290–291
Chanik, Lt Cdr Marty "Streak" 289, 290
Chengdu Aircraft Industry Group, the 134

INDEX

Chinese ADIZ (Air Defense Identification Zone), the   132
CIA (Central Intelligence Agency), the   135
Clark AB, Luzon, Philippines   85, 87, 88, 91–92, 106, 112, 130
Class A uniform (Dress Blues)   107, 108, 109, 148, 151
clearances and background investigations   155
cockpit visibility   142, 221, 244
College of Saint Thomas, Saint Paul, Minnesota   50, 51–52, 53
combat losses   97, 311, 321
Constant Peg project, the   24–25, 87, 108, 119, 126–127, 135, 136, 155, 156, 162, 181, 185, 199, 214, 227, 269, 276, 278, 291, 296, 308, 323
Corder, Maj Chuck   87
Craig, Capt Gary "Goldie"   151, 159, 213, 214, 216, 252, 253, 254, 256–257, 259
cranking   220, 274, 297, 301, 319
Creech, Gen Wilbur "Bill"   12, 118, 123, 162
Cruise, Tom   203

"Dart" aerial gunnery target, the   92
Day, Capt Jim "Meat"   106–108, 109
deaths   151, 172, 175, 178, 179, 265, 270
debriefing sessions   75, 76, 102, 217, 225
Dildy, Capt Doug "Disco"   61
Dishart, Lt Cdr Greg "Hollywood"   203–211
DMPI (Designated Mean Point of Impact) targets   264
DoD (Department of Defense), the   156, 165, 308
"Dogbone" landmark, the   215, 216
dogfights *see* ACM (Air Combat Maneuvering)
Draeger, Capt Rhory "Hoser"   309–310, 311, 313, 314–315, 316, 317, 318, 319, 320, 321–323
Drake, Maj Ted "Gabby"   238, 239, 240, 241, 242, 243, 244, 245, 246, 248, 280–282, 284, 285, 292
Dunn, Lt Col Gil   70

Eglin AFB, Florida   288
EGT (exhaust gas temperature)   237, 273

Eichhorn, Lt Dave   59–60, 62
Ellis, CMSgt Bobby "Daddy"   127, 129–130
emergency procedures   258–261
engines   64, 97, 100, 101, 102, 131, 138, 140, 142, 145, 170, 182, 192, 206, 237, 243, 249, 283, 298, 312
   and afterburner   21, 81, 89, 95, 97, 100, 137–138, 139, 140, 170, 194, 207, 208, 215, 223, 233, 237–238, 240–241, 245, 246, 253, 274, 284, 298, 304, 318
   see also performance

FAA (Federal Aviation Administration), the   52
FCF (Functional Check Flight) pilots   284
Ferris Bueller's Day Off (movie)   229
Fields, TSgt Jerry   261
Fischer, Maj Gen Eugene   123, 148–150, 151, 172, 173, 174–179, 180
flight manuals   277, 278–279
flight simulators   26, 49, 67, 279
flight suits   67, 83, 107, 110, 114, 156, 188, 195
Formation Check Rides   57, 60
Fudula, Maj Gene "Fud"   64, 65, 67
fuel consumption   141, 142, 213, 241–242, 244–245, 246–247, 250, 322
   and "bingo" fuel limit   89, 90, 91, 191, 192, 193, 211, 227, 276, 282, 284, 306
furballs   192, 193–196, 200

G (gravitational force) loads   21, 27, 29, 30, 31, 73, 74, 100, 172, 194, 242, 246, 253, 274, 280, 285, 294, 303, 319
G-LOC (G-induced loss of consciousness)   172, 175
Garcia, Capt Fred "Jose"   261
GCI controllers   89, 91, 106, 109, 123, 140, 143, 151, 191, 193, 198, 214, 232, 239, 247, 252, 253, 254, 293, 297, 298, 301, 302, 312, 313, 314, 316, 318, 321
Geisler, Lt Col Frank "Paco"   154, 181, 185, 188–189, 191–192, 196, 197, 199–200, 201–202, 212, 213–214, 215, 216, 217, 227, 266–268, 281, 287, 288, 289, 292

Gennin, Lt Col George 107, 108, 109–111, 115, 117–121, 122–123, 124, 135, 148, 151, 162, 198, 277
Gilbert, Capt Phil 113, 114
glide ratio 142
Great Depression, the 34
Griffith, Lt Tom 87
"gun's jink," the see jinks

"hard deck," the 22, 73–74, 90, 224
Hasara, Lt Col Mark 68
Have Blue project, the 165
Have Doughnut exploitation program, the 126
Have Idea program, the 126, 127
Have Pad program, the 135, 136, 277
Henderson, Lt Col Earl 130
Herron, Col Kerry 176
Hill AFB, Utah 118
Hoey, Capt Dick "Tooey" 167–169, 271
Hofman, Rich 38–40
Holden, Col Chuck "Brows" 113–114, 115–116
Hollingsworth, SSgt Dave 129
Howell, TSgt Jerry 119, 189, 199, 200–201, 203, 268
HUD (Heds-Up Display), the 28, 299, 300, 301, 304, 305–306, 314, 315, 317, 319, 320, 321
Hughes, Capt Wayne "Huggy" 96, 97–99, 101, 102, 103
Humphrey, Hubert 53
Hurd, Lt Col Joe 80, 81, 82, 84
Hussein, Saddam 309
hydraulic systems 139, 238, 254–256, 257, 258, 260, 261–262

Indonesian Air Force, the 128, 130
Infra-Red Acqusition and Designation System, the 264
Initial Point, the 191, 192, 212, 232, 293
IrAF (Iraqi Air Force), the 126, 211, 311–312, 313–314, 316, 317–318, 319–320, 321, 322
Iraqi invasion of Kuwait see Operation Desert Storm
Iswahjudi AB, Indonesia 129, 130

J. I. Case High School, Racine, Wisconsin 41
Jackson, Capt Mike "Action" 103

jinks 72, 73, 74, 98, 210, 226, 305, 306
Johnson, Maj Aric "Redeye" 170–173, 175
JP-4 jet fuel 92, 242, 309, 310

K. I. Sawyer AFB, Marquette, Michigan 47–48
Kadena AB, Okinawa 69, 70, 91, 92, 106, 167
Kerby, Brig Gen Michael 118, 123, 148
Kinney, Maj Tim "Stretch" 195
KIO (Knock It Off) calls 23, 75, 89, 90, 100, 172, 195, 196, 210–211, 223, 224, 254, 276, 302, 306
Korean War, the 12
Kunsan AB, South Korea 79, 80, 104, 258

landing gear and flaps 65, 133, 138–139, 143, 145–146, 191, 233, 235, 238, 242, 248, 249, 258–259, 295
LaTourette, Col Bob 233
learning to fly 26–27
Libya bombings (April 1986) 217
lie detector tests 160
Liljegren, David 41, 42, 43, 44, 53, 77, 296
Lockheed corporation 165
"low key" position, the 144
low-level tactical navigation 68, 212
Luke AFB, Arizona 67, 77
Lyon, MSgt Don 127–128, 129, 130

MacDonald, Capt Jim "Smack" 194, 212–213, 215–216, 231, 232, 239, 247, 253, 254, 256
Macy, Maj Marty "Fog" 185, 186, 187, 257, 259
Magill, Capt Chuck "Sly" 310, 313, 314, 315, 316, 317, 318, 319, 320, 322
Magner, Col Thomas 61, 62
maintenance and maintenance personnel 13, 110, 119, 120, 121, 122, 123, 127–128, 130, 131, 134, 135, 151, 159, 166–167, 224, 229, 230, 251, 259, 260, 261, 267, 268–269, 278, 281, 282, 283, 284, 285–286, 295–296
Manclark, Lt Col Jack "Mad Jack" 234, 268, 269
M*A*S*H (TV show) 119
Massey Ferguson 35
Matheny, Maj Jim "Thug" 160, 230, 231, 233, 278

INDEX

McCloud, Maj Dave "Marshall"   128
McCort, Lt Cdr Dan "Bad Bob"   282–283
Mercer, Capt Steve "Mace"   89
mid-air collision escape   98–103
Mikoyan-Gurevich MiG aircraft
    (USSR)   24, 31, 78–79, 110, 155,
    156, 166, 218, 310
  MiG-17   64, 119, 126, 127, 136, 185
  MiG-19   128–129, 130
  MiG-21   87, 96, 97, 110, 118, 119,
    120–121, 122, 123, 127, 128,
    129–130, 134, 136, 137–147, 150,
    151, 152, 157, 158, 159, 165, 180,
    181–182, 185, 190, 194, 199, 204,
    213, 214, 219, 220–224, 225, 226,
    227, 239, 244, 247, 249, 250–251,
    252, 257, 278, 280, 292, 295, 296,
    300, 302–307, 312
  F-7 (China)   121, 134, 135, 194, 312
  MiG-21bis   182
  MiG-21F-13   126, 135, 182, 183, 193,
    194, 205–211
  MiG-21MF   157
  MiG-23   87, 110, 118, 119, 121–122,
    123, 131, 136, 151, 190, 192, 227,
    237–250, 251, 277–279, 283–286,
    295, 296, 312
  MiG-23BN   122, 131, 135, 136, 251,
    272, 273–276, 278, 280–282, 285
  MiG-23MS   122, 135, 136, 213, 215,
    230, 231, 232–233, 235, 251, 252–
    258, 259–262, 272, 277, 282–283,
    284, 293–294, 300–302
  MiG-29   244, 311, 312, 313–314, 316,
    317, 319–320, 321, 322
  sourcing and disassembling MiG
    aircraft   126–130, 131–136
  USAF aircraft codes   135, 136
MIL (Military Power) throttle setting,
    the   65, 137, 138, 141, 145, 193,
    216, 220, 237, 240, 245, 246, 248,
    249, 250, 273, 283, 294, 298, 303
military exercises   83, 86
  Blue Air   13, 301
  Cope Thunder   91, 93, 103, 104
  Maple Flag   175
  Red Flag   13, 23, 93, 218
Mitchell, Brig Gen William "Billy"   12, 26
Mitchell Field Airport, Milwaukee   32
Multi-National Operational Test and
    Evaluation program, the   118

Murphy, Larry "Murph"   69, 70
Myers, Maj Burt "Buffalo"   109–110, 111

NAS Miramar, California   203, 204, 211,
    282, 289–291
Nathman, Cdr John "Black"   278
National Lampoon's Animal House
    (movie)   290
NATO   220
  reporting names   73, 157, 239, 272, 312,
    314, 320
NCOs   82, 119, 123, 199, 295
  and NCOICs   127, 289
Neal, TSgt, J. B.   289
Nellis AFB, Nevada   23–24, 78, 83, 87, 88,
    91, 93, 96, 105, 108, 141, 166, 168,
    173, 174, 175, 180, 263, 308
  and Nellis range space   158, 205, 212,
    214, 284
  Threat Training Facility   130
Nevada Test Site (Nevada National Security
    Site)   158–159
Nicholl, Capt Greg "Curly"   168–169, 263,
    264–266, 270
Nicholl, Marcie   168, 270–271
Nixon, President Richard   133
Noriega, TSgt Chico   129
Northrop Corporation   288
notching   314

O'Brien, Maj Pat "P.O.B."   75, 76–78, 79,
    80, 87
O'Clubs (Officers' Clubs)   49, 57, 58, 62,
    103, 150, 166, 173, 180, 193, 197,
    225, 261, 267, 289–290, 292, 308
Officer Efficiency Reports   149
Officers' Wives Club, the   198–199
Operation *Desert Storm* (August 1990 –
    January 1991)   211, 309–322
Operation *Diamond* (1963 – 1966)   126
Operation *El Dorado Canyon* (April
    1986)   217–218
Operation *Just Cause* (December
    1989)   166
Operational Readiness Inspections   264
Osan AB, South Korea   77–78, 79, 80, 81

Pasqual, John   60
Peck, Col Gail   12, 13
Peele, Capt Clarke "Frog"   23, 24, 89–91,
    93–94, 116

Pentagon, the   86, 156, 157, 189, 213
performance   29, 64, 135, 140, 141–142, 146, 206, 229, 240–242, 244, 255, 277, 278, 279–280, 282, 283–285
   and comparisons
      MiG-21 vs F-5E   181–183
      MiG-21 vs F-15   219–225
   see also engines
Phelan, Capt Denny   192
"phone booth," the   182, 205
PLAAF (People's Liberation Army Air Force), the   132
Postai, Capt Mark   87
PP (Performance Profiles)   272, 273
PPL (Private Pilot's License), the   52
pranks and jokes   152–155, 166–167, 184–189, 191, 192
Press, Lt Col Mike "Bat"   104–105
programmable locks on briefcases   153, 154

RAAF (Royal Australian Air Force), the
   No 75 Sqn   103
radar   226, 231, 320, 321
   AN/APG-63 pulse-Doppler   252, 298, 305, 309, 310
   AN/FPS-27A radar   212
   N-019 pulse-Doppler   312, 320
   P-35 "Bar Lock"   312
   RP-23 Sapfir (USSR)   272
   SPO-2 Sirena-3M RWR   316, 317, 319
RAF Lakenheath, England   217
RCOs (Range Control Officers)   264, 265, 266
Reagan, President Ronald   165
recovery procedures and scenarios   74–75, 140, 142–143, 224, 246, 252, 254–262, 279, 280–281
recreation and leisure   103–104, 111, 151, 289–291, 292
Redfa, Capt Munir   126
Republic of Vietnam Air Force, the   182
Robb, Lt Cdr Jim "Rookie"   152–153, 154, 155, 162
Rodriguez, Alex   40
ROE (Rules of Engagement)   99, 220, 307
Roosevelt, President Franklin D.   34
Roy, Capt Mike "Mach"   124, 137, 139, 140, 141, 143, 145, 147
RTUs (Replacement Training Units)   67–68, 77, 84, 177, 178

rules and regulations   190, 196–197, 200, 228
   and pushing boundaries   228, 229–230, 232–236
Running, Lt Col Nels   85–87, 88

SA (Situational Awareness)   69, 90, 99, 103, 231, 291, 313
Saint Edward's Catholic Parish, Racine, Wisconsin   36
Saxman, Capt John   192
Schiavi, Capt Tony "Kimo"   309, 313, 318, 320
Schwall, Capt Art   54, 55–56, 57
Scott, Mike   180
Senior Trend (stealth program)   160, 162–166, 168–169
SFO (Simulated Flame Out)
   approaches   142–144, 241, 246–248
Sheekly, Capt John "Sheek"   72, 73, 74, 75
Shervanick, Capt Larry "Shy"   278
Skidmore, Maj John "Skid"   162, 181
sorties   92, 151, 286, 291, 292, 296
spin recovery   280–281
SPs (Security Police)   153, 154, 156
spy satellites   125, 155, 259
squadron patches   83, 107, 109, 110, 155–156, 227, 292
STU II (Secure Telephone Unit), the   269
Stucky, Maj Paul "Stook"   154, 158, 162, 185–187, 189, 192

TDY (temporary duty travel)
   deployments   103, 104
TEWS (Tactical Electronic Warfare System), the   314, 315, 317, 320
Tittle, Capt George   135
Tollini, Capt Rick "Kluso"   310, 318
TOP GUN (movie)   203, 228, 290
training   12–13, 43, 45, 81, 226–227, 312
   Aggressor checkout program   87, 91, 105, 181, 195–196
   air combat training for a North African country   156–157
   air-to-air   71, 72–75, 76, 77, 79–80, 81, 89–91, 99, 170–172, 190, 203, 220–224, 323
   DACM (Dissimilar Air Combat Maneuvers)   96

INDEX

DACT (Dissimilar Air Combat
  Training) 92, 96–101, 113, 183,
  207, 222, 227, 251, 269, 288
dogfights 21–23
Fighter Lead-In Training 62–69
FWIC (Fighter Weapons Instructor
  Course) 83, 167, 239, 313
FWS (Fighter Weapons School) 23,
  83–84, 96, 110, 118, 152, 181, 185,
  196, 203, 204, 219, 221, 227, 282,
  288, 289
  TOPGUN 12, 13, 181, 185, 203, 204,
    205–206, 211, 282, 289, 292
  in MiGs at 4477th TES 124–125,
    137–147, 151, 277–278
Officer Training School 239
UPT (Undergraduate Pilot
  Training) 45–46, 52, 53, 54–57,
  61–62
  assignment announcements 58–61
TS/SCI security clearances 155, 160, 164
TTR (Tonopah Test Range) 117, 124,
  127, 130, 134–135, 153, 155–156,
  164, 166, 191, 202, 233–234, 259,
  264, 323
Tullos, Maj George "Cajun" 153–155, 185

US Marine Corps, the 63–64, 181, 183,
  185, 190, 291, 310, 323
US Navy, the 34, 43, 152, 181, 183, 190,
  291, 323
  Fighter Weapons School 152, 181,
    203, 204
  VX-4 Air Test and Evaluation
    Squadron 289
US State Department, the 156, 157
USAF, the 43–44, 126, 183
  25th FTS (Flying Training Squadron) 54
  57th FWW (Fighter Weapons
    Wing) 118, 123, 148, 155, 170, 174,
    176, 200
  64th Fighter Weapons Squadron 124
  3246th Test Wing 167
  4450th TG (Tactical Group) 160,
    162–164, 165–166, 167, 168, 263
  4477th TES (Test and Evaluation)
    Squadron "Red Eagles" 13, 24–25,
    31, 87, 107–111, 115, 117–148,
    151–156, 165, 166–167, 180–181,
    184–185, 198, 204, 213, 218, 226,
    239, 277–278, 287, 291–296,
    308, 323
  Accident Board 271
  AFOQT (Air Force Officer Qualifying
    Test) 47, 48, 50
  AFROTC (Air Force Reserve Officer
    Training Corps) 45, 46, 47–49, 50,
    57, 118
    Detachment 410 51
  AFSC (Air Force Systems
    Command) 159, 277
  Air Demonstration Squadron
    (Thunderbirds) 23–24, 86, 118, 139
  Blue Angels 139
  FIS (Fighter Interceptor Squadrons)
    87th FIS 49
    126th FIS 33
  FWS (Fighter Weapons School) 23,
    83–84, 96, 110, 118, 185, 196, 219,
    221, 227, 282, 288, 289
    National Museum 130
  PACAF 71–72, 77–78, 85, 87, 88
  SAC (Strategic Air Command) 48,
    59, 60
  TAC (Tactical Air Command) 123, 126,
    156, 160, 162, 165, 174, 175, 176,
    177, 213, 269, 288
    as Air Combat Command 227
  TFS (Tactical Fighter Squadrons)
    8th TFS 272
    9th TFS 227
    12th TFS 69, 70, 71, 75, 80, 103–104,
      124, 167
    25th TFS 168
    36th TFS 79, 80, 82, 85, 86, 87
    44th TFS 124
    58th TFS 288, 309–310, 313
    67th TFS 89
    80th TFS 104
    90th TFS 96, 102
    94th TFS 307–308
  TFTAS (Tactical Fighter Training
    Aggressor Squadrons) 91
    26th TFTAS (AS) 23, 71–72, 85, 87,
      88, 89, 91–92, 106, 113, 116, 180
    64th AS 151, 174, 180, 181, 288, 292
    65th TFTAS (AS) 87, 91, 104–105,
      170–172, 174, 175, 180, 181, 196, 288
  TFTS (Tactical Fighter Training
    Squadrons)

365

311th TFTS 67–68, 69, 71
426th TFTS 296
TFW (Tactical Fighter Wings)
    3rd TFW 92, 93, 113, 115
    8th TFW 78, 79, 80
    18th TFW 69–70, 92
    33rd TFW 288, 310, 313
    48th TFW 217
    474th TFW 239
TS (Test Squadrons)
    4450th TS 263, 267, 268, 269, 270, 271
    6513th TS "Red Hats" 131, 134, 135, 159–160, 282

Vance AFB, Enid, Oklahoma 53, 54
Venema, Capt Terry 75, 76
Vertical-Scan radar mode 305
Vietnam war, the 12, 43, 48, 64, 68, 86, 97, 110, 115, 118, 225
VOQ (Visiting Officer's Quarters), the 289–290
VPAF (Vietnam People's Air Force), the 97, 142, 225
VSD (Vertical Situation Display), the 298, 299, 300

Ward, Dennis "D" 61
Watley, Maj Monroe 123–124, 195
weaponry 29, 84
    20mm cannon 68, 81, 92, 306
    25lb BDU-33 bomb 264
    AIM-7E Sparrow missile 83
    AIM-7M missile 219, 301, 302, 317, 319, 320, 321–322
    AIM-9 Sidewinder missile 92, 98, 216
    GBU-10 LGB 165
    GBU-10 Paveway II bomb 214
    GSh-23L 23mm autocannon (USSR) 274
    GSh-30-1 30mm autocannon (USSR) 314
    IADS (integrated air defense system) (Iraq) 312
    Mk 82 500lb bomb 258
    Pave Spike LGB (laser-guided bomb) 83
    R-27 (AA-10 "Alamo") missile (USSR) 314
    R-60 (AA-8 "Aphid") missile (USSR) 314, 320

SAM (surface-to-air) missiles (Iraq) 68, 314, 315
Vympel K-13 (AA-2 "Atoll") missile (USSR) 73
Vympel R-24R (AA-7 "Apex") missile (USSR) 272
weights 73, 97, 182, 238
White, Lt Col Phil "Hound Dog" 198, 199–200, 233–234
Wisconsin ANG (Air National Guard) 32–33
World War II 34
Wright, MSgt Bill 131
WSO (Weapon Systems Officer), the 72, 82, 87, 95, 96, 102, 103, 258

Yom Kippur War (1973), the 311

Zettel, Andrew 33, 34–35
Zettel, Capt Rob "Z-Man"
    and the 4477th TES Red Eagles 107–111, 112, 115–116, 308
    and AFROTC scholarship 46, 47, 49, 50, 52
    as Aggressor pilot 85–88, 89–93, 95–103
    and applying to the USAF 44–49
    and Area 51 158, 159–161
    and baseball 38–40
    and career guidance 41–44, 296
    and college years 50–52, 53
    and the F-15 Eagle 287, 296–307
    family background 33–38
    and Fighter Weapons School 83–84
    "furball" engagement and grounding 193–196, 200, 201–202
    memories 32–33, 77, 114
    and MiG-21/TOPGUN sortie 204–211
    and the MiG-23 237–250, 252–262, 271, 272–277, 278, 291, 293–295
    as SOF 231–232, 234, 235, 249, 294
    and training in North Africa 157
    and USAF pilot training 52, 53–58, 61–62, 63–81, 295
        air-to-air combat training 219–225, 227
Zettel, Chuck 38, 42, 62
Zettel, Harriet 32, 33, 34–38, 47, 49–50, 62, 87
Zettel, Mark 42, 44–45, 46, 62, 111